ANCIENT INDIAN TRADITION AND MYTHOLOGY

Translated by
A BOARD OF SCHOLARS

VOLUME 74

ANCIENT INDIAN TRADITION AND MYTHOLOGY

Mahāpurāṇas *Translated into English*

Gen. Ed. DR. G.C. TRIPATHI

Founder Eds. LATE J.L. SHASTRI and LATE G.P. BHATT

PUBLISHED VOLUMES

Vols. 1-4	ŚIVA PURĀṆA *Tr.* J.L. Shastri
Vol. 5-6	LIṄGA PURĀṆA *Tr.* J.L. Shastri
Vol. 7-11	BHĀGAVATA PURĀṆA *Tr.* G.V. Tagare
Vol. 12-14	GARUḌA PURĀṆA *Tr.* J.L. Shastri
Vol. 15-19	NĀRADA PURĀṆA *Tr.* G.V. Tagare
Vol. 20-21	KŪRMA PURĀṆA *Tr.* G.V. Tagare
Vol. 22-26	BRAHMAṆḌA PURĀṆA *Tr.* G.V. Tagare
Vol. 27-30	AGNI PURĀṆA *Tr.* N. Gangadharan
Vol. 31-32	VARĀHA PURĀṆA *Tr.* S. Venkitasubramonia Iyer
Vol. 33-36	BRAHMA PURĀṆA *Tr.* J.L. Shastri
Vol. 37-38	VĀYU PURĀṆA *Tr.* G.V. Tagare
Vol. 39-48	PADMA PURĀṆA *Tr.* N.A. Deshpande
Vol. 49-71	SKANDA PURĀṆA *Ed.* G.P. Bhatt, *Tr. & Annot.* Shridhar Balooni & Pratosh Panda
Vol. 72-73	VĀMANA PURĀṆA *Tr. & Annot.* R.S. Shiva Ganesha Murthy
Vol. 74-76	GAṆEŚA PURĀṆA *Tr. & Annot.* Greg Bailey
Vol. 77-80	BRAHMAVAIVARTA PURĀṆA *Tr. & Annot.* G.P. Bhatt
Vol. 81-82	ŚRĪ VIṢṆU PURĀṆA *Tr. & Annot.* T.K. Narsimhan
Vol. 86	MĀRKAṆḌEYA PURĀṆA *Tr. & Annot.* I.S. Madugula

PURĀṆAS UNDER PREPARATION

Harivaṃśa Purāṇa • Bhaviṣya Purāṇa • Matsya Purāṇa

Devi Bhāgavata Purāṇa • Kālikā Purāṇa • Viṣṇudharmottara Purāṇa

THE GAṆEŚA-PURĀṆA

PART I

Upāsanā Khaṇda

Translated and Annotated by

GREG BAILEY

MOTILAL BANARSIDASS

PUBLISHING HOUSE • DELHI

Email: naraina@mlbd.in* • *Website: www.mlbd.in

2nd Reprint: Delhi, 2023
First Revised Indian Edition: Delhi, 2015
Earlier Published by Otto Harrassowitz, Wiesbaden in 1995

UNESCO COLLECTION OF REPRESENTATIVE WORKS—*Indian Series*
This book has been accepted in the Indian Translation Series of the UNESCO Collection of Representative Works, jointly sponsored by the United Nations Educational, Scientific and Cultural Organization (UNESCO) and the Government of India

ISBN: 978-93-5676-306-7 (Hardcover)
ISBN: 978-93-5676-307-4 (Paperback)

Printed & Published by
Rajendra P Jain *for*
Motilal Banarsidass Publishing House
A-44, Naraina Industrial Area, Phase I,
New Delhi–110 028 (INDIA)
Email: naraina@mlbd.in
Website: www.mlbd.in

PREFACE

This book is a reworking of an earlier work The Gaṇeśa Purāṇa. Volume One. Upāsanākhanda, Otto Harrassowitz, Wiesbaden, 1995. I have revised the translation for this new edition, the Introduction has been sùbstantially shortened and the notes to the translation have been severely truncated.

I have tried to make the translation less literal than in the previous volume and I have been able to correct some mistakes in the initial translation, especially following some good suggestions made by reviewers such as Ludo Rocher and John Brockington.

Greg Bailey,

Melbourne 2103

PUBLISHER'S NOTE

The purest gems lie hidden in the bottom of the ocean or in the depth of rocks. One has to dive into the ocean or delve into the rocks to find them out. Similarly, truth lies concealed in the language which with the passage of time has become obsolete. Man has to learn that language before he discovers that truth.

But he has neither the means nor the leisure to embark on that course. We have, therefore, planned to help him acquire knowledge by an easier course. We have started the series of Ancient Indian Tradition and Mythology in English Translation. Our goal is to universalize knowledge through the most popular international medium of expression. The publication of the PurŒÄas in English Translation is a step towards that goal.

Acknowledgement

It is our pleasant duty to put on record our sincere thanks to Dr. R. N. Dandekar and the UNESCO authorities for their kind encouragement and valuable help in the publication of the volumes in this series.

CONTENTS

A. PUBLISHER'S NOTE v

B. ABBREVIATIONS xi

C. INTRODUCTION

I. The Gaṇeśa Purāṇa xiii

II. Dating and Place of Composition of the Gaṇeśa Purāṇa xv

III. The Idiosyncratic Nature of the Gaṇeśa Purāṇa xxi

V. Content of the upāsanākhaṇḍa xxiii

VI. Traditional and non-traditional material in the upāsanākhaa xxxiv

VII. The upāsanākhaṇḍa as a ritual text xxxix

VIII. A note on the text xlii

D. TRANSLATION AND NOTES

PART I

1 Description of Somakānta 1

2 The Second Chapter 4

3 **Description of Conduct and so forth** 7

4 Entering the City 12

5 Conversation between Sudharmā and Cyavana 16

6 Arrival at Bhrgu's Hermitage 20

7 Description of Somakānta's Earlier Life 24

8 The Restraining of many Birds 27

9 The Tale of Instruction to the King 31

10 Description of Vyāsa's Questions 34

11 The Tale of the Mantra 37

12 The Vision of Gaṇeśa 40

13 Description of Brahmā's Eulogy 43

14	Description of Brahmā's Anxiety	49
15	Description of Gajānana's Worship	51
16	The Entreaty to the Goddess	55
17	Instruction in the Mantra	58
18	The Tale of the Origin of Siddhakṣetra	62
19	Description of Kamalā's Son	66
20	Dakṣa's Eulogy	70
21	Description of the Teaching of the Man	75
22	The Tale of Ballāla and Vināyaka	78
23	The Narration of the Future	83
24	The Tale of the Vision	87
25	Description of the Consecration Ceremony	89
26	Description of the Lineage	92
27	Description of the Consecration of Rukmāṅgada	95
28	The Fasting unto Death	97
29	The Visit of Nārada	99
30	The Violation of Ahalyā	102
31	The Description of Indra's Curse	104
32	The tale of the Mantra	107
33	Indra's Going Forth	110
34	Description of the Sacred Forge of Cintāmaṇī	113
35	Description of the Fate of Kadamba City	117
36	The Tale of Gṛtsamada	122
37	The Tale of the Boon-giver	126
38	The Gift of Boons	130
39	Indra's Defeat	134
40	Description of the Eulogy	138
41	The arrival of Nārada	144
42	Description of the Battle	147
43	Description of the Victory	150
44	Description of the Austerity	153

45 The Gift of a Boon to the Mountain Dweller 156
46 Narration of the Thousand-names of Gaṇeśa in the conversation between Śiva and Gaṇeśa 160
47 Śiva's Victory 181
48 Pārvatī's Appearance 185
49 Description of the Ritual for an Earthen Image of Gaṇeśa 189
50 The Tale of the Vow of the Fourth during the conversation between Pārvatī and Himavat 195
51 The Fifty-first Chapter 197
52 The Traditional Narration in the Conversation between Himavat and Pārvatī 203
53 Description of Nala's Vow in the Conversation between Himavat and Pārvatī 206
54 The Tale of Candrāṅgada 210
55 The Conversation between Indumatī and Nārada 213
56 The Union of Śiva and Pārvatī 216
57 The Conversation between Indra and Śūrasena 220
58 The Short Tale of Bhruśuṇḍi 223
59 Tale of the Vow called the Saṃkaṣṭacaturthī 228
60 The Narrative concerning the Vow of the Fourth 231
61 The Tale of the Aṅgāracaturthī Vow 234
62 Description of the Moon's Curse and favour 239
63 The Tale of the Dūrvā Grass 244
64 The Dūrvāmāhātmya 247
65 The Dūrvāmāhātmya (Contd.) 252
66 The Dūrvāmāhātmy (Contd.) 254
67 The Dūrvāmāhātmya (Contd.) 258
68 The Dūrvāmāhātmya (Contd.) 261

69	Description of the Vow called Saṃkaṣṭa of the Fourth	266
70	Description of the Vow of the Fourth	270
71	The Tale of the Vow of the Fourth	276
72	The Tale of the Vow of the Fourth	278
73	The Caturthīmāhātmya	281
74	The Caturthīmāhātmya (Contd.)	285
75	The Caturthīmāhātmya (Contd.)	288
76	The Seventy-sixth Chapter	292
77	The Caturthīmāhātmya	296
78	The Seventy-eighth Chapter	302
79	The Tale of Kārtavīrya	307
80	The Tale of Kārtavīrya (Contd.)	311
81	The Tale of Rāma	315
82	Relating to Bhārgava	317
83	The Gift of a Boon to Rāma	320
84	On the Solicitation of Kāma	325
85	The Burning of Kāma	330
86	The Tale of Viśākha	336
87	The Tale of Kārttikeya	336
88	The Killing of the Demon Tāraka	338
89	Kāma's Request for a Boon	344
90	The Tale of Śeṣa	324
91	The Tale of Śeṣa (Contd.)	352
92	Description of Various Forms of Worship	357
93	Description of Gajānana's Name	362

ABBREVIATIONS

GnP. —Gaṇeśa Purāṇa,

GN. —ed. Gopal Narayan, Bombay 1892,

GnSN. —Gaṇeśasahasranāmastotra

Krkh. —Krīḍākhaṇḍa

MBh. —Mahābhārata, ed. Sukthankar, V. S., et al, Poona 1933-59.

M —Marathi translation of the GnP. ed. and [Marathi] trans. Bapat, V. and Lele, D. L, Wai 1905-06.

ms. —manuscript (A, B, C, D, I)

MudP. —Mudgala Purāṇa, ed. Nirṇayasāgara Press, Bombay 1976.

Rām. —Rāmāyaṇa, ed. Bhatt, G. H., et al., Baroda 1958-75.

Ukh. —Upāsanākhaṇḍa

INTRODUCTION

I. THE GAṆEŚA PURĀṆA

The Gaṇeśapurāṇa (GnP.) is a Purāṇic text probably composed in the fourteenth or fifteenth century. Its contents derive partially from earlier literature dealing with Gaṇeśa, but also draw on the body of myths found in the mahāpurāṇas and upapurāṇas. It is divided into two books, called Upāsanākhaṇḍa (Ukh.) and Krīḍākhaṇḍa (Krkh.), which are complementary with each other from the perspective of contents. Each book contains many myths and sections of text detailing rituals to be performed to Gaṇeśa, though these are much less common in the Krkh. In addition, the forty-sixth chapter of the Ukh. contains a sahasranāmastotra and chapters one hundred and thirty-nine to one hundred and fifty of the Krkh. contain the Gaṇeśagītā. The presence of both these plus the large body of myths makes this an almost complete devotional text for the worship and theology of Gaṇeśa. Whether the text was developed as a literary expression of one of the Gāṇapatya sects, cannot be determined because of lack of any direct connection between it, and the other Purāṇa dealing with Gaṇeśa–the Mudgalapurāṇa–, and the presence of a distinct sect of Gaṇeśa worshippers located at a specific time and place probably in Maharashtra. Yet there must have been an audience for the text, a growing audience judging from the large number of manuscripts dating from about 1760 until the end of the nineteenth century. In addition, institutional support to fund the initial composition of the text must have come from one or more patrons, conceivably, though speculatively, the family of Moraya Gosavi in Cincwad.

One should not read the extant GnP. in order to find out about the early history of the development of Gaṇeśa as a god,[1] nor should it be read to discover the meaning of the

---

[1] See A. Thapan, Understanding Gaṇapati. Insights into the Dynamics of a Cult. New Delhi: Manohar, 1997.

myths about the early birth of Gaṇeśa, his functioning as Pārvatī's house-guard and his clash with Śiva, subsequent beheading and acquisition of the head of an elephant.[2] As for the first, Gaṇeśa was already a very popular god by the time his Purāṇa was composed and had many sacred places associated with him, though the founding of some of these is provided in the GnP. itself. For the second, the myths of his childhood as they are expressed in the mahāpurāṇas are reinterpreted in the Ukh. and are directly present in the Krkh, but in an extremely muted manner, with the tension between Gaṇeśa and Śiva being underplayed, though still in evidence.

Rather the GnP. must be read as the product of a time when Gaṇeśa had already assumed a status as one of the most popular Hindu gods over much of the sub-continent. The appearance of both it and the Mudgalapurāṇa at similar periods suggests a need was felt by certain groups of Gaṇeśa worshippers to establish Gaṇeśa textually as a god of status not unlike Viṣṇu and his more popular avatāras, Śiva, Hanumān or the goddess. I am not saying there occurred a competition between the worshippers of these gods–especially given the likelihood that many individuals worshipped more than one of them–but that it was considered a god like Gaṇeśa should be represented in a text or texts where he was unambiguously the principal god. This would be a text not only drawing together any myths that might have been developed to expose the unique activities of this god within the larger framework of received mythology, it would also present his theology (through the vehicle of myth and stotra) and collect together as much material pertaining to pūjā as was deemed necessary. It is true that a series of Tāntras dealing with Gaṇeśa had been in existence for some time,[3] but knowledge of them would surely have been restricted to a small circle of adepts.

---

[2] For which see P. Courtright, Gaṇeśa. Lord of Obstacles, Lord of Beginnings. New York, 1985.

[3] G.Bühnemann, Forms of Gaṇeśa. A Study based on the Vidyārṇavatantra. Wichtrach, 1989.

Regrettably we have no direct evidence as to how it was used in a recitational sense, though I heard in October 1983 that recitations from it were being performed in a Gaṇeśa temple in Pune. The sahasranāma stotra has been recorded in compact disc form and vernacular versions of the text have existed since the early eighteenth century. I have easily been able to purchase several summaries of the text in Marathi and copies of the Tamil Viṉayakar Purāṇa can easily be purchased in temple book stalls. Despite this the GnP. seems not to have been widely known outside of a certain intellectual elite and even now, when all the signs suggest Gaṇeśa is becoming a popular god all over India, the text remains largely unknown.

II. DATING AND PLACE OF COMPOSITION OF THE GAṆEŚA PURĀṆA

Determination of the date of any Sanskrit text, except for the most recent is always difficult. Not only is it necessary to date the beginning and end of the compositional process, it is also necessary to date the stages corresponding to the development of new recensions if these arise. In the case of the GnP., the manuscript evidence I have looked at does not suggest the evolution of the text through various stages. Of course this applies only to the manuscript tradition. Any evidence pertaining to the presence of an oral tradition is completely lost to us. The manuscript evidence is consistent in presenting a very late date for the text and does not allow us to establish a stemma for the manuscripts of which there are a very large number.

That so many appear at a particular time (between 1700 and 1850) is in itself a significant development in the dispersal of the text and is one definite indication of the popularity of the god and the systematization of attempts to portray him as a popular god. The existence of both the GnP. and the MudP, with their huge body of myths, metaphysical component and substantial ritual element, reflect a felt need to codify all aspects of Gaṇeśa worship and to universalize a god who must have already been universalized, if we can judge from the dispersion of iconographical evidence. What this means is that any scholarly study of the GnP. will be required to date the text and date the extensive appearance of manuscripts.

We cannot know the prior history of the development of the GnP. if it did in fact exist prior to its earliest manuscript evidence. Obviously, using the epics as a parallel example, a given text can exist either in oral or written form long before its earliest manuscripts but to prove this we need to have external evidence of the kind that includes testimonia. Only in the latest of the Nibandhas (1708) do we find evidence of the use of the GnP. as a source and in the earlier Nibandhas, sources for the Gaṇeśacaturthī rituals are listed as several of the mahāpurāṇas which deal extensively with Gaṇeśa.

Various datings have been given, most centering on the centuries between 1100 and 1400. L. Preston writes that, 'The dating of this Purana between 1100 and 1400 would appear to agree with the apparent age of the sacred sites mentioned by it.'[4] R. C. Hazra[5] also opts for these dates, arguing its lateness derives from the following factors:

a) It mentions the eighteen mahā- and upapurāṇas.

b) It names the Nāradīya and the Nṛsiṅha and it also knows the Liṅga and the Skanda and refers to some of their contents.

c) It is later than the MudP. and the Śāradātilaka because they 'speak of thirty-two and fifty-one forms of Gaṇapati respectively, whereas' the GnP. speaks of fifty-six forms.

d) The GnP. unmistakably refers to the MudP, therefore it is older than it.

e) The earliest manuscript of the GnP. is 1763, of the Gaṇeśagītā 1694, and of the Gaṇeśasahasranāmastotra 1627.

The first two of Hazra's points are certainly true, the third is an unwarranted assumption deriving from the

---

[4] Laurence W. Preston, "Subregional Religious centres in the History of Maharashtra: The Sites Sacred to Ganesh," in N. K. Wagle, ed., Images of Maharashtra. A Regional Profile of India, (Curzon, London, 1980). pp.103-04.

[5] See R. C. Hazra, "The Gaṇeśa-Purāṇa," The Journal of the Ganganatha Jha Research Institute, IX (1951), p.98

fallacy that simpler and lesser is older. The reference he cites to justify his fourth point is 1.9.33 (not 1.9.63) and in my view refers to the sage Mudgala. If it referred to the Purāṇa of the same name, we would expect to find Maudgala, consistent with the forms Laiṅga and Skānda, found in both books of the GnP.[6] Finally, his fifth point is correct but nothing materially alters the dating of the text based on the manuscript evidence. Therefore, I can only assume he reaches his preferred period of dating because he assumes a period of three to five hundred years between the composition of the text and the widespread appearance of manuscripts, even though, as an analogy, manuscripts of the Mbh, and indeed the Skandapurāṇa, date from the 10th century and before and no arbitrary period of centuries for composition appears in respect of them.

A more recent attempt at dating is given by A. Thapan, who writes, 'The Sammoha Tantra (thirteenth/fourteenth centuries ad)[7] refers to a Gāṇapa Tantrika tradition in both the northern and southern class of tantras. It mentions five cults of the Gāṇapatyas and lists the extant body of Gāṇapatya literature which consists of fifty Tantras, twenty-five Upatantras, two Purāṇas and a long list of what seem to be smaller works. ... The two Purāṇas mentioned by the Sammoha Tantra evidently refer to the Mudgala and Gaṇeśa Purāṇas since these are the only two Purāṇas that are devoted exclusively to Gaṇapati.'[8] We can assume with some confidence that this is a certain reference to the GnP. and to the MudP. The question of date is another matter.[9] The Sammoha Tantra is the same as the Chinnamastākhaṇḍa of the Śaktisaṅgamatantra and Goudriaan and Gupta assign the Śaktisaṅgamatantra quite a late date, suggesting that 'dating the text within the last part of the sixteenth or the first half of the seventeenth century cannot be far off the

[6] The same problem applies equally to the two references cited by Thapan, op.cit., p.40. n.56.

[7] Citing N.N.Bhattacharya, History of Shākta Religion, p.123. See also P. C. Bagchi, "The Evolution of the Tantras," in The Cultural Heritage of India, Vol. IV, pp.211-266.

[8] Thapan, op.cit. pp.179-180.

[9] Ibid. pp.179-180.

mark.'[10] Even so I take this as reasonably certain evidence of the text probably existing by 1580.

Another scholar who has tried to date the GnP. is J. N. Farquhar, who dates it between 900 and 1350ACE, whilst giving no reason for his dating.[11] More recently Paul Courtright has dated both the GnP. and the MudP between the 12th and 14th centuries respectively, but without any justification.[12] In a provocative suggestion, Courtright mentions an apocryphal reference to the GnP. in Cincwad in 1659:

> In 1659 Morajā Gosāvī declared to his son, Cintāmaṇī, his intention to pass from the human world... One hagiography of the Cincvad temple recounts the story as follows:
>
> '... After performing the proper rituals in front of the devotees, he led his father to the cave, lighted the lamps and placed a copy of the Gaṇeśa Purāṇa in his lap there...'[13]

The sparse evidence marshalled by Courtright and Thapan is consistent in suggesting a date between 1550 and 1660 for the likely existence of the text. Manuscripts of components of the text certainly existed by that time.

The great majority of the manuscript evidence suggests a text already quite popular, mainly across central and southern India, by the last two decades of the eighteenth century. This is incontestable. More interesting is another body of evidence confirming the text was becoming popular by about 1650, if not earlier. In a recently published[14] commentary of Bhāskara Raya on the Gaṇeśasahasranāma-

---

[10] T. Goudriaan and S. Gupta, Hindu Tantric and Śākta Literature, Otto Harrassowitz, Wiesbaden, 1981, p.69.

[11] J. N. Farquhar, An Outline of the Religious Literature of India, London, 1920, p.226.

[12] P. Courtright, in M. Eliade, ed, Encyclopedia of Religion, (New York, 1987), Vol.5, p.481.

[13] P. Courtright, Gaṇeśa, Lord of Obstacles, p.223. The same hagiography is not mentioned in L.Preston, The Devs of Cincvad: a Lineage and a State in Maharashtra, (Cambridge, 1988), pp.25-33.

[14] Śrīgaṇeśasahasranāmastotram with commentary by Bhāskara Raya, ed. (Tanjore Maharaja Serfoji's Sarasvati Mahal Library, Thanjavur, 1994).

stotra, that scholar in his introduction (pp.3-5) refers specifically to the GnP. and cites several chapters from the Ukh. The editor in his Introduction dates[15] the commentator to the first half of the seventeenth century, presumably meaning before 1650. Nīlakaṇṭha's commentary on the Gaṇeśagītā is dated 1693 and in his Introduction he refers several times to the GnP. Mādhavaswāmi's Marathi rendering of the text should probably be dated about 1700, and the Tamil Viṉāyakar Purāṇa was probably composed in 1730 and used the Ukh. as one of its models.

Further evidence of a mid-seventeenth century date for its popularity can be gleaned from the existence of Cintāmaṇī's Gaṇeśacampū, a text mentioned in the Kavīndrācārya-sūci of Kavīndrācārya who died in 1665. Wakankar argues that 'Cintāmaṇī must be the son of Morayā Gosāvī Mahārāja, the foremost propagator of Gaṇeśa-cult in Maharashtra. This is further strengthened by the word Svānandapuranivāsī (prose portion after verse 44), by which the modern Morgaon was known. Its original name is 'Bhūsvānandabhuvana'. Here Cintāmaṇī, the author, suggests his identity by mentioning the name of the place of his Deity of Worship. Morayā Gosāvī Mahārāja was a Saint and a Yogi. He was born on Māgha Śuddha Caturthī, Śaka 1297, corresponding to 1375 A.D. and took Samādhi on Mārgaśīrṣa Vadya Ṣaṣṭhi, Śaka 1403 (1481 A.D.) and he died on Pauṣa Vadya Caturthī, Śaka 1547 (1635 A.D.).'[16] This date can be disputed, except perhaps for the date of Morayā Gosāvī Mahārāja's death. What is important is that the text in question explicitly claims to be based on the early chapters of the Krkh. It says:

> vilokya gāṇeśapurāṇabālakāṇḍaṃ samuddhṛtya tato 'tiramyāḥ / kathāḥ kṛtaḥ (tāḥ) tābhir ayaṃ gaṇeśacampū....

Two questions are raised by this statement: firstly, was the Krkh. once called Bālakāṇḍa, especially since the

---

[15] Op.cit., p.3.

[16] S. Y. Wakankar, "Gaṇeśacampū by Cintāmaṇī. A Rare and Unpublished Work," in Literary Gems from Sanskrit Literature (A Study of Rare Manuscripts), (Bharatiya Kala Prakashan, Delhi, 2002), p.5

compund bālacarita occurs in the colophons of so many chapters in the Krkh, and, secondly, how long would the gap be between an existing work and the composition of other works explicitly based on it? Finally, a poem about Gaṇeśa's līlās is attributed to 1650.[17] All this evidence points not just to the latest date of the composition of the poem, but to the period when the text began to become popular. If the Śaktisaṅgamatantra dates to the period between 1570-1625, this provides a still older date for the GnP. and the MudP. That it was included in this Tantra along with estimates of the dates of other texts must assume the text was well known or that it was not well known, but that the author of the text was very learned.

A search of manuscript catalogues brings up about seventy references to complete and incomplete manuscripts of the text. The oldest of these is likely to be the one described in the Calcutta Sanskrit College catalogue of 1902 dating to 1763, a text which judging from the colophon may have been composed on the basis of an earlier text.[18] (We could add the mere fact of the presence of variant readings indicates a scribal tradition, implying the existence of earlier manuscripts than those presently extant.) Following this, many other manuscripts date from the 1790s and continued to be produced in considerable numbers until the middle of the nineteenth century. In the final analysis the scraps of evidence do give some support to Hazra's three hundred year period (1100-1400) for the composition of the text, though I much prefer the later date, even as late as 1600. The earlier date corresponds with the likely development of the Gaṇapatya sects and the latter

---

[17] New Catalogus Catalogorum, An Alphabetical Register of Sanskrit and Allied Works and Authors, Madras 1965-, Vol. 5, p.269.

[18] H. Shastri and S. C. Gui, A Descriptive Catalogue of Sanskrit Manuscripts in the Library of the Calcutta Sanskrit College, (Calcutta, 1902), Vol.4, pp.18-19. The relevant section of the colophon reads: Śrigajānana prasunna (?) yādṛśaṃ pustakaṃ dṛṣṭvā tādṛśaṃ likhitaṃ mayā. A similar piece of evidence comes from a manuscript found in the Bhāratīya Itihāsa Saṃśodhak Mandal (notated here as ms.A) which after 1, 61. 5 contains the words: pustakāntare pāṭham, followed by four verses of names of Gaṇeśa not found in other manuscripts.

with the emerging popularity of Gaṇeśa amongst Maharashtrian brahmins.

As for the place of composition, this is also difficult to determine. Whilst it knows much of India except for the deep South, many of the place names mentioned occur in the Deccan, with thirty-seven identified locations. I am confident the place of composition of the Gaṇeśa Purāṇa must be somewhere in present day Maharashtra, and possibly near where the existing aṣṭavināyaka sites are located. However, it is not beyond the realms of possibility that it could have been composed by Maharashtrian brahmins in Benares.[19]

III. THE IDIOSYNCRATIC NATURE OF THE GAṆEŚA PURĀṆA

That the GnP. contains the title Purāṇa (which it takes in all colophons), though calling itself an upapurāṇa in 1,1,8, indicates that for its own recitational tradition as well as for the patrons who paid scribes to transcribe it and, presumably, for its reader/hearers, it fulfilled the conditions they intuitively considered must exist in any text which was to be called a Purāṇa. Leaving aside the putative differences between a mahāpurāṇa and an upapurāṇa, it does contain several features in common with the mahāpurāṇas. A list of them would include the following essentially formal features:

(1) A sophisticated interlocutory system operating at both frame and episodic interlocutory level.

(2) A recitational origin attributed to Vyāsa and at least one level of transmission from the Sūta to the sages in the Naimiṣa forest.

(3) The literary units (khaṇḍa, māhātmya, upākhyāna, gītā) which are the constituent parts of any Purāṇa.

(4) Absence of an architectonic plot of the kind found in the two epics.

---

[19] See Hazra, op.cit., p.98; P. Bisschop, Orientalistische Literaturzeitung, 106 (2011), pp.424-425.

(5) Juxtaposition of mythic and didactic compositional style.

(6) A stock of myths substantially similar, but not restricted to, the traditional body of Purāṇic mythology.

(7) Common Purāṇic imagery.

(8) Techniques of enchainment, embedding and framing.

Other similarities of lesser importance could no doubt be found, but would be increasingly less central to the generic definition of a Purāṇa than those just cited. It is the absence of some of the latter that leads me to consider the GnP. as having an idiosyncratic status in the Purāṇic genre, even within the limits of variation permissible to the mahāpurāṇas.

If the above list does not exhaust the sufficient conditions for a text to be considered a Purāṇa, it contains the necessary conditions for it to be intuitively recognized as such. Accordingly, if the GnP. can be considered a legitimate representative of the Purāṇic genre, wherein lies its idiosyncrasy? Four principal areas can be suggested:

(1) It contains virtually no pañcalakṣaṇa material.

(2) It contains a minimum of dharmaśāstric material in didactic style.

(3) It effects a change in the plot structure of traditional Purāṇic myths brought about by the necessity to include an intervention by Gaṇeśa in every myth. This transforms its myths into something I can only describe as 'metamyths.'

(4) The invariant plot structure of the myths.

The last two features, in particular, produce an idiosyncratic text as much because of the uniformity of plot they create on the surface of the text as because of the intense sectarian character they confer upon the GnP. Many Purāṇas portray a sectarian tone in the sense of giving a deliberately expanded amount of space to the elucidation of the theology etc. of a single deity, but few do so with the singularity of this Purāṇa. The sectarian tone it conveys is not the expression of an explicit superiority of Gaṇeśa over the other deities in the Purāṇic pantheon, all of whom must still perform the traditional roles associated with them in this pantheon. Rather, it comes through in the imperative that it is Gaṇeśa who gives life to these gods, that he is the unity imposing meaning upon human actions in both their pragmatic and transcendental dimensions. This tone is achieved by the unremitting projection of Gaṇeśa at every level of the narrative, a continuous presentation of him unhindered by long didactic sections containing material seemingly having little or nothing to do with the prevailing deity of the text.

IV. CONTENT OF THE UPĀSANĀKHAṆḌA

There is a global meaning discernible across the Ukh. enabling a reader/hearer to interpret its contents and to find a coherence which cannot just be reduced to that of the individual myths themselves. As self-contained plot units generating a range of meanings the myths are the basic source of processed raw material out of which meaning must arise. Concentration on the entire khaṇḍa requires the integration of meaning into a comprehensive whole where the bounded nature of the individual myth is lost sight of under the pressure to find a meaning for the entire khaṇḍa. The name upāsanā defines the contents of this khaṇḍa, much of which is filled with myths explaining why the god should be worshipped and a few lengthy passages describing rituals to the god. In contrast the Krkh. deals with Gaṇeśa's adventures in fighting four different demons, and so the focus moves away from his worship.

Nine Narrative Units – larger bodies of related content combining several myths – can be identified in the Ukh. Below is a brief summary of their distinctive contents:

NU1 Somakānta's leprosy. A king catches leprosy because of bad karma and loses it only after Gaṇeśa's intervention. (1–9)

NU2 Cosmogonic myths involving the three members of the trimūrti. Brahmā's inability to create, the liṅgodbhava myth, Viṣṇu's battle with Madhu and Kaiṭabha. (10–18)

NU3 The story of Bhīma, a sonless king. Difficulties encountered in gaining a child. (19–27)

NU4 The story of Rukmāṅgada. Improper sexual relations. (28–35) Gṛtsamada and Mukundā. Improper sexual relations and the consequences of class mixture. (36–37)

NU5 Tripura. A demon ascetic who conquers the triple-world and is killed by Śiva. (38–47)

NU6 The separation of Śiva and Pārvatī. Pārvatī looks for Śiva when he is absent. (48–56)

NU7 Śūrasena and Indra. Indra's flying vehicle lands in Śūrasena's kingdom but is unable to ascend again because of the low level of merit there. Myths and rituals about the acquisition of merit. (57–78.10)

NU8 The conflict between Paraśurāma and Arjuna Kārtavīrya. (78.12–82)

NU9 Various cosmic disasters. The rise of the demon Tāraka, Skanda's birth, the burning and revival of Kāma, the emasculation of Śeṣa, Kaśyapa's incapacity to create. (83–93)

None of the dominant themes developed in these Narrative Units is unique to the GnP, though this particular grouping of Narrative Units is unique to it. Why these Narrative Units are grouped like this is unclear, nor is it clear whether the grouping is random or determined by an implicit ordering principle.

Not all the Narrative Units, however, are completely separated in every respect. The set of actions narrated in the embedding myths of NU3, 4, 5, and 6 respectively are portrayed as occurring in chronological succession, the whole set of events being presented as kind of a historical linear sequence. Within the Narrative Units themselves this linear sequence is quickly violated as there is no obligation for the internal chronologies of myths they contain to be strictly sequential. This, however, does not effect the chronology of the embedding myths of the Narrative Units and the impression of a strict linear sequence connecting these four is very easily maintained. Apart from this there is nothing else to connect them.

Within the Ukh. and the Narrative Units the myths can be divided into four different types according to content.

i. Karmavipāka Myths:

The compound karmavipāka occurs as early as Ukh. 2.2, but the importance of the mythic frame is determined by the number of myths of this type that occur in the Ukh. A karmavipāka myth consists of a single mythic narrative divided into an embedding myth and an embedded myth. The ripening of an individual's karma provides the surface cohesion for the temporal continuity that governs the two distinct sets of actions occurring in the two parts of this type of myth. Between embedding and embedded myths a clear logical relation emerges in respect of content, and between the units of content which occur in the two mythic units making up the karmavipāka myth there must exist a relation of reciprocity as each myth depends upon the other for its full meaning to become clear. As an example, the sudden change of fortune in the life of the character described in the embedding myth is predetermined by certain actions described in the embedded myth. There is necessarily a temporal openness in the embedded myth because the actions described in it may have their repercussion in the next life or one several times removed, but in whatever life it does occur, dramatic results are foreshadowed. Six narrative components can be isolated in these myths.

In 1.1.23–9.39 and 1.19.4–39; 27.1–27, for instance, two characters named Somakānta and Bhīma respectively, are defined as ideal kings in terms of the typical stock descriptions used of such kings in ancient Indian literature. This description also includes the location of their kingdoms as well as a statement about their wives, and their fall from high status due to bad karma. The ensuing myth, the embedding myth associated with them, contains most of the elements of the karmavipāka myth and follows the recognizable stages, but it is not an independent frame myth.

In the second section of the karmavipāka myth the ripened karma is described. All that matters is that a change has taken place, irrespective of how dramatic this change might have been. Such changes are obviously most dramatic when, as in the case of Somakānta they precipitate a change in the present life of the karma experiencer. What the ripened karma signifies is usually a failure to worship Gaṇeśa at the right time, a failure which must be rectified by the character who is the subject of the myth. This is easiest to comprehend when the ripened karma produces a situation of obvious disaster, something so bad it must be removed even if it is not clear initially how this can be done.

The third section of the myth encompasses the meeting with the sage or whoever it is who will help the karma experiencer find a way to mollify the effect of this karma or rid himself of it completely. This figure is always depicted in such a way that his quite different status from the karma experiencer easily becomes apparent, as it must, since his capacity to read a karmic situation indicates both his superior religious status and a recognition that he is a person who has his own karmic development under control, if he is susceptible to karma at all. In addition, this special status is further indicated (in 1.23-9.39 and 19.1-27,7, for example) by the karma experiencer's recognition that his meeting with the sage was itself the result of previous merit. Thus this meeting is a positive development for the karma experiencer.

The fourth section of the myth can usually be deemed an independent tale (pūrvajanmakathām, 7,7: pūrvakathām, 19,36) in its own right, possessing its own self-contained plot and often a clear devotional element. The encounter with Gaṇeśa experienced by the karma accruing actor in the fourth section of the karmavipāka myth is a much briefer version of what this same actor will experience when his karma has ripened and it also has a direct bearing on certain events in his subsequent life. When Kāmanda, the previous incarnation of Somakānta, has a Gaṇeśa temple built and an image installed in it (8,21–24), he automatically accrues merit from this and when, finally, he dies he is offered the choice of taking his good or bad karma first. He opts for the former and so is born as King Somakānta, becoming a leper when this good karma runs outs and the bad ripens.

The fifth section of the myth covers the receipt and application of the upāya, the instrument that will either negate the bad karma which has ripened, or mollify it if its effect is experienced by someone else (e.g. King Śūrasena, 76, 41–45) other than the actor who accrued it. This upāya can either be a vrata or, as is more frequent, a mantra to be recited after certain austerities have been performed. This section of the myth narrates action seen to be charting a change in the image of the actor who experiences the ripened karma. Instead of remaining a figure who accepts his ripened karma in a resigned manner, he becomes one who is actively attempting to influence the course of his future karma and to modify the effect of his present karma. Finally, it also marks the beginning of the encounter between this figure and Gaṇeśa, an encounter having the effect of turning the former into a devotee of Gaṇeśa as well as removing his bad karma.

The sixth and final section narrates two main events. Firstly, it describes the result of the application of the upāya, this usually being a mantra. The encounter between Gaṇeśa and the karma experiencer in this section is crucial because this part of the myth has been influenced by the bhakti semantic frame, described below. No longer is the karma experiencer the principal actor in the karmavipāka myth, he also assumes one of the two principal roles in the bhakti myth. This is not to say that the plot structure established by the karmavipāka sequence has been entirely abandoned in this section, rather that, as in every myth in the GnP, there is an imposition of a plot which mirrors the shaping influence of the bhakti semantic onto a plot shaped by the karmavipāka myth.

The second event narrated in this section is the removal of the bad karma, an automatic consequence of the successful encounter with Gaṇeśa and the assumption of devotee-ship by the karma experiencer. This event is given very little treatment in the karmavipāka myth. The message implied is the recognition that the problem of karma is now controllable. It has now entered a new dimension because the actor who has experienced the vipāka has encountered in the figure of Gaṇeśa a potentially more powerful force than karma. In addition the status of the actor has changed dramatically from what it was at the beginning of the myth, such that his new status as a devotee must be accorded far more significance than his status as a karma experiencer.

In all of the karmavipāka myths the working of karma is given its due, individuals are required to accrue and experience karma and, when they worship Gaṇeśa, to accrue good merit for the future. Gaṇeśa becomes the principal remover of karma in these myths, although the idea that the individual should also be responsible for his own future is still maintained. The whole set of actions connected with the worship of Gaṇeśa, all of which imply the theological supremacy attributed to him in the stotras offered him by the karma experiencers, are interrelated in that they are productive of good karma which will lead a person to rebirth in Gaṇeśa's world as well as to a desirable situation on Earth.

ii. Gaṇeśa's Family Relations

In the mythology of the mahāpurāṇas Gaṇeśa's role is predominantly developed in the set of myths illustrating his birth and subsequent interrelations with his parents, Śiva and Pārvatī. These myths are built up around the following events: Gaṇeśa's production (he is never born naturally) by Pārvatī or Śiva, his protection of her from Śiva, his confrontation with Śiva, the loss of his head and, finally, his receipt of an elephant's head. The order of these events also mirrors the sequence of their presentation in the myths.

The set of events related in the myths dealing with Gaṇeśa's birth can be partially analysed in terms of the following five sets of relationships:

(1) Pārvatī and Gaṇeśa
(2) Śiva and Gaṇeśa
(3) Pārvatī and Śiva
(4) Śiva and Pārvatī as one group and Gaṇeśa
(5) Pārvatī and Gaṇeśa as one group and Śiva

At its most stark, Gaṇeśa's relationship with Śiva, his social father (in lieu of his lack of a biological father or mother), is marked by distance, tension and sometimes violence, whereas that with his mother is marked by closeness and tenderness. Here is how these qualities are glossed in a study on Gaṇeśa's mythology:

> After Gaṇeśa's arrival, the myth evokes the playful intimacy and warmth between the mother and her newly created son, an intimacy enjoyed while the father remains at a distance. Eventually the mother must let the son go; the son must confront the father and compete with him for access to the mother. In this conflict the son does not stand a chance against the father's overwhelming strength.[20]

Just as in these myths dealing with Gaṇeśa's birth, the triad of father, mother and son, but never daughter, defines the identity of one basic set of characters which forms one element in the social grouping of actors in the myths in the Ukh. that preserve the influence of this triadic grouping of Śiva, Pārvatī and Gaṇeśa.

The triadic group of actors, the range of available relations that can operate between them and the motif of disfigurement provide a general frame for the myths influenced by this frame. There is no requirement that the

---

[20] Courtright, op.cit., p.103.

myths should mimic it exactly. The characters in the Ukh. myths can assume roles quite different from those in the Gaṇeśa birth myths even though the basic constituencies of the relationships still apply. In the Somakānta myth (1.1ff) the relationship between father and mother as a group, on the one hand, and the son, on the other hand, is at first characterized by closeness and tenderness, but as the myth progresses it passes through latent conflict to a situation characterized by distance and respect.

Of all the possible variations in the relationships available as regulating factors between the members of the triad in these myths, conflict is the one most marked. A representative example occurs in Ch.19 where it is narrated how after much effort King Vallabha and his wife, Kamalā, eventually produce a son called Dakṣa whose body is badly deformed at birth (19.41). After twelve years of strenuous effort to rectify his son's condition, Vallabha becomes depressed and banishes his wife and son to the forest. The son and wife subsist together from her begging until after many adventures. Dakṣa is finally made whole again when he gains a celestial body from Gaṇeśa.

The changing relationships between the members of the triad in this myth mirrors the standard sequence of relationships found in the Gaṇeśa/Śiva/Pārvatī myth, exemplifying distance between father and son as one set, between father and son and mother as a single group as another set, and finally, at the end of the myth (26.6) a kind of respect between father and son, though this is implied rather than developed explicitly. The latter is an important pointer to one of the fundamental messages of these family myths in the Ukh. There can only be a shifting of emphasis within the predetermined set of relations defining the interrelationships between the triad of father, mother and son. Any kind of total resolution which implies a fixity of relations is an impossibility.

In these myths the motif of disfigurement occurs frequently and forms the basis of a conceptual opposition between those who are empowered by disfigurement and those who are not. An example of the latter is Ballāla's father, Kalyāṇa, who is disfigured as a result of his son's empowerment and is offered no means of becoming empowered again in the specific sense of his physical affliction being removed.

It is around each of the three members of the triad, that one level of the plot unfolds. The semantic frame I am presently discussing is manifested in the occurrence of a triadic kin nucleus as one of the defining features of the characters in particular myths and in the occurrence of a particular kind of disfigurement in one of the members of this triad. Obviously the normative relations which should operate between the members of this triadic kin group were a subject of continual importance during many periods of Indian culture. What becomes significant in the rehearsing of these relationships in the epics and Purāṇas is the extent of the disjunction between the normative and the actual. In this light, the appropriate myths in the GnP. rest on the normative position governing the behaviour of the family laid down in the Dharmaśāstras, or, simply 'according to dharma' as is the case in some of the myths under discussion.

Equally, the myths in the GnP. show disjunctions in respect of another invariant, that of Gaṇeśa's relations with Pārvatī and Śiva. It is the tension between these two sets of invariants and the disjunctions the myths throw up in relation to each of them that helps evoke the dramatic quality of the myths in the Ukh. It also anchors them firmly within the tradition of Gaṇeśa bhakti as of the śāstric tradition, always such an important component of the Purāṇic narrative.

iii. The Bhakti Semantic System

All Purāṇas contain myths that illustrate the transformation of an individual from a non-devotee into a devotee of a particular god or goddess. These represent an abstract set of themes I have elsewhere called a bhakti semantic frame,[21] one that facilitates both the selection of raw content, including mythic and didactic material, into a Purāṇic recitational tradition, and imposes a set of restrictions on the way this content is organized in order to produ̇ce a 'bhakti text'.

The dominant feature of the transformational model derived from the bhakti semantic system is the formal representation of a transformation plotting the change in a person's status from non-devotee to devotee in respect of a particular object of devotion. There are eight stages to this transformation as thy occur specifically in the Ukh:

(1) Receipt and application of mantra.
(2) Appearance of object of devotion.
(3) Request for refuge.
(4) Object of devotion offers boon.
(5) Devotee's statement of merit.
(6) Devotee requests boon.
(7) Object of devotion grants boon.
(8) Performance of devotional acts.

To show how the bhakti semantic frame manifests itself in its particular way in the GnP. myths I will allude to the myth of Rukmāṅgada and Gṛtsamada as the stages of the bhakti myth described above are derived from it. After Gṛtsamada has been born Vācaknavi raises him and teaches him the mantra gaṇānāṃ tvā (36.19). At length Gṛtsamada ceases to be accepted as a legitimate sage by other non-brāhmaṇical sages, confronts his mother about the truth of his birth and curses her. Subsequently a voice from the sky tells him Indra is his true father and then he goes into the forest to begin meditating on Gaṇeśa (37.4). In reward for his performance of tapas for thousands of years, Gaṇeśa decides to extend (37.9) his favour to him and manifests himself in his presence, assuming a splendid form

---

21 Greg Bailey, "For a New Study of the Vāmana Purāṇa," Indo-Iranian Journal. 29, 1986, pp.1-16.

consistent with the type taken in a darśana (37.10–13). When he sees this Gṛtsamada receives such a shock that he falls insensible to the ground before speculating as to why this obstacle (vighna, 37.16), as he terms it, has been put in the path of his meditation. He then asks the god to protect him from the obstacle and requests refuge (37.18). He tells Gaṇeśa the problem concerning his own mixed class status and then Gaṇeśa reveals his own true identity, announcing his intention to confer a favour, and asks him to pick a boon (37.21). Absolutely overjoyed, Gṛtsamada declares his life to have now attained its result (37.24). Then he requests his boons:

> ... give me knowledge and knowledge of Brahman; devotion to you which is absolutely rock solid and which I will never cease to recollect; and the highest position of devotee amongst all your devotees, Gajānana. And beneficient God, there is one other boon I request. Give me that special place for your worship which will be capable of attracting the inhabitants of the triple-world, which will be famed in the three worlds and which will be worthy of homage from gods and men. (37.29–31).

He then nominates the Puṣpaka forest as the place he wants to become famous and Gaṇeśa agrees to give him this and everything else for which he has asked. Finally, he makes him the sage of the mantra gaṇānāṃ tvā, a status conferring on him pre-eminence amongst the sages and in so doing, remove the problem of his mixed-class birth. After this Gaṇeśa disappears, Gṛtsamada constructs a temple and erects an image at the same spot which is subsequently named Puṣpaka. His final act is to worship the image and at this point the myth ends.

The resolution of the original problem – not being a devotee of Gaṇeśa – is essential for the myth as a whole because (a) it establishes one of the fundamental boundaries of the myth, and (b) it fulfils one of the didactic intents of the text, namely, to convey the lesson that obstacles can be removed by appeal to Gaṇeśa. Nonetheless, the traditional denouement almost becomes an after-thought, an excellent illustration of this being 48.1–56.46, where Pārvatī's separation from Śiva following his defeat of the demon Tripura is narrated. Here the denouement of the original plot, Śiva's reunification with Pārvatī, occupies only nine 56.35–44 of the four hundred and five verses of these chapters, much greater prominence being given to the description of the performance of various vratas employed in the propitiation of Gaṇeśa.

V. TRADITIONAL AND NON-TRADITIONAL MATERIAL IN THE UPĀSANĀKHAṆḌA

The analysis of the mythic and didactic material of the Ukh. in terms of semantic frames does not exhaust the analysis of the contents of the text. Another avenue of analysis is suggested by the phenomenon of the juxtaposition of traditional and non-traditional material in the narrative of the GnP. I use hesitantly the terms 'traditional' and 'non-traditional' as adjectives to describe Purāṇic contents. All Purāṇic material is traditional. The composers of a particular Purāṇa take great pains in demonstrating that the events they are narrating happened long ago in respect of the external chronology of the text and the internal chronology of the Purāṇic bard in relation to the narrated action of the text he is reciting. In addition the actorial roles found in the myths and the themes they present are those typical of Sanskrit narrative literature from the time of the Mbh, a narrative tradition far older than that of the GnP. This does not preclude innovations from occurring in the Purāṇas, it simply recognizes that a virtual requirement of the genre is the incorporation of material into it in such a guise as to preserve its apparent antiquity on the standard set by the epics and the earliest mahāpurāṇas. There are many myths in the GnP. found elsewhere only in the MudP, the other gānapatya Purāṇa, and a priori these would have to be judged as non-traditional in relation to many other myths considered as variants of well known Purāṇic myths.

Of the approximately thirty-eight distinct mythic units in the Ukh, twenty-one can be considered non-traditional on the grounds of not being found in any Purāṇa other than the MudP. Note that the themes raised in both categories of myths are virtually identical. The difference between them is that the traditional group is characterized by a certain degree of fame contingent upon their received status as well known texts within the culture, a characteristic probably not possessed by the non-traditional myths. Here is a list of such myths. The myth is named according to the name of its chief protagonists, rather than by its colophon title.

Somakānta 1.23–9.39
Kāmanda 7.8–8.37
Bhīma 19.4–39; 27.1–27
Dakṣa 19.40–22.7; 23.41–25.1; 26.3–31
Ballāla 22.8–23.40
Rukmāṅgada 27.28–29.25; 34.43–35.47
Mukundā and Gṛtsamada 36.1–37.48
Kardama 51.49–52.22
'Poor Kṣatriya' 51.58–52.19
Candrāṅgada 54.1–56.32
Śūrasena 57.1–57.25; 59.1–6; 74.1–7; 74.27–76.45; 78.1–10
Bhruśuṇḍin 57.26–38; 58.2; 48–57
Kaivartaka 58.1–47
Sāma 60.8–17
Sulabha and Samudrā 63.4–46
Āśrayā and Kauṇḍinya 64.9–16; 68.33–40
Janaka and Gaṇeśa 66.7–67.21
Cāṇḍāla woman 74.8–26
Budha 77.1–77.62

In total this probably covers about one third of the text, so it is a significant body of new material. The fact that such an amount of new material exists might simply mean the recitational tradition of the GnP. made liberal use of oral material not previously utilized in Purāṇic composition. Yet the question of its provenance differs from the effect on the perceived meaning of the text engineered by the juxtaposition of traditional and non-traditional material. The question of meaning arises when one considers the juxtaposition of the traditional and non-traditional material across the entirety of the text. Traditional myths intersect non-traditional myths in a way preventing the reader/hearer from being subjected to a continuous recitation of a non-traditional myth for more than about four mythic units or nine chapters (e.g. 19–27 which contains four non-traditional myths).

The traditional myths found in the Ukh. are amongst the most famous in the Purāṇic repertoire, e.g. the Paraśurāma myth, the liṅgodbhava myth, and the myths of Nala and Damayantī and Arjuna Kārtavīrya. Their recurrence in conjunction with the recurrent application of the bhakti semantic frame as a transformational model shaping the plots of these myths suggests the juxtaposition of traditional with non-traditional myths might have been intentional. Despite the surface variations the traditional myths exhibit in their various Purāṇic versions, the deep plot structure and its semantic underpinnings allow of minimal variation. Yet this principal is violated in the GnP. where the traditional plot structure is always transformed under the influence of the bhakti semantic frame. Given the consistency with which this occurs, one might describe the resulting process as encompassing a reinterpretation of traditional Purāṇic mythology from a gāṇapatya perspective.

Circumspection is needed, however, in the use of the word 'reinterpretation' as it could imply distillation of meaning according to arbitrarily determined hermeneutical principles. This sense of the word does not summarize the intention of the composers of the GnP. Rather, the traditional myths in the Ukh. exhibit a very specific style of reworking designed to make didactic points about certain theological aspects of Gaṇeśa within the broad context of Purāṇic mythology which these composers have inherited. Those responsible for the recitational tradition of the GnP.

were faced with the problem of presenting a complete theological image of a deity who in the mahāpurāṇas had been presented as performing a narrow range of functions broadly defined within the conceptual limits of the creation and removal of obstacles.

Moreover, the portrayal of him in these terms was already restricted as it had been carried out through the medium of a specific set of myths centred on family relations. In the symbolic universe made explicit in the mythology of the mahāpurāṇas Gaṇeśa is, therefore, accorded a quite specific role, one certainly retained in the GnP. where it remains one of the central planks in his theology. At the same time, however, an attempt has been made to broaden his ambit theologically. The new theological imperative of the Gaṇeśa worshippers demanded an integration of Gaṇeśa's traditional image – the troublesome son of Śiva – in Purāṇic mythology with his new image as the theological centre of the Purāṇic universe including his attendant nirguṇa and saguṇa aspects.

Appropriation and modification of traditional myths by the composers of the GnP. recitational tradition foregrounds Gaṇeśa into the universe of Purāṇic mythology in a way permitting the construction of an image which takes him far beyond his dramatic role contingent upon his being Śiva's son. In the application of the specific GnP. variant of the bhakti myth the retention of the traditional alongside of the new image of Gaṇeśa was quite possible. He could be presented in the traditional myths as the power behind the functions traditionally performed by other gods in Purāṇic mythology. As an example, Gaṇeśa did not need to personally perform the creation function customarily performed by Brahmā, he could simply be portrayed as the deity who removes the obstacles which threaten to prevent Brahmā from successfully accomplishing this task (See 13–15). Nor does he need to displace Śiva's function in the Paraśurāma myth where Śiva empowers Paraśurāma to be able to remove all kṣatriyas from the earth twenty-one times. In the Ukh. version of this myth, Śiva does give a boon (83.7–21) to Paraśurāma which indirectly empowers him with great destructive power, but the final empowerment is the responsibility of Gaṇeśa. For the boon Śiva gives Paraśurāma is a six-syllable mantra to be used in the propitiation of Gaṇeśa with the subsequent benefits this will confer on the agent of the propitiation. Gaṇeśa is able to empower (83.26–48) Paraśurāma without violating the traditional role Śiva plays in this myth. In this way many of the famous roles performed by a variety of characters in Purāṇic mythology are anchored in the power made available by Gaṇeśa.

Acquisition of this power requires recognition by its recipients of Gaṇeśa as the supreme deity in the universe and, like Śiva and Viṣṇu in the mahāpurāṇas, acknowledgement that his is the ultimate power in the universe. The composers of the GnP. have legitimized this image of Gaṇeśa by the best means available to them and one long accepted as viable within the culture. This is the utilization of highly valorized narratives, i.e. traditional myths, to effect a set of innovations in Purāṇic mythology. The success of this was guaranteed as much because these myths met the demands of a specific set of devotees as because the innovations were cloaked in a guise long sanctioned by the culture.

Given the theological imperative as providing one possible explanation of the incorporation of traditional and non-traditional material in the same text and the ready availability of traditional narratives to provide legitimation for Gaṇeśa as the theological centre of the Purāṇic universe, another limit on the selection of materials for inclusion into the recitational tradition of the GnP. suggests itself. From this perspective the text would be required to contain a certain amount of traditional material in its narrative if the theological requirements are to be met. This is a specific requirement, perhaps exclusive to the GnP. itself, and a more general restrictive force working on its process of composition would be the necessity to include traditional material in order to furnish it with the external trappings of the genre to which its name lays claim. Here the conservatizing influence intrinsic to genre as a cultural entity, guaranteeing predictability and consequent recognition as part of a particular order, acts as a restriction on the form of a text which would remain part of the genre.

VI. THE UPĀSANĀKHAṆḌA AS A RITUAL TEXT

The anukramaṇikā of the GnP. given at 10.29–30 sets out the didactic parameters of the text as well as providing the reader/hearer with a guide for the reading of the text. It establishes a very broad organizational grid designed to assist the reader/hearer in creating his own frame of meaning, albeit one which will be tempered by his own retrospective summary of what he finds in the text and whatever else he might bring to it. If we were to make an assessment of the success of the Ukh. in fulfilling the treatment of topics listed in the anukramaṇikā, it would have to be a positive one. Gaṇeśa's theology is developed in full, both by the presentation of thirty-eight dramatic situations where his practical interventions in the affairs of the inhabitants of the triple-world are continually presented, as by the formal theological statements contained especially in stotras and the invocatory parts of pūjās and in the occasional description of the god himself where he is equated with the neuter Brahman of the Upaniṣads. Additionally, and certainly of great moment given the emphasis in this and other bhakti texts directed towards the personal nature of the bhakti relationship, the appearance of Gaṇeśa with an elephant head to those who become his devotees has strong theological and ritual implications. This is his 'real appearance' and, understood as an act performed only for his devotees, becomes part of the conversion process for these very devotees. That it occurs in what can only be described as a ritualistic context where it is the high point of the devotee's experience of Gaṇeśa raises the whole question of the status of the GnP. as a ritualistic text.

Rather than treating both khaṇḍas in this way, yet still recognizing the large quantity of ritualistic material in the Krkh, the name upāsanā would incline the reader/hearer to expect a strong component on ritual in this khaṇḍa as a reflection of its concern with worship. The only reason we might conclude that the Ukh. is not a ritual text (or a 'ritualistic text', the term 'ritual text' implying texts such as the Āgamas or various types of Paddhatis) is because it is mostly filled with mythic narratives.

This objection is substantially tempered by the acknowledgement of the dominating influence the bhakti semantic frame has had on the individual myths in the GnP. and on their configuration across the text as a whole. The portion of the myth dealing wth the devotee's encounter with Gaṇeśa strongly evokes a ritualistic context. His performance of austerities in the forest sets the scene for the recitation of the mantra which will provoke a darśana from Gaṇeśa. Once the deity does appear the vocal exchanges between deity and devotee are formal and conventionalized. When these exchanges are completed and the deity has disappeared the final stage of the bhakti myth is enacted, the construction of a temple to Gaṇeśa and the placement of a mūrti before which the new devotee performs pūjā.

In the bhakti myth the transformation in devotional status of the character who will become Gaṇeśa's devotee brings into play strong ritualistic actions. Apart from the formalized behaviour and the formalized speech acts, the bhakti myth in the GnP. is begun and concluded with a ritual act: the performance of tapas and the recitation of the mantra as the initial stage, the erection of the temple and the worship of the image as the concluding stage. These are quite different ritual acts possessing quite different aims. The first is a self-interested act designed specifically to rid the potential devotee of an obstacle preventing the completion of a precisely defined aim. It is not an act of devotion as such, rather it engages the transactional contract of the brāhmaṇical sacrifice, conforms to no notion of ritual time and is private. Quite different from this, the second is performed as an expression of devotion to the deity, certainly not to achieve any self-interested goal. It is a public act and does not imply the transactional model. The differences in these ritual acts reflect the differing status of the character at the beginning and end of the transformational process which will change his status, but for the present argument the important point is the enclosure of the transformation process by two rituals.

The ritualistic elements of the bhakti myth are strongly complemented by the passages in the Ukh. composed in didactic style where prescriptive descriptions of rituals are given. Six chapters are relevant here:

3.6–28 Purification rituals to be performed by a twice-born man in the morning.

49 The Gaṇeśapārthivapūjā.

50. 2–7 The use of mantras in rituals.

8–23 Results achieved from worshipping different numbers of images.

24–32 Mahotsava on the fourth day of Bhādra. Utsarjana.

60.21–38 Saṃkaṣṭacaturthī. Performed on the fourth day of [the dark fortnight of] each month.

70.6–60 Saṃkaṣṭacaturthīvrata.

88.1–10 Varadacaturthīvrata.

13–20 Mahotsava. Utsarjana.

Collectively these chapters produce a comprehensive description of Gaṇeśa rituals, both the public and private rituals, such that Chs. 49 and 60 are sufficiently comprehensive to be used as precise guides for their respective rituals. The didactic intent of each chapters is deliberate, but this and their existence in the text are not sufficient reasons to describe the Ukh. as a ritual text, even if this is what its composers intended it to be. Whilst the didactic chapters could be removed from the mythic chapters in which they are embedded and still be quite comprehensible because of the pragmatic nature of their contents, it is their appearance in association with the mythic chapters that makes the Ukh. a ritual text.

The myths in the Ukh. obviously provide a narrative and an ideological context for the rituals described in the didactic passages which are themselves embedded in the myths. More specifically it is the bhakti myth that sets the context, but only the final stage is really appropriate here. If the bhakti semantic really has had a prominent influence in determining the choice of contents in the GnP, it must be possible to relate these didactic ritual passages to that semantic frame in order to show how they have been brought into the text by it. However, because the bhakti myth in all its stages manifests strongly ritualistic elements, the process of conversion from non-devotee to devotee in particular being highly formalized, this is not sufficient to account for the occurrence of these didactic passages. Instead we must point to a specific stage of the bhakti myth to see if its narrative expression could be taken as producing the didactic passages. The best candidate for this is the eighth stage, 'Performance of Devotional Acts,' as it covers the devotee's behaviour towards Gaṇeśa.

VII. A NOTE ON THE TEXT

This translation is based on the editon of the text published by Gopal Narayana and Sons in Bombay in 1892, and two other editions virtually identical to it. Each has ninety-two chapters. However, I have also consulted five manuscripts and a study of them has led me to break the text into ninety-three chapters.

I have also slightly modified the text in many places, full details of which can be found on pp.583-600 of the first edition of this translation.

CHAPTER ONE

Description of Somakānta

The Sages said:

1-3. Very wise bard of bards, who is skilled in the Vedas and the śāstras, repository of all knowledge, you are the only reciter we have found. You are omniscient and good and you have appeared because of the great merit we have acquired in this and previous lives. Our life in this world is auspicious and we are very fortunate as are our deceased ancestors, the Vedas and śāstras, our austerities and our hermitage.

4-5. We have heard the eighteen Purāṇas at length and now, best of brahmins, we want to hear the others as well. For twelve years we have been engaged in Śaunaka's great sacrifice and our only reason for stopping is to drink the ambrosia of your tale.

The bard said:

6-7. "Illustrious ones, due to your meritorious actions you have asked well. The request of those who are virtuous and even-minded is beneficial to people. Brahmins, I too experience delight when reciting these tales, especially so if I will be reciting to men of virtuous conduct.

8-12. There are, however, eighteen minor Purāṇas such as the Gaṇeśa, the Nārada, the Narasiṅha, etc. Amongst these, firstly I am going to recite the Gaṇeśa Purāṇa. It is rarely heard, especially by someone in the world of mortals. Simply by hearing it a man will achieve his goal. Neither Brahmā, nor Śeṣa can describe its majesty, yet with your acquiesence I am going to tell it in summary. Those who have acquired merit over many births will hear it, but heretics, non-believers or evil-doers will not hear it.

13-15. Since he is really eternal, without characteristics and has no beginning, nobody seeks[1] to describe his real appearance. However, those who are devoted to his worship can describe that appearance of his which has characteris-tics. The blessed one has the form of Om and is stationed in the first syllable of the Vedas. The sages and the gods led by Indra always recollect him in their hearts and Brahmā, Śiva, Viṣṇu and Indra continually worship him, the cause of all worlds, the cause of all causes.

16. At his command Ka creates the universe,
At his command Viṣṇu protects it,
At his command Hara destroys it,
At his command the Sun, Lord of the day, moves around.

17. At his command the wind blows too,
At his command the waters flow to the various directions,
At his command the stars shine on the Earth,
And at his command fire burns in the triple-world.

18-22. His adventures are secret and are not told to anyone, but as I am going to tell them to you, listen attentively, brahmins. Previously Brahmā narrated it to the immeasurably splendid Vyāsa, he narrated it to Bhṛgu and he to Somakānta. Myriads of merit arise for those who visit sacred places, give gifts, perform austerities, sacrifices and vows, but for those who hear the Purāṇa called Gaṇeśa, wisdom grows, excellent brahmin, and their minds turn neither towards worldly existence, nor to land, wives and sons. They are excellent sages, attentive to the tale of Gaṇeśa, Lord of the peacocks. So hear about its greatness in the case of Somakānta.

---

[1] "nobody seeks" kenāpi neṣyate: GN has the easier reading śakyate, but is unsupported by any of the manuscripts.

23-31. In Devanagara in Surāṣṭra there was a king named Somakānta who understood the meaning of the Vedas and the śāstras and followed closely the meaning of the Dharmaśāstras. Twenty elephants, two thousand horses and six thousand chariots followed him when he marched out and he also had uncountable foot soldiers, some of whom carried fire-weapons and others who carried a bow with a pair of quivers. He surpassed Bṛhaspati in intelligence and Kubera in wealth, and in patience he surpassed the Earth and in depth the ocean. And that king surpassed the sun in brightness, the moon in splendour and he surpassed the fire in heat and the god of love in handsomeness. His five ministers were powerful and firm in fortitude, and they understood the true meaning of the treatises on political conduct. They were crushers of enemy kingdoms. The first one was called Rūpavat and another one was called Vidyādhīśa. There was also Kṣemaṃkara, Jñānagamya and the fifth was called Subala. Due to their great prowess they overran various countries, and when decked out in a variety of clothes and ornaments, they were very handsome. Ever engaged in the king's duties they were exceedingly endeared to the king.

32-36.The king had a wife named Sudharmā who was endowed with good qualities. Straight after they had beheld her form Rati, Rambhā and Tilottamā were embarrassed and though they expressed disdain towards it[2] they could not find happiness anywhere. On her ears she was wearing splendid golden earrings studded with many gems and on her neck she wore a golden ornament and pearls. On her hips there was a girdle made of jewels and anklets of similar type were on her feet, and on her fingers, toes and hands, she wore rings of unsurpassed beauty. She possessed clothes by the thousands of many colours and of great value, and was dedicated to revering her illustrious lord and to being generous and honouring guests. Day and night she served her husband and always obeyed his command.

---

[2] "they expressed disdain towards it" na ca menire: That is, disdainful towards her beauty.

37. These two had an excellent son named Hemakaṇṭha, who had the strength of a myriad of elephants, and who was wise, courageous and instilled distress in his enemies.

38. Such was Somakānta, best of kings on the Earth. When the king had reduced everything to his submission, he established a kingdom on the earth, and he was ever intent upon the law, a sacrificer and a liberal gift-giver, excellent brahmin.

CHAPTER TWO

The second chapter

The bard said:

1-3. Sages, you must all hear about Somakānta's bad deed.[3] As a consequence of the ripening of his karma that virtuous king began suddenly to ooze with leprosy and this gave him great pain. Whether it be good or bad, karma never leaves a man. Whatever is done in any condition becomes karma which living beings certainly experience in other conditions.

4-7b. As if he were a boat in the ocean, he became sunk in an ocean of sorrow and he experienced much pain as though he were bitten by a snake. The king was completely covered with many wounds from which blood was trickling and, full of purulent blood, he became distressed because of the worms on his body. Seemingly filled with consumption the king became merely bone, was deranged with anxiety and experienced pain in all his senses. Then, having checked his mind with effort, the king spoke to his ministers.

---

[3] "bad deed" duṣkṛtam: Strictly speaking this word denotes the results of Somakānta"s previous evil activity, the coming to fruition of which is described in the present chapter.

The king said:

7c-11. Damn my kingdom and my appearance! Damn my strength, my life and my wealth! What has caused this calamitous karma to manifest? In splendour I have excelled Soma, hence I am called Somakānta, and I have protected the good, the wretched, those who are versed in the Vedas, the hermitages as well as the nations and other beings, as though they were my sons. And with my arrows I have defeated enemies of ferocious appearance and I have brought the entire Earth under my control. And with my mind restrained and with no evil attachments I have correctly worshipped Sadāśiva, the Supreme Self.

12-15. Previously my body was redolent of fragrant scents, but now, because I stink foully, my life is worthless. For that reason, with the approval of all of you, I will go to the forest. For the sake of my kingdom, you must all consecrate Hemakaṇṭha as king, my valourous and intelligence son, and protect him courageously. I will now never be able to show my face in the world. For me there is no point in having a kingdom, nor wives, nor life, nor regal splendour. Prime-ministers, I will work for my own good in the forest.

The bard said:

16-18. After he had said this, covered with a stream of warm, purulent blood, he fell to the ground like a tree struck by the wind, excellent brahmins. Then the ministers and young women made a tremendous noise and for a moment the people made a dreadful cry of distress. But with the use of quick acting herbs, the ministers' application of sacred formulas and by fanning him and wiping him with a cloth, they revived him. After the king had been restored the ministers said this.

The ministers said:

19.Through your favour happiness equal to that of Indra
Has been enjoyed spontaneously by each person.

How are we going to live without you now?
And how can we subsist like cattle slaughterers?
20. Your only son must rule!
He is strong, a killer of enemies and his wealth is great.
Leaving behind all happiness, King,
We are now going to go with you to the forest.

The bard said:

21. Then Sudharmā, his chief wife and a real heroine,

Made a declaration to serve the king in the forest:
'I will go with him unto the end, but you should not!
In conjunction with my son you must rule the kingdom as I would!
22. Of a person's previous activity there is not simply one who experiences
What is unpleasant and another who experiences what is pleasant.
A person is attached to the result of particular actions,
Since such a thing must be experienced by him alone.
23. He enjoyed this kingdom with pleasure,
And I too had various kinds of pleasurable experiences.
Women should accompany their husbands in this world and the next,
So it is prescribed by the sages.'
24. Then at that very moment her cultivated son, Hemakaṇṭha, who was filled with grief, made this speech to Somakānta.

Hemakaṇṭha said:

25-26. Without you, Tiger amongst men, I have no value in the kingdom, wives, life or abundant wealth. Just as a lamp without oil and a body without breath are useless, so too is this kingdom without you, Protector of the Law.

The bard said:

27. After he had drunk of the ambrosiacal words of his ministers, his son and Sudharmā, the delighted king addressed his son concerning the law.

The king said:

28-32. That son who is ever devoted to his father's command and faithfully performs the funeral ceremony, and who offers a funeral oblation in Gayā is indeed called a son. He indeed is a son who has his own son and who knows the meaning of the Dharmaśāstras, who understands correct political conduct, who sustains everyone and who sustains the deceased fathers. Therefore, in accordance with correct political conduct, rule this kingdom at my command. In conjunction with the ministers, command all these subjects as if they were sons. Oozing with leprosy and beyond contempt, I am going to the forest with my wife, Sudharmā. Assent to this, firm-vowed son.

CHAPTER THREE

Description of conduct and so forth

The bard said:

1-4. After getting up from there and taking his son's right hand, the king took him to an upper room of his palace where he always took counsel. There was a golden lion's throne in there bedecked with many precious stones and inlaid with pearls and corals, shining like Indra's palace. Father and son sat there, and though there was only two of them, they appeared as many, because they were reflected in every gem and so appeared to be covered with a mass of gems. Filled with concern[4] for his son

[4] "filled with concern" karuṇāyukta: The noun karuṇā often renders "pity" or "compassion", both of which seem inappropriate here where the king is

and for the sake of his family's glory, the king spoke firstly about personal conduct and then about the various forms of political conduct.

Somakānta said:

5-6. A man should wake up when only three hours of the night is left, and after he has left his bed and sat in a clear spot, he should recollect his teacher. After having asked of the Earth, "World, accept patiently the touch of my feet," and having contemplated his chosen deity, he should bow and accompany this with a eulogy:

7. At daybreak I give obeisance to Gaṇanātha,
Who is the cause of everything,
Who gives boons to gods such as Brahmā and so forth,
Who abounds in all the Āgamas,
Who grants the results of accomplishment in the law, power and sensuality,
Who is the cause of liberation for humans,
Who is beyond words, who is the beginning
And who has innumerable appearances.

8. At daybreak I make obeisance to Śiva, husband of the mountain's daughter,
Who has the moon on his diadem,
Who is dressed in a tiger-skin,
Who is pitiless towards the mind-born Kāma,
Who gives boons to Viṣṇu and Indra,
Who is loved by the gods and perfected beings,
Who carries the ḍamaru drum, the trident and snakes,
Who is Pura's enemy.

9. At daybreak I make obeisance to Viṣṇu, husband of Lakṣmī,
Who has mighty strength,
Who has engaged in several incarnations

---

giving his son instruction in practical matters about kingship for the sake of preserving his own lineage and the kingdom.

For the protection of his own people,
Who dwells on the Milk ocean,
Whose kinsman is overlord of the gods,
Who is the Lord, the destroyer of evil,
Who defeats enemies and is the cause of liberation for all beings.

10. At daybreak I make obeisance to the Sun, Lord of the day,
Who removes evil,
Who removes deep darkness,
Who is praised by exalted people,
Who is the three Vedas,
Who by means of illusion expelled the gods' enemies,
Who is the unique cause of knowledge,
Who possesses great power and is of noble character.

11. At daybreak I make obeisance to Pārvatī, the mountain's daughter,
Who causes prosperity, who brings to the other shore
Those centred in the ocean of worldly existence,
Who possesses three eyes,
Who is the cause of the elements of creation and so on,
Who by means of illusion expelled the gods' enemies,
Who consists of illusion,
Who is praised by the Lords of sages and gods, who is Sureśī.

12-20b. After he has recollected other gods and groups of sages in the same way and mentally worshipped them with ritual practices,[5] he should request forbearance in case of mistakes. Then, taking a water pot, he should go in a

---

[5] "and mentally worshipped them with ritual practices" mānasairupacārais: The upaçāras are specific ritual acts (See P. Courtright: op.cit., pp.184-85; Ukh. 70,17ff and P. Kane: History of Dharmaśāstra, 1962, Vol.5.2. pp.35ff., for a description) to be performed in a personal ritual (pūjā or anuṣṭhāna) to a deity. Like many other practical forms of worship which are often prohibitive in terms of time and expense they are regarded as equally efficacious if merely thought about in the mind.

southwesterly direction from the village, and he should also take clay – pure white for a brahmin, red for a kṣatriya, and black for a vaiśya and a śūdra. But he should never dig it from a river bank, nor from an anthill or the house of a brahmin. After he has covered the ground with grass etc., and has emptied himself of urine and excrement whilst facing north or south, whether in the night or day, a man, having first cleaned his bottom with grass or soft wood and so forth, should then wash himself five times with water and clay. Then immediately after, his left hand should be washed ten times in this way and then both hands seven times. Then the penis once and the left hand three times. When he has emitted urine he should wash his hands and feet twice. For a householder it is prescribed that this should always be done once, but one performing a vow should do it twice, a forest dweller three times and a wandering ascetic should do it four times. For purification day and night a woman and a śūdra should do one eighth of the latter.

20cd-28. After that, having sipped water and taken a piece of wood from the milk or thorn tree, he should clean his teeth and tongue, accompanying this with a request, 'O Lord of the forest, give me strength, power, glory, energy, cattle, intelligence, wealth, wisdom and knowledge of Brahma.' Then, having first taken a bath in cold water to remove dust, he should perform the saṃdhyā worship with prayers and benedictions for the household. And after that he should utter prayers, offer an oblation, practise Vedic recitation, offer a libation for the deceased ancestors and perform personal worship. And he should feed all the gods and guests whilst under the eye of the brahmins, listen to Purāṇas and give gifts, but he should avoid slandering others. With ambrosial words, energy and money he should be benevolent to others, but he should neither hurt others nor engage in self praise. Nor should he practise treachery towards his teacher, nor lay scorn on the Vedas, practise heresy or frequent with evil doers, eat what should not be eaten or have intercourse with another's wife. Nor should he avoid his own wife but approach her for sex at the right time and he should also act dutifully towards his mother and father, his teachers and cows. He should give food and clothes to the weak, the blind and the poor and he should certainly not behave in such a way that involves forsaking the truth.

29-31. Those who are virtuous enjoy the king's favour and protection, but when he has studied the Dharmaśāstras with regard to offences and has consulted with the wise, experienced in political conduct, the king should mete out punishment. If he does not inspire confidence, one should never have confidence in him. One who wishes to survive should not have excessive confidence in one who is always confident, nor should one ever have confidence in one who is always confident, yet is violent.

32-33. Through application of the six measures[6] he should make his own kingdom prosper and he should make gifts according to his capacity, or otherwise he will become weak. When others are confused the king should condemn the worst path. It is he who should apply punishment and he who should speak through ambassadors and be of agreeable appearance.

34-41. Only through fear of punishment do people adhere to their own duty, otherwise it is said, 'There would be no agreement about what is right for oneself and what is right for another.' If some vile man were to slander or praise him, he should be neither angry nor pleased, for what is the worth of reproach and what is the worth of praise. If in the past someone has injured another or if in the past someone may have been rich, yet now comes for refuge, he should always be accorded refuge. The advice of spies should always be utilized for it is the foundation of the kingdom and having abandoned the six enemies such as sensuous desire, etc., he should conquer the others. The excellent king should not cause the loss of livelihoods, the deprivation of his subjects, the deprivation of the gods or the deprivation of pleasure gardens and shrines. To attain renown he should give gifts and donations during the periodic change of the moon. He should not issue commands to friends, nor should he divulge a secret amongst women. He

---

[6] The six measures are listed at Manu-Smṛti. vii,160.

should extract a cow from mud and a brahmin from debt. Never should he utter a lie. Never should he abandon the truth. He must captivate the hearts of his ministers, subjects and dependants and he should always do homage to brahmins and gods.

42-48. When he had taught his son, Hemakaṇṭha, everything else about that conduct called 'Political Conduct' as it is taught in the Veda and in respect of its standard usage, which brings peace, has a pleasing form and is the overlord of the sciences, the king summoned his ministers, observing that the hour was auspicious. They immediately procured many Veda knowing brahmins, skilled in sacrificial rites, who were in their houses. Then the king invited the great kings and queens, his own friends, the chiefs of the city guilds and the citizens to witness the consecration of his own son, a killer of enemies. After he had worshipped Gaṇeśa and his chosen deity according to the rite, and had asked for a blessing whilst honouring his mother, and had then performed the obligatory funerary ceremony, refreshed the brahmins with some juice and caused the completion of his son's consecration to the accompaniment of the sound of hymns, Somakānta then made this statement to his three principal advisers.

49-50. The king said, Here is my son! Ministers, be prudent! My son is assigned into your hands alone. Since those who are skilled in politics carry out my orders, so should they too, including the principals of guilds, obey his order.

CHAPTER FOUR

Entering the City

The bard said:

1-4. When the consecration began, the king honoured the brahmins and gave them jewels, pearls and coral, and myriads of excellent cows. He also gratified them all with elephants, cows, horses, money and fine clothes. The clothes came from various regions and had gold concealed within them. To the kings, queens and heads of villages he gave clothes from Kashmir, large and of many colours, and to his dependants and those of good character he gave things according to what they deserved. Then to his ministers he gave some villages and large amounts of money.

5-9. After that, full of grief and pain, and exceedingly dirty and impure because of faults acquired in former lives, the king left for the forest. Once the king had departed a great cry of distress arose amongst the people, and, each one having instantly abandoned his own job, they – all – ministers, the queen and Hemakaṇṭha, surrounded by his friends – went toward the overlord of men. When he left he was getting up, falling, stumbling, fleeing and weeping. But the distressed ministers and townspeople surrounded him when the king had gone two gavyūtis[7] and had become very tired. Seeing a lake of cool water surrounded by many trees, he spoke to all the ministers, towns people and his kinsmen.

10-16. Please forgive the offence I have caused you during my long reign. People, with my hands joined in salutation I am now making obeisance. Have compassion on my son and on me who has become like this because of fate. I request all of you not to lose affection for me. Everyone who has come, including women and the elderly, must go back to the city. You are being protected by my son and so you will be free from worries. All of you bid farewell to me. I am resolved to go to the forest and when you have all left, my mind will become steady. All of you kindly do this great favour for me, for although I want to die and am in great distress, I am unable to speak harshly to you. Only I have acquired this great evil from my other births, so for the people who bring about good I have separated myself from this kingdom. As I am oozing from leprosy, what else can I do?

[7] A gavyūti is a measure of about six miles.

Each person experiences his own deed, be this a good deed or a bad deed.

The bard said:

17-20. After they had heard this speech the king's friends were dumbfounded and some who were greatly distressed struck their heads with the palms of their hands. Some who were clever and others who were learned consoled each other about the king by telling the adventures of men who had lived previously. But others, having looked closely at his unspeakable condition, became like yogins who become accomplished in knowledge when they have understood their true nature. Then some who were courageous, having calmly checked their distress, spoke to the distressed Somakānta who was longing to go to the forest.

The people said:

21-25. Because you have nourished and protected us it is not fitting that you should leave. In the same way that coldness does not leave water, nor heat fire, or as the ocean does not abandon its shores or the sun leave brightness, so how can we enter the city without you, Beloved of the people. Indeed, King, like the starry heaven without the moon, this city will have no splendour without you, Harasser of enemies. We shall go with you to two or three sacred fords. By visiting a sacred ford your appearance which was splendid will be splendid again. Then, preceded by bards chanting eulogies and filled with great joy, we shall together enter the banner-filled city.

The bard said:

26-27. Having heard their speech, yet still full of anger and anxiety, the king, although bowing to them, said repeatedly, "No! No! Then Hemakaṇṭha, accompanied by the ministers, spoke to the beloved king with appropriate propriety and a feeling of compassion and affection.

His son said:

28. I cannot bear to go and rule the kingdom and to live without you. How can I bear to be separated from you, something I have never experienced before?

The king said:

29-35. It was for this very reason that previously I instructed you in the learned Dharmaśāstras which contain so much about good political conduct. Please don't allow that to become useless! It is said that once a descendant of Jamadagni who was knowledgeable in respect of good conduct and very wise struck his mother in compliance with his father's order. And Rāma too, having left his kingdom went to the forest with his younger brother without having asked and Lakṣmaṇa causelessly abandoned Sītā in the forest.[8] Therefore, at my command, Hemakaṇṭha, go quickly to the city with my three ministers and rule the kingdom I have entrusted to you. Just as when a wise man is intent upon his appropriate task, his mind remains on the Supreme Self, or, just as the mind of an ordinary person goes onto wealth when it is displayed, so when I have left for the forest my mind will go onto you. When good fortune has arisen again through the power of fate, I will go to my house. The law will certainly continue to operate if you are acting in accord with my command, but if you accompany me this will not be so. Therefore go and I will depart.

The bard said:

36-38. The townspeople, ministers and his son were very miserable and when they had decided to depart they made obeisance to the king. He dismissed them and they returned to the city after having praised him with prayers and circumambulated him. Subsequently, after he had assembled a great army with foot soldiers, chariots, horses and elephants, the

---

[8] Presumably the implication of this verse is that these two figures acted without their father''s permission and so disaster followed.

proud Hemakaṇṭha, holding parasol and banner, went to the city.

CHAPTER FIVE

'Conversation between Sudharmā and Cyavana'

The bard said:

1. Then having come up to his mother, he said to her eagerly, but with a mixture of affection and embarrassment, "Mother, how can you abandon one who is without fault?

Her son said:

2-3. You should say to father, 'Your son must go with you'! If in compliance with your command he will take me, I will serve you two. I am not inclined towards the kingship. Will this kingdom give me happiness when I am without you two?

Sudharmā said:

4-5. Even though he is racked with so much grief and misery the king will not issue this command to me. Therefore, great-armed son, depart with my permission! Child, I am obedient to the rule of loyalty to one's husband. For a wife there is no other god than her husband and he alone must be esteemed.

The bard said:

6-9. When he had heard this, that kind-hearted son made obeisance to his mother, obtained her assent and circumambulated her, then returned to the city. Like Indra's city its moistened roads were opulent with fragrant scents and it was adorned with blossoms, flags and banners. After he had given betel nut and clothes to his subjects and sent them away, the joyous, but grieving, king entered his splendid home. He ruled the kingdom by the law, protecting his subjects as he would a son, and consistent with the teachings he put his mind onto the law, power, sensuality and liberation.

The sages said:

10. But what happened to Somakānta? Did he reach the forest? Did he have a companion and did he engage in any activity? Tell us in detail!

The bard said:

11-20. All right, faultless sages listen carefully and I will tell you how Somakānta did what he had to do after he had gone to the forest. With his lawful wife, Sudharmā, and two of his ministers, Subala and Jñānagamya, he entered the inaccessible forest. In front went the two ministers, in the middle the king and like Sītā behind Rāma, his lawful wife Sudharmā went behind. Eating the same food, the four were of one mind concerning dwelling and resting places and they went from forest to forest, indifferent to happiness and misery. Terribly tormented by fatigue, hunger and thirst and from going up and down pathless hills, they sought the shade and settled down somewhere. Then, going further into the forest they saw a large lake where dwelt tortoises, and crocodiles which were like Mataṅga, and where there were beautiful trees including the palmyra, the Khadira, the Pine, the Priyāla, the Bakula, the Breadfruit, the Roseapple, the Nimb and the Fig trees infested with multitudes of creepers of many varieties. And where the darkness was thick like the inside of a mountain cave, and where the breeze feels pleasant and carries the odour of the lotus and of kādamba geese, and from where the sages gather their lotuses and fruit. And where there were swans, herons, hawks, parrots, crows and cuckoos, sārikas and cranes, all making different cries.

21. And where for those who dwell in the many arbours of creepers and flowers
There is neither twilight nor sunbeam, heat nor cold.

Just as for those who possess merit
There is no hunger, thirst or death in heaven.

22-24. When they had reached there they all drank some cold water to dispel their fatigue, and when they had bathed and performed the obligatory rites they enjoyed some fruit. For a while then, the king slept on a pleasant sandy bank whilst his lawful wife, Sudharmā, stayed by to massage his feet and the two ministers, having received his assent, left to gather tubers, roots, flowers and lotus shoots.

25. Then Sudharmā saw a boy of marvellous appearance,
Fierce, powerful and blazing with splendour.
Because of his conspicuous appearance she thought,
'This boy was previously born as Kāma.'
26. Straight after she had seen him Sudharmā rejoiced,
And believed that he must be the bringer of good.
Realizing that her heart was agitated, yet still,
And that he could cause evil or be of assistance, she spoke.
27. She asked him, 'Who are you and why have you come?
Whose son are you and who is your mother?
Friend, speak ambrosial words to me
And delight my ears now!'

The bard said:

28. So questioned the boy addressed
The king's daughter with ambrosial words.
'Beautiful woman, Bhṛgu is my father and Pulomā is my mother.
I have come here from my house to get some water.

29-33. Beautiful woman, I am called Cyavana and I am carrying out my father's order. Who are you and is this man with you? Why has he come to this forest? Why are your limbs sweating like small streams on a mountain in the rainy season? And what karma has caused this revolting smell? Tell me! Having been so charming yourself with your beautiful eyes, your great delicacy, your face clear and lovely and every splendid limb charming, why are you waiting upon him who is completely covered with masses of worms. A person as eminent as him has never previously been known by your father, friends, brothers and the brahmins, yet now he is a leper overburdened with a mass of worms. Why were you chosen as his bride and why have you come to this inaccessible forest?'

The bard said:

34. When that intelligent son of a sage had questioned Sudharmā, who was filled with grief and joy, she explained everything to him.

Sudharmā said:

35-41. In the region of Surāṣṭra there is a great and famous city called Devatā. My husband Somakānta lived there and ruled the kingdom. He was very proud, munificent, of great courage, mighty and heroic, possessed innumerable troops and was a crusher of the kingdom's enemies. He performed sacrifices, was most handsome, of regal splendour and brought bliss to his friends. He was discriminating in all his duties and proficient in the treatises on political conduct. For a long time, Excellent brahman, the king enjoyed his own kingdom, a position attained due to the ripening of earlier karma. Accompanied by his two ministers, he has come to this forest. Since he has presented the kingdom to his son, I have been wandering, sticking to his back. I have come here with two ministers called Subala and Jñānagamya. Having received the king's assent those two went into the forest in search of fruit. Rākṣasas, spirits of the dead, ghosts and birds and beasts of various kinds terrify us here. But why haven't they eaten us?

42-49. I could not bear to experience his misery, yet I am standing here before him. Nor can I see an end to his misery or to his bad karma. When he was surrounded by brahmins he did not find pleasure in oily, sweet, acidic, salty or bitter food, but he does now with fruits, roots and tubers of sour and harsh flavours. Whereas cooked food is ample nourishment for the poor and for him, for the prosperous there is not much strength in cooked food alone. He used to sleep in a hevenly soft bed, but now behold everywhere in him the reversal caused by time. His lovely fragrances of many kinds had spread in all directions, but now he is foul smelling and smeared with purulent blood. Surrounded by wise men he was immersed in an ocean of bliss, but now he is covered by worms and is in an ocean of misery. I don't know how we will cross over this ocean of misery, Son of Bhṛgu. But like a boat on the deep ocean for those who are sinking, you must be like a boat for him.

CHAPTER SIX

Arrival at Bhṛgu's Hermitage

The bard said:

1-2. After Bhṛgu's son, Cyavana, had heard that speech, he quickly picked up his pot which was filled with water. Distressed, he silently returned home in great sorrow. Bhṛgu then asked his son what had caused his delay.

Bhṛgu said:

3. You look like you're trembling. Have you seen something extraordinary? Why are you late? Son, tell me from the beginning!

His son said:

4-9. Sage, in the region of Surāṣṭra in a city known as Devatā, there was a lotus-eyed king called Somakānta. He ruled a large kingdom, protecting his subjects by the law. Yet because of fate, misfortune befell him and having bestowed the kingdom upon his son he has come here, tormented by his extreme sorrow, with his wife and two ministers, Subala and Jñānagamya. Oozing with leprosy and covered with worms he rambles about, moving with difficulty. He has become an Indra who acquired one thousand vaginas from the sage, Gautama.[9] Some time passed whilst I was asking about what had happened to them, with questions such as, "How did delicate limbed Sudharmā come to this? And how did her husband come to be oozing with leprosy?" But their pitiful words made my heart choke up and after I had filled my pot I quickly returned.

The bard said:

10. He reported to him everything she had related in her speech and after he had heard it, Bhṛgu again spoke to his son.

Bhṛgu said:

11. Son, you have my permission to go. Quickly bring them all to me. I want to see these curiosities and I will show myself to them.

The bard said:

12-13. Urged on thus by his father, Cyavana, a very repository of compassion, went from pond to pond, anxious to find Sudharmā. At that very moment the two ministers, Subala and Jñānagamya, laden with fruits and tubers, came to the king.

14-18b. Then the sage spoke to the delicate-eyed Sudharmā, "My father invites all of you to his hermitage, Firm-vowed woman." When she had heard his speech, Sudharmā, agitated with grief, became depressed and her body looked as though life had left it. After the very virtuous wife of the king had drunk in the ambrosia of his words, that delicate-limbed woman left, accompanied by the two ministers. With her husband Somakānta she was guided by the sage's son, like Śiva and Śivā accompanied by Gaṇeśa and Skanda. She looked splendid in the middle of the path as she went before the sage.

---

[9] The point of the comparison is that Somkānta"s reaction to leprosy is identical with that of Indra when, for being caught attempting to seduce Gautama"s wife, he was cursed by that sage to become covered with one thousand vaginas. See Chs.30-34 below for a telling of this myth.

18c-21. They reached the area of Bhṛgu's hermitage, filled with the sound of mantras and strewn over with various kinds of flowers and creepers. It resounded with the cries of many birds, and cats, mongooses, hawks, elephants, cows, rats, snakes, birds, lions and tigers play there. No wind blows fiercely there, nor does the sun shine fiercely there. It does not rain fiercely there and the clouds rain only at his wish. Going before the sage's son, they entered there happily.

22. She saw the wondrous Bhṛgu there,
Clad in deer and tiger skin, the image of the sun.
Accompanied by his wife and two ministers, the king
Bowed and with his hollowed hands joined, he spoke.

The king said:

23. My blessings proclaimed by the brahmins have come to fruition,
As has my accumulated good work and austerity.
Since birth I have been completely pure and
Life has been good for my mother and father.
24. Masses of merit acquired in previous births
Caused a sight of you which instantaneously destroys evil.
It causes future blessings, Indra of sages,
And renders birth pure in the past, present and future.
25. In the region of Surāṣṭra, sage of unerring sight,
In a city called Devatā I ruled a kingdom
By utilizing prudent politics, by honouring gods, brahmins and so forth,
And by dread of evil, Indra of sages.
26. But what was my unforeseen evil
Which manifested itself most terrible and miserable,
By which I was led into such a terrible state?
I know of no possible remedy for it![10]

---

[10] "no possible remedy for it" na kiṃcit pratikāram atra: With the first occurrence of the words pratikāra and upāya, which appears in the next line, a central motif in the plot of the myths of the GnP. is encountered. Pratikāra has the literal sense of "counter-action," upāya that of "arrival, approach,"

27. Remedies were tried but came to nothing.
I now seek the remedy of your compassion as a real remedy.
We have come for refuge to your hermitage
Where natural enmities attain concord.

The bard said:

28. Having heard this speech, firm-vowed Bhṛgu became filled with compassion, and after looking at Somakānta, he thoughtfully spoke.

Bhṛgu said:

29-31. King, I will tell you a remedy. Don't worry! Men who are in my hermitage experience no misery. Excellent king, I will talk to you about what you did in a previous life and about your evil, which has forced you into this condition. But firstly you must all have a meal as you have been looking for food for a long time. From one forest you have travelled exhausted into this forest and your faces are severely emaciated.

The bard said:

32-34. After he had said this he had him bathe, with his body rubbed with fine oils. Then he had him eat large quantities of food seasoned with the six flavours. At the command of Bhṛgu, the eminent sage whose splendour is immeasurable, they ate, duly prepared, well bathed and rested. Having lost their unsurpassable anxiety they slept on soft beds provided by the sage, as though back in their own kingdom.

---

with a semantic extension to the sense of "attainment of one"s goal" and therefrom to the "means of attaining one"s goal".

CHAPTER SEVEN

Description of Somakānta's Earlier Life

The sages said:

1-2. What did Somakānta do after he arrived there? And what remedy did the omniscient Bhṛgu suggest? Excellent brahmin, tell this tale to us listeners. We never have enough of drinking in your ambrosial words.

The bard said:

3-5. You have asked appropriately, Very fortunate sages! You are certainly oceans of knowledge. Brahmins, if the listener or the reciter does not get to the end of the tale, the reciter should recite from the written book or the hearer should take it with him. If a pupil does not ask a question and if, when questioned, the teacher does not reply, then both are considered by people to be deaf and dumb, Excellent brahmins. Now listen, because I am going to tell Somakānta's story.

6-7. When night had passed away and the sun, Lord of the day, had risen, the best of the Bhṛgus, having completed his early morning bath, the muttering of prayers and the offering, began to tell the king[11] the tale of his previous life. With his wife and two ministers he had also bathed and completed the muttering of prayers.

Bhṛgu said:

8-14. In the delightful city of Kolhāra, located near the Vindhya mountains, there was a famous vaiśya called Cidrūpa who was very wealthy. His wife called Atisubhāgā was famous for her beautiful eyes and was very virtuous, of generous disposition and faithful to her husband's commands. In a previous life you became her son, Best of kings, and as

---

[11] That is, Somakānta.

proclaimed by the brahmins these two named you Kāmanda. But your parents had become senile and day and night they individually showered excessive affection on you and over-fondled you. Then in an auspicious ceremony involving the giving of wealth, they married you to a woman known by the name of Kuṭumbinī[12] who had doe eyes and was very delicate in limb. She was deeply attached to you and was always devoted to guests, the gods and brahmins, and she was very beautiful, a veritable jewel amongst women. Her name Kuṭumbinī was deemed appropriate for her because she had five daughters and seven sons. Was she not as lovely as Kāma's wife?

15-18. After a long time your father died and your good mother burnt herself with him and went to heaven. Then with a group of friends you dissipated great wealth. Of whatever money was obtained, some was lost and some spent, until the lot was gone. Your lawful wife became very anxious and divorced you, but you ignored her command and then sold the house. She was allowed to depart, and without you, a thorn in the lineage, she went with her children to her father's home in order to nourish her offspring.

19. Then you became arrogant and intoxicated like a drunkard, acted improperly in the city and behaved like a rutting elephant.

20. You took others' property, were a paramour of women,
A thief in villages, a trouble maker amongst people,
A chief amongst gamblers, the heart of a torrent of deceit,
You roamed about doing harm, a hero without strength.
21. All those people, slaked with their attachment to pleasure,
You stole from those townspeople,
Using every possible pretext–friendship, pledges, the ancestors,
And you became maddened by this great wealth.
22. You mouthed every curse and falsehood
And gave witness to the cheating of wanton women.

[12] Kuṭumbinī "wife of a householder."

So all the people became frightened,
As though a highly venomous snake had gone into their house.
23. That made you became unbearable to those people,
Just like a thorn in a dish made of milk.
Then after they had gained the king's permission,
The people banished you from the city.
24. A murderer of many people,
You were always killing women, children and the old.
But just as when a wolf or a deer sees a lion,
You fled on seeing a great body of men and stayed in the forest.
25. Fish, cranes, swans and wild cocks,
Wolves, deer, monkeys, cuckoos, rhinoceros, hares
And iguana you needlessly killed.
In this way you wickedly nourished your own body.

26-27. After you had ridded a mountain cave of lions, tigers and jackals, and had assembled some absolutely unbearable thieves from many places, you built an excellent house there with wood, lumps of earth and stones. It was broad, a krośa[13] in length and decorated with many curiosities.

28-30. Because your wife's father was afraid of the king and the people, he made her come with her children to your cave dwelling. The children wore a variety of clothes and adornments and your wife shone splendidly like a goddess and you were there accompanied by thieves. You had returned to the cave after having killed and robbed some miserable people on the road, and with the thieves, your wife and children, you shone like a king in there.

31-33. On one occasion you saw a learned brahmin called Guṇavardhana quite alone in the middle of the road at midday. After seizing his right hand, you held the brahmin and he began trembling, knowing by the assault what your intention was. Then realizing what was in your heart he became filled with a

[13] Measurements of a krośa vary in length, but it may be about 2 1/4 miles.

wish for life and he spoke to you, communicating with words of extraordinary pity and reason.

Guṇavardhana said:

34-41. You already have good fortune and wealth, so why do you wish to kill me? You are not one to rob a brahmin who is a peaceful husband and has injured nobody. Leaving behind your evil inclinations you should resolve upon righteous duties. My first wife has died and in order to requite the debt to my fathers and for the advancement of a righteous lineage I have obtained another lovely wife, one who is of good conduct, very generous, virtuous and endowed with all the virtues. She has worked with great zeal in endeavouring to master the practice of the householder. Our lives would be pointless without each other. Become my father and mother and I will become your son, since in the treatises it is proclaimed that the father is the saviour from fear and the giver of life. Even thieves protect a brahmin who seeks refuge, so you must release me, a brahmin who is seeking refuge. If not, you will descend into the underworld for a thousand kalpas, and all of your sons, women, friends and subjects will enjoy your wealth. Your thieves will remain happy and will not share in your evil, but I have no idea for how many births you will experience that evil.

CHAPTER EIGHT

The Restraining of many Birds

Bhṛgu said:

1-3. When he had uttered this speech tinged with pity, he immediately became languid, but when you heard it your heart was not softened. Could Brahmā have made you even harder than a diamond? By killing many creatures and humans by the thousands, you have developed a hardness akin to the mentality of an ungrateful person. Then as hard as Death, you spoke to him.

The thief said:

4-8. Evil man, it is useless to direct your collection of sayings at me. Erudition in one who is not listening is like water in an overturned pot. Stupid man, here we have my intelligence, there we have your advice! Just as a drinker has no concern for the truth, so this does not impress me. A person who is addicted to wealth has absolutely no concern for his paternal kinsmen, in the same way that a person sick with desire has neither fear nor shame, Sage. Have you ever seen purity in a crow, truth in a gambler, courage in a eunuch, the waning of sensual desire in a woman or patience in a snake? Through the power of fate, the Ordainer[14] has sent you to me whilst I am not engaged in anything. I will never release you.

Bhṛgu said:

9-11. After you had said this and taken a sharp sword in your right hand, you cut off his head, just as a cat does with a mouse. Really, the number of murders of brahmins you have committed cannot be calculated, nor, above all, that of the murder of living beings, women, children and the elderly. But one who calculates the evil of others takes a share of those evils himself.

12-17. After a long time had passed, Kāmanda, you became old. Then you experienced tremors, hiccups, sweating, languor and phlegm. You became fatigued and your fatigue did not go away even when you were seated or asleep. And then your sons, female servants, attendants, friends, bards, grandsons and even your close friends, showed you no respect. There was only one brahmin there who was considered trustworthy, who could keep a secret and whose movements would be unhindered. You sent him to invite all the sages dwelling in the forest and they came at the brahmin's command because they were afraid of you. After having made obeisance to them you said, "Accept gifts from me!" But they said, "We will not accept your gifts because

[14] The Ordainer is the god Vidhātṛ.

you are evil. Evil is transferred onto another by sacrificing, teaching, birth, personal association, talking, walking together, sitting and eating."

18-24. Disquieting you with these words, they all bathed fully clothed and then muttered Vedic hymns after they had returned to their own hermitage. Then in your heart, Kāmanda, there arose a sharp pain caused by your own disease, your abandonment by your own kinsmen and by the brahmins' rejection. And after you had pondered over your own vast wealth consisting of base metals, jewels and so on, you developed a strong desire to restore an old temple. In an old temple in a little wood the brahmins, under your orders, placed an excellent and beautiful image of Gaṇeśa that had existed from eternity. The temple was long, broad and had four beautiful doorways, four portals and was adorned with four spires. It was inlaid with many columns, filled with many altars and contained a beautiful courtyard inlaid with jewels, corals, strings of pearls and so forth. It was filled with many flowering trees, was decorated with fruit trees and was glorious with ponds of sweet water located at the four directions.

25-31. Because you had renovated this temple your wealth began to diminish and some of it was also taken by your wife, your sons, friends and kinsmen. Then after a very short time you died and Yama's messengers bound you and struck you severely with strokes of a whip. Your whole body was pierced by thorns, crushed on a stone and sunk in a ferocious hell of slime, blood and pus. In such a state these messengers led you into the presence of Yama and Citragupta, and Yama asked, "Will you utilize your merit or your evil?" You said, "Yama,[15] born from the sun, I will utilize my previous good merit." Thereupon, you were appointed king in the country of Surāṣṭra. In reliance upon power derived from austerities and because I am

---

[15] Yama is the Lord of the dead and Citragupta keeps a record of good and evil deeds, making him a kind of karmic administrator. Yama's question boils down to a request for Somakānta (i.e. Kāmanda) to live out the accrued karma reflecting either his evil or his good actions.

compassionate[16] towards one who has sought refuge I have told you of your previous birth which caused this evil. Because you constructed that lovely temple you have become King Somakānta. You have a most charming wife who in loveliness is as beautiful as Śacī, Indra's wife.

The bard said:

32-36. That most wretched of kings, Somakānta, having heard what Bhṛgu said, was beset with doubts about his speech and became still as a stone. But because he placed doubt on the word of that ascetic Bhṛgu who knows the meaning of the Vedas and the śāstras and knows the past, present and future, in less than a moment birds of many shapes and colours came forth ferociously out of his body and pecked the king. Flying here and there they pecked the breast of the king with the hard points of their beaks, and cutting off bits of flesh willy nilly, they ate them near the sage. Thereafter he returned to take refuge, his body suffering terribly. In miserable words he spoke to Bhṛgu, a repository of austerity and knowledge.

The king said:

37-38. How is it that in your forest there exists no fear amongst species hostile by nature, but that in your presence they seek to kill me? I am a miserable leper who is devoted to your feet. I have come for refuge, so free me now, sage who gives security for all living beings.

The bard said:

39-40. Addressed in this way, Bhṛgu, who was affectionate towards the miserable, spoke again to him. This happened to you because you doubted my word, King. I will tell you the

---

[16] Bhṛgu"s compassion gives him the will to help Somakānta and his power (bala) derived from austerities gives him the special vision to see a person"s past lives.

remedy[17] and you will instantly become normal. Merely at the sound of my hum these birds will leave.

The bard said:

41. When those birds heard the sound of that brahmin's hum they disappeared. The king was satisfied as were his wife and ministers.

CHAPTER NINE

The Tale of Instruction to the King

The bard said:

1. After considering the misery caused by his previous karma, Bhṛgu became extremely perturbed and having momentarily reflected, he spoke again to the king.

Bhṛgu said:

2-3. Here we have your evil, there we have the remedies I have mentioned! Still, I will tell you one particular remedy for destroying that evil. If you will listen expeditiously to the Gaṇeśa Purāṇa, then you will certainly be released from the ocean of misery. No doubt of it.

4-7. After he had said this to him and muttered the excellent one hundred and eight names of Gaṇeśa and had consecrated the water with charms, he sprinkled the king. As soon as he had sprinkled the water, a small figure with a black face fell onto the ground from his nostril. He grew instantly. His gaping mouth measured seven talas[18] and it was frightful, his tongue was terrible and he was red eyed, had long arms and wore braided hair. Straight away a huge fire began spewing from his mouth as did pus and blood, causing the eyes to be blinded, as though it were another darkness.

---

[17] This is the remedy first requested in 5, 26.

[18] A tala is equal to a span measured by the thumb and middle finger.

8-12. After spotting that marvellous being who was filling all the directions with the gnashing of his teeth, all the dwellers in the hermitage fled. The eminent brahmin[19] then questioned that male who was before his eyes, "Are you intelligent? Tell me who are you and what your name is?" He then replied to that sage, the brahmin who had questioned him, "I exist in the body of a single human being and my name is Pāpapuruṣa. As a result of your application of consecrated water on the king I have come out of his body. But I am sick with hunger and I want some food, so give me some food! If you don't I will eat the people and Somakānta in front of you, sage. But tell me about this charming dwelling spot and from where I have come."

13-16. The sage spoke to him again, "Now that you have come out of him, go at my command, stay in the hollow of that straight, sapless mango tree and eat the leaves that fall down. If not I am going to reduce you to ashes. My word is never false, vile creature." When the sage had finished speaking he touched the dry tree and merely at his touch the tree became ashes, brahmins. And as a result of the sage's steadfast gaze that terrified male vanished into ashes. When he had vanished the sage turned to Somakānta.

Bhṛgu said:

17-18. By hearing of this Purāṇa your merit has appeared, Excellent king. Until that vanished tree arises here again you must remain, day after day, in its ashes. When this tree has grown up, King, your evil will have gone.

The king said:

19. I have neither seen nor heard of the Gaṇeśa Purāṇa before. Where was it composed, brahmin, and who was its creator, sage?

---

[19] The eminent brahmin is Bhṛgu.

The sage said:

20-21. Brahmā first told it to the wise Vedavyāsa and to me Vyāsa communicated this Purāṇa, which destroys evil. I will narrate it to you. But now, perform your ablutions in that sacred water, and Firm-vowed man, make the resolution that "I will hear this Purāṇa."

The bard said:

22-25. Urged on by Bhṛgu and having bathed in the famous Bhṛgutīrtha, Somakānta was filled with joy. Then he undertook his resolution, saying, "Henceforth I will listen to any Purāṇa about Gaṇeśa. As soon as he made that resolution the king became free of illness. Through Bhṛgu's favour the king lost his colour and became free of his wounds and worms. On recognizing him, Bhṛgu went to the king who was amazed, but thrilled. After sitting down in his own seat, he then offered the king a seat. When seated that excellent king, divinely splendid, spoke to him.

The king said:

26. Through your favour and merely by a resolution,
All my crushing anxiety has gone.
Recite in its totality this marvellous Purāṇa
Of Dviradānana.

Bhṛgu said:

27-32. Listen carefully. After you have become composed I am going to recite this Purāṇa. The desire to be able to hear it arises in men because of the possession of masses of endless merit. It is not otherwise. For evil men, merely by giving ear to that Purāṇa, evils which are slight, gross, wet or dry and great, though they might be acquired over seven years, are destroyed instantaneously because of Gaṇeśa's favour, he who is imperishable, immeasurable, without qualities, without form, who is imperceptible by speech and mind, and whose form is bliss alone. Brahmā, Śiva and the rest of the gods do not know his real appearance and even one as judicious as the thousand-faced Śeṣa is unable to describe his greatness, excellent king.

33-36ab. That Purāṇa, which gives such great merit, I heard in the words of Vyāsa of immeasurable energy who has knowledge of the self, just as Dakṣa, when sick with grief after the destruction of his sacrifice, heard it from Mudgala. Only that person should listen to this whose devotion to Gaṇeśa, giver of all success, is rock-solid, but never should such a one communicate it to others. If everyone were to perform service[20] to Gaṇeśa, however then could the masses of obstacles ramble about freely and who would experience misery brought about through various forms of separation?

36cd-39. Vyāsa, a knower of the past, present and future, composed it of old for those people without knowledge of the meaning of the Vedas, who have not studied the Vedas, who are lacking in that conduct circumscribed by the classes and stations of life and those who cause the mixture of classes. Observing that people were dishonest, evil doers in the Kali age, he composed the eighteen Purāṇas for the preservation of the Law. As many Upapurāṇas existed also and these people knew their meaning, but only from it did these people know Gaṇeśa's appearance.

CHAPTER TEN

Description of Vyāsa's Questions

Bhṛgu said:

1-6. There was a great sage, Vyāsa, son of Parāśara, born from a portion of Nārāyaṇa, who knew the meaning of the Vedas, the past and the future. After he had divided the Vedas

---

[20] The point being that Gaṇeśa is the remover of obstacles, a task he performs for his devotees. If everyone worshipped Gaṇeśa, nobody would encounter any obstacles.

into four parts in order to facilitate the understanding of its meaning, he began to compose the Purāṇa because of a conceited arrogance about his own wisdom. But he had not first performed any auspicious ceremony for accomplishing its completion, nor any act of obeisance, nor any eulogy to Gaṇeśa or anyone else. Being overcome by ignorance because of that, he could recollect no purpose at all. He became quite confused about which path of conduct was worldly and which was unworldly, and about the obligatory, periodical, optional, śrauta or smārta rituals, even though he was omniscient, the expounder of the Vedas and the śāstras. Like a snake whose poison is neutralized by mantras and herbs he became torpid, but he did not quickly discover the cause of his own condition.

7-9. Then he went to Satyaloka to question Dhātṛ respectfully and the sage, Parāśara's son, was shy, his heart overcome with amazement. After he had made obeisance to the hosts of gods, divine sages and to Brahmā, whose seat is the lotus, he was in turn honoured by Brahmā and sat in a splendid chair he had offered him. The great sage, son of Parāśara, then touched Brahmā's feet with his hands and having bowed down reverently, he began questioning him.

Vyāsa said:

10-15. Brahmā, has fate caused this astonishing thing to happen to me? My intention was to compose the Purāṇas that contain the meaning of the Vedas. This was after observing all these beings in the Kali age who are devoid of knowledge or virtue, engage in senseless activity, and are dull, non-believers and scorn the Vedas. They will only understand the precepts and the prohibitions by what I say. But my knowledge has just disappeared and I ramble as if I have become drunk. I can see no reason for it! How could this have happened so suddenly?[21] I

---

[21] Vyāsa''s reversal and his surprise at its suddenness parallels that of Somakānta (2, 6-8). The motifs of this reversal, lack of the attributes (i.e. a perfect body) required for kingship and lack of great knowledge, correspond to the image of warrior and brahmin respectively. Moreover, the

have come to ask you about the cause of its manifestation and the reason for it. Four-faced Brahmā, besides you, who else can I turn to for refuge? You are omniscient and the creator of everything. Remove my confusion! Even though I am omniscient, constantly engaged in correct conduct and am of Nārāyaṇa's own form, tell me the cause of my confusion Brahmā!

The bard said:

16. Having given ear to this speech and having pondered, Brahmā, smiling and a little surprised, addressed that bowed sage.

Brahmā said:

17-18ab. Look here! Having carefully considered that activity must be undertaken and that it is good and bad, and that a man can do a deed in either one or another way, I am going to tell you about the subtle path of actions.

18cd-20. The wise man should accomplish difficult and easy deeds with honesty, application and intellect, but without pride and selfishness. Because of pride the Lord of monkeys[22] became a vehicle of carriage, and because of selfishness Dhṛtarāṣṭra, Ambikā's son, destroyed everything and formerly, because of selfishness, Rāma Jāmadagni destroyed the kṣatriyas.

21-23. There is a god who has neither beginning nor end, who is the creator of the universe, who comprises the universe, who is the ordainer of the universe and the sustainer of the universe including the existent and nonexistent, the manifest and the imperishable. He is always able to produce something, undo it and alter it. The gods led by Indra are always subject to his command and believing, "I am Viṣṇu, Rudra, Sūrya, Agni,

---

apprehension of fate having possibly caused the reversal is another feature linking the two events coming up in different myths. Finally, we are already given a hint at the reason for Vyāsa"s confusion, namely, his failure to propitiate Gaṇeśa in any way before embarking on his enterprise (see vs.3-4).

[22] A possible reference to Sugrīva of the Rām.

Varuṇa and the rest," he destroys obstacles for devotees and builds up obstacles for others.

24-28. But relying on the power of your own wisdom you, omniscient as you are, have acted arrogantly and it is because of your conceit that you have not worshipped him, nor made a recollection of Gaṇeśa or anyone else in respect of your undertaking. If he is not recollected in respect of the undertaking of any duty, or when entering and departing a house, whether it concerns a śrauta, a smārta or a worldly activity, he creates an obstacle. Those who expound the meaning of the learned treatises and the Vedas speak of him as supreme bliss, they speak of him as the supreme path and they speak of him as the supreme Brahman. Child! Go respectfully for refuge to Dviradānana. If the illustrious god is kindly disposed he will do what you wish. But if not, you will not obtain your wish in a thousand years.

Vyāsa said:

29-31. Who is this Gaṇeśa? What is his real appearance[23] and how can it be known? To whom has he previously been kindly disposed, Four-faced god? How many are his incarnations and what deeds did they perform? Who previously worshipped him and in respect of what deed was he called to mind? I have asked this, though my mind is scattered, so Great-grandfather, receptacle of compassion, tell me all this in great detail.

CHAPTER ELEVEN

The Tale of the Mantra

Bhṛgu said:

1. Wishing to answer the questions put in this manner,
Four-faced Brahmā spoke again.

---

[23] "real appearance" rūpam.

"After considering the multiplicity of Gaṇeśa mantras,
I am going to describe everything sequentially."

Brahmā said:

2-11ab. Sage, since the mantras of the great Gaṇeśa are endless, I will tell you about the worship of him who brings quick success. In Gaṇeśa's sacred text there are seven myriads of great mantras. Sage, I know something of their secret, so too does Śiva. A six-syllable and a one-syllable mantra are the best of them and by the mere recollection of those two every success comes into one's hand. Sage, by worshipping him those fortunate people who are liberated whilst alive are honoured and worshipped even by the gods. By way of devotion to him the perfected men engage in servitude to them and heartily manifesting devotion to Gaṇeśa, they move at will, are omniscient and can assume any form at will. But the life of those who do not even have a snippet of devotion is worthless. One should not look at the faces of those who are adverse to Gajānana, for there will be obstacles at every step merely due to a sight of them. Seeing one of his worshippers causes all obstacles to disappear and beings, both moving and unmoving, make obeisance to them.[24] Accordingly, I will tell you about that auspicious mantra consisting of one syllable and just by performing it you will certainly obtain what you desire. I will describe its performance just as Śambhu described it to me.

11cd-16. After the pure man, a very wise adept, has had a bath and clothed himself in a clean garment, and has made a seat for himself out of kuśa grass, cloth and a black antelope skin, and having placed himself on it and effected the purification of the elements and the checking of the breaths, he should attentively observe the rite of depositing the syllables internally and externally. Then he should restrain his breath in the heart whilst reciting a root mantra. After that the twilight verse should be recited as prescribed in the Āgama. Having meditated on the

[24] The implication being that whoever uses this mantra will be accounted a worshipper of Gaṇeśa, and accordingly, will receive obeisance.

god from head to foot with mind motionless, he should, when well composed, worship him with ritual practices in the mind. Then performing the rite of repetition of mantras, he should recite as much as he is able. Gajānana will be well disposed to give gifts will manifest himself in his real form for as long as a person is absorbed in recitation.

Bhṛgu said:

17-18. Having said this to the sage and considering the day to be auspicious, Brahmā taught everything about Gaṇapa's great mantra -- with its single syllable and single vowel -- to that confused sage.

Brahmā said:

19-21. When you see that god, who resembles a thousand suns, come to give a gift, then make your heart firm, thinking, "Gajānana, be ever firm in my heart." You should ask for a boon, which he will undoubtedly give. And when your heart becomes fixed on god, you will gain divine knowledge.[25] You will also know the past, present and future in its entirety. Child, having got rid of your deep confusion you will be able to compose many texts.

Vyāsa said:

22. Father, your instruction has caused my confusion to vanish. With your assent, Grandfather,[26] I will undertake this performance.

Brahmā said:

23-28. Mighty sage, recollecting Gajānana, undertake this performance in a lonely place where there are no people and no

---

[25] I presume "divine knowledge" is knowledge of the god's self-manifestation, something normally only granted to individual devotees.

[26] Here the names "father" and "grandfather" are epithets of the god Brahmā.

cause of distraction. When an atheist, an abuser, a pitiless person, one lacking in good conduct, a mischief maker, a rogue or such like come for refuge, the great mantra must not be spoken. But you must impart it to one whose devotion is solid, to one who has faith, to one who comports himself well, to one desirous of it, to one who is not hardhearted and to one who knows the śāstras. If imparted where it should not be imparted, it causes the great mantra's reciter, his ten ancestors and his ten descendents to go to hell. But whoever applies it with devotion obtains the result he desires as well as sons, grandsons, money and wealth. And having obtained unblemished knowledge through the power of the single-tusked Gaṇeśa, he will obtain liberation, after he has first experienced all worldly enjoyments on earth.

CHAPTER TWELVE

The Vision of Gaṇeśa

The bard said:

1. After he had heard that speech issued from Brahmā's mouth, the sage was filled with great rapture and he questioned him again.

Vyāsa said:

2-3. Brahmā, having drunk your ambrosial words I have become attentive. I want to hear about this great mantra. Who has recited it. Did he gain success from Gajānana? As you are my only teacher, resolve my uncertainty!

Bhṛgu said:

4. Excellent king, when he was questioned in this way by the sage, Brahmā, best of speakers, spoke tenderly to the stooped Vyāsa.

Brahmā said:

5-11. Good! You have asked well. That means you now possess merit.[27] Those who are without merit, Brahmin, show no concern for hearing a tale. I will teach you the correct method of worship, for nothing can be kept from a devoted student who is very wise. You have been told that the illustrious Gaṇanāyaka exists in the syllable Om. Those not wishing for any obstacles worship Vināyaka in this way in respect of all tasks, because if they do not he causes obstacles. Accordingly, there are mantras found in every Āgama which possess the group of syllables for the beginning om and the syllables for the concluding om, but others give no results at all. Gaṇanāyaka encompasses everything that exists and does not exist, both manifest and unmanifest. Accordingly all the gods, siddhas, sages, demons and kiṃnaras, celestial singers, wandering bards, snakes, yakṣas, gūhyakas and humans, as well as all the worlds, both moving and unmoving, are worshippers of Gaṇeśa. Hence, there is certainly no one superior to Gaṇeśa.

12-21. I will tell you a certain traditional tale as to how Gaṇeśa was caused satisfaction through the recitation of this king of mantras. Once upon a time when, due to the force of fate the cosmic destruction had begun, the mountains were shattered by winds and fell in every direction. Twelve suns were burning, having dried up the great ocean, and a huge fire, garlanded with flames, burnt everything. Then the great Saṃvartaka clouds showered water everywhere, their jets of water resembling those which come from an elephant's trunk, Excellent brahmin. The oceans and the rivers overstepped their boundary. In this way everything was destroyed, beginning with Brahmā down to the immoveable things. And so when this evolute composed of māyā had been destroyed, Gajānana alone existed somewhere,

---

[27] "that means that you now possess merit": That is, when Vyāsa puts this question (vs. 2-3) to Brahmā it is a sign of his having accrued sufficient merit to give him the wisdom to ask such questions.

having assumed a form much smaller than the atomic particles. Then after a very long time had passed in a state of intense darkness, there appeared the one syllable filled with the Brahma sound. It existed once again in a modified form consisting of bliss and then having become an evolute in conjunction with māyā, it became Gajānana. Straight after that the qualities – sattva, rajas and tamas – came into being from him, and after that arose three gods – Brahmā, Viṣṇu and Śiva, and through his māyā the entire triple-world, both moving and unmoving, was constructed.

22-26. Then because of his māyā the three gods rambled about confused. Sage, each was anxious to see and to question his own father, because they wished an answer to the question "What duties should we perform?" Having investigated twenty-one heavens from top to bottom, back and forth across the sky, they subsequently came to the underworld. But still not seeing the Supreme self, they performed a severe austerity. For one thousand years they devoted themselves to uttering mantras and fasting. Exhausted, wearied and pondering, they returned to earth in order to investigate forests and groves, rivers, seas, mountains, peaks and caves.

27-29. However, they saw a huge lake filled with many aquatic animals, was surrounded by trees and had a great variety of birds. It reverberated with the sounds of ducks, swans, geese and cranes, which delighted in eating fragments of lotus root fibres. After they had bathed and rested on its bank, they crossed it and went forward to the great lake. It rippled with many waves and was exceedingly dangerous for men to cross, filled as it was with crocodiles and large fish.

30-39. Then they saw a terrible sight resembling the fire of cosmic destruction. Before them was a mass of fiery energy resembling a myriad of suns, fiery energy which took away their sight and so they became extremely anxious. But they emerged from the midst of that fiery energy by the way of the sky. Worn out with hunger and thirst, puffing and panting constantly, reviling and cursing themselves, they became perturbed. Then Gaṇeśa, overseer of the worlds, who is filled with a surplus of compassion and who knows the meaning of everything, appeared to them in a form pleasant to the eyes and the mind. The filaments of the red lotus were surpassed by the splendour of his feet, fingers and nails, and the disk of the sun at dawn was surpassed in mass of splendour by his red garment. The peak of Hemādri[28] was surpassed by the splendour of the texture of his girdle. He had four handsome arms resplendent with spear, bow, shield and lance, and he possessed a beautiful nose, a lotus-like face which in beauty surpassed the full moon and beautiful eyes, surpassing the lotus and he was splendid day and night. His head was shining with a diadem, surpassing many suns in brilliance, and he wore an upper garment surpassing the beauty of the heaven embossed with its multitude of stars. Glorious with a single tusk surpassing in splendour the tusks of Varāha, he had a superb trunk more fearful than those of the world-protectors, Airāvata and so forth. Straight after they had seen this those joyous gods immediately bowed, sage.

CHAPTER THIRTEEN

Description of Brahmā's Eulogy

Vyāsa said:

1. He has five faces, four faces and even a thousand faces! How did they eulogize that boon-giving god with the elephant's face?

Brahmā said:

2. By glimpsing from the corner of their eyes the compassion of Vighneśa, his face prepared to grace them, Brahmā, Viṣṇu and Śiva obtained clarity of intellect, then praised him.

---

[28] "golden mountain" hemādri: Possibly Mt. Meru.

The seers said:[29]

3. The unborn who is free of change, shapeless, the one,
Independent, non-dual, bliss-filled,
The supreme, having no characteristic, no distinction, no desire,
Whose form is the supreme Brahma, Gaṇeśa we will worship!

4. He who is beyond all characteristics, the first, his form intellect and bliss,
Whose intellect is splendid, all-pervading, attainable by knowledge,
Whom sages must contemplate, whose form is space, the supreme Lord,
Whose form is the supreme Brahma, Gaṇeśa we will worship.

5. The cause of the universe, whose origin is unknown,
The origin of the gods, origin of happiness, origin of the yugas, Gaṇeśa.
Who pervades the universe, is praised by all, Lord of the gods,
Whose form is the supreme Brahma, Gaṇeśa we will worship.

6. Who takes Brahmā's form due to rajas, who knows the Veda,
Who is ever engaged in tasks, whose form is to be pondered in the heart.
The creator of the universe, repository of all knowledge,
Whose form is the supreme Brahma, to Gaṇeśa we have bowed.

7. Always grounded in sattva, sporting playfully,
Destroying the gods' foes, protecting the universe.

---

[29] "The seers said" ṛṣaya ūcuḥ: This does not refer to the seers who, together with the bard, constitute the primary set of interlocutors in all Purāṇas. Rather, it designates Brahmā, Viṣṇu and Śiva in their capacity as seers of Gaṇeśa in his revelatory form.

Of whom there are many incarnations, who removes innate ignorance,
Who continually assumes Viṣṇu's form, to Gaṇeśa we bow.
8. Who is tamas, the yogin, having Rudra's appearance, three eyed,
The destroyer of the universe, saviour, cause of knowledge,
Who on account of his many teachings is enlightening his own people,
Who continually assumes Śiva's appearance, to Gaṇeśa we bow.
9. Who removes the mass of darkness, removes people's ignorance,
Who is the essence of the three Vedas, Supreme Brahma, the other shore.
Who brings knowledge to sages, whose transformation is far away,[30]
Who continually assumes Brahmā's form, to Gaṇeśa we bow?
10. Refreshing plants with streams of his own rays,
And the hosts of gods with portions of flowing nectar.
Removing heat from the sun's rays, Lord of the brahmins,
Whose real form is the moon, to Gaṇeśa we bow.
11. Whose real form is light, who has the form of clouds and the wind,
The primary cause of transformation, who exists as the divisons of time.
Whose real form contains many powers and activities,
Who continually assumes Śakti's form, to Gaṇeśa we bow.
12. Whose real form is creation's foundation, having the form of the Great.
Whose form is the cloud and whose primary form is Lord of the world.
Whose real form is existence and non-existence, cause of the world.

---

[30] "whose transformation is far away" vidūre vikāram: Here I follow M, but I am uncertain as to the precise meaning of this phrase.

Who continually assumes the form of everything, to Gaṇeśa we have bowed.

13. Whichever person will direct his mind onto your two feet,
Will not experience annoyance from multitudinous obstacles.
Whoever is devoted to that powerful Gaṇeśa whose image shines like the sun,
How could that person be enveloped by pain?

14. We were entirely confused because of our ignorance,
And we had still not reached your feet after one thousand years.
But through your favour we have now come.
Now, Gaṇeśa, sustainer of everything, protect your supplicants continually.

15. Gaṇeśa became very pleased when he was eulogized in this way and with the deepest compassion he began to address them.

Gaṇeśa said:

16-17. You have taken much trouble for this purpose for which you have come here. So choose a boon from me because I am happy with that eulogy. And since you cultivated gentlemen have composed this eulogy, with my blessing it will become renowned as the ¯King of eulogies.

18. Rising early, a wise person who is pure and always filled with devotion,
Should recite it at the three divisions of the day.
He will obtain all his desires including prosperity and sons.
At death he will assume the form of the Supreme Brama.

19. After they had heard his speech, these, who at his inlination had arisen from the qualities – rajas, sattva and tamas, were very pleased and spoke to him.

The three said:

20-21. If you are pleased, Lord of the gods, creator and destroyer of the creation, then let us undertake unswerving devotion on your lotus feet. Moreover, what should we do? Command us! This is the only boon we desire, Dviradānana.

22-25. After he had heard their speech Gajānana spoke once more, "Your devotion towards me will be rock-solid, very fortunate gods! Accordingly, you will overcome even the greatest difficulties and now, to please you, I will speak to each of you in turn about your duties. Brahmā, since you have arisen from the rajas quality, be the creator. Viṣṇu, by virtue of your connection with sattva, undertake protection everywhere. Hara, since you have arisen from the tamas quality, destroy everything.

26-27. The illustrious Gaṇeśa then gave Brahmā the Supreme self, the Vedas, the śāstras and the Purāṇas, the capacity to create and other knowledge. He gave Viṣṇu the power to take the form of his own choice by means of yoga, the single syllable and six-syllable mantras as well as all the Āgamas. And to Śiva, the illustrious god gave the power to destroy.

28. Then having cupped his hands in respect, the dejected Brahmā spoke to Ibhānana, the boon-giving world-preceptor, Lord of the triple-world.

Brahmā said:

29-30. But this power I have received does not discriminate between what should and should not be named, and as I have never anywhere seen a creation which has diversity, how can I achieve one having a cave here, a pond there? Yet equally, how can I break the Lord's command?

31. Thereupon, having given him the divine eye the Lord Gajānana spoke to the confused Brahma, knower of the Vedas and the śāstras.

Gaṇeśa said:

32. Brahmā, behold now the incalculable Brahmā's eggs moving about in my body, from its innermost to its outermost part.

33-38. Then Gajānana who was snorting like the wind led Brahmā into his belly, and there, Brahmā the Placer, saw Brahmā's eggs in great numbers, like fruit on a fig tree and mosquitos on these fruit. He then split one of these with his own powerful fiery energy and the lotus-born Brahmā saw the entire creation within it. There was another Brahmā in it and another Viṣṇu, Indra, Prajāpati, Śaṅkara, Bhāskara, Vāyu and Varuṇa, protector of waters, rivers and forests. There were also oceans, yakṣas, heavenly minstrels, nymphs, kiṃnaras and snakes. There were also sages, meritorious people, sādhyas, humans, mountains and trees and creatures who were germinating, womb-born, sweat-born and also egg-born. And there was also the Earth, seven hells and twenty-one heavens.

Brahmā saw everything that existed and did not exist and that moved and did not move.

39. Then Gaṇeśa split every conceivable egg,
And in each one Brahmā saw everything.
But having seen this he became confused as before,
Because he was completely unable to reach the end of those eggs.

40. Lotus-born, Brahmā was unable to stand or move, so having seated himself he eulogized Dviradānana.

Brahmā said:

41. I praise that god who is the god of gods, Gaṇeśa,
In whose body there is no numbering of Brahmā's eggs.
Who can number the atoms in the sky,[31]
The large fish in the ocean, or the pebbles on the shore?
42. Now that I have beheld your lotus feet,
I feel no shame,[32] praiseworthy Lord of the gods.
I have wandered in the tranquil repository of knowledge
Where even liberation is trifling. Can one say anything at all?

---

[31] "atoms in the sky" abhre'ṇūnām: An easier reading found in GN and D is abhroḍūnām "stars in the sky".

[32] "I feel no shame": That is, no shame at not being able to find the end of Gaṇeśa"s stomach. The tranquil repository of knowledge is Gaṇeśa.

43. Lord of the gods, in your belly with its many things,
I have seen that multitude of Brahmā's eggs.
I am unable to stay here, yet I cannot leave,
44a. So I will not go for refuge to anyone but you.

44b-d-46. Then the illustrious Gajānana, whose image endures forever, became calmed and turned out the mentally weary Brahmā through the hole in his nostril, with Viṣṇu following him. And the god Gajānana, the Lord, turned out the blackish Hara, who had gone in with Brahmā, through the hole in his ear. Viṣṇu and Śiva both slept comfortably on his body.

CHAPTER FOURTEEN

Description of Brahmā's Anxiety

The king said:

1. What did Brahmā do after he had seen the eggs in their thousands? And how did he accomplish the creation after he had been commanded by Gajānana?

Bhṛgu said:

2-4ab. A feeling of arrogance sprang up in him and he reflected, "I know the śāstras, the Vedas, the Purāṇas and the Āgamas. I possess intuitive and discursive knowledge and I can curse and bless. In addition I have seen the Brahmā's eggs and the dispositions of creation[33] and so now I am absolutely capable of undertaking the creation."

4cd-8. The lotus-born Brahmā being filled with this kind of arrogance concerning the creation, many kinds of obstacles appeared in their thousands, King. After surrounding Brahmā, like bees at a honeycomb who are maddened by the honey of

[33] "the dispositions of creation" sṛṣṭīnāṃ racanās: The sense here is that the eggs are embryos in which the fully formed creation exists in miniature. For example see Kūrma Purāṇa, 1.4.4.

flowers, these dreadful things stayed. Some had three eyes and five trunks, pitted faces and seven hands, whilst others were three footed and had five snouts, and still others had seven snouts and six feet, whilst some had ten faces and five feet. fangs the size of the palm of a hand and the belly of a wolf. These massive beings were of many shapes and could not be counted.

9-14. After hearing their distinctly hostile shrieks, he trembled. Some of them turned and struck him with their fists, whilst others shouted and seized him by the four tufts of his beards and roughly shook his four faces to and fro. Others laughed at him, whilst some scorned him and praised him, and some stayed close to him. Some bound him, whereas others freed him again, yet when he was set free again others dragged him about to and fro. Some embraced him whilst others kissed him as if he were a child and, one danced around, having seized him by his eight beards and moustaches.[34] And so the helpless Brahmā became filled with anxiety and anguish and let go all of that arrogance about the creation which had come into his mind. Unconcerned about his own life, he fell into a great stupor, but when only a moment had passed he recollected the Lord in his mind. Almost weeping because of his distress he propitiated Gajānana.

15. Though I have a long life,
My mind is intent upon a creation with variety.
I bow to the stainless one, he who saves from the ocean of existence,
The knowledge of whom is the truth.
When I have achieved birth on Earth
Through devotion to you,
I will attain the highest carnal enjoyment or
That liberation which is unequalled happiness, universal preceptor.

---

[34] Brahmā has four faces and on each one there is a beard and moustaches. The eight beards and moustaches refer to the total number of his beards and moustaches, not to eight of each.

16. Honoured by your immortal glance this devotee sits before you, Mighty god. I am long-lived. May I experience shame before you, but not death!

17-25ab. Whilst he was propitiating him in this way, he heard the words, "Perform austerities!" uttered in the sky. He propitiated him once more. And as soon as he heard the words from the atmosphere the obstacles – hugely virile creatures of various shapes – disappeared. All except him, lotus-seated Brahmā. Once freed the lustrous lotus born Brahmā, wondered, "Without a mantra and without a location, how can I perform a great austerity?" His mind confused about this, he roamed about in the centre of the water and thought, I will bow to Gajānana, meditating on him with undivided attention. Him whose auspicious body is smeared with red sandalwood paste, his vermillion coloured head resplendent with a diadem engraved with jewels and pearls, who wears a snake as his brahmanical thread and who is ornamented with many ornaments made of priceless jewels. Him who is splendid with finger rings shining with glittering emeralds and a huge belly splendid with a great navel enclosed within a great snake. Him around whose hips is a shining thread enlaced with brilliant jewels, who is clothed in red garments flashing with golden threads. Him whose hands are the best, whose tusk shines brilliantly and who wears the moon on his forehead.

25cd-26. He meditated on him in this way and again there came some words from the heavens, "Behold the banyan tree! Behold the banyan tree!" But after he had heard this lovely utterance, Brahmā once again became filled with anxiety.

CHAPTER FIFTEEN

Description of Gajānana's Worship

Bhṛgu said:

1-7. Then Brahmā had a great vision, Excellent sage. Whilst wandering here and there he saw a large banyan tree in the water, but he had this misgiving, "Since this universe, both moveable and immoveable, was destroyed by water, heat and a great wind, how could one solitary large fig tree have remained?" On a leaf of that tree there was a small boy. He had four arms, a beautiful tiara, he was resplendent with earrings and he was wearing a necklace made of pearls and jewels shining brightly on his neck. He had a half moon on his brow, red clothes and also a thread around his waist. After seeing him like this he wondered how that boy with his one tusk, his human shape and his elephant's face glowing brightly, could be there. Then with his trunk the boy threw water onto his head, after which Brahmā, filled with both anxiety and joy, laughed loudly. When he laughed, the boy got down from the banyan tree and, coming onto Brahmā's lap, he spoke in a mellifluous voice.

The boy said:

8-11ab. In spite of your venerable age you are foolish and more simple than a simpleton. You are overwhelmed with anxiety about the creation because you have struck obstacles and, very anxious about your austerities, you have been continually wandering around in this water. Four-faced Brahmā, I will teach you this mantra of mine. It consists of one syllable and is the remedy for the removal of all your anxieties. Recite it one million times with a preparatory ritual[35] and then I will become visible and give you the utmost capacity to create.

11cd-15. After he had seen that marvellous thing in a vision, Brahmā, whose seat is a lotus, came to his senses and he lamented, "When will I have a sight of the highest Lord? For, sunk in an ocean of joy was I when I experienced that vision." Then after he had bathed, he stood with one foot on a lotus, meditating on Gajānana and recited that supreme mantra for many days. And for a thousand years he performed a great austerity with his senses conquered, his wish for food conquered, stationary like a wooden stick or a stone. Then from

---

[35] On the puraścaraṇa "preparatory ritual" for the offering of a mantra, see Kane, History of Dharmaśāstra, 1962. Vol.5.2, pp.1107-12.

out of his mouth came dangerous flames which severely injured all beings.

16-17. After Gajānana had seen Brahmā's firm devotion he was satisfied with his deep devotion and appeared before him. His splendour was that of a myriad of suns and like Agni he was garlanded in flames. He was all but burning the three worlds and all but destroying heaven and earth.

18. He holds a lotus and an axe, he is ornamented with divine garlands,
He removes all difficulties and his body is entirely beautiful.
A resplendent trunk on his lovely face, he nourishes his devotee's wishes.
The sole destroyer of all obstacles for gods, men and sages.

19-20. After he had seen that mass of fiery energy, Brahmā shook tremulously and became terribly anxious, his mind so distracted that he ceased reciting. He covered his eyes and the recollection[36] faded, but having regard to his particular condition, Vighnarāja spoke immediately.

Gaṇeśa said:

21-23. Do not be afraid, Lord of the Worlds! It is indeed I who have come, I who taught you this auspicious one-syllable mantra in a vision, because of which you have attained success. I have come to grant you a boon and I have assumed my placid appearance, so choose a boon, firm-vowed Brahmā! I am pleased, so I will give you whatever is in your heart, for when I am pleased anything can come about. There is no doubt of it.

The sage said:

24. Having heard this pure speech of Gaṇanātha
Brahmā rejoiced whilst reflecting upon the Supreme.

---

[36] "recollection" smṛti: This word must have the sense of "vision" here. Often when a devotee has an initial vision of the deity, he is able, at will, to recollect a vision of the deity again. The verb smṛ "to remember" is always used in these circumstances.

And having bowed to the teacher of those who are moving and non-moving,
His heart calm, he said, "My birth is fruitful."

Brahmā said:

25-29. The Lord who is never accessible to the yogins who know the Vedas and the śāstras, and all the Upaniṣads, he who has neither beginning nor end, who is eternal, immeasurable and without qualities, has now become visible to me because of my stores of merit. If you are pleased, Lord of gods, Vighneśa, Bringer of compassion, give me that rock-solid devotion towards yourself in consequence of which trouble will not touch me. Give me, immediately, the capacity to undertake a creation with variety and when you are satisfied Gajānana, let all these obstacles be removed.[37] By a mere recollection on my part you must always cause all my duties to be completed and at death give me certain liberation, knowledge and purity.

Gaṇeśa said:

30-31. Yes! You must produce that vast creation with its variety of kinds. After having recollected me, all obstacles will disappear from everywhere and due to my favour you will have rock-solid devotion and auspicious knowledge. Fearlessly, perform all your duties, four-faced Brahmā.

The sage said:

32. Brahmā obtained that very boon and worshipped the Lord. Whatever he conceived in his mind certainly appears.

33-37. Due to Gaṇeśa's favour, two young girls appeared at just the right moment to be presents in Gaṇeśa's worship. Both

---

[37] When Gaṇeśa is satisfied with Brahmā's devotion, only then will he cause the obstacles to be allayed. Even though vighnāni "obstacles" is the subject of yāntu here, the implication is that they are allayed as a result of Gaṇeśa's agency.

were glorious, their faces and eyes charming and tranquil. They were adorned with various ornaments embossed with many jewels, they were redolent of celestial fragrances and adorned with celestial clothes and garlands. Brahmā decreed that these two should be a present for him. He offered him a handful of celestial flowers and burning lamps in plantain wood. And having eulogized him with his thousand names, he then performed a circumambulation of him. After paying homage he propitiated him with the words, "Be beneficent towards those who are wretched." In this way Brahmā, the supreme Lord, worshipped him.

38-39. Then, the illustrious Gaṇeśa who removes obstacles became pleased and having taken these two – Siddhi and Buddhi – the Lord disappeared. And at the command of the supreme Lord and by virtue of his favour, Brahmā, tranquil in mind, produced that creation, laid out as it had been before.

CHAPTER SIXTEEN

The Entreaty to the Goddess

The king said:

1-2. After hearing this tale about Gaṇeśa my heart is filled with delight. Once again recite an immortal tale, Sage of the priests, as I have not had enough. After the illustrious Gaṇeśa, who is the Supreme, had disappeared, how did Brahmā create the creation? Describe that, Lord!

The sage said:

3-9. First of all Brahmā created seven small sons from his mind and he said to them, "To help with the creation you must create from your own minds." But after hearing his command they resolved to engage in austerities and when they had performed a very great austerity they attained the supreme Brahman. Prajāpati then created another seven sons, but possessing an overabundance of wisdom, they too did not create the perfect creation. Having consideration for Sanaka and the rest, he himself began to create and from his own mouth lotus-born Brahmā emitted the priests and fire. From his arms, thighs and feet came the other three classes and from his heart came the moon, from his two ears the sun and from his ears the wind and the breath. And from his navel came the atmosphere and from his head the sky. The earth and the directions he formed from his feet and the other worlds from his ears, and everything else high and low, moving and unmoving, oceans, rivers, mountains, grass, shrubs and trees.[38]

10-11ab. Then after a certain number of days had passed, Excellent sages, two huge demons were born from the ears of the huge Viṣṇu who was sleeping. In the triple-world these two were known by the names Madhu and Kaiṭabha.

11cd-12. Their faces gaped with teeth, their eyes were reddy-brown and their noses were long, both had huge bodies, immense strength and were as tall as mountains. Their voices roared like the clouds in the rainy season and they were terribly arrogant.

13-15. These two malevolents scoffed at him in many words and they ridiculed the śāstras, the wise, the sages, gods and the priests. The Earth trembled because of their noise as did Śeṣa too and the entire creation was terrified by their sound. Their eyes red with anger, they began to eat absolutely everyone.

16-17. Then in order to awaken Viṣṇu for the destruction of Madhu and Kaiṭabha, lotus-seated Brahmā eulogized the boon-giving goddess Sleep who had gone into Viṣṇu's eyes and was the cause of Viṣṇu's stupefaction.[39] Having duly considered and

---

[38] Cf. Ṛg Veda 10, 90.

[39] "the cause of Viṣṇu"s stupefaction" viṣṇumohanakāriṇīm: The word mohana "stupefaction" is difficult to translate here. Its usual meaning centres on perplexity or confusion and one who is subject to moha is contrasted with one who possesses intuitive knowledge (jñāna). Here it may convey the idea that Viṣṇu as the protector of the universe, has, under the influence of sleep, fallen down on the job in not killing the two demons. Thus he is confused or deluded in respect of his correct duty.

then correctly realized that those two would be killed by Viṣṇu's hand due to Gajānana's favour, he became filled with both delight and anxiety.

Brahmā said:

18. You take the form of the svāhā and the svadhā, you are immortal,
Your form is the sound of the short syllable and half a short syllable.
You are the creator, destroyer and mother of people,
You alone are the power of what exists and what does not exist.
19. You are the revealed texts, the accent, the destructive night,
You are without beginning or end, you are the night,
You are the mother of the universe, the ordainer of the universe
The cause of creation, destruction and stability.
20-26. And you are the Sāvitrī verse, the twilight, the great illusion, hunger and thirst. Of everything you are the essence and you are the power in beings, Pārvatī. And here is Hari, creator of the triple-world, your Lord, the crusher of daityas and dānavas, whose mind is filled with sleep, yet who still possesses discursive and intuitive knowledge. He creates, protects and destroys this universe, yet at critical moments in his incarnations you have guided him. You must delude both of these evil daityas, Madhu and Kaiṭabha, and then, because they are so dangerous, give him the knowledge to kill them. In a previous birth they propitiated me tirelessly for a boon and so I gave them boons of many types. It is because of me that they are both inviolable. Since then I have endured their loud and soft words and wanting to kill me, they have chanted with many kinds of hymns. Also, because they are evil they have never stopped striking me. Therefore, I am propitiating you, the goddess, to awaken Viṣṇu.

CHAPTER SEVENTEEN

Instruction in the Mantra

The sage said:

1. Until Viṣṇu gets up these two will overrun the heavens and the residences of Indra, Yama and Kubera.

2-6. The gods just wanted to flee anywhere after they had seen those two and some of them tottered and fell, others fainted and stumbled. Then the goddess Sleep released Lord Viṣṇu and after he had roused up all the gods, he fought with those two in order to prevent their overrun of all the gods, the snakes led by Śeṣa, the sages, yakṣas and rākṣasas. Viṣṇu looked splendid. He was holding his club, his discus and his conch, he wore earrings and a diadem and his thick skin was like a dark cloud. The illustrious Viṣṇu then blew his conch with great vigour and caused heaven and earth to shake because of its sound.

7-10. On hearing the sound of Pāñcajanya their heart was pierced and terrified with fear of it they then said to one another, "We completely overran the Earth, the underworld and the twenty-one heavens, but we had not then heard that sound which has made our adamantine hearts tremble. Hence we will have to fight with this very powerful man for victory or defeat in order to bring an end to our itch for battle. We will kill this enemy or die!"

11-12ab. Having made this resolve and eager for battle they both said to Viṣṇu. "You have appeared, Viṣṇu, supreme person, in order to bring an end to our itch for battle. But how will you obtain supremacy over us if we can see you?"

The sage said:

12cd. After he had heard their speech the far-famed Viṣṇu spoke.

Hari said:

13. Well said, great demons! Fight with me if you wish, for nobody looks for his own death.

The two said:

14ab. You have four arms, Lord of the gods, so give us an arm wrestle!

The sage said:

14cd. Viṣṇu gladly said, "Yes," after they had addressed him in this way.

15-18. Having left his weapons aside he fought them only with his four arms. They struck his head with their foreheads and his shanks with their shanks, his elbows with their own elbows, and his arms with their arms, his ankles with their ankles, his buttock with their buttocks and his nose with their noses, his fists with their fists and hi ack with their backs, and their arms were tearing apart and shaking in circles. In this way the fight between them continued for a long time then, and five-thousand years passed, great sage.

19-27ab. However, the imperishable Hari was unable to defeat them, so he took the form of a heavenly musician who was skilled in music. Going into a forest he made the sweet note of a lute and deer, wild beasts, humans, gods, heavenly musicians and rākṣasas became utterly engrossed with it and they all left their respective activities. Śiva, Lord of the mountains, heard its note when he was on Mt. Kailāsa. Straight away Śiva, destroyer of Bhaga's eyes, said to Nikumbha and Puṣpadanta, "Someone is singing in the forest. Bring him to me quickly!" After they had left and caught sight of him they said to him, "Śiva has heard the sound of your singing and is thrilled. Faultless one, the god summons you to sing. So leave quickly with us and we will go to him." When he had heard their speech the heavenly musician, who was devoted to Hara, went with them to where the god Maheśvara was located. He saw Pārvatī's husband wearing a diadem shaped as a half-moon, a garment of elephant and tiger skins and ornamented with a garland of headless bodies. With his yellowish braided hair and a snake as his sacred cord, he was resplendent.

27cd-28. He bowed to the ground before the Lord of everything, the one who destroys the pains of those who are obeisant to him. Then helping him up with his own hand, the Mountain-dweller offered Viṣṇu, born from under an axle, a seat and honoured him.

Then Hari said:

29-31. "My life has now become fruitful, because this vision of you – which gives accomplishment in the law, sensuality, power and liberation – has occurred." And with lute-like sounds, soft stanzas and a variety of melodies, the heavenly musician satisfied that god who was so engrossed with his singing, and he also satisfied Skanda, Gaṇeśa, the goddess Pārvatī, the gods and the sages.

32-33ab. Then with delight, Śiva publicly embraced Hari and he said to that auspicious god clothed in yellow and holding a lotus, mace, discus and club, "Hari, ask of me all your desires. I will give them since I have attained the highest happiness from your song."

Bhṛgu said:

33cd. Hari then told him about the previous course of events concerning the two demons.

Hari said:

34-36. Whilst I was asleep on the ocean of milk, Madhu and Kaiṭabha arose from my ear secretions and came to eat Brahmā. Brahmā eulogized Sleep, splendid Śiva, and she awakened me. I then engaged in battle with those two and a wrestling match ensued. I was unable to conquer them so I did this.[40] Now, Śiva, repository of compassion, tell me the way to kill them.

Śiva said:

37-39ab. You went to the battleground without having worshipped Vināyaka, and so you had no strength. Consequently, you've got real problems. Worship Gaṇeśa and set out for battle, respectable god! With his power of illusion he will delude those two and through my favour you will kill those two malevolents. There is no doubt of it!

Hari said:

39cd. Śiva, tell me, how I should worship that god, Vināyaka?

Īśvara said:

40-41ab. Seven myriads of Gaṇeśa mantras have been recited. Even amongst them there are great mantras and amongst them too there is a great one-syllable mantra and a six-syllable one. Illustrious Viṣṇu, I am going to tell you about one of these two.

41cd-43ab. Then, having set aside the one syllable mantra in consideration of the power of his discus and the Siddhāri mantra, and having paid out a monetary debt, he told him that great six-syllable mantra of Gaṇeśa which is auspicious and grants every success.

43cd. "Merely by[41] performing it your task will be successful." Then Viṣṇu left quickly to perform it.

---

[40] "I did this": That is, Viṣṇu became a heavenly musician and sang a song.

[41] "Merely by...": This must be an insertion into the narrative of Śiva's direct speech. It is recited by the narrator, not by Śiva himself.

CHAPTER EIGHTEEN

The Tale of the Origin of Siddhikṣetra

The King said:

1. How and where did Viṣṇu recite that excellent mantra and did he obtain success? Tell me this in detail!

The sage said:

2-7.There is a celebrated place of the highest quality called Siddhikṣetra which gives success on the earth. The great Viṣṇu went there and performed a severe austerity. Whilst meditating on Vināyaka he propitiated that god in accord with the procedure for the six-syllable mantra. After having diligently conquered his senses, he carefully fixed the boundary of the eastern area with his weapon, an arrow, and completed the purification of his body and the stilling of his breaths. And he completed the ritual placing of letters progressively within his body beginning from the lower part of the body, and the ritual placing of letters progressively outside of the body beginning with the head. He restrained his breaths and meditated on the god Gajānana with the basic mantra and having worshipped him in the mind with the gestures – beginning with the invocation gesture – as well as with a variety of objects and the sixteen kinds of ritual behaviour, Viṣṇu, Lord of the lords of yogins recited that supreme mantra.

8-10. After a period of one hundred years had passed, the supreme self, Gaṇādhipa, who was like a myriad of suns and fires, became visible. Completely tranquil in heart, he spoke to Viṣṇu, on whose banner is Garuḍa. "Ask me for those boons that you want, Viṣṇu. I will give them all because I am satisfied with your austerity. If I alone am worshipped first, victory will certainly be yours."

Viṣṇu said:

11. Brahmā, Śiva and the gods led by Indra
Cannot see you just through their austerities.
I see you Gaṇeśa in your many forms, your one true form,
And in your form that is both manifest and unmanifest.

12. You are the one whose true form is smaller than the atoms,
Your real form is greater than what is great, such as the heavens.
Repeatedly through the power of fate.
You cause the creation, destruction and preservation of living beings.

13. Self of everything, omnipresent, the power in everything,
Pervading everything, the maker of everything, the highest Lord.
You see everything and of everything you are
The ordainer, protector, maker, destroyer, the leader of all, the father,

14. By seeing one like you I will experience success in all things, god.
However, I am still going to tell you about one thing.

15-18ab. At the end of my yogic sleep Madhu and Kaiṭabha sprang up from the dirt in my ears. These two great warriors strove to eat Brahmā. Then I fought with them for many days, but because my strength is waning I have come to you for refuge. So think about how I will destroy these two, as the highest renown exists in victory over other demons.[42] Supreme Lord, give me now your inexhaustible devotion, through which my unmatched fame will cleanse the triple-world.

Gaṇeśa said:

18cd-19ab. Viṣṇu, you will certainly get whatever you request. You will have glory, strength, the highest fame and no obstacles.

---

42 "over other demons": That is, demons who have already been killed. Madhu and Kaiṭabha are nothing special.

The Sage said:

19cd-23. Having said this to the great Viṣṇu, Lord Gaṇeśa disappeared from there, but Viṣṇu was filled with joy as he considered these two demons to be conquered. There he built a crystal palace luxurious with jewels, a glittering gold spire and four very splendid domes. Then he set up an image made of jewels taken from the Gaṇḍakīya river. The gods and sages spread its fame under the title of Siddhavināyaka, since Hari obtained a splendid success there. Thereafter, it became famous as Siddhikṣetra, the "Field of Success," all over the earth.

24-25. Then Hari went to where Madhu and Kaiṭabha were and after they had seen Hari coming they jeered and ridiculed him. "Why has your face, dark as a cloud, reappeared before us now? Once more we will give you a huge send-off[43] from here, mischievous god. You've gone stupid! Why have you come back for battle?"

Hari said,

26-27ab. Just as a small fire by itself can burn everything quickly, and just as a small light removes much darkness in the night, so I can now certainly destroy both of you who are drunk with pride.

The sage said:

27cd-31ab. On hearing his speech Madhu and Kaiṭabha became very angry, and suddenly with their fists they struck Viṣṇu hard on the heart. Then there was another wrestling match between him and them and that battle went on for many days. But eager to give a boon to them both, Hari said to Madhu and Kaiṭabha in a silky voice, "For many years you two have

---

[43] "huge send-off" mahāmuktim: I am uncertain of the precise meaning of this and take it to mean they will defeat him again. M gives a literal translation of the verse.

endured my blows, bulls of daityas, and I am pleased with your manly endeavour. Two such as you have certainly not been born before and will not be born again."

The two said:

31cd-32ab. Request boons from us! We will give you many of them Hari, since we are both perfectly satisfied with you and your fighting.

The sage said:

32cd-33. Having given ear to and heard the speech of those two who were deluded by illusion, Viṣṇu said, "You daityas are

trying to give me some boons, so come, and I will kill you! That is the only boon I choose."

34-36ab. Then after looking at all the water, Madhu and Kaiṭabha, now terribly happy, said, "Death at your hands is auspicious. By thinking of you at death we will immediately attain eternal liberation. Kill us where your two thighs are not covered by water, Viṣṇu, descendant of Madhu! We are giving up everything except truth. Everything is based on truth."

The sage said:

36cd-39ab. After hearing their words, he lifted both of them up onto his
thighs and cut off their heads with his razor sharp discus. The gods then rejoiced, flowers showered down, all the heavenly musicians sang and the apsaras danced. Viṣṇu too was then filled with delight and after going up to Brahmā, the Supreme Lord, he told him the whole story.

Hari said:

39cd-43. When I was powerless to conquer those two, I went to Śiva, the mountain dweller, and Śaṅkara taught me that excellent six-syllable mantra. I propitiated the mighty god,

Vighneśvara, with it and he gave me boons which themselves give fruition to many desires. It was through his power that I killed the evil Madhu and Kaiṭabha, but as soon as he had been eulogized and worshipped, that mighty god disappeared. The greatness of the great Gaṇeśa is celebrated. Through Śaṅkara's favour I will kill the daityas and dānavas.

44-45. After all the gods and sages had eulogized Gaṇeśa, Brahmā, Śiva and myself they went to their own homes. Whoever should listen constantly to this "Glorification" that destroys evil, will not be afraid of anything and obtains everything for which he has wished.

CHAPTER NINETEEN

Description of Kamalā's Son

Vyāsa said:

1-2. That was the glorification of Siddhikṣetra, and especially of Gaṇanātha, which when heard removes evil, gives all desires and increases merit. But once more, Brahmā, tell me a small tale about Gaṇeśa, for even though I have been drinking the nectar of those tales, I have not had enough.

Brahmā said:

3. Son of Parāśara, I am going to tell you this expansive and auspicious tale of the Lord Gaṇeśa, the god who presides over all the gods.

4-6. In the country of Vidarbha there was a magnanimous and exceptionally courageous king. Wise Vyāsa, he dwelt in the city of Kauṇḍinya and he had generous vassals[44] and other kings as feudatories. Ten myriads of horses, elephants, footsoldiers and chariots moved in front and behind him when he was

---

[44] "he had generous vassals" sāmantā varadā: The word varada is difficult to construe here in the meaning of "feudatories". The variant reading karadā in GN (6) is certainly easier.

advancing. Thousands of brahmins depended on him and were happy.

7-9. His most illustrious wife was named Cāruhāsinī and her lotus face blossomed, whilst her eyes were the eyes of a young deer. Ever devoted to the gods and brahmins, utterly obedient to the Law, she was loyal to her husband, her life was her husband and she was always obedient to her husband's command. Because of fate she had no son, yet she was a beautiful woman.

10-12. Then once when Bhīma was watching her, all her charming limbs radiant, the excellent king, distressed since he was without a son, spoke these words, "After giving up this kingdom we are both going to the great forest. The fate of a man who is without a son is definitely not heaven nor happiness, nor indeed do the gods accept his offering or the fathers his food oblation. My mother, my birth, my father, my house, my wealth and my family are worthless and in the same way that a goose without water is useless, so too is my karma."

13-17. Having made this resolve he summoned two advisers, one of whom was named Manorañjana and the other Sumantu. Both were conversant with the polity, the three Vedas, current affairs and the sixty-four arts. Coming at once they bowed to the king, sage, and then Bhīma said to them both, "Protect my kingdom. Evil produced in a previous birth of mine or my wife's has appeared and because of it there is no lineage on either side which will bring happiness. If I return again you must give it back to me. But if not, after I have divided my kingdom, you two must take it." The king settled this with a svastivācana[45] rite.

18-22. After he had made many gifts to the brahmins, the excellent king left the city with his young wife and his ministers. When he had gone the length of a field he dismissed them all, but his two advisers said, "King, we are going with you." Their friends and the townspeople wept as they were

---

45 "svastivācana rite": A small rite performed at the beginning of any ritual. The sacrificer requests the brahmins to bless him with the word svasti, after which he proceeds with the rite.

bitterly distressed, but he said to them, "Fear not! The two ministers will do the king's jobs for you. These two will protect you just as I have done. And sighing continually the king spoke once more to the two ministers. "I have given this kingdom to you two! By all means return to the city."

23-28. Accordingly, having given away everything, he left the city with his wife and whilst wandering about he saw a pond replete with lotuses, filled with various kinds of aquatic animals and adorned with trees in flower. On its bank those two, the king and his wife, saw a charming and auspicious hermitage where all was bliss and prosperity. Species of animals hostile by nature – such as elephants and lions, mongooses and snakes, cats and mice – did not engage in hostilities there. In there, on a seat of kuśa grass, the two saw the tranquil sage Viśvāmitra surrounded by pupils earnestly engaged in study of the Vedas. Bowing before that great sage with their hands folded, they both held his feet and repeatedly expressed obeisance. The tiger of sages, Viśvāmitra, repository of austerities, made them stand up and knowing the situation, he spoke in gentle words to the king.

Viśvāmitra said:

29-30. King, you will have a son of great renown who will possess all the qualities. Tell me where have you come from and what your city is called. After that, Excellent king, I will work hard to destroy your evil.

Bhīma said:

31-33. Lord, my city is called Kauṇḍinya and it is in the region of Vidarbha. My name is Bhīma and this is my wife, Cāruhāsinī. We have tried diligently to obtain a son by vows, gifts, austerities and so on, but because of an evil act committed in an earlier birth compassion[46] has not arisen in any god. Having left the kingdom, I have come to the forest where we both saw your footsteps. Whilst wandering through many

---

[46] That is, no god has had the compassion to grant them a son.

forests, I was made to come here by fate, as association with the good immediately gives an excellent result.

34-35ab.For this reason your blessing on me who has undertaken Vedic recitation,[47] sacrifices, gift-giving, austerities, vows and mantras has destined a son. No doubt of it. As a result of your compassion and restraint, my wish will not now be in vain.

35cd-36ab. But what was that absolutely foul evil I committed in a previous birth, Sage? Tell me what counteraction you have devised for me in this matter, Omniscient sage?

Brahmā said:

36cd. The great sage, Viśvāmitra, having listened to his words, carefully told that king an ancient tale.

Viśvāmitra said:

37-39. You abandoned the rules of the family – which are based on the Vedas, the śāstras, the Purāṇas and worldly custom – because you were blinded by a lust for prosperity. All your ancestors constantly worshipped Gaṇanāyaka, but on account of his anger[48] no offspring has been born to you. I am going to tell you how Gajānana became your family deity. Great hero, listen to this carefully from the beginning.

40-44. King Bhīma, the seventh man before you was a king who had one child only after a very long time. Even then he was deaf, mute, a hunchback and his very pitted body was streaming pus and stank terribly. When his mother Kamalā saw him she became very distressed and in her own heart she wondered, "Is it right to be in this world without a son? But to have a son like

---

[47] The point being that Vedic recitations etc., have allowed him to meet Viśvāmitra, whose power is such by itself to cause the birth of a son.

[48] Gaṇeśa is angry because Bhīma has not followed the family ordinances. The king has not recognized that he has an obligation to create a lineage (saṃtati: here translated "offspring"), because he is obsessed with his own concerns.

this brings little pleasure and causes great trouble. Why doesn't Brahmā bring death to me or to him now? How will I now show my face to my good friends?" Wailing in this way she cried terribly because of her pain.

45-50. On hearing her weeping, her husband, knowing the ways of karma, went to the lying-in chamber. After seeing his very distressed wife and the child in such a condition, he spoke in a gentle voice, comforting her, "Do not be distressed, Good lady! Such is the course of karma. A man's share of pain arises from evil committed in former lives and the man who experiences pain, after having found happiness, experiences happiness, but attains pain again. This child will not be good for us if we simply lament. If a previous deed is attached to him, he will experience it in the future. We will apply ourselves with excellent herbs, mantras, jewels, austerities and recitations in accord with the precepts relating to pilgrimage and worship of the gods. Beautiful-browed woman, do properly whatever is recommended for the boy."

51-52. The good woman understood that and having got rid of her grief over the boy and cleansed him with water, she rejoiced with her friends. He performed a rite[49] that was entirely appropriate for his son's birth, and he respectfully honoured the brahmins whilst she honoured their wives.

CHAPTER TWENTY

Dakṣa's Eulogy

Brahmā said:

1-9. He invited the good brahmins, who were grounded in the Vedas and knew the destiny of men, first honoured them with

---

[49] "performed a rite": The word for rite is abhyudaya which designates a special kind of rite for "worldly prosperity". See Kane, History of Dharmaśāstra, 1962, Vol.5.2., p.1037 n.1671.

wealth, clothes and jewels, consulted with them and then gave his son the name of Dakṣa. He then gathered a collection of herbs and undertook the offering of mantras and the recitation of prayers. For twelve years he himself performed a severe austerity for the removal of his son's illness and for the prosperity of his own lineage. But when the king saw that his son was not freed from the disease he became depressed and seething with anger he said, "Leave my palace with your son, Queen Kamalā! From now on I am unable to look at you and this son." After Vallabha reproached her in this way, Kamalā then departed from the city for the forest, taking her son. Weeping, falling to pieces with grief, wiping away the tears of pain, carrying him on her back, she became ravaged by fatigue, thirst and hunger. She went from one village to another, living by beggary and suffering terribly, and thieves plundered her clothing, jewellery and such like. And so going into a village she would leave her son in a Śiva temple and this beloved of the king would wander into a city for alms.

10-15. On one occasion she went with her son to beg in the city and by virtue of making contact with breath from the mouth of a certain brahmin – who Lambodara had caused to appear there because of his exceptional devotion – the young boy acquired a celestial body with eyes and ears. Having lost all her pain, Kamalā rejoiced after she beheld him making charming and delightful utterances. But Kamalā wondered, "Why didn't he become whole as a result of the efficacious herbs, mantras, personal service and vast sacrifices? Why did my son become whole by virtue of contact with his breath and where will I find this man who can destroy bad karma?" After she had said this and had embraced her son, her anguish gone.

16-17. Once again, collecting her son, she went into the city to beg. The townspeople respectfully welcomed them both and fed them with various kinds of cooked food and vegetables and such like, candied sugar, ghee and food prepared with milk. Eating happily in this way day after day they also obtained lovely new clothes and money each day.

18-26. Then the chief of the town asked him, "Tell me your father's name! What is your country? What is your town? Who are your kinsmen and what is your livelihood?" After giving ear to those words he told him his name was Dakṣa. Then he questioned him further about his mother, father, city, family and what had happened, and he replied, "My beloved father is in the city of Bhānu in Karṇāṭaka. He is a great kṣatriya, strong, famous and a crusher of enemy troops. This is Kamalā his wife and I am his son called Dakṣa. Brahmin, when I was born blind, deaf and filled with many sores, my mother tried to abandon me. She made a great effort but my father prevented her and then my father performed austerities for twelve years and offered the merit of that. But when my father could not see anything right in my body, he banished mother and me, townsman. Now I have become good looking by virtue of contact with somebody's breath." In this way Dakṣa told him everything he had heard from his mother, after hearing which the city dweller left and Dakṣa too left quickly and gladdened his mother.

27-34. In that city a brahmin of compassionate heart then instructed these two in the rules for the propitiation of Gaṇeśa, after which Kamalā and Dakṣa attained supreme calm, both intent upon the propitiation of Gaṇeśa by means of the austerity of standing on one toe. Completely engrossed in devotion, these two were reciting that excellent mantra of eight syllables in which the name of god is in the dative case and is preceded and followed by Om. On seeing them living on air, their bodies emaciated, the illustrious Vināyaka, an ocean of compassion, appeared in front of them. He was four-armed, huge in body, elephant-faced, very handsome, of the appearance of many suns and like the sun arisen in the night. His head was glittering with a diadem set with jewels, gold and pearls, he was dressed in yellow silk and ornamented with golden bracelets on the upper part of his arms. Reclining on one knee, he was seated on a large seat and he was wearing a golden girdle and a jewelled ring. On his stomach there was a large snake and he carried one sk, half that of an elephant.

35. Both of them saw this very form and then once again the form of a brahmin.[50] The brahmin said to these two, "I am satisfied with your calm and I have come to give you a boon. Choose your heart's desire!"

The sage said:

36. When the pleased Vighneśa became visible in the form of a brahmin, Dakṣa bowed to him with deep devotion and spoke with his hands folded.

Dakṣa said:

37-38ab. Merit performed in a previous birth has borne fruit for me, excellent brahmin, because I have seen your form which is vast and superlative in its duality as Vināyaka and as a brahmin. Now my birth has become significant.

38cd-48. You are the highest of causes and you are the cause of the Vedas, the supreme knowledge, the Supreme Brahma who is eternal and is to be sought through the Vedas. You alone are the witness of everything and you are the inside and outside of everything. You alone are the agent of actions in bodies both subtle and gross. Having many forms and having only one form, you can be defined, yet you are without shape. You alone are Śiva, you alone are Viṣṇu, Indra, Agni and Aryaman. Your own form is the Earth, Atmosphere and Heaven and you have the form of the Pleiades, the Moon and water. You are the maker of everything, the protector of everything and the destroyer of everything, you are the preceptor of beings moving and non-moving and the protector, and you possess intuitive knowledge and discriminative knowledge. You alone are the past, present and future and you alone are the deity of the senses. You are a kalā, a kāṣṭhā[51] and an hour, prosperity, firmness and patience.

[50] "once again the form of a brahmin": because Gaṇeśa had transformed his "theophanous" form into that of a brahmin.

[51] A kalā is the equivalent of 1.6 minutes and a kāṣṭhā 3.33 seconds.

You alone are Sāmkhya and Yoga, the śāstras and the Veda, the Purāṇas, the sixty-four arts as well as the Upaniṣads. You alone are the brahmin, the vaiśya, the kṣatriya and śūdra. You are this country and the foreign country, the field and the fields of merit. You are the measurable and immeasurable, and the field of knowledge for yogins. You alone are heaven, hell, the forests and the groves, herbs, creepers, trees, bulbs, roots and fruits. You comprise the living beings that are egg-born, born from a woman, sweat born and those which sprout. You are desire, anger, hunger, avarice, deceit, pride, compassion and forbearance. You are sleep, exhaustion and pleasure, laughter and grief.

The sage said:

49. After hearing Dakṣa's speech Vināyaka was very pleased. Almost smiling he spoke to him in words deep as the rumbling of clouds.

Gajānana said:

50-53. Very fortunate one, I am pleased with this profound eulogy. Though longing to grant a boon, I can, however, not give you one. Were I to give you a boon, a devotee might become angry with me, thinking, "He will give a boon merely because someone has a mangled body." You have obtained a celestial body and you have eyes and ears. I can say that the name of him from whom you have really been born is Mudgala. That Lord of brahmins will reveal his true form merely at a thought. What desires you desire, he will give all of them to you.

54-56. After saying this the supreme Gaṇeśa disappeared from there instantaneously. After he had disappeared Dakṣa was very distressed and wept just like when a beggar obtains a treasure and loses it or as a calf screams loudly when a cow has died. And whilst shedding tears from both his eyes he fell onto the ground, constantly muttering, "Where has Vināyaka gone? Where has he gone?

CHAPTER TWENTY-ONE

Description of the Teaching of the Man

Viśvāmitra said:

1-3. Terribly agitated, Vallabha's son was wandering around and running to and fro, but he could not find his lost clothes and jewels. On the road he questioned brahmins and trees about Vināyaka saying, "Where has Vināyaka gone? Has he been seen anywhere? Tell me about the celestial hermitage of Mudgala, an exceptional devotee who is devoted to Gajānana. It is excellent and gives security to all his followers."

4-7. Wandering about and mentally reflecting on Mudgala, he went to his charming hermitage of many wonders which surpassed Alakānanda.[52] In there on a very splendid seat he saw the brahmin, Mudgala, who knew the truth of the Vedas and the Vedāṅgas, was skilled in all the śāstras, possessed the sun's splendour and, because of the power deriving from his yogic exercises, a variety of forms. In accord with the procedures of the sixteen forms of ritual he was worshipping a large image of Vināyaka. It had three eyes and was made out of gold and jewels and adorned with many ornaments.

8-21. On seeing him Dakṣa bowed prostrate on the ground, shedding tears from his eyes and sighing repeatedly. Mudgala asked him, "Who are you and where have you come from? How can I remove your pain? Leaving nothing out, tell me everything!" After hearing the brahmin's words and having collected his wits, Kamalā's son then spoke to that bull of the brahmins. "In your presence, brahmin, I am going to speak only the truth about my purpose. In the country of Karṇāṭaka there was a king in the city of Bhānu. He was named Vallabha and he understood correct political conduct, was wise, gave gifts and was compassionate. But when his wife Kamalā gave birth to me, I had a runny nose, my blood-filled wounds stank, I was blind, a

---

[52] Alakānanda is Kubera's city.

hunchback, deaf, dumb and racked with coughing. When the townspeople saw me they said, "Get rid of him!" For twelve years my father made considerable effort, but he did not achieve his goal from Maheśvara, namely, a remedy for making my body whole. Then because of the violence of his inner feelings he banished me and Kamalā, my mother. Thereafter, in her distressed condition, my mother began wandering from town to town. She came with me to the city of Kauṇḍinya and being tormented by hunger, she began to wander around begging. Due to the power of her previous merit we experienced this vision of you. It was just like sight for a blind man. And due to the touch of your breath and the power of your limbs, my blemishes have disappeared, just as happened in the past to Ahalyā when she touched Rāma's foot. Through your favour I have obtained a celestial body, Strong-vowed sage. Yet this was something I did not understand, nor could my mother explain it to me, but I was amazed and I resolved in my heart, "Since I have gained this celestial body by virtue of the breeze from his body, then whenever I see him I will assume this body.

22-25. After wandering around for many days with this intention, Gaṇeśa, the repository of compassion, appeared before me, resembling a myriad of suns. Gajānana, the god of gods, was satisfied with our austerity and on seeing him, Kamalā gained the desires she had wished for in her heart. Then in a mellifluous tone the pleased god said to me, "Since you have become exhausted from wandering around as a result of having undertaken a vow for a particular aim, I Mudgala, an excellent brahmin, have appeared to you."

26-30. After I had heard that speech my heart thrilled and then I eulogized Gajānana with many eulogies and then, pleased, he said, "Wise boy, choose a boon!" So I told him of all my mind's desires and he had abandoned his form as a brahmin and took another form. He was four-armed, large in body, his head was covered with a large crown and in his hands he carried an axe, a lotus, a garland and sweet meats. He was wearing celestial garments and the tip of his trunk, his trunk and his tusk were shining. On his ears he wore some earrings which were like the orb of the sun, a snake was encircled around his body, he wore celestial ornaments and he was attended by kiṃnaras, groups of heavenly musicians and divine sages.

31-37. Then after I had seen that form I became filled with joy in the same way as the ocean has a full tide after seeing the full moon. But at that very moment the form disappeared before I could look at it properly just as when one is awake one does not see everything that has occurred in a dream. I then became utterly depressed, swooned and fell to the ground. When I became conscious again, I was thinking about the request that I choose a boon and I asked the Lord of the god of gods, the Lord who pervades everything, "May there be permanent prosperity in my house and may my devotion to you be the same. If it was because of previous merit that I saw you, then give these two things to me." I then heard the words, "It is given," come from a voice in the atmosphere, after which, brahmin, thrilled in heart I came to you. Mudgala, you are the elephant-faced god and the elephant-faced is Mudgala. Thus does Gajānana illuminate everything that is visible in my mind.

Bhṛgu said:

38-43. Having heard his speech, Mudgala spoke these words. "Son of Kamalā, you have done your duty successfully and you are devout. Nobody can describe the glory of your devotion. I performed rock-solid austerities for one thousand years, yet I have never seen a god like this who is the Lord of all worlds, the teacher of beings moving and non-moving, the teacher, the constant guide[53] of rajas, sattva and tamas and the foundation of the guṇas. Who creates the bodies of Brahmā, Śiva and Viṣṇu, who is the creator of beings and the manifestations, the basic elements of creation, the senses and of intelligence. Neither the gods, nor the Vedas, nor the sages know him completely. But such indeed is that Gajānana who you have manifestly seen. I praise your feet as you are really devout."

---

[53] "constant guide": these words may denote the ahaṃkāra.

44-48. Then they bowed to each other and embraced and the teacher and his friend, being of one mind, met together for a long time. Beginning with recitation and meditation, Mudgala taught the one-syllable mantra to the compliant prince. Day after day he told him of this one-syllable mantra, saying, "Undertake personal service and he will be pleased with you. Gajānana will give you those desires you wish for in your heart. If you let go of this mantra, you will be utterly destroyed, but if, however, you practice devotion for a long time in this world, you will, as one of Gaṇeśa's hosts, become subservient to the world protectors, Indra and so forth. After you have enjoyed all carnal enjoyments here, you will attain liberation at death."

CHAPTER TWENTY-TWO

The Tale of Ballāla and Vināyaka

The king said:

1-6. I am absolutely astonished at what has been narrated about the behaviour of that child, Dakṣa. It is truly marvellous, excellent sages. He was blind, hunchbacked, of putrid smell, flowing with blood, dumb, impure and virtually just a cough. How could he gain a celestial body from the breath coming from Mudgala's body? By what merit has this occurred and from what evil has it arisen? He performed the highest austerity for one thousand divine years, so why didn't he achieve the vision which comes from a god's satisfaction? In what manner did Ibh ānana, god of gods, become visible to Vallabha's son and was he without afflictions in a previous life? Remove this doubt of mine that has just arisen, omniscient sage! Obeisance to you! Though constantly drinking the nectar of Gajānana's tales, I have still not had enough.

The sage said:

7. You asked that well, king. I will duly tell you everything and your doubt will be removed. Listen single-mindedly, King.

8-12. In the country of Sindhu there was a very famous city called Pallī,[54] where there was an excellent vaiśya named Kalyāṇa. Munificent, prosperous and wise, he was absolutely obedient to the gods and the brahmins. His celebrated wife, who was known as Indumatī, had a beautiful face and she was loyal to her husband, her life was her husband and she was obedient to her husband's word. In time an excellent son who possessed the qualities was born of these two. Kalyāṇa then bestowed many presents upon the priests including gold, jewels, ornaments, clothes and cows. And in accord with what was proclaimed by the astrologers he gave his son the celebrated, auspicious sounding and powerful name of Ballāla.

13-21. A long time passed and on one occasion, Ballāla, ever devoted to the worship of the gods, joyfully left the village accompanied by his friends and he led the young boys into the forest. They occupied themselves playing various games, then bathed, set up a beautiful precious stone and worshipped it with beautiful blossoms and shoots, intending it to be Gaṇeśa. And some who were disposed to meditation undertook a recitation of his name. As was their inclination others danced out of devotion to the god, whilst some sang songs appropriate for the satisfaction of the god. Some enthusiastically erected a covering with branches and fresh young leaves, others built a protective wall around it and some an excellent hall. And there were those especially happy ones, who, after offering incense and a lamp, food offerings and honorariums of betel nut and fruit, some by performing rituals in the mind, others by using such things as flowers, creepers etc., duly worshipped him. And others who were learned recited the Purāṇas then, whilst others expounded the Dharmaśāstras and some expounded other books. In this way all spent their time for many days devoted to god, and

[54] Pallī: Almost certainly the modern day Pali which is one of the eight aṣṭavināyakas, sacred sites located around Poona. For other details see L.Preston, "Subregional Religious Centres in the History of Maharashtra. The Sites Sacred to Ganesh," in N. K. Wagle, ed., Images of Maharashtra: A Regional Profile of India, London 1980, pp.110, 125, n.45.

because they were devoted to god not one of them knew hunger or thirst.

22-24. One day, however, their fathers sought out Kalyāṇa the vaiśya and all of them angrily said, "Stop Ballāla! He calls together the young boys and goes into the forest every day, but they do not return to eat in the morning, nor at midday, nor in the evening. Consequently our young boys have become weak. You must now give guidance to your own son! From now on if he is not restrained we will strike him and then, after consulting the Lord of the city, we will expel you."

25-29. On hearing their unprecedented words, Kalyāṇa's eyes became like the japa flower because he was full of anger. After picking up a large club with which to strike his son he left and as soon as he reached the pavilion he really smashed it with one blow of the club. King, all the young boys then fled everywhere. Only Ballāla remained firm in rock-solid devotion. Seizing him with his clenched fist, Kalyāṇa thrashed him so severely with the club that streams of blood came forth from all over his body, just like the torrents of water coming from a mountain in the rainy season. Afterwards he threw the god, beautiful with its vermillion, far away.

30-32. Having completely lost his affection for his son and as if he were another messenger of Yama, he tied the child tightly to a tree with pālāśa creepers and he could be freed neither by teeth, hands nor feet. Later on he said to his son, "The god will free you. It will be up to him to give you food, drink and protection and if ever you return home, then truly you will die."

The sage said:

33. When he had smashed the god's temple,
The enraged vaiśya, Kalyāṇa, left immediately for his own home.
And by binding his own son to a tree in the forest,
He became quite evil due to the force of fate.
34. After he had gone, the vaiśya's son grieved
And in his mind he wondered,

"How did the god get this name Vighnāri,[55]
Which is chanted by all the people?
35. Since you do not destroy obstacles and evils,
How is it that you are celebrated as being the destroyer of evils?
Just as Śeṣa does not abandon the Earth, nor Savitṛ the light,
Nor the Moon ambrosia, nor the fire heat,
36. So one should not abandon one's own devotees.
If you had abandoned them how could you be so famous in the Vedas and śāstras?"
Lamenting in this way, he cursed his own
Very evil father Kalyāṇa.

37-39. "This unsurpassed temple of mine has been ruined by him and he has thrown away the Gaṇeśa image and struck me. If my absolutely rock-solid devotion towards Dviradānana is unsurpassed, he will certainly become blind, deaf, humpbacked and mute. What I said then is the truth. Everything I have declared will happen to him. He whose mind is on devotion cannot be in bondage, even though he might be bound in a body.

40. Reflecting on god with undivided attention
I am going to abandon my body in this peopleless forest.
Since I have not attempted escape,
This body can only be offered to god."

41-44. Having understood that this was his intention, Gajānana appeared in the form of a brahmin because of Ballāla. And just as the splendid sun on the eastern mountains brings an end to night's darkness, so were his bonds loosened by his fiery energy.[56] Bowed straight, he then made homage to him and his body became beautiful, having neither blood nor wound. The appearance of the god of gods caused his knowledge to became pure and he eulogized Gajānana with various words as seemed fit.

---

[55] Vighnāri, "Enemy of obstacles".

[56] "loosened by his fiery energy": That is, loosened by Gaṇeśa's fiery energy.

Ballāla said:

45. You alone are the mother, the father and the kinsman.
You alone are the creator of the moving and unmoving.
You create evil, mischievous and good people and
You assign birth in a womb or not in a womb.
46. You alone have the form of the extent of the whole world, the atmosphere,
The earth, the ocean, the high mountain, time and the wind.
You have the form of the sun, the moon, the stars, the planets, the world-Protectors, the classes, the objects of the senses, herbs and the elements.

The sage said:

47. After he heard that eulogy, Gajānana became very pleased and having embraced him, his own devotee, he spoke in a refined voice.

The god said:

48-50. The person who smashed my temple will fall into hell and with my assent your curse against him will take effect. When my curse[57] has taken effect there can be no doubt that he will become blind, deaf, mute and a hunchback discharging fluid. His father will banish him and his mother from his home. Request now another wish for yourself and I will grant you something that is difficult to get.

---

[57] "my curse" mama śāpam: Though Ballāla uttered the curse, its effectiveness is due to Gaṇeśa's power and so it is consistent for Gaṇeśa to say "my curse!"

The sage said,

51. Then Ballāla said to the god, 'Let my devotion to you be rock-solid and whilst staying always in this sacred place,[58] you must protect people from obstacles!'

Gaṇeśa said:

52-54. Hereafter my name will always be preceded by your name and will be auspicious to the people. It will be known in this city as Ballāla-Vināyaka. Your heart will stay firm on me and your devotion unswerving. And I will grant the wishes of those who will perform my festival in the bright half of the month of Bhādra in the town called Pallī.

The sage said:

55. After giving these boons the god disappeared from there. Then after Ballāla had erected an image of Vināyaka in conjunction with the brahmins, he erected a temple of many lustrous colours.

56. This small tale called "Ballāla and Vināyaka" has now been recited. After hearing it one obtains one's desires and is freed from all evils.

CHAPTER TWENTY-THREE

The Narration of the Future

Bhṛgu said:

1. After he had heard Viśvāmitra's speech, Bhīma questioned him further.

---

[58] "staying always in this sacred place, you must protect people...": Presumably this means that the people who come to this place will be protected from obstacles. It is not a general recommendation for protection from obstacles.

Bhīma said:

2ab. From hearing the adventures of Dakṣa my mind has calmed, but tell me, what was the fate of the vaiśya Kalyāṇa?

Viśvāmitra said:

2cd. Listen single-mindedly Bhīma, as I am going to tell you that tale.

3-6. Blood flowed from Kalyāṇa's body because of Ballāla's curse and besides having innumerable flowing wounds, he suffered from deafness and blindness, and became dumb, with a foul stink emanating from his body. Indumatī[59] saw this unexpected condition and in response to it she grieved, saying, "What is this? What is this? How did this condition befall my guiltless husband who is wise, munificent, devoted to the gods and the brahmins, well grounded in the meaning of the Dharmaśāstras and fully satisfied with his own wife?"

The sage said:

7-9. After lamenting much in this way she began sighing repeatedly, but on hearing that he had bound her son in the forest, still weeping, she went into the forest with the townspeople to where her son was bound. In the temple that was there she saw the god Gaṇanāyaka with his four arms, three eyes and his vermillion coloured body, and her son Ballāla who was worshipping Gajānana there.

10-12ab. Noticing that he was freed, that he was without wounds and his body unmutilated, Indumatī spoke angrily to the townspeople, repeatedly abusing them, "Why did those who speak the truth abuse me in my husband's presence? Having left such a man as him, I have come here because I love my son. Look at my son manifesting such devotion to god!"

---

[59] Indumatī is Kalyāṇa's wife. See 1.22.9.

The sage said:

12cd-14. They were all astounded by him and afterwards could barely speak, but after seeing his body reddened with vermillion, smeared with red sandal wood paste, clothed in red, splendidly adorned with red flowers and garlands, without the thought of "I", without ego, as though he were Vighnapa without a trunk, someone said, "Who could understand the glory of this great devotion?"

15-23ab. She lost her grief after seeing her son like this and rejoiced, then she embraced him, affection streaming from her breast. She said to him, "Let us go to our own house which has been devastated as a great misfortune has befallen your father. You must provide some remedy for it, wise son? We are the most fortunate pair in the world in having a son like you. There are wounds all over his body, it flows with blood and emits a putrid smell, his face is black and he is emaciated, deaf and blind. That's how your father is! I have come to inform you about him. He struck you as is a father's right and even if that was frivolous it is not a transgression according to the Purāṇas, the revealed and the remembered texts. Consider the duties of a son and reflect on his good health. Your father loves you, so in public[60] you must praise your father most highly. A good son who is renowned should carry out his parent's command and he should respect, nourish and protect them both. Devise a remedy[61] using herbs and mantras and the petitioning of the gods, and then fix your vision on me, son. You will have renown in this world and I will have happiness, son."

23cd. After he had heard her words Ballāla made this speech.

Ballāla said:

24-31. What of the mother! What of the father! What of the son! and what of the friend! Everything is done by Vighnarāja

---

[60] "in public" loke: For this meaning of loka in the Rām see Pollock, S., The Rāmāyaṇa of Vālmīki, Volume ii. Ayodhyākhaṇḍa, Princeton 1986.p.364.

[61] That is, devise a remedy for restoring good health to Kalyāṇa.

and it is traditionally said that everything depends on him. Therefore, fortunate woman, Vināyaka is my father and mother. One attains the appropriate result according to the activity one performs. I have entrusted my life to Gajānana, god of gods and because of his profound devotion he has given me knowledge and life. Because he destroyed the temple, cast away the god and struck me, who is so devoted to Vināyaka, he has experienced the appropriate result. In consideration of the fact that you are not my mother, nor he my father, but that the god Gajānana is the mother, father and god of everything, that he alone is the giver of knowledge, the protector and destroyer – when he takes the form of time –, that his own form is everything, that he is the Lord of the gods and embodies Brahmā, Viṣṇu and Śiva, my being struck by that cruel, evil man is as pointless as his casting away of the god's image and his destruction of the temple. Looking at his face will constitute a major offence. Casting aside your affection for me, serve your husband!

Viśvāmitra said:

32ab. After she had heard her son's words she addressed him again.

His mother said:

32cd. As a favour kindly and affectionately utter a counter curse![62]

Her son said:

33-39. In a future existence, you, the boon-seeker, will be his mother and one like him will be your son, strong-vowed woman. He who is called Kalyāṇa will become a bull of the kṣatriyas named Vallabha and you will be known by the name

[62] "counter curse" ucchāpam: This is a counter curse in the sense that it will reverse the earlier curse or, at the least, put limits on its effectiveness.

of Kamalā. Your son will be known by the name of Dakṣa. Vallabha will perform austerities for twelve years, remaining in the highest condition of restraint, in order to remove Daksa's blindness, deafness, muteness and his wounds. Failing to achieve his result, beautiful-faced woman, he will ban you and your son from the house and then you will live in a foreign country. Fortunate woman, as a result of fate – the will of Dviradānana – your son will become whole by virtue of touching some excellent brahmin. Gaṇanātha will appear there just then and Dakṣa will obtain a celestial body from Dviradānana.

40. Everything about the cause of that curse has now been related, beautiful woman, and you have also been told what will happen. Understand it as you will.

Viśvāmitra said:

41-42. Saying this he turned his mother away and she then left, full of grief and unhappiness and a certain feeling of outrage. Ballāla ascended a celestial carriage produced by his devotion as decreed by Gajānana and then he went to heaven.

43-44. Now I have explained everything about which you asked. The vaiśya obtained that destiny after two births and everything then happened just as Ballāla said. She was born and became Kamalā, he became a bull of the kṣatriyas.

CHAPTER TWENTY-FOUR

The Tale of the Vision

Bhīma said:

1. Where, how and for whom, tiger of sages, did the wise prince, Dakṣa, perform that personal service? Tell me in detail, for though I have been listening, I have still not had enough.

Viśvāmitra said:

2-6. Near the city of Kauṇḍinya there was a huge forest, which was delightful and filled with many trees, teemed with various beasts of prey and many hosts of birds, and was resplendent with creepers and palmyra trees. It was resplendent with ponds and lakes of pure water and it was also resplendent with an image of Gaṇeśa standing in the midst of a dilapidated temple. Remaining there, he[63] performed austerities in order to please Gajānana. For a period of twelve years he caused satisfaction to that god, utilizing the one-syllable mantra Mudgala had taught him.

7-12. With the use of baths, garments, perfumes, garlands, incense and lamps he performed a food offering made of radishes and food that he had begged. And the bull of kṣatriyas mentally contrived an honorarium for the sacrifice. In this way twenty-one days passed for him, King. When it next dawned he saw in a vision a single, huge red elephant. It was splendid with its cheeks oozing ichor, good looking, the semblance of a mountain, its face charming and tranquil, its tusk resplendent. Strewn over with Bhramara bees and with its great belly it was virtually another Gajānana. In the appropriate place on its neck it had placed a garland of jewels. Then raising up the elephant-king placed him on his shoulder and the elephant went to the city, adorned with emblem and standard.

13. Then he awoke[64] and questioned his own mother, "Mother, Kamalā, tell me the meaning of this now, whether climbing onto the elephant's shoulder was good or bad?"

His mother said:

14. You are fortunate because you have seen Vināyaka in the form of an elephant. There can be no doubt that you will acquire a kingdom as a result of your ascent.

---

[63] Dakṣa

[64] "he awoke": That is, he came out of the vision.

Dakṣa said:

15-16. If I should acquire a kingdom I will give you a palanquin, villages, a lamp and a garland of pearls, and I will enact the law in respect of gifts of gold and cattle, vows and restraints and many other kinds of gifts.

The sage said:

17-18. Having heard this, Kamalā, full of joy, spoke to her son, "When you occupy the kingship, son, I will be supremely happy. Whilst you are supporting what is best, make sure your mind is intent on the good law. Have a rich life and be devoted to the honouring of the brahmins and the gods!"

CHAPTER TWENTY-FIVE

Description of the Consecration Ceremony

Viśvāmitra said:

1ab. Listen king, and I will talk about something auspicious that was caused by fate.

1cd-2. In the city of Kauṇḍinya there lived the very wise King Candrasena, who, with the maturing of his own karma and the force of time, died and went to heaven on the heavenly path because of his abundant righteousness.

3-6. On hearing of this the townspeople all made a tremendous noise and leaving their various occupations, they went there on the run. They saw the dead king and drawn with grief, they faltered, collapsing and striking their heads with their hands. Taking hold of his feet, they bowed and gave way to folly and distress. Some took his hand and placed it on their heads, whilst some made loud sounds with their mouths on the back of their hands and others fell down deathlike because of their great affection for him.

7-13. His wife Sulabhā was terribly distressed and cried in a mournful tone, whilst striking her heart with her hands. Then she became faint and fell to the ground, her jewels scattered about, but she was lifted up by three women of the city who were facing similar disasters. Candrasena's beautiful wife then wailed shamelessly and heartlessly, crying out indistinctly, "Lord! Lord! Disposer! You have no compassion! Your behaviour is childish! When people are in love you unite them, but you separate them before their purpose has been achieved. King, I have not yet asked you, so tell me where you have gone, repository of compassion! I will go to that blessed spot everyday if you tell me to, beloved What transgression of mine has brought you into this cruel state now? Forgive that, and free of shame, I will make obeisance in the midst of the people. Wherever you have gone take me, your sonless wife who brings you love! Without a husband the triple-world looks empty."

The sage said:

14-17. His ministers were Sumantu and Manorañjana and they too lamented about him, saying, "What will happen to the kingdom? Where has the excellent king gone without consulting the two of us? Why don't you speak king? Why have you remained silent? Can't you see that your beloved wife has become distressed like a widow! King, we will come too after we have given up everything including our status as householders. But now that this city is without a Lord who will protect the kingdom?"

The sage said:

18-22. On that occasion a very wise brahmin who knew the truth of the Vedas and the śāstras uttered some sharp words on that very subject. "You are all self-interested and nobody here is trustworthy. The tear drops of friends fall onto the face of the deceased and a dead body becomes a burden for the earth, but will anyone else in this round-shaped universe follow the dead? And here is Queen Sulabhā weeping with a wish for his life, but never does her heart weep for going after him.[65] Moreover, all you townspeople are all just obsessed with the progress of your own concerns. Have not the kings of the Lunar and Solar dynasties died?[66]

23-25ab. Look! After you have got yourselves up, you must prepare the king's body. Only the closest relative, and no other, can perform the funeral rite and for this very purpose people are very eager to have a son. In consequence of this, bring a son who is appropriate to the law or some other, for he must begin the rites and everyone must give him a benediction of sesamum."

The sage said:

25cd-28ab. Admonished by that brahmin, all the townspeople, the two ministers and the women performed his funeral rite. Sumantu did everything and everyone gave a benediction of sesamum and after they had bathed again, at length, they all entered the city. Then they ate the leaf of the nimb tree, after which having bowed to the Lord[67] and consoled Sulabhā, they each went to their own abode.

28cd-32. At the same time as this all the townspeople, the two ministers and the king's wife were puzzled about the job of protecting the subjects. But at that very moment the sage Mudgala, who knew everyone's intentions, came there and said, "The king has a large elephant named Gahana. He must take a garland made of lotuses into the assembly where he will cast it onto the neck of somebody, who will then become king." All of them said "Yes" and by saying "Good! Good!" they honoured the words of the delightful Mudgala who possesses knowledge of what is beyond the senses.

---

[65] "for going after him" anugatyartham: That is, placing herself on the funeral pyre with her husband.

[66] The sense being that because these kings of famous dynasties have died, the death of Candrasena should be easier to bear.

[67] "having bowed to the Lord": That is, to the deceased king.

CHAPTER TWENTY-SIX

Description of the Lineage

Viśvāmitra said:

1. On a certain day associated with an auspicious plant,
And at an auspicious time on that auspicious day,
With an auspicious conjunction productive of a good result,
And the people of various kinds were assembled in the town,
The queen, King, placed a garland
Of jewels on the elephant's trunk,
2. Having asked the elephant, "Choose a king,
That one amongst the people of whom you think most highly."
Having taken that garland, the Lord of elephants,
Made crimson by the secretion of fluids,
Wandered all over the place
As commanded by groups of singers, bards and brahmins.
Perceiving by smell that he was surrounded by various
Kinds of musicians, mercenaries and men who sought the kingship,
He went out of the town
To the assembly hall which was filled with the populace.
3. After placing their husbands and young boys in the forefront,
The women assembled in the city
For the sake of the kingship as did many kinds of men
And many leaders of guilds.
But when the elephant went to an inaccessible place
All of them became utterly disconsolate
And returned to their own houses,
Whilst others left the city.
4. However, the elephant went to Kamalā's son
Who was worshipping Dviradānana.
Seeing only him, he placed the garland on him

Whilst the gods in the sky and the people were looking on.
5. When they realized the feeling of the citizens,
Of the queen and both ministers,
The people then gave clothes,
Garlands and ornaments to Dakṣa.

6. Many sets of instruments, both terrestrial and divine, were played and the joyful gods released an auspicious shower of flowers.

7-9. These people were then introduced in due order according to their appropriate status and they bowed to king Dakṣa and his two ministers. The king then gave betel leaf and clothes to the people and after honouring and giving many gifts to the brahmins, honouring his mother with such things as ornaments and clothes, he gave presents to the brahmins in accord with the precepts.

10-12. Placing her in the palanquin, he himself mounted the elephant and putting himself before his two ministers who were mounted on horses, he went to the city adorned with banners and flags and its roads moistened. The town-heralds were eulogizing him, the apsaras were dancing before him and the heavenly musicians who were skilled in the song rushed up and walked before him. Sounds of victory, sounds of adoration and musical notes went to the sky.

13-17. After they had reached the king's gate some people went home, but the innumerable kings all entered the assembly hall. Then the very wise king sent the palanquin, the umbrella, the banner, the chowrie and his minister Sumantu to Mudgala. When he saw Mudgala coming he left his own throne and bowed to him, his crowned head placed before his feet. He then invited him to sit on his own throne and was himself directed by him onto another seat. When he was seated with the assemblage of kings, the very wise king, Dakṣa, honoured the sage and also gave a cow to the brahmin[68] who was there.

---

[68] "to the brahmin who was there": I am uncertain whether this refers to Mudgala or to the brahmin, first introduced in 25,17, who set in process the train of events leading to Dakṣa becoming king.

18-20. Then he said to him, "Ah! Mudgala, great sage, these people now appreciate your great glory. By means of your favour I have gained a kingdom and beauty in body. Consider what my previous condition was and consider a kingdom such as this, Sage! I know that you must certainly be Vināyaka. Excellent sage. Brahmin, place your lotus-like hand on my head again, so that I may partake of all my wishes for a long time, Sage."

21-25. Having given ear to his speech, Mudgala said to him, "You will never experience the fear that is caused by an enemy and you can wish for any wish you want and you will have it!" Then he gave him villages, clothes, jewels, wealth etc., as well as herds of cows and clothes to the other brahmins and after they had applauded him with benedictions, the brahmins went to their homes. He then gave many villages to the two ministers and the householders and had a very large temple of Gaṇeśa built. The king then dismissed the assembly and entered his house.

26-29ab. Vallabha came there after he had heard the news from the people. Then to the great king Dakṣa, whose name was famous in the triple world, King Virāsena, as commanded by Gaṇeśa in a dream, gave his own beautiful daughter who had been wanting a husband. His son in her was known as Bṛhadbhānu, his son was Subhāla, Padmākara was his son and Vapuṛdīpta was his son. Citrasena was his son and you came from Citrasena.

Vyāsa said:

29cd-30. After he had heard the complete succession of the lineage from Viśvāmitra's mouth and had satisfied and approached the sage again, he questioned that bull of the brahmins.

Bhīma said:

31. When will Vināyaka be pleased with me, great sage? Lord, tell me the way for me to obtain his favour, when, after having seen Gajānana, I will accomplish what must be done.

CHAPTER TWENTY-SEVEN

Description of Rukmāṅgada's Consecration

The sage said:

1. Tell me, what remedy did the intelligent and compassionnate sage, Viśvāmitra, tell to Bhīma?

Brahmā said:

2. He did tell Bhīma a remedy. Hear about the great one-syllable mantra the sage told to Bhīma.

3-5. Viśvāmitra who knows the good law was pleased and said to him, "Propitiate the deity, the Lord Gaṇanāyaka, with it and perform personal service in the temple that Dakṣa built. Vināyaka will be pleased and will give you all your wishes, whether they pertain to accomplishment in the law, power, sensuality, liberation or anything else that is desired. Return to your city Bhīma and don't worry about anything."

The sage said:

6-9. After he had said this and had made obeisance to him the king then left, accompanied by his wife, and he rejoiced when he saw his own town. The two ministers went with the army and the citizens to the king, and they embraced the king, whilst some bowed at a distance, others close by. Accompanied by them all, the king, on whose banner there is a bee, reached the city. It resounded with many musical instruments, had its roads moistened and a fragrant smell about it. People said to each other, "Like a woman who has gained a husband or a blind man who has gained sight this town is now resplendent."

10-12. He stood in the palanquin listening and so too did Cāruhāsinī. Both were adorned opulently with clothes and jewels and, being praised, both were full of joy. Both entered that delightful city that was filled with many kinds of wealth and showered all the people with pearls, ornaments, clothes and betel nut, and after they had left, both went to their own abode.

13-19. Then on an auspicious day the king went to Dakṣa's temple where at all times he worshipped the mighty Vināyaka and became constantly occupied with fasting and the setting of his mantra in motion. When he was eating, sleeping, moving speaking or just breathing, the king, his attention undivided, was always thinking about him alone. The king saw the unsurpassed Vināyaka in water, on the ground, in the atmosphere, in heaven, in a god, in a man, in a tree, in smoke, in food and in drink. He praises whomsoever he sees him in, intent upon a tight embrace. All the people in the city took him for a piśāca. Then Vināyaka arrived and holding the king on the palm of his hand, he said to him, "King you are freed! Tell me what you want." The king said to him, "I know nothing other[69] than your lotus feet," and then Vināyaka said, "Through my favour you will have a handsome son endowed with good qualities who will have a golden body, King. Go to your own home and devote yourself to the worship of the priests and the gods."

20-26. After he had gone to his home the king did exactly that and undertook the worship and the feeding of the gods with all his heart, thinking, "May Gaṇeśa be pleased." After only a short while a splendid son was born to him and on account of his son's birth he gave many gifts and named him Rukmāṅgada as authorized by eminent brahmins. Like the moon in the bright half of the month, the young boy grew prodigiously and for his education the king put his son under the care of a teacher.

---

[69] "I know nothing other..." nānyaṃ jane: He is only interested in washing Gaṇeśa's feet. Anything else is irrelevant to him.

Simply by hearing it he understood what his teacher proclaimed and since Kapila, the repository of all knowledge, had taught it, he too became a repository of knowledge, virtually another Gajakarṇa. Rukmāṅgada was exceedingly powerful and skilled in all the śāstras. He performed a tiara coronation for him who possessed many qualities and to the principal brahmins he gave clothes, jewels and money.

27. After that he too performed an additional large devotion to Vināyaka and day after day he recited the one-syllable mantra he had obtained from his father.

28-29. One day the heir-apparent entered the forest, went hunting and killed many gayal and deer. When he became quite exhausted he saw the hermitage of a certain sage, a veritable lattice of various kinds of trees and creepers and full of animals no longer hostile towards each other.

CHAPTER TWENTY-EIGHT

The Fasting unto Death

The sage said:

1-6ab. Then Rukmāṅgada saw the good sage, Vācaknavi, and his wife, Mukundā, talking to him with affection and charm. The exhausted king then made obeisance to both of them and when the sage had gone to bathe, the excellent king pleaded, "O mother, Mukundā, give me the best cold water, for without water my vital breaths will go to Yama's abode." Having given ear to his speech, she said, sick with lust, "Nowhere amongst the gods, snakes or the mass of yakṣas and heavenly musicians can I see a man like you who is even more handsome than Kāma, so pleasing in all his limbs. I am completely set on you, desirable man, so give me your heart and a drink of the nectar of your lips."

The sage said:

6cd-9. But immediately after he had heard this offensive statement,[70] terribly distressed because of his fatigued condition, but with his senses subdued he said to that superb Tilottamā,[71] "Don't be so bold! Because of Gaṇeśa's power my mind is never inclined towards adultery since it is reprehensible. I do not want to drink water offered by someone as depraved as you. I came thinking this was a sage's hermitage, but I will leave here, ugly woman." But seizing his hands, the suffering woman spoke to him as he was preparing to leave.

Mukundā said:

10-12ab. A man who wishes forcibly to ravage the wife of someone else certainly goes to hell, even if he does not himself engage in sexual relations with her. Brahmā proclaimed independence for women in the Kṛta and Tretā time periods. If you do not obey my command, you will become ashes, or you will become a forest wanderer who has lost his kingdom.

12cd-16. Rushing up to him after she had said this, she embraced him impetuously and forcibly kissed him on the face, tormented as she was by Kāma's arrows. But Rukmāṅgada then forcefully pushed her away and she fainted and fell to the ground like Rambhā struck by the wind. His mind indifferent towards another man's wife, he then spoke to her when she had got up. "Illustrious woman, ignorant wife of a sage, a woman whose heart is set on another man will certainly dwell in hell. My heart would never waver, even if the great ocean were to dry up."

---

[70] An offensive statement because she makes out that she loves him when really she is only interested in sex and because she is deceiving her own husband.

[71] "to that superb Tillottamā": That is, he spoke to Mukundā who is beautiful like Tillottamā, a famous nymph of great seductive beauty.

17. Spurned in this way by him, she cursed him angrily. "Just as I have become miserable, you too will get your leprosy. From now on your heart will be hard and you will be heartless."

18-26. After the king had copiously rebuked her for speaking in that way, he quickly left the hermitage, terribly distressed. He saw that his own body had become pale like a crane's body and that it was full of leprosy, without beauty, utterly vile. At that moment, whilst he was immersed in a sea of anxiety, he said this to Gajānana, "Have I offended you? Why have I become like this now? How did I have this encounter with this depraved wife of a sage? Assuredly, Gaṇeśa, Lord of Perfections, you have caused this evil person to prosper dramatically, yet you undertake incarnations for the protection of the good. This woman is conceited because of her beauty, she is wanton and she is depraved, yet she is not ruined. But how is it that my body –previously so lovely as to rival gold – has come into this condition or by what evil action? Just as before I am always practising devotion to you according to the precepts, elephant-faced Lord and I go to none other than you for refuge. I cannot show this body or this face to the people, so I will dry up this body by fasting unto death." After he had made this decision he sat near a banyan tree.

27. Servants rushed hither and thither, but they could not see the king. And when night came each one returned to his own home and the condition of the king and his servants was like that of two Cakravāka birds.[72]

CHAPTER TWENTY-NINE

Nārada's Visit

The sage said:

1-7. One day whilst sitting under a banyan tree, the king, from afar, saw the divine sage Nārada, a bull of the sages. He

[72] "...two Cakravāka birds": Cakravāka birds are famed for their grieving when separated. See Rām. 1.1. for the classic illustration.

bowed to him and requested, "Rest for a moment." Then Nārada, a repository of compassion, descended from his atmospheric path. After he had honoured the sage to the extent of his capacity he respectfully addressed him, "I am named Rukmāṅgada, Bhīma's son of vast strength. I was engaged in the hunt and came to Vācaknavi's hermitage where I made a request for water because I was thirsty, Faultless sage. After the sage had gone to bathe, his exceedingly depraved wife, who was sick with desire, kissed me. With a mind corrupted by evil and herself tormented by the arrows of Kāma, she said, "Enjoy me!" But because of god's favour I have conquered my senses, so I repulsed her. Then that extremely hurt woman, her mind cruel, cursed me terribly, saying, "You very evil man, you shall become leprous because you are rejecting me who desires you."

8-9. After I had heard that wicked speech I left the hermitage and became a pale leper. Tell me my expiation, sage! Bhīma too will most certainly be immersed in an ocean of sorrow because of my absence from him.

10. Having heard that speech of his the omniscient Nārada was filled with compassion and spoke about the way to destroy his leprosy.

Nārada said:

11-17. Whilst I was coming hither I saw something that was utterly marvellous. In Vidarbha there is a famous city named Kadamba, in which there is a temple where there is a really excellent and auspicious image of Vināyaka called Cintāmaṇī and it gives every wish to everyone. In front of the temple there is a large tank which was previously one of Gaṇeśa's footprints. King, a certain śūdra who had eruptions of the skin and was worn out with old age came to Kadamba town on the occasion of a pilgrimage. Immediately after he had bathed in the Gaṇeśa tank he gained a celestial body, however, and ascending an excellent flying vehicle brought from heaven by the hosts who had Gaṇeśa's real appearance, he went to the highest heaven, on reaching where nobody grieves or ever falls back. Indra of kings, I myself have seen that place which is fit for bathing. After having bathed and worshipped the mighty god who grants desirable things, give gifts to the brahmins and you will immediately become purified. And once you have completely cast off your withered skin, like a snake you will become very handsome.

The sage said:

18-19. After he had heard this very speech uttered by Nārada, the excellent king said nothing at all, immersed as he was in an ocean of bliss. But when the bull of sages, Nārada, got ready to leave, he addressed him, after he had respectfully bowed to and honoured the sage again.

Rukmāṅgada said:

20-24. Faultless sage, who previously gained good success in that sacred place and who erected that beautiful image made of jewels and precious stones which is called Vināyaka? Tell me! My curiosity is very great, Sage, and the inclination of ascetics like you is to help others, otherwise there would be no point in you wandering amongst people. In the worlds the cloud rains, Śeṣa supports the Earth and the sun too moves around continually for the benefit of people, brahmin. In front of you, who is impartial in respect of all beings and omniscient, what should one say who is lacking in sophistication and stupid, Repository of compassion? Nevertheless divine sage, I am still asking you to resolve this doubt.

Nārada said:

25. King who brings blessings to his people, you have asked a good question. I am satisfied with your statement and I will tell you everything.

CHAPTER THIRTY

The Violation of Ahalyā

Nārada said:

1. Once I went to see Indra at Amarāvatī, and after he had honoured me as prescribed, severely stooped down, he spoke.

Indra said:

2. Sage, tell me something wonderful that will give me pleasure. You wander all the worlds and so you know everything.

Nārada said:

3-8ab. In the world of mortals I saw Gautama's large hermitage with its lattices of various creepers and trees and its flocks of various birds. I saw Gautama there with Ahalyā, but after seeing her beauty, I became agitated with lust. Because of her beauty, she was known in the world as a Sāvitrī, a Śacī, a Lakṣmī, a Girīndrajā, an Urvaśī, a Menakā, a Rambhā, a Tilottamā by whom was produced children like Brahmā and Śiva. She was also an Anasūyā, an Arundhatī, a Chāyā who is Saṃjñā, wife of the Sun and an Āditi, wife of Kaśyapa. Not even a single one of them was like her, nor could there have been anyone amongst the wives of the nāgas. I came quickly to visit this excellent Amarāvatī. But look at this lovely lady. Without her Amarāvatī is insignificant.

The sage said:

8cd-11. Speaking thus to Śakra, the sage who was fond of song disappeared. When the illustrious Nārada, best of sages, had disappeared, Indra, killer of Jambha, swooned as he had been wounded by Kāma who has a fish on his banner. He thought, "When will I see the wife of the sage Gautama and after I have experienced the nectar of her lips when will I be free of passion's fire? I see nothing else to live for except for a lovely embrace with her."

12-14. Having arrived at this plan, the killer of Jambha became Gautama[73] and thinking only about her on the way, he came to the sage's hermitage and saw Ahalyā at a time when, however, Gautama had gone to bathe. He went inside and said, "Wife, prepare a lovely bed for us!" Then she said, "Why have you stopped reciting scriptures and come home now? Why did you make this reprehensible request for sex during the day?"

Gautama said:

15-17. As soon as I began to bathe a lovely nymph came there to bathe alone and appeared naked in front of me. Her lower lip was like the bilva fruit, her body was quite beautiful and she had beautiful full breasts. Lovely lady, my heart oppressed by Kāma's arrows and I could not stick to muttering prayers. So I came back to the hermitage. Give me sex now wife! Would you see me dead somewhere, burnt by desire's fire? I will curse you or I will depart and severely curb my heart.

Ahalyā said:

18-19ab. Having abandoned your Vedic recitation and worship of the gods, why are you asking for sex? This is inappropriate for you brahmin sage, however, I will obey your command, because for a woman there is never another duty than obedience to her husband.

The sage said:

19cd-28. Believing that he was her own husband because of his voice, shape and demeanour, Ahalyā got into the bed to have sex with Indra, the thunderbolt- bearer. Without hesitation the killer of Jambha, in the shape of Gautama, dallied with her,

[73] "He became Gautama": This means that he changed his appearance to that of Gautama.

kissing and embracing her, unfastening her skirt and so on. But when she smelled his celestial fragrances she became very frightened and trembled. In her mind she pondered, "Does he have a false body? Could he become a severe stain on me like the one on the moon? If both my families were ruined because of my intercourse with this depraved man, how could I show my face, darkened by disgrace, in the world? But to what fate will my dear husband, the sage, bring me?" Then angrily she asked that rogue, "Who are you who takes a false body? I was unsuspecting because of my husband's body. Speak! If not, I am going to curse you!" Addressed in this way, he manifested his own body because he was frightened of a curse. It was decked with celestial ornaments, had a diadem and gold bracelets and his lotus-like face was glittering because of earrings of astonishing splendour. Then he said to her, "Know that I am Śaci's husband. Your lovely appearance has made me become agitated with passion's fire and because I could not get any satisfaction anywhere, I have done this. Therefore, you should respectfully enjoy me, the Lord of the triple-world."

29-31. After she had heard his speech the sage's wife was filled with anger and almost belching flames from her mouth, she spoke to Indra, Lord of the thirty, "Because his body was yours, fool, when my husband arrived, I was unaware what the situation might be, Performer of one hundred sacrifices, dolt! You have shattered my fidelity to my husband and I have committed a monstrous evil. Into what condition will I enter as a result of the curse which will come from Gautama's voice?"

CHAPTER THIRTY-ONE

The Description of Indra's Curse

Rukmāṅgada said:

1. What happened when Gautama returned, great sage? Tell me everything as I am very curious to know.

Nārada said:

2-12. Immediately after having completed his obligatory rituals, Gautama went back to his hermitage and he called his own wife near, saying, "Give me some water to wash my feet. Why haven't you appeared in front of me straight away as before? Why haven't you brought a seat and why aren't you saying something pleasing?" After she had heard his words she began trembling like a creeper and emerging with face downcast she immediately came to the sage and prostrated herself on the ground, her head placed in the direction of his feet. Distressed and afraid of a curse she then spoke softly to the sage, "At dawn you left to have a bath as is your usual practice. Assuming your appearance the depraved Indra, Lord of the gods said to me, 'After I had seen a beautiful woman who was amorous and even more beautiful than the nymphs, my mind would not remain firmly fixed on recitation to the gods during the obligatory rituals. I have turned back and returned, so give me sex, lovely lady.' Thinking that it was certainly you, in error I obeyed your command exactly. However, after having smelt those celestial fragrances I had a misgiving once again[74] and said, "Evil man, if you do not want to become ashes, tell me who you are." Because he was afraid of this curse Indra, destroyer of armies, became visible. However, I did not come quickly as soon as I heard your command, Excellent sage, because I was ashamed. Forgive me this transgression.[75] It is not a fault when made known by oneself, but it is a fault when made known by another. One should not publicly display gifts, honour and dishonour, herbs, sex, prosperity, household quarrels, long life and spells."

13-15. After he had heard this, his senses swirling with anger, the sage cursed his own wife, "Ill behaved woman, you will

---

[74] "I had a misgiving once again": The first misgiving being her surprise at Gautama"s request for sex during the day.

[75] "Forgive me this transgression": That is, the transgression of not coming out to meet him when asked.

become a rock! You will recognize neither my own body, my demeanour, nor my gestures, because your very lustful heart has been fixed on another man. You will regain your own body only when touched by the foot of King Rāma, son of Daśaratha, when he is wandering from forest to forest."

Nārada said:

16-23ab. Straight away she became a rock due to the power in the words of that repository of austerity. When he had heard about her curse, Indra, chastiser of Pāka, trembled just like the mountain Himavat when it is met by a hurricane. In his mind he wondered, "What should I do now? If I were to stay hidden in the ocean, a pond, a pool or a lotus, then that sage would find me." Therefore, Indra, the thunderbolt- bearer, roamed about in the form of a cat and Gautama could not see him in the door, in the house nor in the hermitage. And he wondered, "Where has Indra, enemy of the dānavas, gone, the one who defiled my wife?" But through meditation the excellent sage perceived him instantaneously and said, "Because you are the Lord of the gods I will not turn you into ashes, yet since you are a rogue, Husband of Śaci, I will curse you. Be possessed of one thousand vaginas. For as long as this speech uttered in anger by this sage is heard your own body will look as though it is stamped with one thousand vaginas." Immersed in an ocean of misery, Indra, killer of Vṛtra, grieved.

Indra said:

23cd-28. Many times have I been taught various teachings by the eminent, but I have not given careful consideration to the statements of the eminent because one's own opinion brings benefits, whereas everything uttered by another is conducive to ruin. The opinion of an elderly person is very sound, but the whimsy of an amorous woman leads to ruin. In view of

Nārada's declaration how can I go to that blameless woman[76] and, being the king of the gods, how will I show my face to my people? Where has my celestial body gone now? Whatever am I going to say to my wife? Damn me! and damn Kāma through whom I have come to this contemptible condition. Whether karma is good or bad, it is experienced by living beings, so after being born as an animal I will destroy this vile self. Taking the form of an Indragopa beetle, I will stay in a lotus filled with buds.

CHAPTER THIRTY-TWO

The Tale of the Mantra

Nārada said:

1-3. After Indra had gone into the lotus, however, I came to his city where I met the gods who were led by Bṛhaspati. I told them all about why the two were cursed, about the intercourse of Indra with Ahalyā and of their deformity, about how Indra, because of his outrage against Ahalyā, acquired one thousand vaginas from Gautama's curse, and gods, about how she became a stone by having intercourse with him.

The sage[77] said:

4. All the gods were filled with sorrow after they had heard what Nārada had said. They were so unhappy that they were weeping with agitated sighs and exhalations.

The gods said:

5-10. He performed one hundred sacrifices, he conquered demons, he protected the triple-world and he enjoyed Indra's

[76] "In view of... , how can I go...": That is, how can Indra approach Ahalyā who has now become a stone.
[77] The sage who speaks here is probably Bhṛgu.

excellent heaven. As a result of this the many gods who are honoured and the brahmins who are well versed in the Vedas have enjoyed various kinds of things difficult for others to obtain. Where will that god now stay? How will he eat and how will he sleep? To whom can we now go for refuge for ourselves or even for him? Who will protect us and the heaven belonging to Indra and Śacī? How might the excellent sage Gautama be appeased, since he is now thinking angrily about the offence committed against his own wife whilst he was separated from her? We can think of no other remedy than Gautama's favour. Therefore, Nārada, we will go and appease the sage Gautama.
11. Accordingly, these gods left with Nārada, and on meeting Gautama, to whom they had come for refuge, their hands cupped, they praised him alone with various words.

The gods said:

12-19. We do not have the capacity to describe your power, sage. Who could describe the weight of Meru and of Himavat or the drops of rain in clouds, the dust particles on the Earth or the sands of the Ganges? What fool would try to calculate the water in the ocean or Viṣṇu's qualities? You caused an abundance of corn to grow by noon from seeds just planted in the morning and previously you protected the excellent sages. And the Vālakhilyas created another Indra by performing a sacrifice, when they were requested to do so by Brahmā and the rest who made him king of the birds.[78] Also when someone consumed the

[78] "... made him king of the birds": This alludes to a myth recited at Mbh. 1.27, especially vs.11-13, 19-20. The Vālakhilya sages have been offended by Indra, so by means of a sacrifice they create another Indra. However, the creation of this second Indra violates Brahmā"s command regarding the disposition of the divine positions of authority in the triple-world, according to which there can only be one Indra who is king of the gods. To alleviate this situation and to maintain the status quo Brahmā asked the Vālakhilyas to make the second Indra king of the birds, thereby preventing the problem of confused roles in the world.

ocean with one hand,[79] intelligent son produced another creation, and the great Cyavana supported Indra's power. Therefore, serving men of pure heart like you, who are devoted to helping us and exercise favour towards the weak, as well as making obeisance to you, looking at you, speaking with you, honouring you and touching you, causes evil to be destroyed. So be kind to us who for Indra's sake have approached you for refuge.

Gautama said:

20-22. The sight of you certainly does not occur to the naked eye. It bestows wishes upon men and has occurred because of my merit. Indeed, because of seeing you my birth, toil, austerity, gifts, body, self and vows have become worthwhile. Now, detail to me what you seek and if I can, I will do anything by means of the power gained from recollecting you.

23-24ab. Having heard this speech the heaven-dwellers were delighted, just as the ocean gets an extraordinary thrill at moon-rise or as parents become filled with joy when their infants talk. All the gods then made a request to the great sage Gautama.

The hosts of gods said:

24cd-26. Kāma became ashes because of a transgression against Śiva,[80] but you have not deprived the evil-doing Indra of his life. Sage, by our command let him immediately regain his proper position and bear patiently his transgressions. Indeed, when this favour has been extended we will have achieved our wish.

---

[79] "someone consumed the ocean": Presumably a reference to Agastya's act of drinking the ocean at the request of the gods. See Mbh. 3,102-103.

[80] "a transgression against Śiva": This alludes to Śiva's burning of Kāma when the latter tries to make the former fall in love with Pārvatī. For a telling of this myth see below Chs.89, 1-90, 20 and for other versions see O'Flaherty, W, Hindu Myths. A Sourcebook. Translated from the Sanskrit, Harmondsworth, 1975, pp.154-59, 326.

Nārada said:

27. After hearing the speech of the collection of gods, Gautama laughed and responded with this to the entire host of gods.

Gautama said:

28-34. Not even the name of that wicked one who has committed this offence should be pronounced. There is no difference between deceit, fraud and evil action and for one who lacks remorse there is certainly no expiation. However gods, due to your direction I will act favourably. Sirs, if you are angry, let your curse fall on me. There is, however, one pure being who is sought after by many, hence I am now going to recite a single mantra which you must direct towards him. He is the creator of all, the destroyer of all, the protector of all, a repository of compassion, Vināyaka, god of gods, who consists of Brahmā, Viṣṇu and Śiva, and he has a mantra of six syllables which gives great success. When it is recited he will certainly gain a celestial body, he will have as many eyes as he has vaginas and he will regain his own kingdom. I speak the truth to you!

35-36. Having thus addressed the gods Gautama became silent. However after they had honoured him, they made obeisance, filled with joy. The gods circumambulated him repeatedly, obtained his permission to leave, and went to where Indra, killer of Bali and Vṛtra was located, praising the sage with the words, "Nobody else exists who is as virtuous as Gautama, the one accomplished in knowledge."

CHAPTER THIRTY-THREE

Indra's Going Forth

Nārada said:

1-7ab. The gods said to the killer of Vṛtra, "Come out, Indra, performer of hundred sacrifices, for we are here with Nārada, the divine sage. We went to the sage Gautama and appeased him, and we have come here to you. He has prescribed a remedy and has granted a boon even to you. When a fault occurs good people announce it to the public and they enact an appropriate remedy for causing its removal. If a fault is hidden it grows, but if it is announced it should disappear. Therefore, Lord of the gods, after you have come out you too must announce it. Speak to the gods' sage[81] and enact the remedy enjoined by the sage. Accept the Vināyaka's great mantra of six syllables. At the marriage of Pārvatī, daughter of the mountain, with Śiva, Brahmā saw her big toe and then he spilt his semen. Ashamed he turned his face down and left, but knowing this, Maheśa went up to him and, with that remedy, made him without flaw."

7cd-12. Straight after he had heard this eloquent speech uttered by the hosts of gods and sages, Śakra, who had listened carefully to the words of all the gods who were there, came out of the lotus, King. His limbs were smeared with purulent blood, he was dirty and smelled putrid. When they saw him in such a condition, all the gods bowed to the Lord of the gods and, Excellent king, after they had dressed his stinking fissures with bits of cloth, Bṛhaspati, Lord of the word, taught the great six-syllable mantra of Gaṇeśa to Indra who had bathed well and sipped water again. When he had recited it he obtained a celestial body. He was glorious, possessed one thousand eyes and shone as if he were another sun.

13-16. The regions and intermediate regions then resounded with the songs and the music of the heavenly musicians, the gods' shouts of victory and the sounds of their musical instruments. The joyous gods all released showers of flowers and then all the sages led by Nārada offered benedictions. The joyous gods embraced him and others praised him. Still others, who were well pleased, said to him, "You protect us, but like a moonless sky we cannot shine in your absence. Without their

[81] The gods'' sage is Nārada and Gautama is the sage who has enjoined the remedy.

own parents young children become unhappy in every way, similarly, without you we can never have security."

The sage said:

17. On hearing this speech of the gods the killer of Jambha really rejoiced and, pleased, he told the facts to the gods.

Indra said:

18. Using the beguiling speech of the divine sage,
I committed a very bad deed.
It produced an unbearable result,
But now all of you have lifted me out of the great mire of evil.
19. I bow to all the most excellent of the immortals
And to all the sages whose majesty is so great.
Therefore, you must all rescue me,
You must all save me as I have come to you for refuge.[82]
20. How did you manage this effort
Of Gautama's pacification?
How did he recite this supreme mantra for me?
Tell me everything about this.

The gods said:

21. After we had placed the sage and the teacher[83] before us,
We left after we had bowed respectfully to the sage.
He was conciliated with lovely ambrosial words,
And when requested he recited his own mantra.
22. By reciting it you have become thousand-eyed
For the good of all, god.
Proceed, god, to your own Amarāvatī.
Rule the worlds and the gods!

---

[82] The sense of the last two pādas of this verse is that even though he has emerged from hiding, he must still be protected from Gautama.
[83] The sage and the teacher are Nārada and Gautama respectively.

Śakra said:

23. I will not proceed to my own city
Without Gaṇeśa's favour, Excellent sages and gods.
The substance of your task has been completed,
So return to your own celestial abodes, dallying joyfully.
24. I have appeared long enough in public,
Immersed in shame and experiencing dire misfortune.
This sage with his fierce fiery energy has been conciliated
And by your favour I have become one thousand-eyed.[84]

CHAPTER THIRTY-FOUR

Description of the Sacred Ford of Cintāmaṇī

Nārada said:

1. In the highest posture at the base of a kadamba tree,
Having directed his eyes onto the tip of his nose,
Jambha's enemy, having checked his mind,
Recited this six-syllable mantra.
2. One thousand years passed
Whilst Indra, Lord of the Maruts was eating air.
Thickets and anthills appeared on the body of him
Who was still as a mountain.
3. Thereupon the illustrious Gaṇeśa became pleased,
He who is all-pervasive, omniscient, endowed with terrible splendour.
Whose own splendour conceals the splendour
Of the sun, the moon and fire and covers everyone's eyes.

---

[84] That is, as a result of the conciliation of Gautama the gods have been able to win his favour and hence through him, and only secondarily through the gods, has Indra become one-thousand eyed.

4. Who has four arms, who is crowned with a jewelled diadem,

Who has beautiful arm bracelets and earrings adorning the side of his face.

Who is wearing a chaplet composed of pearls and has two anklets,

And a valuable waist band high on his hips.

5. Whose eyes are lotuses, whose huge belly is like a broad lotus,

Who wears a garland furnished with lotuses.

Whilst wearing red clothes and having the form of all the gods,

He manifested himself in Maghavan's presence.

6-7. He saw him and was terrified with fear, thinking, "What is this? What is this that has come here? How can I survive whilst I am only air and bone? What is this great impediment? I do not know who created it just now. My body is streaming with sweat and shakes like the leaf of a banyan tree."

8. The Lord Vināyaka who sees everything noticed his bewilderment and spoke this charming speech to the great Indra.

Vināyaka said:

9-12. Fear not, Lord of the gods! Do you not know me, god, when I am without form, without characteristic, blissful in mind, eternal, beyond cause, unmanifest, the cause of the cause of the world, the god upon whom you continually and immoveably meditate with that mantra. You have toiled for a long time, so I have come in person, because I am satisfied with your austerity and have come here to give you a boon. Know this: the protection, destruction and origin of the infinite number of Brahmā's eggs[85] is due to me alone! So choose whatever you wish, Blameless god.

---

[85] "Brahmā's eggs": That is, universes.

Nārada said:

13-14. After he had heard his delightful speech, Indra, slayer of armies, recognized that huge body as the illustrious Vināyaka, god of gods. He bowed with deep devotion and after he had quickly stood up, Indra, husband of Śacī, spoke to him who now appeared in the form of a brahmin.

Indra said:

15-29. Even the gods led by Brahmā and the Lords of the directions don't know your characteristics and your activities as creator, sustainer and destroyer, Great-armed god. But this is an artificial situation[86] which has beset me because of my performance of a hundred sacrifices, yet even now many obstacles still remain for me. However can I know your majesty, Gajānana, for only he who can know your majesty, Great Lord, will gain the fullness of your favour, Vighnakāraṇa? He will have the ability to describe your forms and your qualities. You are without support, yet you are the support of everything, constant in knowledge, undecaying and immortal, possessing illusion, perishable and unique. You are the imperishable and supreme self, the shape of everything and the Lord of all. Sanaka[87] and so forth, renounced after knowing you by means of their fierce austerities, but through the power of the six-syllable mantra you can be seen, Supreme Lord. Previously Brahmā had recited this mantra to me just as a favour and Brahmā said to me, "When you forget this, straight away you will fall from your position and your situation will become really difficult." Then, however, full of lust and in the power of an evil fate, I ravished the sage's wife and so I came into this misfortune. Due to this mantra recited by Bṛhaspati, I have once

---

[86] I understand this verse to mean that Indra considers Gaṇeśa's appearance before him to be essentially artificial, in the sense that he still does not understand how Gaṇeśa got there and that obstacles still impede his acquisition of a full knowledge of the god.

[87] "Sanaka...": This refers to the well known sons of Brahmā who became renouncers instead of engaging in the activity of creation.

again seen your real appearance, Lord of the gods, and so now I have one thousand eyes. Its performance has achieved a result because your lotus-like feet have appeared. But now, Vighnapa, give me whatever boon I request. Ensure that I will not forget you and let my mind constantly rest joyfully on your lotus-feet, mighty god. Because you give cherished desires, I am requesting something else: that the city of Kadamba should be called "Cintāmaṇī city." Henceforth, it must become famous in this world, Gajānana, and this lake should become famous as the sacred ford called "Cintāmaṇī." Those beings who bathe in it and are generous will become accomplished in liberation, power, sensuality and the law, due to the favour of the World-teacher.

The sage said:

30. After he had heard Indra's speech, the Lord of obstacles, who is Lord of the worlds, his voice deep like a rumbling cloud, spoke in a silky tone.

Vighneśa said:

31-35ab. Everything you have requested will come about, Mighty god. Let there be one other boon for you: that you will be consolidated in your own position. Also, Lord of the gods, you will never forget me and whenever you might be in a tight situation, you must recollect me, Indra of the Vasus. By manifesting then, I will ensure success in every task of yours. This city called Cintāmaṇī, which was called Kadamba city, will be celebrated on the Earth and will become the sacred ford called Cintāmaṇī. Success will stay in the hands of all who bathe in it. Whatever is thought of, I, the Vināyaka of Cintāmaṇī, will grant.

Nārada said:

35cd-40. After he had obtained this boon from him, Viṣṇu brought the Ganges, and having performed the consecration with her he worshipped the illustrious, mighty Gajānana who was accompanied by his attendants. Worshipped by Indra, Lord of the gods, the mighty god then disappeared. Indra then carefully erected a crystal image of Vināyaka, auspicious, celestial and beautiful in every limb. Śakra also constructed a large temple out of gold and jewels, after which, having bowed and made a circumambulation, he returned to his own abode. The huge lake Cintāmaṇī became celebrated on the Earth and to this day, following Śakra's command, the auspicious water of the Ganges always goes to her own home after performing the consecration on his image.

41-42. In this way the majesty of that sacred place has been narrated to you. Its wondrous appearance takes away all faults, is splendid, auspicious and gives all wishes. After going there, King, protector of the Earth, you should bathe according to the injunction and you will become freed from all faults. No doubt of it.

43. Then the sage quickly left after he had inquired after the king and had respectfully saluted Rukmāṅgada with benedictions.

CHAPTER THIRTY-FIVE

Description of the Fate of Kadamba City

Vyāsa said:

1. What did King Rukmāṅgada do after the gods' sage had gone? Tell me that charming tale!

Brahmā said:

2. After the sage named Nārada had gone,
Having undertaken that momentous instruction,
Rukmāṅgada was filled with happiness
And beheld his own army with its four corps.

3. Yet to the army the king appeared to be deformed,

He who was formerly like Kāma, he whose splendour was golden.

Being uncertain how he could become like that.

It asked the king the reason for it.

The army leaders said:

4-6ab. After having wandered over mountains, forests and lakes, we have returned hungry and thirsty, Lord of kings, but very desirous of seeing you. We were searching everywhere and have now reached your lotus-feet, but after seeing your condition we feel very sorry. Tell us, Excellent king, what caused it?

The king said:

6cd-14. When I was thirsty and hungry I saw the house and hermitage of Vācaknavi in front of me and hurried to it. When I got there I saw his beautiful faced wife, whose name was Mukundā. I asked her for water, but she was evil and wilful and in a lovely voice she said to me, "Have sex with me! If you don't I am going to curse you." However, my mind pure, I forcibly drove her off, but with her husband gone to bathe that evil woman cursed me angrily. After that, in a state of extreme distress, I found myself seated at the foot of a tree and because of the power of previous merit I saw the sage Nārada. He told me the best way to get rid of my misfortune and he extensively described the majesty of Gaṇeśa's sacred ford located in the sacred place called Cintāmaṇī. The sage with the divine eye then told me how to bathe in it and so I am going to bathe there in order to remove my blemish. All of you must accompany me if you wish to bathe in it, and after we have bathed, given gifts according to our capacity and worshipped Vināyaka, we will return to our city, purified by the favour of the god and the sacred ford.

Brahmā said:

15-20. Having understood his intention they left, following the king, and after having gazed upon the sacred ford called Gaṇeśa and bathed there, the king became right again,[88] his colour like burnished gold just as before, Lord of sages. After that King Rukmāṅgada was now convinced the speech made by Nārada to be the truth and after bathing there again, Rukmāṅgada filled with the highest joy, gave many gifts to the brahmins. After he had worshipped Vināyaka he saw a mass of splendour, as did the brahmins and his servants, which was a flying vehicle, the image of the sun. It was filled with groups of Vināyakas, nymphs and kiṃnaras. After he had bowed to them he asked, "Who are you, from where have you come, whose messengers are you and what is your task here? Tell me carefully!"

Brahmā said:

21-23. After they had heard these pleasing commands from the king, Vināyaka's messengers who were in the flying vehicle said, "You are generous, Excellent king, since with all your heart you have meditated upon the Lord who is Cintāmaṇī. With the appropriate act of pilgrimage and a gift given according to the rite you have worshipped Cintāmaṇī and you have done correctly what had to be done. Because he gives whatever is thought of, he is traditionally called Cintāmaṇī.

24-28ab. And by meeting you, Well-vowed man, we have accomplished our duty, but we do not know the greatness of your devotion, Excellent king. By means of body, mind and intellect and even by offering your life, you have propitiated the god Vināyaka who is the leader of all the universes. We are his messengers and he has sent us, King, and though we were in rapid flight, he said impatiently to us, "Bring my devotee

---

[88] "became right again" samyakbabhau: or "appeared as normal": This statement means that his leprous condition incurred as a result of Mukundā's curse has now been lifted.

Rukmāṇgada to me in a flying vehicle." After hearing this we have come, so you must ascend the path to heaven! Go speedily with us to the god Vināyaka!

Brahmā said:

28cd-32ab. On hearing their speech, King Rukmāṅgada said, "Envoys! On the one hand here am I, a half-wit, and on the other hand there exists that imperishable mighty god of perfect body, who is immeasurable, indefinable, consisting only of mind, who is the cause of creation, stability and destruction, but who is himself beyond cause. I do not know why he is he respectful towards me? Is this excellent merit which has come to fruition for me a result produced from a sacred ford in an earlier birth? The appearance he has manifested before you is auspicious and gives extraordinary results, hence you are exceedingly fortunate because the Lord is perceptible to you night and day.

32cd-35ab. After he had said this and bowed, he worshipped him who was born from the lotus-feet and asked them all, "My father named Bhīma is an excellent kiṅg who is fond of the brahmins, speaks the truth and possesses formidable power. How can I return to my sweet-smiling mother without him? She propitiated Vināyaka, the god who is the god of gods, and all her life she has honoured that deity and never another."[89]

The messengers said:

35cd-36, In that case make them both also bathe in the sacred ford and happiness will be given to your mother and father. We will then lead those two, mounted on an excellent flying vehicle.

Brahmā said:

37-39. When he heard this speech and had made a substitute image[90] out of kuśa grass, he uttered this mantra to all of them

[89] "the one born from the lotus feet" = Gaṇeśa?

[90] "substitute": That is, a substitute of a stone or metal image of Gaṇeśa.

successively, "You are Kuśa, you are the son of Kuśa who was created by Brahmā in the past. When you are bathed, he is bathed. This is the tying of the knot." In the sacred ford called Gaṇeśa situated in the sacred place called Cintāmaṇī, the king then performed the ceremonial ablution for all the village people.

40-41. Then at the command of the messengers King Rukmāṅgada and his army, having climbed into that excellent flying vehicle, arrived at the city of Kauṇḍinya amidst the strains of music, the sounds of prayers and the singing of heavenly musicians and nymphs. The heaven resounded with noise in all directions because of that flying vehicle.

42-46ab. King Rukmāṅgada, who had attained prosperity by bathing in the Vināyaka ford, conferred prosperity upon his mother, father and all beings. Just as soon as this prosperity produced by the bathing of the kuśa grass image of Gaṇeśa was firmly bestowed, other flying vehicles arrived together at the command of Vināyaka. Each one ascended and one by one they moved in the sky, and in this way Rukmāṅgada, his mother Cāruhāsinī, Bhīma and all the people went to wherever Vināyaka was located. That entire city, from a small boy to one who cooks dogs, attained a good fate from the merit acquired by bathing in Gaṇeśa's sacred ford.

Brahmā said:

47. Now I have narrated absolutely everything that you asked about, Sage. The man who listens devoutly to the glorification pertaining to the sacred ford situated in the sacred place of Cintāmaṇī will also attain a good destiny

CHAPTER THIRTY-SIX

The Tale of Gṛtsamada

Vyāsa said:

1-2. Lotus-seated Brahmā, I have heard the glorification of the sacred ford of Gaṇeśa and the story of Rukmāṅgada and the inhabitants of Kauṇḍinya city. However, Brahmā, tell me the good story of Mukundā.

Brahmā said:

3-5. After Rukmāṅgada had gone she blazed with passion's fire like the open space in a huge forest during a forest fire in summer, son. Mukundā gained no comfort in that spot in the forest covered with flowers and creepers where a cool breeze blew, nor from moonlight and sandalwood. Nor did she find any pleasure in laughter, dance, song, storytelling, food or drink. But in spite of her anxiety and agitation about him, sleep came instantly to her, fatigued as she was from hunger and thirst, Lord of sages.

6-10. Indra became aware that the young woman asleep in the deserted forest was sick with desire and agitated because of Rukmāṅgada, son. Assuming Rukmāṅgada's appearance, he sexually enjoyed that lustful woman and gladly embraced her. Mukundā became very aroused. She too fiercely kissed Rukmāṅgada, son, and with a firm hand he squeezed her two full breasts. Naked, he unhesitatingly enjoyed sex with that naked woman. Then, a little ashamed, she returned to her own home and Indra, who had been Rukmāṅgada, immediately disappeared from there, sage.

11-13. Rukmāṅgada considered himself freed from her, but she conceived from him and at the appropriate time in the ninth month she produced an auspicious son whose pleasant body, which was completely without fault, exceeded that of Kāma in appearance. He fell onto the ground with a huge noise and all the directions, heaven, earth and the underworld resounded. All the birds flew around, flying up and about all over the place.

14-18. After he had finished his own obligatory ritual Vācaknavi returned, but he never became aware of Mukundā's adventure and with great joy he performed everything, beginning with the birth ritual. In accord with his capacity he gave gifts to the brahmins according to their status and when the tenth day came the sage performed the naming ceremony. The brahmins who were occupied with astrology named him Gṛtsamada, and then in his fifth year he conducted the rite of the giving of the sacred thread. He made the acquisition of the four Vedas the consecrating ritual for that boy, who, merely by their recital, comprehended them instantaneously due to his brahmanical power. He also became a repository of the Vedas and śāstras and his own karma was auspicious.

19-21ab. Once at an auspicious hour the father, Vācaknavi, instructed the son in that great mantra of the Ṛg Veda beginning with the words "gaṇānāṃ tvā."[91] He said, "This is the great Vedic mantra which gives every success, and it alone is the best among the mantras uttered in the Vedic scriptures." He said, "Meditating upon the god Gajānana with your mind immoveable, recite this, and straight after attaining the highest success you will become famous in the world."

Brahmā said:

21cd-22. Then after he had obtained the mantra from his father's mouth, the brahmin Gṛtsamada, having become disposed towards personal service, became engrossed in meditation and recitation. Much time passed in this way for that bull of sages.

23-26. Now, in the region of Magadha there was a king named Magadha who was of handsome appearance, very proud, a munificent man and a crusher of enemies. Richly endowed with various splendid ornaments he was seated upon a throne of great worth and on that throne of the good law that hero was like

---

[91] gaṇānāṃ tvā "You are one of the hosts": This mantra is originally found in Ṛg Veda, 2.23.1.

another Indra, the one often invoked. He possessed an army consisting of four corps, he was wise, respectful towards the learned, and his two ministers were repositories of wisdom, superior in their qualities to Bṛhaspati. His wife Ambikā was of beautiful appearance, superior in virtue, loyal to her husband, illustrious and forbearing to both the favoured and the cursed.

28-30. Led by Vasiṣṭha and Atri, the great sages who were fully conversant with the Vedas assembled for the funerary rite of the king's father, summoned as they had been by the king. The ascetic Gṛtsamada who was pure in mind was also invited. He then spoke confidently on the subject of the śāstras, but in the presence of the other sages Atri said to him, "Shame! Shame! You may possess austerity, but because you were born from Rukmāṅgada, you are not a sage. Ponder on your birth from a prince! You are unworthy of respect in our presence, so go from here to your own hermitage."

31-32. When he had heard Atri's speech he blazed with anger as if he were burning, and he really was almost burning the triple-world and almost consuming those sages, some of whom fled like deer who have spotted a lion. After that he addressed those sages led by Vasiṣṭha who were at that meeting place.

Gṛtsamada said:

33. Lord of sages, if I cannot be Rukmāṅgada's son, I will turn the rest of you into ashes with a fire curse.

Brahmā said:

34-36. Having said this to all those sages he went to his mother. Gṛtsamada asked her, "Speak! You excessively lustful, depraved woman. Tell me who my father is, Mukundā! If not you will be burnt to ashes." After she had heard this speech of his Mukundā became terribly agitated and trembled like a bud-filled plantain tree in the wind. With her palms clasped in obeisance, that woman spoke in a pitiful voice.

Mukundā said:

37-39. When he became separated from his retinue whilst he was utterly absorbed in the hunt, I saw the excellent king, the good Rukmāṅgada who is prosperous in the triple-world. Whilst my beloved husband Vācaknavi was occupied with his personal ritual, and, remembering Brahmā's statement that "Women are irresistible," my heart became stuck on that king. He is your father.

40. After he had heard her speech the sage became silent and with his head hung low in shame he placed a curse on his mother.

Her son said:

41. Stupid depraved woman! Obsessed with evil, become countless fruits in the forest that are thorny and shunned by all living beings.

42-43. Full of anger she too placed a curse on her son, saying, "Since you have cursed me rogue, irrespective of my being your mother, I am going to curse you, son. Your son will be much more cruel than you. He will be a very powerful demon who will bring fear to the inhabitants of the triple-world." In this way these two, mother and son, cursed one another.

Brahmā said:

44-45. Straight away, having lost her human body, she went into the Badarī forest where she was shunned by the multitudes of birds, by the bastards[92] and by the egg-born creatures that were there. Then there was a voice in the atmosphere, "Gṛtsamada was born from Indra." But, brahmin, Gṛtsamada had gone to perform a personal ritual.

46. That excellent person who hears this story of Gṛtsamada never encounters difficulty and obtains everything that is desired.

---

[92] "bastards" jārajair: This is a literal translation identical to the one given by M. I am, however, unsure of its exact meaning.

CHAPTER THIRTY-SEVEN

The Tale of the Boon-giver

Brahmā said:

1-6. First of all the wandering sage visited the forest called Puṣpaka. It was filled with many trees and creepers, was beautiful with multitudes of flowers and was adorned with the waters of mountain torrents and the best young sages. Gṛtsamada bowed to them and with their permission he dwelt there. After he had bathed there, he undertook a recitation, whilst standing on the tip of his big toe and, with his mind still, meditating on the mighty god, the Lord of obstacles. With his vision fixed on the end of his nose, looking neither here nor there, his senses subdued, his breath subdued, his entire self subdued, feeding on air, he performed austerities for one thousand divine years. But when the sage Gṛtsamada opened his eye and it looked about, there arose from the eye a fire which completely scorched the thirty gods, and the apprehensive gods then wondered, "Who might possess this characteristic?"

7-10. Then undertaking a supreme effort and eating only one fallen leaf and nothing else he became an utterly stationary pillar. His mind immoveable, he performed austerities for fifteen thousand years and after Vināyaka had seen his unbearable distress,[93] he manifested himself, shining brightly, in order to show favour to him. Just as a cow runs quickly after hearing the cry of her calf, so too the god Gaṇeśa went quickly to Gṛtsamada, whilst illuminating everything with his fiery energy, the equivalent of one thousand suns.

---

[93] "unbearable distress" tapanaṃ ... durghaṭam: What to Gṛtsamada is austerity is distress to Vināyaka.

11. Elegant with his huge tusk, his flapping ears were moving.

Shaking pleasurably with joy, his forehead was a glittering moon.

Garlanded with huge lotuses, foundation of the universe's cause,

Lotus stalk in his hand, an assembly of servants was bowing.

12-15. He was mounted on a lion and was ten-armed, his sacrificial thread a snake. He was smeared with saffron, aloe, musk and sweet smelling sandalwood, was accompanied by Siddhi and Buddhi, and he was glorious, greater in splendour than a myriad of suns. Though his own form was indescribable he appeared before that sage because of his divine play[94] and his fiery energy consumed the fiery energy of the great sage just as the sun does in respect of the splendour of the moon and the planets. Closing his eyes the sage shook tremulously because he was so agitated, and insensible, he fell to the ground, the good result of his meditation forgotten.

16-19. But once again whilst he was meditating in his mind on the salubrious Gajānana, the bewildered sage was really pondering the cause of his obstacle. "What has caused this unexpected agitation to appear? From now on will all my austerities prove to be in vain? Lord of the gods, universal self, protect me from this dreadful obstacle! To whom else besides you can I go for refuge, Lord of the universe? God, I constantly experience massive distress because Atri said about me, 'He is not to be respected in our company,' and that burns my heart."

Brahmā said:

20ab. After hearing him lamenting in this way, Vināyaka spoke.

---

[94] "divine play" līlayā: Līlā is the doctrine in medieval Hinduism which asserts that god, aloof and detached from the world, will manifest himself in the world of mortals because of a playful affection he holds for the world he has created.

Gaṇeśa said:

20cd-22. Know that it is I, Gaṇanāyaka, who has come to confer a favour. This has never been attained by Sanaka and so forth who took an austere restraint for a long time. Abandoning your fear, declare whatever you wish for, Excellent sage. I am satisfied with your unending austerity on your great toe.

Brahmā said:

23. After he had heard the god of god's splendid speech he became sunk in his own bliss and bowed prostrate to him. Supremely happy, he spoke to the boon-giver, Vināyaka.

Gṛtsamada said:

24-26. My life of restraint and austerity has now attained its fruit. Here is he whose body is wholly bliss, who is without form, yet who is Brahma embodied. (And releasing tears from his eyes he danced with joy and was filled with a mental bliss that was inaccessible even to the Vedas and śāstras). Now that I have seen you in person, what can I possibly request, Lord? Even so, with your permission I will request one thing, Dviradānana.

27-34ab. God, humans are the very best amongst the eight million, four hundred thousand species and amongst humans, Illustrious one, the classes are the very best. And of them the brahmins are the best, and of them those who are wise are superior, and amongst the wise those who are devoted to personal service, and amongst them those who know Brahma. Lord of the universe, give me knowledge and knowledge of Brahma; devotion to you that is absolutely rock-solid and which I will never cease to recollect; and the highest position of devotee amongst all your devotees, Gajānana. And, Beneficent God, there is one other boon I request. Give me a special place for your worship, one capable of attracting the inhabitants of the triple-world, which will be famed in the three worlds and will be worthy of homage from gods and men. Bringer of all desires, if you are satisfied, do this for me, Vighneśa, and cause the forest called Puṣpaka to become renowned, Lord of the gods. Staying there, always fulfil the wishes of your devotees and cause this city of Puṣpaka to become especially famous across the four directions by the name of Gaṇeśa City, Gajānana.

Brahmā said:

34cd. Having heard this speech, Dviradānana spoke.

Gaṇeśa said:

35-40. Good! Good! Great-armed man. When I am pleased, Bull of the sages, nothing in the three worlds is difficult for devotees to obtain. Whatever you request, brahmin, you will have, and because I am pleased brahmin, you will acquire what is difficult to obtain. Sage, because you recited the Vedic mantra, "gaṇānāṃ tvā", you will become the sage of that mantra.[95] You will be famous everywhere and you will achieve the highest eminence amongst the gods led by Brahmā and the sages led by Vasiṣṭha. Those who practise recollection, firstly to you and later to me, will attain success in all activities they undertake. Without knowledge of the hymns to the sages and the gods activity is fruitless.

41-42. You will also have a powerful son who will frighten all the gods and achieve great fame in the three worlds. Except for Rudra none of the gods will be able to defeat him and he will be devoted to me, his life will depend on me, he will be grounded in me and he will be wholly intent upon me.

43-44ab. And this city will be named Puṣpaka in the Kṛta age, Maṇipura in the Tretā age, Bhānaka in the Dvāpara age and in the Kali age it will become famous in the world under the name of Bhadraka. By gift-giving and bathing there one will obtain all of one's wishes.

---

[95] "the sage of that mantra": in the sense that it will be known as having been revealed and taught by the sage Gṛtsamada, who is the ṛṣi of Ṛg Veda 2.23. The devatā is Bṛhaspati.

Brahmā said:

44cd-47. Having given these very boons to him the Lord immediately disappeared from there, and after he had disappeared the sage erected an image of Gaṇeśa there and also built a beautiful temple. He determined that its name would be Varada for evermore, but eventually due to the favour of Gaṇeśa it became Siddhisthāna, yet because it nourishes everybody's wishes it is called "The Puṣpaka sacred place." Filled with a feeling of devotion he then worshipped that image.

48. Whoever might hear this tale of the excellent appearance
Of the splendid Vighnarāja, Lord of sages,
Will obtain all his wishes, and rock-solid devotion towards Gaṇeśa,
And he will be released from transmigration.

CHAPTER THIRTY-EIGHT

The Gift of Boons

Vyāsa said:

1. Lord of the gods, what happened to Gṛtsamada then? Lotus-born Brahmā, I have full confidence in you, so tell me this carefully.

Brahmā said:

2-4. All the groups of sages respectfully bowed to and honoured that very best of sages, Gṛtsamada, brahmin. Due to Gaṇeśa's boon they solicited[96] him in the rite performed for any undertaking and recollected him at the beginning of the worship of Gaṇeśa. As such that sage became famous and undertook the highest devotion to Gaṇeśa, reciting the mantra whilst remaining perfectly still.

---

[96] The sages solicited Gṛtsamada and recollected him through their recitation of the mantra described in 37.37.

5-6. Once, Vyāsa, the sage sneezed terribly, filling the directions, the sky, the earth and the mountain caverns with noise. Straight away he saw before him a frightening young boy, whose complexion was red, who roared loudly and was like the japa flower in colour.

7-11ab. On seeing a young boy like this, a veritable mass of fiery energy constantly dazzling the eye's line of sight, he trembled as he was agitated with fear and in his mind he wondered, "What is this impediment which has come here? I do not know. Might it be a wonderful son Gaṇanātha has given me?" Again he beheld his son, his face handsome, his eyes delicate, wearing a lovely golden bracelet on his upper arm, a lovely diadem, a pretty ankle bracelet and his loins shining because of a lovely thread around his hips. The sage asked him, "Who are you, to whom do you belong and what do you want to do? Tell me where your parents are and where your home is child of great splendour."

Brahmā said:

11cd. When he had heard this speech of his, the young boy spoke to the sage.

The young boy said:

12-14. You know the past, the present and the future, so why are you questioning me? Even so, as I am subject to your command I will speak. I was born from your sneeze and as you alone are my mother and father, be kind to me! Father look after me for several days, Sage. I am capable of subduing the tripleworld and I am going to bring the Lord of the gods into a state of subjection. There is no doubt of it. Look at my strength!

Brahmā said:

15-17. After he had given ear to his speech the sage Gṛtsamada was filled with both joy and apprehension and uttered this polished speech, "If he really is capable of tormenting people in the triple-world even though he has just been born, then I will give my son his own mantra. The god, Vināyaka, Lord of the world, will be completely gratified by it and so will give him what he wishes, and I too will become famous."

18-19. Pondering this in his mind, he then taught him his own mantra namely, "gaṇānāṃ tvā," and he then said to him, "Whilst respectfully performing personal service, and after fixing your mind on Gajānana, you must recite this Vedic mantra. When he is fully satisfied with you son, he will give you all your wishes."

20-27ab. Now that he had gained this great mantra in this way he went to the forest to perform austerities. With his senses subdued, he stood on one toe and ate no food, and half a myriad of years passed during which, his mind still, he was reciting and meditating on the god Gajānana. Then out of his mouth there came a fire which began burning the regions and so the gods, demons and dwellers of the underworld became frightened. Thereupon, Gajānana, who was satisfied with his austerities, manifested himself, spreading a circle of lustre, thereby causing the regions to be free of darkness. Full of joy, he was swinging his trunk and his lovely tusk, yet when he heard his booming sound the young boy became a little agitated. Opening his eyes, he beheld that god who stood before him, four armed, huge in body and splendid with a variety of jewels. In his hands he was carrying an axe, a lotus, a garland and sweetmeats, and though overpowered by his fiery splendour, having gathered courage, he bowed. And when he had made obeisance with the palms of his hands clasped he made a request to the Lord.

The young boy said:

27cd-28ab. I am devoted to the gods and have come to you for refuge, so why are you overpowering me? Be very kind, God, and give me every wish!

Brahmā said:

28cd-32. Having given ear to his speech, he checked his own glory and very pleased he said, "Small boy, take heed! That one on whom you meditate day and night is I who will now give you a boon. Here is my highest form which is self-luminous and contains the world. Brahmā, Śiva and so on, do not know it, so in no way will humans know it, nor the gods, nor all the sages, nor the other royal sages, nor the demons, nor the accomplished sages and the heavenly musicians, nor the snakes, nor the dānavas. But I am bound by your austerity so I have come here to give you a boon. Request of me any boon your mind desires!"

Then the boy said:

33-36ab. By seeing you I am fortunate, so too is my father very fortunate and my austerity and my life are now meaningful. Because of my youth, Lord of the gods, I do not know how to compose a eulogy. However, you are the creator, the protector and destroyer of all worlds. Through your brightness the sun, fire and the moon shine, and through your majesty you make moving and unmoving things attentive, Very wise god. Not even Brahmā and Śiva know your exceptional greatness.

36cd-41ab. If you are going to give me a boon, Gajānana, then give me this: Lord, give me a special capacity to subdue the triple-world. Gods, demons, heavenly musicians, humans, snakes and rākṣasas, as well as wandering bards, kiṃnaras and sages must always be subject to me. Whatever I conceive mentally must always be realized. The protectors of the world who are led by Indra should at all times offer me servitude and whilst I am on Earth you must bestow various enjoyments upon me and liberation at death. Also, in accord with your command I request this city as another boon from you. Let it become famous, since it has been here that I performed this fierce austerity. Let it become famous amongst people under the name of Gaṇeśapur.

Gaṇeśa said:

41cd-44. You will achieve the conquest of the three worlds, you will be afraid of nothing and everybody will always be subject to you. I will give you a triple city made of gold, silver and iron which will be indestructible to all the gods except Śiva and it will move where it wishes. Also, your name Tripura will become famous in the world and you will attain liberation only when Śiva destroys your city with a single arrow. Entertain no doubt about that. Everything else you have wished for will also come about through my favour.

Brahmā said:

45-46. Having given such boons the Lord disappeared from there, but the demon called Tripura became dejected because he was separated from that god. After gaining boons consonant with his wishes, he attained great happiness and strove physically to bring about victory over the triple-world.

CHAPTER THIRTY-NINE

Indra's Defeat

Vyāsa said:

1. What did Tripura do after he had been made arrogant by his boons, Brahmā? Please tell me everything since it is all of interest to me.

Brahmā said:

2-6. He then had an image of Gaṇeśa made of stone from Kashmir erected as prescribed by brahmins who were skilled in mantras. And in the midst of Gaṇeśapur he built a beautiful temple which was huge, celestial and golden, decorated with jewels and pearls. He then worshipped the Lord with the sixteen ritual practices and countless acts of obeisance, eulogies and solicitations. After he had requested forbearance from the Lord of the god of gods and requested permission to leave, he went outside and gave many gifts to the brahmins in accord with their status. Because of that, that abode of Tripura located in Bengal was called Gaṇeśapur and it confers every success upon everyone.

7-11. The demon Tripura, who had become full of pride because of Gajānana's boon, now governed the human worlds but was obsessed with conquering the gods. In order to serve him, very powerful men came from everywhere with their foot soldiers, horses, elephants and charioteers. By his favour kings became his servants, but those who were inimical died because they could not fight him. Having in this way conquered the Earth, he went to Amarāvatī. There Indra was surrounded by hosts of gods who were adept at various kinds of battle and armoured up, he mounted Airāvata and departed for battle.

12-15. The mighty demon then split his army of four corps into three parts. After he had beheld the great demon Bhīmakāya who was skilled in fighting with the bow, the club and the sword, and the demon, Vajradaṃṣṭra, who was adept at fighting with missiles and wrestling, the bull of the demons said to Bhīmakāya, "Become overlord of the human worlds." And to the venomous Vajradaṃṣṭra the powerful Tripura said, "Go to the underworld with one third of my army and by my authority, render subservient all the snakes led by Śeṣa. With the other third I will conquer Indra and all the gods."

Brahmā said:

16-19. Vajradaṃṣṭra and Bhīmakāya both set out as commanded and he began enjoying himself with his army of four corps. Capturing the divine soldiers, they smashed the celestial trees and after he had established himself there, the demon king despatched messengers to Śakra, saying, "Either bring Indra here quickly for a meeting or declare this command of mine, 'Go immediately to the world of the dead or give me

Amarāvatī[97] and I will willingly look after you. But if you intend to fight, then advance towards me quickly.'"

20-24. When they met Indra they described what the demon Tripura had done and after hearing their speech he was like a mountain struck by a thunderbolt. Indra, enemy of Cācala shook like a tree in the wind and wondering what had happened, he became wound up with anxiety. Eyes completely inflamed, he blazed with the fire of anger as if he were turning the world into ashes or drying up the clouds. He told the messengers to leave quickly and get ready for battle. Indra, killer of the god's enemies, himself mounted Airāvata and roared, shaking the triple-world with that great roar. After hearing his speech the messengers left as they had come.

25-27. All the gods armoured up and in their hands they held swords and various weapons. Some had short javelins in their hands and some had spears and pikes in their hands, some were carrying hammers and swords, others had bows and arrows in their hands, whilst some were armed with hunting clubs and others had staves in their hands. Accordingly, to the accompaniment of the sounds of various instruments, Indra, the thunderbolt bearer, went forth with the hosts of gods, his path blessed by the brahmins.

28-29. However, from his messengers' statement Tripura knew Indra to be preparing for battle, and so he armed and roused his four-limbed army. After he had gathered together that numberless army, he marched out, mounted on his horse.

30-35. Adorned with heroes, the two armies beheld each other and a huge noise ensued because of the booming of their battle cries, their roars, the neighing and the strains of music. Then merely by the sound hum, Tripura urged them on and those heroes fought with the gods and a great battle ensued. Not knowing whether one was ally or enemy, they killed each other and in this way many demons died in that tumultuous battle, but the gods fell too, tormented by the demons' weapons. The

---

[97] "Give me Amarāvatī": Amarāvatī is a metonym for the kingship of the gods.

soldiers seemed to be spotted like kiṃśuka flowers and some lay down, but not on beds, and others – camels, elephant-masters, chariot hordes and foot-soldiers – because they had no feet. But then, like deer looking for food who have unexpectedly seen a lion, the demons fled and went in all directions.

36-43. After that, having checked his army, that most eminent of enemies, blazing greatly because of the fire of his anger, became himself without rival and rumbled like a cloud. All but devouring heaven and earth he went to Indra and with his own sword he violently struck the hand of the Lord which held the thunderbolt. Then, miraculously, the thunderbolt fell from his hand and taking it, the demon struck the elephant Airāvata with it. Being struck, Airāvata left and fled. With his fist Indra then struck the bull of the demons, who momentarily fell to the ground, but getting up swiftly he struck Śakra with his fist and felled him to the ground. Getting up, Indra angrily said to the demon, "Get ready to wrestle now, Lord of the demons." But completely surprised and arrogant with power, he said, "Why are you so unconcerned about your own life, Lord of the gods? Even worms, insects and flying insects consider life to be exceedingly precious. God, go to the Earth! That is your appropriate place which I offer to you."

Brahmā said:

44-50. After he had heard that speech, Indra, killer of Bala and Vṛtra, said, "Enemy, if indeed I do not liberate you from life, I will certainly go to Earth in obedience to your command, vile demon. But now, rogue, you will go the Earth without your head." After the Lord of the gods said this, the evil demon-king struck him on the heart with his fist. A battle between them then took place and like Kṛṣṇa and Cāṇūra, both sought victory over the other. These two struck heart with heart, hand with hand, and they struck the part of the leg between the thigh and knee with their two knees, head with head and elbow with elbow. They struck back with back and feet with feet, but the demon, having got hold of Śakra's feet and swung him around repeatedly, threw him far away to a place that was known by none and he himself mounted the four-tusked Lord of elephants.[98]

51-55. Thereafter all the hosts of gods became distressed because of their fear of the demons and went to the caves on Mt. Himavat, searching for Śakra. Wandering around thinking, "Where has this god fallen, however will we find the Lord?" they met the Lord of the gods, his face downcast, who had turned up just then. Some groups of gods bowed to him, whilst others embraced him, some honoured him, whilst someone else fanned him and some devotedly rubbed his feet. All the gods dwelt right there then, their bodies hidden.

56-57. However, the demon, having ascended Airāvata, went to Amarāvatī and when he himself was in Indra's place, he gave the places of the gods to the demons, allocating them one by one to the enemies of the gods as had been previously arranged. Listening to the voices of the heavenly musicians accompanied by the music of celestial instruments and being served by kiṃnaras, he dallied with the groups of apsaras.

CHAPTER FORTY

Description of the Eulogy

Brahmā said:

1-2ab. After he had seized the god's residences the demon went to Brahmā's heaven, but having already heard from Agni about the courage shown by the demon, Brahmā went to Viṣṇu who was at the Milk Ocean.

2cd-8. The demon had two sons called Pracaṇḍa and Caṇḍa who were born from his mind. He installed Pracaṇḍa as overlord in Brahmā's world and then made Caṇḍa the lord in Viṣṇu's

---

98 "Lord of Elephants": This is Indra' s elephant and Tripura' s mounting of it indicates he now holds the position of king of the gods.

world. Then he himself went to Kailāsa[99] and shook it with his forearms. Terrified with fear, Pārvatī, the mountain's daughter, embraced Śaṅkara tightly, but Mahādeva was pleased with the demon's courage and so being one who confers happiness upon his own devotees, he went outside to grant a boon. He saw the demon Tripura and said to him, "Choose a boon!" and he asked, "If you are pleased give me Kailāsa now and go straight to the top of Mandara mountain. That is my wish!" So Śiva temporarily gave him Kailāsa and Śiva, the mountain-dweller, himself went to Mandara mountain with his hosts. Atop the peak of Kailāsa the demon Tripura was ecstatic.

9-12. Having brought the gods into subjection in this way he returned to the underworld and on Earth the powerful Bhīmakāya forcibly brought the kings into subjection and fettered all the sages. He quickly smashed all the fire holes which satiate the gods and above all, the hermitages and sacred fords. He harassed the ascetics by putting them into a place of confinement and, utterly arrogant, he was constantly hostile towards men of good conduct, towards those who utter the exclamations svāhā, svadhā and vaṣaṭ and those who study the Vedas.

13-14. Then Vajradaṃṣṭra brought the seven hells into subjection and he also brought Śeṣa, Vāsuki, Takṣaka and all the snakes, both poisonous and non-poisonous, under his control. Vajradaṃṣṭra then coiled up Ratnajāta and sent him away.

15. For amusement and pleasure,
He dallied lustfully with the snake maidens.
Whilst he experienced these carnal enjoyments,
He gathered many kinds of jewels and went to Tripura.

16-17. Then whilst he was declaring loudly that the hells had been brought under control, he acquired many servants, villages, valuable clothes and an excessively high opinion of himself. And after he had brought the triple-world into subjection in this way the demon Tripura rejoiced.

---

[99] Kailāsa is the mountain where Śiva resides.

18-21. Day after day, now dwelling in caves, all the gods wondered, "How will his death occur and when will it be? We do not know why or from whom he obtained this boon?" Excellent sage, all the gods being confused about this Nārada came there whilst he was wandering freely over the triple-world. When he saw the miserable gods he descended from the atmospheric path and on seeing him they all stood up out of respect and in turn they bowed to him, embraced him and honoured him. Whilst he was resting they questioned him about Tripura.

The gods said:

22-23. Tripura has conquered the triple-world, both moving and unmoving. He seized our homes and defeated Brahmā and Śiva. To whom shall we turn for refuge now? How will he die and who gave him the boons? Sir, tell us about Tripura!

Nārada said:

24-27. I will tell you in full the extensive activities of the demon. For one thousand years he performed severe austerities and then he propitiated the Lord Gaṇeśa, leader of the gods. He gave him some boons which could not be warded off and which were terrifying to everyone. With the sole exception of the mighty Śiva, he was given safety from the deceased ancestors, the fathers, sages and gods, piśācas, rākṣasas, yakṣas and snakes. Everyone must respectfully propitiate and strive to win the favour of the Lord of gods, Dviradānana, Vighneśa, who gives every success.

The gods said:

28. How can one win the favour of that wise god of gods? Sage, kindly tell us what should be done.

Nārada said:

29-31. I am going to declare a mantra of ten syllables to everybody and you should perform a personal devotion with this mantra I have devotedly given to you. You must all be steadfast in mind and as soon as the god Gaṇanāyaka becomes visible he will tell you all the way to kill that demon. You must follow my advice as I cannot see any other way.

Brahmā said:

32-34. The sage Nārada, who was addicted to the sound of the lute, left immediately after he had said this and all those excellent gods became engaged in meditation on Gaṇeśa. Some stood on one foot, some remained in the lotus position, some were in the heroic position and others had their eyes closed. Fasting and controlling their breaths they muttered the mantra the sage had uttered.

35-38. Then after a considerable time had passed and having observed that the gods' personal devotion had continued for a long time, Gajānana, ocean of compassion, Gaṇapa, giver of boons, manifested himself before them. He was adorned with pretty earrings and wore a diadem of flashing gold. His trunk was resting on his tusks, he wore a beautiful armlet and a shining hip girdle and in his arms he carried a rope, an elephant goad, an axe and a lotus. He was ornamented with a vermillion moon and musk of red sandalwood. He was shining splendidly like flashing lightning, his splendour like that of a myriad of suns.

39-41. After seeing this salubrious god Vināyaka, all the gods were overpowered by his splendour, yet nobody was frightened. Some of the gods instantly bowed before Dviradānana, whilst others honoured him, their voices faltering with joy. And to remove their distress some eulogized the Lord who removes difficulties, the god whose face is pleasant, whose pleasant face is tranquil.

The gods said:

42. Obeisance! Obeisance to you, whose form is the supreme truth!

Obeisance! Obeisance to you, the cause of everything!

Obeisance! Obeisance to you, the creator of everything,
To you who resides in all the senses!

43. Obeisance! Let there be obeisance to you who consists of beings.

Obeisance! Obeisance to you who creates beings, Lord of the gods!

Obeisance! Obeisance, you who understands all wisdom!

Obeisance! Obeisance to the cause of the universal dissolution!

44. Obeisance! Obeisance to the maintainer of everything, Lord of all!

Obeisance! Obeisance to the cause of causes!

Obeisance! Obeisance to the one who appears to those who know the Vedas.

Obeisance! Obeisance to the one who gives all boons.

45. Obeisance! Obeisance, you who are word and reflection!

Obeisance! Obeisance to the remover of obstacles!

Obeisance! Obeisance to the one destroying the wishes of non-devotees!

Obeisance! Obeisance, knower of your devotee's wishes!

46. Obeisance! Obeisance! Lord of the devotee's wishes!

Obeisance! Obeisance, expert in the arrangement of the universe!

Obeisance! Obeisance, cause of the demons' destruction!

Obeisance! Obeisance to the remover of difficult situations!

47. Obeisance! Obeisance to the most supreme amongst the compassionate.

Obeisance! Let there be obeisance to you who are knowledge.

Obeisance! Obeisance to the destroyer of ignorance.

48. Obeisance! Obeisance to the destroyer of the non-devotee's power!

Obeisance! Obeisance to the liberator of devotees!

Obeisance! Obeisance to the binder of non-devotees.

Obeisance! Obeisance to you whose image takes various forms!

49. Obeisance! Obeisance to the organ of understanding the parts of
reality![100]
Obeisance! Obeisance to the pre-eminent knower[101] of the parts of reality!
Obeisance! Obeisance to you, witness of all actions!
Obeisance! Obeisance to you, guide of the qualities.

Brahmā said:

50. In this way the gods eulogized the god, the Lord Dviradānana. Utterly delighted he spoke excitedly to the excellent gods.

Gaṇeśa said:

51. I have achieved complete satisfaction with your eulogy and austerities, gods. I am going to give you everything you ask for. Therefore, choose, Lords of the gods.

The gods said:

52-54ab. If you are satisfied, Lord of the gods, kill the demon Tripura, because after having seized the offices proper to us,[102] he is standing firm. You gave him safety from the entire collection of immortals, as a consequence of which we have fallen into this difficult situation. Free us from this difficult situation immediately as we have come to you alone for refuge, and this is our only request.

---

[100] "parts of reality" tattva: The word tattva refers to the twenty-five principles of the cosmogony which in Sāṃkhyan thought are depicted as being manifested in an evolutionary manner.

[101] "pre-eminent knower": I take this to refer to the Puruṣa who witnesses and is antecedent to the appearance of the tattvas.

[102] "the offices proper to us" adhikārān no: This refers to the gods" positions in the triple-world, positions sanctioned by dharma.

Gaṇeśa said:

54cd-56. I will certainly bring an end to all your fear of this dreadful demon. This eulogy you have performed has brought me much pleasure and so it will become celebrated as the "Remover of Distress." It gives every desire to those men who recite it and hear it, and whoever recites it at the three divisions of the day will never experience distress.

CHAPTER FORTY-ONE

The Arrival of Nārada

Vyāsa said:

1. What did Gaṇeśa do, he who is the boon-giver, Lord and creator of everything? Tell me that as requested, Brahmā!

Brahmā said:

2-4. Taking the appearance of a brahmin, Gaṇeśa went to Tripura and he saw that most excellent of brahmins seated on a splendid seat. After he had arisen and performed obeisance, the demon invited him to sit on his own seat, and once he had honoured him, he asked, "Where have you come from brahmin? What do you know and what is your name? Tell me that as requested. And what is your aim? If it can be achieved, the two of us will do it."

The brahmin said:

5-8ab. Demon, we are omniscient, we know everything and, as we roam about at will, we make our abode wherever we are when evening comes, wandering out of a wish for the good of beings. In the triple-world we are famous under the name of the Kalādharas. We want to see your grandeur, so we have now come to your home. Now that we have seen all your wealth we are satisfied. Such wealth does not exist in Kailāsa, Vaikuṇṭha[103] or in Brahmā's world, nor has such wealth as yours ever been seen in Indra's heaven.

The demon said:

8cd-10. Brahmin, since you are just a Kalādhara, can you really appreciate that wealth? All beings have wealth, but you must extol my wealth over their wealth and display this gargantuan wealth in their midst, if you can. If you display it I will give you exactly what you want, brahmin, even life itself. Nothing I say is false, even if it is in jest or fantasy, sage.

Kalādhara said:

1-14. Having seen the wealth of others, what more could you want, Enemy of the gods? I am, however, happy with your conduct, so I am going to give you a triple-city made of gold, silver and iron which is shaped like an arrow. Enjoy yourself there secure for as long a time as you please! The gods, heavenly musicians, humans and uragas will be unable to pierce it, it will bestow any imaginable aim, go where you wish, give wishes and be auspicious. When in the course of time, it is pierced by one single arrow, then Hara will destroy it, demon.

Brahmā said:

15-16. Having said this he took up a bow, firmly placed an arrow in it and then created the triple-city which was like the three worlds. It had a variety of delightful palaces adorned with pleasure groves and lanterns, and whilst bestowing every wish, it moved through the sky accompanied by different groups of birds.

17-20. Deluded by māyā, the demon stood on it, rejoiced ecstatically and thundered like a cloud, shaking the triple-world. Filled with arrogance and pride he made the triple-world shake

---

[103] Kailāsa and Vaikuṇṭha are the abodes of Śiva and Viṣṇu respectively. Hence Tripura's wealth is unimaginable as it outmeasures that of Brahmā, Viṣṇu and Śiva.

and he thought, "Nobody is better than me." Then he said to the brahmin, "Excellent brahmin, ask for something that is really difficult to get and I will give it to you." Though he was without desire,[104] that brahmin who had just been addressed spoke to the demon.

The brahmin said:

20-23. I went to Kailāsa and saw Śiva correctly worshipping an image of Gaṇeśa which grants any wish that can be conceived. Have it brought and give it to me, if you can, Lord of demons. In my wanderings over the triple-world I have never seen such an image, so my heart is set on it, excellent demon, and once I have got it I will have achieved my aim, Lord of demons. Then I will proclaim your fame in the triple-world with its moving and unmoving beings, namely, that there is no one more generous than Tripura in giving what is desired.

The demon said:

24. I regard Śiva as a servant and I take no account of the gods, so when I have retrieved that image I will give it to you, Bull of the brahmins.

Brahmā said:

25-28. After he had said this he respectfully honoured Kalādhara and gave him ten villages, cows, clothes ornaments and jewels, coral and woolen coverlets as well as large pearls and others which were highly valuable. The demon also gave him good horses and chariots with golden axles and guardrails as well as one hundred male and female servants adorned with many jewels. Taking what had really been forced upon him, Kalādhara went to his own hermitage, exciting his wife and all those who dwelt in his hermitage.

---

[104] "Though he was without desire" ni`spṛho "pi san: This does not just mean that he wished for nothing then, rather as a brahmin renouncer his existential situation was one without inherent desire.

Brahmā said:

29. Nārada narrated the whole story to the gods and without regard for time they allowed the days to pass.

CHAPTER FORTY-TWO

Description of the Battle

Vyāsa said:

1-2. What did the demon do after Kalādhara had gone? Was the auspicious Cintāmaṇī image given to him after it had been brought? Tell me everything in detail, four-faced Brahmā, as I remain dissatisfied with just a brief hearing of Gaṇeśa's games.[105]

Brahmā said:

3-8. After he had gone, Excellent sage, the demon did everything that I am going to narrate to you. Listen attentively, Sage! He sent two messengers to Śiva who was on Mount Mandara and he ordered them as follows, "After you have reached Śiva, respectfully declare this command of mine to him, 'In your house there is an auspicious image of Cintāmaṇī which gives all wishes. Śiva, husband of the mountain's daughter, give it willingly to the demon-king.' That demon has forcibly brought into his own house every conceivable thing in heaven, hell or the world of men that is extraordinary. Bring the image quickly, god, as we are going back to that powerful demon. If you do not give it willingly the bold demon will seize it by force, causing you to suffer pain."

---

[105] "Gaṇeśa's games" līlāgajānanīḥ: That is, the joke Gaṇeśa is playing on Tripura by appearing in disguise. But it also has the broader sense of providing the very motive i.e. divine play, for Gaṇeśa's appearance on Earth.

9-12. After he had heard the messenger's speech, Śiva seethed with anger and thinking that the two of them were only messengers, he said to those two messengers, "I will overlook your speech. I am sure you would not like to be turned into ashes like Kāma. What's to be done with that demon who is but straw to me, the Lord? If he wants to die he should come to me and there will certainly be a battle! Even in one hundred lives he will not get this image! Can the fire of destruction be abated in the sun? What can a person who has fallen from Meru do if he only has the strength of a mouse? Could the ocean be dried up by the loss of its countless drops of water?"

Brahmā said:

13-17. After they had heard Śiva's speech the two demons left as they had come and they told their master the statement Śambhu had uttered. After he heard that, the demon, conversant with the import of such statements, blazed and flamed with fiery anger, almost scorching the triple-world. He ordered his own army with its four corps to make ready for battle and the army hastily appeared opposite Mount Mandara. Being unbounded like the ocean, it covered the Earth's surface with hoards of swords which, when unsheaved, looked like many suns and it was roaring like a ferocious cloud, causing Death's heart to shake.

18-22. After he had mounted the triple-city that resembled an aerial vehicle, was huge yet rapid as thought, the demon then left, itching to fight Śambhu. He wore a large, splendid jewelled suit of armour, as well as earrings, armlets, a garland of pearls, rings with seals on them and a golden girdle. The precious diadem he wore was radiant with its embedded jewels. His great roar shook Śiva's heart and with his bow and quiver, a shield of tortoise shell, a massive sword and celestial daggers, that bull of demons looked resplendent. Hosts of apsaras and heavenly musicians were singing and dancing, whilst bards and wandering singers went joyfully in front of him.

23-27ab. Śaṅkara having heard from a messenger's statement that the demon had arrived with his uncountable armies which were itching for battle and were drawn on by Death, the Trident-bearer, after he had worshipped, bowed to and circumambulated Dviradānana,[106] and had placed him in front of that huge army due to his power, his eyes burning with anger, he came from his own home to the battlefield where heroic soldiers with their powerful voices were roaring in every direction. Then they advanced with their weapons, each wishing to kill the other and both armies clashed in a confusion of dust and gloom. Without knowledge of who was their own man or an enemy, both fought in the van of the battle and a tumultuous battle ensued in which nothing at all was known.

27cd-31. The blood of the slain warriors, charioteers, horses and elephants lay on the earth and once the dust had settled warrior fought individually with warrior. Some used darts, some used stones and some used arrows sharpened on a stone, whilst some used spears, some fists and others used lances and axes. Warriors, horses and foot soldiers were slain there and a river of blood, shining with hairs resembling the green moss plant, appeared and it was adorned with tortoise-like shields, fishlike daggers and heads like lotuses. It also carried headless bodies resembling trees and umbrellas which were like whirlpools and to vultures and jackals it brought ecstasy and for the heroes it was a cause of satisfaction.

32-34. But once he had seen this river, the powerful Śiva, Lord of the mountains, went straight up to the demon and the demon himself, mounted on Tripura, went straight up to him. Then after they had seen their two leaders come into contact, the others came in pairs and the demon troops and Śiva's troops fought each other in an orderly way, using many weapons, celestial daggers, swords and tree-trunks. I will briefly tell you the names of these battles.

---

[106] I assume that the mention of Dviradānana here refers to an image.

CHAPTER FORTY-THREE

Description of the Victory

Brahmā said:

1-5. Two by two they fought, Śiva and the demon leader, Pracaṇḍa with six-faced Kārttikeya and Caṇḍa with Nandi. The heroic Puṣpadanta fought with Bhīmakāya, Bhṛṅgiti with Kālakūṭa and Viṣavat with Prāṇahāri. Vīrabhadra and Vajradaṃṣṭra, both of great strength, fought, and the heroic Indra fought there with the demon's minister. Battle-mad Jayanta fought with Bali, the demon's son, whilst the gods' teacher who was highly skilled with weapons fought there with Kāvya. In this way the gods and demons formed many pairs. I could not describe them even in a hundred years.

6-8. Charioteers fought with charioteers, elephant drivers with elephant drivers, horsemen with their equivalents and foot soldiers with footsoldiers in that fierce battle which resounded with the noise of various musical instruments, neighing, the trumpeting of elephants and the din of carriages. Some of them engaged in various kinds of wrestling, whilst others, once they had lost their swords in battle, struck body against body.

9-17. Then Pracaṇḍa shot at the six-faced Kārttikeya with nine stout arrows which had been brightened on a stone and released after they had been drawn back to the ear. But splitting them with very smooth arrows before they had arrived, Kārttikeya struck him with five arrows. His mind reeling, Pracaṇḍa fell senseless onto the ground. Caṇḍa too was struck by Nandi with five sharp arrows, became senseless and instantly fell onto the ground. Then Bhīmakāya launched ten arrows at Puṣpadanta, but in battle the latter split those arrows with his own sharp arrows and, whilst resting on the ground, he struck him with three arrows. Bhṛṅgiti felled Kālakūṭa with five arrows and then, full of anger, the very powerful Vīrabhadra hit Vajradaṃṣṭra with four sharp arrows. After averting them he himself shot three arrows at Vīrabhadra, but in an instant

Vīrabhadra split those flying arrows with three other arrows and vigorously felled Vajradaṃṣṭra with three arrows. And Indra felled the demons' adviser with a stroke of the thunderbolt.

18-19. Lifting up his sharp sword the demon's son advanced on Jayanta, wishing to kill him, but after spotting him coming amidst the fallen heroes, Jayanta split his sword with an arrow and then quickly struck the demon's son with three arrows. Once struck by them, he fell, vomiting blood and fainting.

20-24. With defeated soldiers all around, some Pramathas, filled with victory, pursued some demons wounded by the hosts of gods whom they had seen intent upon flight. The gods being victorious in this way and his own army dispersed, the demon, ruler of Tripura, came himself, alone, to Śiva. Initially engaging in a sword fight, they both fought with magical weapons. The demon released the magical weapon called Varuṇa and there was a ferocious shower of rain. In the ensuing battle there was so much mist that nothing was known, but whenever there was a lightning flash enabling a man to recognize himself from the other man, a tumultuous battle occurred, unparalleled in its ferocity.

25-31. On witnessing that entire army harassed by wind and rain and with his own army scattered in all directions because of its fear of falling stones, Śiva, the mountain dweller quickly released the magical weapon called Vāyu. When that great wind struck the clouds, they were scattered into pieces in the sky, the wind buffeted the demon's army round in all directions and the heroes' turbans disappeared into the distance as if they were bird's feathers. Fallen elephants, chariot horses and foot soldiers were pulverized and uprooted trees and creepers covered the soldiers. Then the demon warded off the wind with the magical weapon called Garuda and after drawing the bowstring back to his ear and taking an arrow, enchanted with the magical weapon called Anala, he shot it at Śiva's army. Instantly a hot rain fell, burning everything. Everyone was tormented by garlands of flames and thought it was the cosmic destruction.

32-39ab. From the blazing flames there came a man who induced great fear. Huge in body, scraping the firmament with his head, his mouth gaping with teeth, his cries loud, he was sick with hunger. Flourishing his ferocious tongue, one hundred yojanas in width, he agitated the fighting elephants with the violent wind from his nose. Then he devoured that army in the way the king of the birds does with snakes and when harassed by the man the splendid army fled. Coming up behind Śiva it said, "Save us! Save us!" After removing the army's fear with the words, "Don't be afraid," Śiva, husband of the mountain's daughter restrained the fire at that very moment by discharging the magical weapon called Parjanya. He then felled the ferocious man with a single arrow, but after getting up, the man devoured Śiva's armies. Distressed with fear, the Pramathas went away, intent upon flight and they trembled whilst they were faltering, falling and puffing. Even Śiva went into a cave because he had nobody to help him and all the heroes led by six-faced Kārttikeya followed him.

39cd-42. Wishing to abduct Pārvatī, the mountain's daughter, who he thought was alone on the mountain, the demon went alone to Kailāsa after leaving the battlefield. The mountain's daughter saw him coming in the distance and she trembled. After going to her father she said, "Will the demon carry me away?" After he had heard her statement and had led her to a cave that was difficult of access and unknown to anyone else but himself, he left her there in safety.

43-47. With a view to seizing her, the demon came to the golden mountain, but he did not see the mountain's daughter anywhere, Excellent man. Yet whilst wandering there he did see a single, auspicious image of a Cintāmaṇī which resembled a thousand suns. After taking it he immediately went to his own home. Powerful and universally victorious, he went from there to Pātāla surrounded by bards singing eulogies to the accompaniment of a variety of musical instruments. However, whilst the demon was moving along, the image of the Cintāmaṇī disappeared from within his hand. It was as though a miracle had occurred, and considering it to be an inauspicious omen, he re-entered his city and, exceedingly dejected, he became terribly anxious.

CHAPTER FORTY-FOUR

Description of the Austerity

Vyāsa said:

1. After Tripura had defeated him, what did Śambhu do to the victorious demon Tripura who was filled with victory and how did he do it?

Brahmā said:

2-6. After that, whilst thinking about the state of the Earth now that it was without the sacrificial formulas called svāhā and svadhā, he experienced severe mental anguish[107] and he wondered, "When will the gods be able to live in their own abodes without feeling oppressed and by what means can he be defeated when he is really so difficult to defeat?" Whilst he was suffering anxiously in this way, the excellent sage Nārada, who had come to visit the gods, unexpectedly came upon Śaṅkara. When he saw him the god rejoiced ecstatically, as though he were a mortal who has just gained immortality, and in accordance with the ritual he honoured him once he had accepted the prepared seat. After he had embraced him, yet still suffering terribly from anxiety, Śiva spoke to him, seeking the welfare of the gods and the killing of the demon.

Śiva said:

7-8. The powerful demon has undertaken the destruction of all the gods and in battle with him their confidence was broken and they fled, going in all directions. Brahmin, I do not know who is where. Also, he broke my weapons into a thousand pieces with his weapons.

---

[107] "he experienced severe mental anguish": That is, Śiva is worried because of the absence of the sacrifice on the Earth, a situation which is a symptom of the adharmic condition into which the triple-world has descended.

Brahmā said:

9. After he had heard Śiva's speech the excellent sage spoke, whilst musing on the great wonder of the defeat of Śiva, Lord of the triple-world.

Nārada said:

10-12. Look! You are omniscient, the Lord of all knowledge, the protector, destroyer and controller of everything, you are capable of producing something, undoing it and changing it, you possess the eight kinds of magical powers such as smallness and so on, and you enjoy yourself through the six supernatural powers. What can I say? I am just a sage who is devoted to music and wanders continually over the triple-world, whereas you, god, are the most eloquent of all speakers. Still, in consideration of your request I will speak to you.

13. After he had said this and had thought for a moment the sage again addressed Śiva.

Nārada said:

14-16ab. In your eagerness to go to battle you neglected to worship Gaṇapa. In consequence, you were defeated fire-eyed Śiva, holder of Pināka. But now, after first worshipping Vighneśa, who wards off all obstacles, propitiating him and gaining a boon from him, go diligently into battle. You will conquer that demon. Have no doubt about it.

Brahmā said:

16cd-18. Previously that demon propitiated the god Gaṇeśa with great austerities, as a result of which Vighnaughahāri gave him this boon: "Except for Maheśvara, nobody will be able to kill you." Accordingly, Mountain-dweller, with one single arrow you must split open this triple-city which moves at will. Gaṇeśa has declared this as the means of victory.[108]

---

[108] The speaker of vs.18. is Nārada, although his words are being narrated by Brahmā.

19. After Śiva heard the sage's remedy he became immeasurably happy and once he had heard the words that Gaṇeśa had previously spoken, he addressed the sage.

Śiva said:

20-22. You have spoken the truth, brahmin. Because of your speech I now remember that once in the past he taught me a mantra, Sage, which included a six-syllable and a one-syllable mantra, both of which take away all difficulties. But because my mind was entirely occupied with fighting I neither recited nor recollected those two and so Gajānana, the remover of all obstacles, the cause of everything, the creator, protector and destroyer, Vināyaka, was not recollected.

The sage said:

23. Mahādeva, you must please the great-god Gajānana.

24-27ab. Then dismissing Nārada, the god Śiva left to perform austerities. At a spot in Daṇḍaka forest, he recited the mantras whilst in the lotus position, and then, having restrained his senses by the force of his meditation, Śaṅkara performed a fierce austerity for ten years, utterly absorbed in meditation. Then out of his lotus-mouth there came a superior man who had five faces, ten arms, a moon on his forehead, and he was radiant as the moon. On his shaven head there was a garland, he was ornamented with serpents and was adorned with bracelets on his upper arms as well as with a diadem. Moreover he was concealing himself with ten weapons, the splendour of which was like that of the sun, fire and moonbeams.

27cd-31. Overpowered by his radiance the god Śiva saw standing before him the fierce Vināyaka who had five faces and five mouths. Indeed he was another Śiva. On seeing him the god Śiva conjectured, 'Have I become double, or has Tripura come here in my form or is there another amongst the thirty-three myriads of gods who has five faces? Or else did I watch him for a long time in a dream or has Gajānana come to give me a boon? I am going to meditate day and night on the god who removes every obstacle!

Brahmā said:

32-35. After hearing that speech Dviradānana said, I am the Lord Vighnahara who you have contemplated in your heart. Brahmā, the gods and the sages do not know my real appearance, how much less those who do not know the Vedas, the Upaniṣads and the six śāstras.[109] I am the creator of the entire world, its organizer and its destroyer. I am the Lord of all those moving and unmoving beings beginning with Brahmā who are comprised of the three qualities and I am satisfied with your austerity, so I have come here to grant you a boon. Mahādeva, choose as many boons from me as you wish.

CHAPTER FORTY-FIVE

The Gift of a Boon to the Mountain Dweller

The sage said:

1. The Lord of the gods, Vighneśa, Vighnahāri, was pleased and wished to give boons to Śarva. What did Sadāśiva request?

Brahmā said:

2. After hearing Gaṇeśa's speech and recollecting the real appearance of the boon-giver Gajānana, Śiva made this speech.

Śiva said:

3. By worshipping you now,
My ten eyes and ten arms have become auspicious.
By eulogizing you, God, my five heads have become auspicious,

---

[109] "the six śāstras": That is, the Vedāṅgas.

And so too have my five faces by bowing to you.
4. You are earth, water, air and the directions,
Fiery energy and time, and your nature is that of causing.[110]
You are the atmosphere, taste, form and smell,
Touch, word, mind and the senses.
5. You are the heavenly musicians, yakṣas, deceased fathers, humans,
The celestial sages and all the hosts of gods.
You are Brahmā, Indra, Śiva, the Vasus and the Sādhyas.
Beings, both moving and unmoving, were produced from you.
6. By means of the rajas quality you create everything, Unique god,
You protect all this by means of sattva.
By means of the tamas quality you destroy it, Lord of the qualities.
Yet you are always indifferent, a witness to every action.

Brahmā said:

7. Then with Śiva's permission I too spoke to the god Gaṇeśa and I recited his names. Listen to all this, very wise man.
8. You indeed are the first seed syllable of the vowels,
And in the form of the exclamation oṁ you are the basis of the Vedas.
May you also have the name Gaṇeśa,
Since you are the mighty Gaṇeśa.
9. When Gaṇanayaka had said om,
Śarva became satisfied and gave some boons, saying,[111]
'Whoever will recollect you in respect of all his duties, Lord,
Will achieve his goal without any impediment.

---

[110] "your nature is that of causing" kalanātmako: I am uncertain of the precise meaning of the first part of this compound. M translates it as gaṇanārūpa, "whose form is that of the hosts".

[111] I assume that Brahmā recites Gaṇeśa's proclamation of Om as recorded in the first two lines of this verse and that Śiva takes up the speech again thereafter. This is what the context suggests and vs.12 makes it clear that Śiva is speaking there, at least.

But by not recollecting you, nobody, not even a worm or an insect,
Will obtain success in the goal for which he aims.
10. Worshippers of Śiva, of yourself, of Viṣṇu,
Of Śakti and of the sun god, should, in respect of every duty,
Whether it be good or bad, religious or worldly,
Zealously worship you first of all.
11. Whatever is auspicious amongst all beings,
Including gods, yakṣas, vidyādharas and kiṃnaras,
Of that you are the Lord and you become the embodiment of auspiciousness,
Since you bring auspiciousness for your own devotees.
12. You were not recollected at the start of the battle with that eminent demon,
Because I neither praised nor honoured you, Lord,
And you have defeated me.
So now I have come to your feet for refuge.[112]
13. All-powerful, forgive my offence!
Give me victory on the occasion of every battle.
Even those who never worship you, God,
Beggars and dullards, must be allowed to prosper!

Brahmā said:

14. On hearing this, Gaṇeśa, knowing the substance of all speeches,
Made this statement to Śiva, the mountain dweller:
"On whatever occasion you should recollect me,
I will come to you, Śiva, Lord of Umā.
15. Consecrate the single arrow with the seed syllable of my name,
And with that alone throw down the triple-city,

---

[112] "You have defeated me": Thus Śiva now attributes his defeat not to the superiority of the demon, but to his own omission in not worshipping Gaṇeśa before the battle.

Rendering it and the demon into ashes
By means of my power, Maheśa."
16. Gaṇādhipa was completely satisfied in his mind.
To Śiva as he bowed correctly and devoutly,
He then recited one thousand of his names,
That which grants victory and accomplishes people's desires,
17. And he said to him, "Recite it on the occasion of battle,
And you will immediately kill the demon.
Men who recite it at dawn, noon and sunset
Will have success in all their most cherished desires."
18. After he had heard the speech of Dviradānana,
And had duly worshipped him, Śiva rejoiced ecstatically.
He installed a huge Gaṇeśa image there,
Then immediately constructed a massive hall
19. After he had satiated the gods and the group of perfected sages,
Given gifts to the bulls of brahmins and
Repeatedly worshipped the god,
Śiva, Lord of the mountains made obeisance to Gaṇeśa, the boongiver.
20. He said to everyone, "This is Maṇipūr.
It must become famous all over the world."
When all of them and the god had pronounced their assent,
They all disappeared, preceded by Gaṇanātha.
21. After Gaṇeśa and the hosts of gods and sages had disappeared,
Śiva went to his own home accompanied by his own hosts,
And by multitudes of yakṣas, heavenly musicians and goddesses.
Quite joyfully he told his own story to the mountain's daughter.
22. After hearing all these immortal words from Śiva, the mountain dweller,
These Lords of gods, sages and Lords of yogins, and their wives, rejoiced.
They thought about their own homes and the destruction of Tripura,

Which would be accomplished by the favour of Śiva, the mountain dweller.

CHAPTER FORTY-SIX

Narration of the Thousand-names of Gaṇeśa in the conversation between Śiva and Gaṇeśa

The sage said:

1. How did Gaṇeśa specify those one thousand names? Concerned as you are about the welfare of beings, tell me how it was given to Śiva!

Brahmā said:

2-5. Previously that god had been obsessed with achieving the destruction of the triple-city, but because he did not worship Gaṇeśa there arose a veritable mass of obstacles. Yet after he had concentrated firmly in his mind he saw Vighnakāraṇa and when he had devoutly worshipped Mahāgaṇapati according to the rite, he asked the indefatigable god the way to allay the obstacles. Mahāgaṇapati was completely gratified by Śambhu's worship and to him he then recited his own thousand names which gives results for all desires and is the special allayer of all obstacles.

6ab. Of this mantra which is a garland consisting of one thousand names of the illustrious Mahāgaṇapati, Gaṇeśa is the seer, Mahāgaṇapati is the deity, the metres are of various kinds, "Hum" is the introductory syllable, "trunk" is the power word and svāhā is the wedge syllable. Its purpose in a recitation is to please Mahāgaṇapati who is the doorway to the removal of all obstacles.

Mahāgaṇapati said:

6cd-173. Om, Lord of the hosts, whose past-time is the hosts, Lord of the hosts, Overlord of the hosts, who has a single trunk, who has a curved trunk, who has an elephant's face, who has a great belly, who has a pendulous navel, who is smoke coloured, who is huge, who is the leader of hosts, whose face is good, whose face is bad, who is intelligent, who is king of obstacles, who destroys evil, who is ferocious, delightful, joyful, the delight of the gods, who is excessively proud, who is Heramba, Śambara, Śambhu, who has pendulous ears, who is very strong, who is gladdening, who grants prosperity, who is ferocious, who roars like a cloud, who is a conqueror of the hosts, Vināyaka, Virūpākṣa, a Lord, who is brave, a boon-giver, who is the great Lord of hosts, who is the intellect, who is perfection, who gratifies quickly, who is liked by the Rudras, who is overseer of hosts, Umā's son, a destroyer of evil, who is Kārttikeya's elder brother, who is Īśāna's son, whose vehicle is a rat, who is loved by the perfected ones, who is Lord of the perfected, who is the perfected one amongst the perfected, Vināyaka, who is unimpeded, who is Tumburu, who has a lion for his vehicle, who is loved by seductive women, who is scratched on the hip,[113] who is a prince, who is a descendant of Śākala, who is appeased, who is immeasurable, who is the origin of the hymn invoked by the Kūṣmāṇḍas, who is invincible, who conquers easily, who is victory, who is Lord of the Earth, Lord of the worlds, the Lord of creatures, who is undecaying, who is the maker of the universe, the destroyer of the universe, who has the form of the universe, who is the receptacle, who glows, who is a poet, who is a bull of poets, who is conducive to the brahmins, who is beloved of those who know Brahma, who is the eldest king, the Lord of treasures, the Lord of those who like wealth, who is liked, who exists within the city of gold, who exists in the midst of the Sun's disc, who has scattered the waters of the

---

[113] "who is scratched on the hip" kaṭaṃkaṣo: I have no idea of the meaning of this compound. The vr. kaṭaṃkaṭo is attested in GN and B and is an epithet of Śiva.

ocean by striking his trunk, who split Pūṣan's teeth, who grew up playing on Umā's body, who grants liberation and preserves the lineage, who wears a coronet, who wears ear-rings, who has a garland of pearls, who wears a garland of flowers, who consists of the mind, who destroys the prosperity of demons by averting his face, who overcomes the Earth with the gait of his foot, who is very young, whose girdle is made of muñja grass and gold, who removes bad omens, who removes bad dreams, who pacifies, who is endowed with good qualities, who is established in sounds, who is handsome, who resides in everyone's eyes, who wears shining anklets, who wears yellow clothes, who carries a sword, who resides in the month of April to May when the moon is not full, who has a bright-coloured body, who has dark teeth, who has the moon on his forehead, whose arms are oblations,[114] who is the Overlord of the yogins, who is in the eye, who is the man, who has elephant's ears, who is the great king of the hosts, who is victory, who is firm, who is Lord of elephants, who has a banner, who is god of gods, who is Kāma's life, who is a lamp, who controls the air,[115] who is learned, who is a boon-giver, who roars, whose roars split the clouds in the large sky, who has boar's teeth, who conquers death, who is clothed in a tiger skin, whose being is power and desire, who is the saviour of the gods, who is the crusher of the demons, who was born from Śambhu's mouth, who was born from Śambhu's anger, who causes Śambhu's laughter, who possesses Śambhu's fiery energy, who removes Śiva's grief, who causes happiness to Gaurī, who was born from the impurity on Umā's body, who has a person's body, who makes a great roar, whose body is a mountain, who has a beautiful face, who is the self of everything, who is the self of all the gods, who has

[114] "whose arms are oblations" havirbhujaḥ: This is a difficult reading but it is attested by all the mss. GN and GSN. contain the easier reading caturbhujaḥ. Could it be possible to take havirbhujaḥ as a special formation from havirbhuj, a name of Agni?

[115] "who controls the air" vāyukīlakaḥ: Bhāskarāya (GSN. p.17) gives the following explanation for the meaning of this epithet: "arresting the breaths in the body which has nine apertures."

Brahmā's head, who is the Lord of the regions, who acquires the pot which is Brahmā's egg, who has the shining heaven on his forehead, whose hair is truth, the opening and shutting of whose eye is the birth and death of the universe, whose three eyes are the moon, the sun and fire, whose single tusk is the Lord of the mountains, who is righteousness, who is strengthened by the Sāma hymns, whose teeth are the Pleiades and the planets, who has a voice and a tongue, whose nose is Indra, who has a necklace in the midst of his brow, who delights in astrology, whose shoulder is the Kula mountain, whose bells are the sun and the moon,[116] who has Rudra's head,[117] whose arms are the male and female rivers, whose fingers are snakes, whose nails are the stars, whose hip is the Earth, whose penis is embraced, who is a mountain, whose knees are inferior to those of Rudra,[118] whose buttocks are hell, whose feet are the sages, whose thumb is time, whose body is the three Vedas, whose finger is the stellar sphere, who is motionless because of the fire in his heart, whose home is the lotus pericarp in the heart, who has the sky as a lake for sports, whose elephant's heel chain is meditation for true devotees,[119] whose restraining rope is the act of worship, who is majestic, who is Kaśyapa, who is a ruler, who is an astrologer, who is sluggish, who is powerful, who is renowned, who is lawful, who is a conqueror, who is a Pramatha, who is Lord of the Pramathas, who is the thought-jewel, the Lord of wealth, whose home is in a forest of wishing trees, who stands in a circle of jewels, who rests on a jewelled lion throne, who rests his foot on the head of Tīvrā, who is caressed by Jvālinī's head, the splendour of whose seat is

---

[116] "whose bells are the sun and the moon": This refers to bells kept hanging on the sides of elephants.

[117] "who has Rudra"s head": Possibly satirical since Śiva chopped off Gaṇeśa's head when the latter refused him entry to Pārvatī's house.

[118] "whose knees are inferior to those of Rudra" rudrānujānukaḥ: My translation is a guess.

[119] "whose elephant's heel chain is meditation for true devotees": Presumably this means that his heel chain is an object of meditation for this devotees.

blessed by Nandā, whose seat was decorated by Bhoginī, whose seat is Kāmadāyinī, who rests on a seat supported by the glittering Ugrā, of whom the gem in his head is called Tejovatī, who is garlanded with the goddesses Satyā and Nityā,[120] whose seat is the remover of obstacles, who rests on a lotus which has the form of all the śaktis, who assumes the lotus position on a syllable, who rests in the three holes which contain the sacred fire, who has the tip of his toe bent upwards, whose ankle is not prominent, whose heels are covered, whose buttocks are fat, whose knees are joined together, whose thighs are thick, whose hips are upraised, whose navel is deep, whose stomach is gross, whose chest is corpulent, whose arms are huge, whose shoulders are corpulent, whose neck is like a conch shell, who has a large underlip and a long nose, whose left tusk is broken, whose right tusk i's raised high. who has a huge jaw, who has three small eyes, who has flapping ears. who has a firm head, the top of whose frontal prominence is like a bunch of flowers, whose diadem is a jewel, who is independent, whose waistband and necklace consist of snakes, whose sacred thread is a snake, whose hair ring is a snake, whose armlets and neck-chains are snakes, whose girdle and belly tie are snakes, whose upper garment is the king of snakes, who is red, who wears red garments, who is adorned with a red garland, whose eyes are red, whose hands are red, whose palate is red, whose lips are like tender leaves, who is white, who wears white clothes, who is adorned with a white garland, whose splendid umbrella is white, who is fanned with a white chowrie, all of whose limbs are flawless, who is endowed with all characteristics, who is opulent with all kinds of ornaments and decorations, who possesses absolute splendour, who confers happiness on all those who are auspicious, who is the cause of all causes, whose unique trunk gives all things, who is an archer, who is filled

---

[120] GSN. p.24 takes all the proper names occuring in this verse as referring to the personified śaktipīṭhas.

with seeds,[121] who bears a club, whose body is white, who makes beings auspicious, who has a fine sacred thread, whose lineage prospers, who wears a diadem, who wears ear-rings, who wears a necklace, who wears a garland of wild flowers, who has auspicious arm bracelets, who holds a bow made from sugar cane, who has a pike, who has a discus in his hand, who carves a lotus, who holds a noose, who has a blue lotus, who holds rice husks, who holds flower buds, who holds his own tusk, who holds a creeper that grants all desires, whose unique trunk gives security to everyone, who is independent, who holds a string of rosary beads, who possesses the knowledge of hand gestures, who has a mallet as a weapon, whose pot is the Earth, who holds a conch, who causes delight to swarms of bees, who holds an orange, who carries a mango bud, who has an axe, who showers multitudes of gems from the pot of gold on his trunk, who is Lord of the beautiful lady of speech, who is fond of playing with the king of birds, who loves Mahālakṣmī, who is enchanted by Siddhalakṣmī, whose upper body is Ramā and the Lord of Ramā,[122] whose lower body is Maheśvara and Umā, the left half of whose body is the Earth and the boar, the hind part of whose body is Rati and Kandarpa, who creates fragrance and pleasure, who gives pleasure to joyful people, who increases the wealth and prosperity of those whose great fortune has already prospered, whose tusk is happiness and cheerfulness, who is a repository of abundant beauty, at whose feet Madanāvatī rests, whose tusk is both pleasant and unpleasant, who is a shelter for those who have even the slightest difficulties, who always flows with ichor when sexually aroused, whose docile feet remove obstacles, who possesses the power called Drāviṇī, whose tranquil eye is Tīvrā, whose one eye is cherished by Jvālinī, who attracts Mohinī, who is adorned with the beauty of Bhogadāyinī, the beauty of whose face is like the beauty of Kāminī, one of whose eyes has settled on Tejinī, who has a passion for wealth,

[121] "who is filled with seeds" bījapūrī: I am uncertain of the meaning of this word. Bhāskarāya gives no commentary on it, nor does M give a rendering of it.

[122] Ramā and the Lord of Ramā are names of Lakṣmī and Viṣṇu.

who roars, who is Lord of the treasure called Mahāśaṅkha, at whose stooped head Vasumatī bows, who is Lord of the great Southern elephants, who must be served by all the gods and teachers, who resides in the heart of the three sacred fires, who is Īśāna's head, whose tuft of hair is the Lord of demons, who is Vāyu's son, whose eye is not fierce, who is celestial, who possesses divine weapons, whose body has one hundred joints, who is fond of choosing the elephants such as Airāvata and so on who stand at the ten directions, who has a scabbard which holds weapons such as the thunderbolt, who is the powerful supporter of the hosts, whose retinue is victory and defeat, who brings about victory and defeat, whose lotus feet are worshipped by those who are victorious, who is garlanded with the eternal and the transitory, who is perfectly radiant of Vilāsinī, who is ornamented with Śauṇḍī's beauty, who gives eternal happiness to Śeṣa, who confers auspicious things onto auspicious people, who sustains rites, the sacrifice and knowledge, who is served by those who have desires, whose feet rest on Subhagā, who is the refuge of the beautiful Lalitā, who protects Kāminī, who is desire, who enjoys sporting with Kāminī, who is the refuge of Sarasvatī, who is Gaurī's son, who is the mansion of prosperity, whose feet are concealed by teachers, who is accomplished in speech, who is the husband of the goddess of speech, who is Mālinī's lover, who is Rāma, who is the eldest brother of Vāmā, who is captivating, whose lotus feet are embossed with garlands of pearls, whose initial syllable is Hum, whose power is prominent, who protects and creates the universe etc., who has a feminine consort named Svāhā, who possesses the wedge syllable, who has made his abode in the ocean of immortal nectar, whose eyes are rolling about because of immortal nectar, whose eyes are rolling about because of alcohol, who calculates the remains of what is left, Gaṇeśa, Lord of the hosts, who is absolute perfection at all times, who is to be worshipped always, who is naked, who is deathless, whose vision is without end, who is immeasurable, who is immortal and does not suffer from old age, who is pure, who is indestructible, who is imperishable, who is the immorta and the undecaying, who is unknowable by reason, who is undecaying, who is unconquerable, who is independent, who is salubrious, who is pure, whose perfection is immeasurable, who is not dual, who is friendly, whose mind is immeasurable, who is without shape, who is a smokeless fire, who destroys strength, whose characteristics are unmanifested, who supports the pīṭhas, who is a support, who does not need a support, who has a rat on his flag, who fulfils desires, whose large chariot is a rat, whose perfection is without guile, who is non-dual, who is immeasurable, whose face is immeasurable, who stands in the midst of an ocean of sugarcane, who eats sugar-cane with milk, whose splendour surpasses that of the god of love, whose splendour is equal to that of Indra's bow, whose splendour is similar to that of the Indragopa beetle, whose lustre is that of a sapphire, who is dark like the petal of the Indivara, who is adorned with the disc of the moon, who is loved by fuel,[123] who shares the iḍā libation, whose name is the iḍā libation loved by Indirā, who destroys obstacles for the Īkṣvākus, who is desired by the parts of the ritual, who has Īśāna's head, who is Īśāna, who is loved by Īśāna, who destroys plagues, who is the destroyer of the three desires, who is devoid of even an atom of desire, who is Viṣṇu, who has the digit of the moon on his forehead, who likes moonbeams, whose face is uplifted, who is lofty, who is the foremost of the noble thirty gods, who is vigorous, whose body is blazing, who is beyond inference and argument,[124] whose eyes are the Ṛg, Yajus and Sāma Vedas, who gives success and prosperity, who is easy to obtain by one whose clear mind is intent, who frees one from the three debts, who has destroyed obstacles for good devotees, who has destroyed the powers of the gods' enemies, who has destroyed the prosperity of those who are indifferent to his

---

[123] "Who is loved by fuel": Bhāskarāya, GSN, p.39, comments, "You are loved by fuel because you have the form of fire in the śrauta and smārta sacrifices."

[124] "who is beyond inference and argument" īhāpohavivarjita: The idea here is that inference and argument will not necessarily bring a person to knowledge of Gaṇeśa, the implication being that devotion is more important for the achievement of this goal.

worship, who destroys boils and skin diseases, who stands on a seat which is a round stool, who has adopted the posture of standing on one foot, who upsets the prosperity of the daityas, who shelters all from agitation, who is the repository of the lordly powers, who is sovereignty, who grants wishes to those belonging to this world and the other world, whose blink is identical with the light of sheet lightning, whose face resembles that of Airāvata, who should be called the syllable Om, who is the syllable Om, who has vitality, who is Lord of plants, who is the repository of nobility, who has forbearance towards arrogance, whose sound is loud, who is the goad of the celestial elephants, who exists in the demon's goad, who is proclaimed in all the phonemes ending with visargas including the aḥ, who holds a water pot, who is a kalpa, who wears braided and knotted hair, whose face is that of a young elephant, who is the witness of actions, who is the success of actions, who gives the results of good and bad karma, whose shape is round like that of the blossoms of the kadamba tree, who is leader of the Kūṣmāṇḍa hosts, whose body is compassion, who is reddish, who is a narrator, who wears a girdle round his hips, who is crippled, who loves those who are crippled, who stands in a hole dug by swords, who is pure like the sky, who is bald, who resides in tusks, who has the khaṭvāṅga club, who is as difficult as the sky to seize, who is opulent with good qualities, who is impenetrable bliss, whose prose and verse is an ocean of immortality, who loves singing and prose, who roars, who is song, who was born before the god of love, who is intent upon secret conduct, who is secret, who is described in the secret texts, whose abode is secret, who is an ocean of molasses, who is accessible through a teacher, who is the teacher's teacher, who is garlanded with small and large bells, whose frontal lobes are like pots, who is pot-bellied, who is called the letter ṅ, who is the letter ṅ, whose trunk is the shape of the letter ṅ, who is passionate, who is Śiva's friend, who is the Lord of Caṇḍa, who is of fierce valour, who is father of the moving and unmoving, who is the thought-jewel, who is eager for solid food, who is the sacred text, who consists of the sacred texts, who can only be described with difficulty in the sacred texts, whose body is the sacred texts, who is the origin of the universe, who is the witness of the universe, who is victory, who is defeat, who is complete victory, who is Lord of the lion throne in the sense of the tongue,[125] whose splendour shines when his ears flap, on whom swarms of bees hum, whose howling makes a loud uproar, whose jewelled anklets clang, who is named the final syllable and visargaḥ, who gives great success for every mantra, whose bald head is a drum, who is a Lord of the female demons, who loves the ḍiṇḍi drums, who is gladdened by the sound of the large drum, who is Ḍhaṅka, who is Gaṇeśa as Ḍhundhi, who can be named by the syllable ṇa, who is the Lord of speech, who is the soul of the universe, who is the creator of the universe, who, of the material principles, is the material principle called prakṛti, whose material principle can be described in words, who rests within the eyeball, who is the rescuer, who is Tāraka's killer, who is Sthāṇu, who is loved by Sthāṇu, who is the establisher, who is what is moving and stationary, who is the extinguisher of Dakṣa's sacrifice, who is the giver, who is generous, who is the origin of compassion, who is compassionate, who possesses celestial power, who carries a staff, who is leader of the army, who has shattered the garland of clouds into pieces with his tusk, who restrains the demon's elephants, whose elephant's pot clings to his tusk, who subdues the gods' enemies, who possesses self-control, who is wealth, who is Kubera, who is a kinsman,[126] who gives wealth, who holds up the Earth, who becomes manifest only through meditation, who should be meditated upon, who is the object of meditation, who is engrossed in meditation, who is the

---

[125] "who is Lord of the lion throne in the sense of the tongue" jihvā-siṅhāsanaprabhuḥ: I am quite in the dark about the meaning of this name. Here is what GSN. p.46 gives in comment: "His name, being renowned, stands on the lion throne of the tongue. He gives the four ends of man (puruṣārtha), hence he is the Lord of the lion throne in the sense of the tongue".

[126] "who is a kinsman" bandhuḥ: This reading is attested by all the mss. An easier reading given in GN 99c and GSN is dhanyo "who is wealthy".

primordial sound cit, whose girdle contains a row of created universes, who should be described loudly, who loves loud sounds, who is sound, who is situated in sound, who is complete, who is pure, who is perpetual, who is both perpetual and impermanent, who is healthy, who is the highest heaven, who is the supreme abode, who is the supreme self, who is the highest refuge, who is higher than the high, who is Paśupati, who is Lord of beasts, who frees the soul from fetters, who is full of bliss, who is the highest bliss, who is the primordial supreme person, whose face is a clear lotus, who destroys the ignorance of those who are humble, who is beyond analysis and proof, who removes the injuries of the humble, who has a snake in his hand, who is Lord of snakes, who hisses like a serpent, who likes sugar cane, whose pair of feet are worshipped by Bāṇa, who plays with children, who is curious, who is Brahma, whose feet are worshipped by Brahmā, who is a brāhmaṇical student, who is Bṛhaspati, who is the largest, who is intent upon Brahma, who is friendly to the brahmins, who is loved by those who know Brahma, who gives prosperity with a glance, who is auspicious, who is splendour, who removes fear, who is the illustrious one, who is easy to obtain through devotion, who gives wealth, who increases wealth, who is the future, whose abode is the past, who gives what is pleasant, who is to be meditated upon from the spot between the eyebrows, who is a mantra, who is Lord of mantras, who possesses a mantra, who is intoxicated when in rut, whose rut is massive, whose tusk is the supreme Lord in Mekhala, whose eyes appear to be heavy when he is in rut, who is very strong, who has great courage, who has great vitality, who is magnanimous, who is the sacrifice, who is Lord of the sacrifice, who is the protector of the sacrifice, who gives the results of the sacrifice, who is Lord of the sacrifice, who is accessible by yoga, who is Lord of cows, who is loved by beggars, who is flavour, who loves flavours, who should be enjoyed, who gives amusement, who is loved by Rāvaṇa, who protects kingdoms, who contains jewels, who gives happiness to kingdoms, who is a goal, who gives lakhs of wealth, who can be defined, who exists during the destruction,[127] who loves sweet meats, who likes elephant stables, who is obsessed with dancing, who causes gain, who is famed amongst beings, who is the best, whose mouth is fire, who should be praised, who is accessible through the Upaniṣads, who is the slaughterer, who has eyes everywhere, who is the ordainer, who has mouths everywhere, who is the pleasant god, who is the leader of everything, who restrains the thunderbolts of the thunderbolt wielders, who is Vivasvat's kinsman, who is the support of everything, who is Lord of everything, who is the Lord, who is the sound Brahma, who can be attained through equanimity, who is the Lord of Śambhu, Śakti and the hosts, who is garlanded with the flowers of the six seasons, who is the six supports, who is the six syllables, who is a doctor in respect of saṃsāra, who is omniscient, who is the healer of all healers, who is playing when he is destroying, preserving and creating, who destroys a bed of arrows, whose great frontal prominence is reddened, who imparts discrimination between good and evil, who is the witness, who churns the ocean, who is intelligible to himself, who has gifts, who is independent, whose wishes are the truth, who is devoted to the chanting of the Sāma Veda, who is happy, who is the goose, who is Lord of the elephant demons, who is the oblation, who eats oblations made to the gods and ancestors, to whom sacrifices should be offered, who is ecstatic, who is in the midst of the mantra having the syllable hrīm, who is Overlord of the sacred places, who is the Earth's husband, whose highest obsession is patience, who quickly confers peace, who finds happiness in peace, who is the divine tree on the Earth, who gives accomplishment in the law, who gives accomplishment in power, who gives accomplishment in the sensuous, who increases good fortune, who gives knowledge, who gives power, who gives the fruits of liberation and carnal

---

[127] "who exists during the destruction" layastho: That is, the destruction that occurs between two periods of creation according to the scheme of the Purāṇic cosmogony.

enjoyments as results, who confers what is pleasing, who is a hero, who gives prosperity, who gives victory, who subdues everyone, who destroys faulty embryos, who gives sons and grandsons, who removes Lakṣmī's sorrow who destroys misfortune, who supports all the powers, who paralyses the mouths of opponents who clarifies disturbed minds, who neutralizes an enemy's evil spells, who removes distress, who gives liberation from bonds, who is a moment, who is half a second, who is a minute period of time, who is forty seconds, who is two seconds, who is a blink, who is a very rapid blink, who is an instant, who is a period of twenty-four minutes, who is a period of forty-eight minutes, who is three hours, who is the day, who is the night, who is a period of day and night, who is a fortnight, who is a month, who is a half-year, who is a year, who is twelve thousand divine years, who is thirty-six thousand divine years, who is the period of the great destruction, who is a sign of the zodiac, who is a fixed star, who is a lunar day, who is a lunar period of two and a half hours, who is the turn of the day, who is an astrological division of the day, who is a quarter part of a lunar mansion, who is the first astrological house, who is half of a zodiacal sign, who is the wheel of time, who is Mt. Meru, who is the seven stars of Ursa Major, who is the pole star, who is the eclipse, who is Saturn, who is Venus, who is Jupiter, who is Mercury, who is Mars, who is the Moon, who is the Sun, who is the destruction, who is the creation, who is stability, who is everything which is unmoving and moving, who is earth, who is air, who is fire, who is air, who is the heavens, who is individuality, who is primordial matter, who is the masculine principle, who is Brahmā, Viṣṇu, Śiva, Rudra, Indra, Śakti, Sadāśiva, who is the thirty gods, who is the deceased ancestors, who is the perfected ones, who is the yakṣas, who is the rākṣasas, who is the kiṃnaras, who is the accomplished ones, who is the vidyādharas, who is the ghosts, humans, animals, the birds, who is the oceans, who is the rivers, who is the mountains, who is the origin of the past, present and the future, who is Sāṃkhya, who is Pātañjalayoga, who is the Purāṇas, who is the Vedas, who is non-Vedic literature, who is the limbs of the Vedas, who is good conduct, who is Mīmāṃsā, who is Nyāya, who is Āyurveda, who is the Veda of archery, who is music, who is drama and dance, who is a follower of Vikhanas, who is a follower of the Bhagavat, who is a follower of Manu,[128] who is a follower of the Pañcarātra, who is a follower of Śiva, who is a follower of Paśupati, who is a Kālamukha, who is the instructions pertaining to Bhairava, who is a follower of Śakti, who is a follower of Gaṇeśa, who is a follower of Sūrya, who is a follower of the Jains, who is the sacred texts of the Jain saints, who is truth and falsehood, who is the manifest and the unmanifest, who is the sensible and the insensible, who is bondage, who is liberation, who is happiness, who is carnal enjoyment, who is Yoga, who is truth, who is small, who is large, who is the term for salutation, who is the sound huṃ, who is the sound phaṭ, who is the benediction svadhā, who is the benediction svāhā, who is the ritual exclamation śrauṣaṭ, who is the ritual exclamation vauṣaṭ, who is the ritual exclamation namaḥ, who is intuitive knowledge, who is discriminating knowledge, who is bliss, who is understanding, who is consciousness, who is equanimity, who is restraint, who is unique, who is the support of the single syllable, who is engrossed in the syllable Om, whose mind is fixed on one object, who is a unique hero, whose real appearance is one and many, who has two forms, who has two arms, who has two eyes, who has two tusks, who protects islands, who has two mothers, who has two faces, who is non-dual, who is beyond duality, who is the Sun, Moon and fire, who produces the three worlds, who is the three fires, who gives the results of following the three paths, whose own self is the three guṇas, who is the origin of the triple-world, who is the Lord of the three powers, who has three eyes, who has four arms, who has four tusks, who

[128] "who is a follower of Manu" mānuṣam: Usually this word simply means human. An easier reading is sātvatam, "a worshipper of Kṛṣṇa", found in GN. 132d and GSN. p.63 but it is not attested in any of the manuscripts. I remain uncertain of my own translation.

represents the four souls,[129] who has four faces, whose stratagems are of four kinds, who resides in the four social classes and the four stations of life, who practises the four kinds of speech, who is the instigator of change, who is delighted with the ritual of the "Fourth," who is the origin of the day called the "Fourth." you are the five syllables, who has five forms, who has five faces, who possesses the five best accomplishments, who is the five supports, who is the five colours, who is intent upon the five syllables, who is five tālas high, who is one and a half feet high, who is the vowel of the five Oms, whose sudden appearance consists of the five Brahmas, who is surrounded by the five subordinate deities, who likes the five foods, who is the god of Love, who is himself the five Śivas, whose stool has six corners, who dwells in the six cakras of the body, who splits the six knots, who destroys the darkness over the six limbs, whose navel is six finger breadths in depth, who has six faces, who is the brother of six-faced Skanda, who is surrounded by six śaktis, who destroys the six hostile groups, who destroys the fear of the six waves of existence, who is beyond the six systems of philosophy, who performs the six activities of a brahmin, who possesses the six qualities, who resides in the six flavours, whose feet are the seven underworlds, the circumference of whose thighs are the seven islands, whose diadem is the seven heavenly worlds, who gives gifts to Sūrya, who gives happiness to the kingdom with its seven limbs, who is praised by the hosts of the seven sages, who is the repository of the seven meters, who has seven sacrificial priests, who resides in the seven musical notes, who has the seven oceans as the basis of his playful activities, who is served by the seven mothers, who experiences rapture through his enjoyment of the seven metres, who is the seven metres, who is Lord of the sacrifice, whose image should be meditated on in the form of eight images,[130]

---

[129] "who represents the four souls" caturātmā: According to Bhāskarāya (GSN. p.66) these ātmas are the ātmā, antarātmā, jñānātmā and paramātma.

[130] "whose image should be meditated on in the form of eight images" aṣṭamūrtidhyeyamūrtir: Bhāskarāya. GSN. p.71, takes aṣṭamūrti to refer to

who is the cause of the eight primary elements of creation, from whom arises the fruit of the eight-limbed yoga, whose seat is on the lotus which has eight petals, whose splendour is equal to that of the eight śaktis, who strengthens the eight sovereign powers, whose splendour consists of the eight sacred seats and the lesser seats, who is protected by the eight mothers, who is seated on a seat consisting of nine snakes, who rules over the nine treasures, who returns to the city of nine doors,[131] whose mansion is supported on nine pillars, who is eulogized by the nine Nārāyaṇas, who is served by the nine Durgās, who is the great Lord of the nine lords, who is ornamented with nine snakes, whose body is adorned with nine jewels, who is supported on the head of the nine śaktis, whose being is tenfold, who has ten arms, who is praised by the ten Lords of the world, who consists of ten chapters,[132] who has the ten vital breaths, who possesses restraint over the ten organs, whose great mantra has ten syllables, whose body pervades the ten regions, who is eulogized by the eleven great Rudras, who possesses the eleven syllables, who has twelve very strong arms, whose mansion is on the cakra that lies on the forehead, whose different parts have thirteen designations, who is the presiding deity of all the gods, who gives boons to the fourteen Indras, who is the Lord of the fourteen Manus, who is richly endowed with the fourteen primordial knowledges, who is Lord of the fourteen worlds, who is the fifteen kinds of Sāma hymns, who is clear like the moon when it has fifteen digits, whose abode has sixteen supports, who is the syllable of the sixteen vowels, who resides in the seventeen digits of the moon, who is the sixteen principal vowels, who is the seventeen Tantric arts, who is the seventeen syllables, who is Lord of the eighteen islands, who composes the eighteen Purāṇas, who creates the eighteen herbs, who has

---

Śiva (aṣṭamūrtiśivas), but does concede that the image can be meditated upon in eight separate forms.

[131] "city of nine doors": A metaphor of the body.

[132] "who consists of ten chapters" daśādhyāya: Bhāskarāya, GSN, p.73, takes this to refer to the four Vedas and the six Vedāṅgas.

recollected the eighteen forms, who creates the eighteen forms of writing, who creates the eighteen heterogeneous castes, who is the twenty-first man, who has twenty-five fingers in the form of young leaves, whose self is the twenty-four material principles, who is the Puruṣa, who is the twenty-fifth part, who is Lord of the twenty-seven stars, who causes the twenty-seven junctions, who is overlord of the thirty-two fierce forms of Śiva, who is the thirty-four deep pools, who is the source of the thirty-six material principles, whose body is the thirty-eight digits, who is not impeded by the group of forty-nine bowing Maruts, who is the series of fifty syllables, whose body consists of the fifty Rudras, who is Lord of the fifty śaktis of Viṣṇu, who is part of the fifty syllables, who is the series of fifty-two elephants, who resides in the sixty-three syllables, who introduces the sixty-four syllables, who is the repository of the sixty-four arts, who is praised by the group of the sixty-four perfected yoginīs, who is manifest in the sixty-eight great sacred fords and sacred places of Bhairava, who is himself the sacred places of Bhairava, who is himself the ninety-four mantras, who is Lord of the divinities who number more than ninety-six, who is the bliss of the one hundred, who is the support of the one hundred, whose eyes are as broad as the one hundred lotuses, who has one hundred armies, who has one hundred for support, who has one hundred very sharp weapons, whose abode is on a lotus, who is ornamented with Śeṣa, who is the Puruṣa of one thousand heads, who has one thousand eyes, who has a thousand feet, who should be eulogized with the one thousand names, who removes the strength of Indra, who has made his seat on the king of serpents who has a thousand hoods, whose eulogy is recited by the eighty-eight thousand primordial great sages, who is the support of lakhs of wealth, who has enjoyed four lakhs of recitation, who expounds the four lakhs of verses in the Purāṇas, whose life resides in the eighty four lakhs of beings, who resembles a myriad of suns, who is as pure as beams from myriad moons, who is leader of the myriads of followers of Vināyaka who are controlled by Śiva and PārvatĪ, whose limbs are splendid through being charmed by seven myriads of great mantras, to the impressions of whose feet the rows of thirty-three myriads of gods bow, who is the friend of endless numbers of śaktis and who is eulogized by endless numbers of sages, who has endless prosperity in his endless names, who is endless, who gives endless happiness, who is served by the eternal gods, who is praised by an endless number of mouths. In this way have the thousand names of Gaṇeśa been declared.

174-178. The man who recites this daily at the hour sacred to Brahmā will have in his grasp all the rewards which pertain to this and the other world: long life, good health, lordly power, patience, heroism, strength, renown, intelligence, wisdom, fortitude, beauty, good fortune, handsomeness, truth, compassion, forbearance, tranquillity, dexterity, positive disposition towards the law, control of the world, conversation with everyone, sharpness in speech, erudition in the assembly, magnanimity, profundity, holy splendour, strength, fiery energy, a good family, good conduct, splendour, courage, honour, intuitive knowledge, discriminating knowledge, belief in existence, stability, trust-worthiness, prosperity in wealth, grain etc. These will occur immediately in consequence of its recitation.

179-184. A king, a queen, a prince and a minister, by reciting it, attain the power to subject utterly a person to their will in four different ways, but whoever recites it for the purpose of subjecting a person to his own will, he becomes a slave. Effortlessly it gives accomplishment in the Law, power, sensuosity and liberation. It removes fear of possession by yakṣas, rākṣasas, Durgā's attendants and female demons, produces happiness in the empire and utterly crushes the arrogance of rivals. It fosters the seed of friendship which has been consumed and destroyed by any quarrels, it calms the effects of bad dreams and soothes the mind of an angry husband. It gives knowledge of the three time periods, the eight perfections and the six activities as well as bringing about the cessation of an enemy's black magic and crushing enemy armies. On the field of battle it alone brings victory for everyone, it destroys the blemish of barrenness for all and it is the sole cause of the protection of embryos.

185-191. This eulogy of Gaṇeśa is to be recited daily, but not in a place where there is famine, plagues or dangers. The house where this eulogy is recited will be prosperous and there will be a decrease in leprosy, urinary diseases, haemorrhoids, diseases of the anus, indigestion, abdominal swelling, disease of the spleen, gall stones, dysentery, distention of the belly, coughing, respiratory problems, intestinal wind, colic, diseases arising from morbid swelling, etc., headache, vomiting, inflammation of the neck glands, loss of appetite, fever produced by wind, the bowels or phlegm, from two of these or from disorders of all three, and those diseases which arise from accidental misfortune, cold and heat, those which last for one day or more, those which are known and unknown etc., and those which arise from disorders of bodily fluids, etc. The recitation of that eulogy terminates them all immediately, and women, śūdras and degraded people immediately gain perfection by reciting it. Accordingly, this mantra of one thousand names should be recited in order to gain good health.

192-196. By reciting this eulogy of Mahāgaṇapati a person filled with desire enjoys all his earthly desires in this world in his chosen manner. Then in charming celestial sky vehicles which represent the result of his desires, he wanders as he wishes through the abodes of the Moon, Indra, the Sun, Viṣṇu, Brahmā and so on, taking whatever form he wishes, giving what he wishes and having the capacity to give what he wishes. Then after he and selected relatives have enjoyed enjoyments according to their wishes and after he has become a follower of Gaṇeśa, that attendant of Gaṇeśa is favoured by Gaṇapati. And because he is on the same level as Nandi and Śiva etc., he is gladdened by all the hosts and through the kindness of Śiva and Pārvatī he is cherished as if he were a son. Loved by Śiva, his desires fulfilled because of a boon from Gaṇeśa, he remembers his previous births and is reborn as a universal king devoted to the law.

197-199. But the person without desire who is completely engrossed in Gaṇeśa and constantly and devoutly recites it, he abides in a state of detachment and intuitive knowledge once he has attained the highest yogic accomplishment. Now that he has become perpetually without bonds, is declared to be in supreme bliss, has passed beyond the universe, is the highest, perfected and without rebirth, he dies and always remains joyfully in Vināyaka's dwelling place.

200-202. This eulogy gives all the lordly powers here and in the next world to all those who mutter, recite, teach, hear, expound, repeat, contemplate, consider and praise it. Even a person who wanders at will, yet keeps this eulogy in mind will be protected in battle by eight myriads of Śiva's hosts. If the eulogy is written down in a book it should be honoured as if it were a mantra, since the highest good fortune remains in it forever.

203. All the gift-giving, all the vows,
All the sacred fords and all the sacrifices,
Never give the instantaneous result coming
When Gaṇeśa's one thousand names are remembered.
204. The person who constantly recites his thousand names
Everyday when the sun rises,
In the evening, at midday,
Or at these three times,
Becomes foremost in lordly powers,
More powerful in strength, extends his fame substantially,
Destroys poverty, subdues the universe,
And prospers splendidly with sons and grandsons.

205-206. In addition, a poor person who is single-minded, disciplined and moderate in eating, yet recites this for four months whilst totally engaged in the worship of Gaṇeśa, will obtain great prosperity in the manner laid down by the supreme goddess, having first completely extirpated poverty in respect of his seven subsequent births.

207. Whoever constantly recites this entire eulogy of Gaṇeśa,
Will have in his grasp longevity,
Good health, a family utterly without blemish,

Wealth for the sick, auspicious fame,
Pure speech the beauty of which is natural,
Good sons,
A virtuous wife,
And anything else he desires.

208-211. "Conquering-the-hosts, Gaṇapati, Heramba, Earth-bearer, Mahāgaṇapati, Granter-of-lakhs, Quick-to-favour, Unfailingly perfect, Immeasurable, Mantra, Thought-gem, Repository, Very-auspicious, Seed, Filler-of-the-directions, Boon-giver, Time, Son-of-Kaśyapa, Rejoicing, Accomplished-in-speech, Ḍhuṇḍhi-Vināyaka." A man who has his mind on me, who is concerned with propitiating me, can eulogize me with these twenty-one names and some sweetmeats. Yet I am really eulogized by the one-thousand names, no doubt of it.

212. Obeisance! Obeisance to him whose feet the best of gods worship!

Obeisance! Obeisance to him whose auspicious self is without equal!

Obeisance! Obeisance to him, uniquely perfect with expansive trunk!

Obeisance! Obeisance to you who has the face of a young elephant

213. Him whose feet ring with hosts of small bells,
Who effects the removal of weighty problems[133] by manifesting himself,
Onto whose cheeks rut juices are driven by waves,
May he, Gaṇapati, named king, suppress evil.

---

[133] "weighty problems" gurum iti: lit. "heavy weights". I have chosen the translation "weighty problems" for this compound as a reflection of Gaṇeśa's role as the destroyer of obstacles which impede success. Many of these obstacles are presented as problems and Gaṇeśa"s first step towards their resolution is to manifest himself before his devotee who has the problem.

CHAPTER FORTY-SEVEN

Śiva's Victory

Vyāsa said:

1. Tell me, Brahmā, what did Hara do when the eulogy of one thousand names had been completed and Gajānana had become pleased?

Brahmā said:

2-3. Ecstatic because Gaṇeśa had given him a boon and because he had been taught the one thousand names, Śiva danced around and let out a great roar. Calling his own hosts and the gods he laid down the opportune time for battle and very joyfully the gods went to Śiva.

4. Brahmā, Kubera, Indra, sacker of cities, Agni,
Vāyu, Soma, Varuṇa and Aryaman,
Yakṣas, the heavenly musicians, the plants and kiṃnaras
All eulogized him after they had made obeisance to him.

The gods said:

5-6ab. Mahādeva, Lord of the universe, giver of bliss in the worlds, when will we see you kill that demon? We have fallen from our own positions because he is damaging everything.

Brahmā said:

6cd-8. On hearing the gods' speech, Śiva, the trident bearer, departed joyfully. Whilst meditating in his mind on Gaṇeśa he resolved to fight, and, accompanied by the gods and heavenly musicians, he soon reached home. In the meantime the demon's spies described the course of events to him.

9-11. Then the husband of the mountain's daughter came for battle with his army of gods and his armoured troops were armed with swords and stabbing knives. But roaring loudly and adorned with the adornments of battle, the demon gladdened his warriors with gifts of money, ornaments, garlands and garments. Then standing in the midst of the many chariots of those warriors, the great demon himself ascended Tripura, roaring in every direction.

12-16. Then occurred a great battle between both armies in which iron swords of many kinds were used as well as arrows which pierced the vitals. The constant river of blood which ensued obstructed the roads and the soldiers who were struck shone like kiṅśuka bushes in flower. Some, intensely hostile, killed prisoners who had been taken alive, whilst others, seizing men by the hair, slit their throats. Very soon dust from the pounding feet of fleeing charioteers, warriors, horses and elephants filled the heaven and earth and in that terrifying darkness nothing could be discerned. So those heroes with their multiplicity of titles engaged in fierce battle, and casting aside their wish for life they resolved to die.

17-23. When the wind had caused the dust to disappear the gods appeared to have died and with the divine army in flight, the demon's army rejoicing, Indra, sacker of cities, came forth, thunderbolt in hand and battle-proud. But as soon as they saw Indra's thunderbolt the daityas and dānavas ran away. Then Indra, the thunderbolt bearer, pulverized the demons with his falling thunderbolt and under the blows of that cruel thunderbolt they died. Yet some only had shattered feet, some had broken necks, some had their stomachs torn asunder and others had arms cut from their shoulders. Some had thighs broken and others were struck on the shanks, some whose ankles were pierced fell, whilst still others fell under false pretence. Many rivers sprang up from the falling blood of the heroic slain charioteers, the warriors and their wounded horses. Nevertheless, the fortitude of those warriors who were seeking victory increased.

24-26. Growling softly, the demon Tripura saw his army being struck repeatedly, so he came to do battle with Indra. On seeing Indra he said, "Why do you want to die? Though I will not hit you from behind, Indra of the Vasus, you are certainly going to lose your life from this battle. Are you strong enough to do battle with me Indra, husband of Śaci? Tell me if a goat would do battle with a lion? If you are strong enough come and fight! If not, go where you wish!"

27-31. After he had said this and Indra still stayed there, the demon, stringing his bow, rained down many arrows and struck the divine army. From just one enchanted arrow countless arrows came forth which filled heaven and earth, pulverizing the gods and heavenly musicians. These never-ending multitudes of arrows caused it to become dark again and the gods, disfigured by his arrows, fell to the ground. Then Indra, Vala's destroyer, fell to the earth, struck by powerful blows. When all those eminent gods had swooned, Maheśvara found pleasure in him when he was boasting much, roaring and fighting in the sky, and Śambhu mentally praised the demon's valour.

32. At that very moment Nārada came there for a visit and after he had been honoured, he said to Śiva, "Listen, dark-red Śiva."

Nārada said:

33-37ab. Don't be anxious about the killing of Tripura. I will tell you the way to kill him and then you do it, Maheśvara. Previously he performed an austerity in Puṣkara and Brahmā propitiated Gaṇeśa for him.[134] Without thinking that god gave him what he asked for, namely, a huge triple-city which can move where it wishes, which rests on a single arrow,[135] which can not be split by the gods and which is free of the wind's path.

---

[134] Normally Brahmā is propitiated by demons and directly offers boons himself (See G.Bailey, The Mythology of Brahmā, Oxford University Press, Delhi, Ch.9). This relationship between Brahmā and demons is an invariant one in Hindu mythology, so the composers of the GP. were unable to change it, yet they could modify it to bring it into consistency with their theological image of Gaṇeśa as the absolute in all spheres of activity. Accordingly Brahmā becomes the means by which Tripura obtains his boon rather than being the source of the boon.

[135] "which rests on a single arrow" ekabāṇāśritam: It is not at all clear why this should be here except that it foreshadows the essential fragility of Tripura, which, as any Purāṇic audience would know, is eventually destroyed by a single arrow.

But in secret he proclaimed this, "There is one person who will split your triple-city with a single arrow. Your death will occur because of him."

Brahmā said:

37cd-39. When that excellent sage, Nārada, had gone after having said this, Śiva brought those swooning gods back to a state of alert. Then through Nārada's reminder he remembered Ibhamukha's speech. Capable of destroying everything, the god heartily undertook great exertions in order to kill the demon-king.

40. Śiva made Earth the chariot, Sun and Moon the wheels,
Brahmā the driver,
Meru the bow, Viṣṇu the arrow,
And he harnessed the two Aśvins as the horses.

41. Purifying himself with water and pondering mentally on the god,
He recited the one thousand names
Linked with the one-syllable mantra as he had prescribed it.
With that he enchanted the mighty Pināka.

42-44. When Śiva enchanted the huge arrow shaped like Viṣṇu, the Earth shook, so too did Śeṣa, the forests and the mountains. At the sound of his bow all of his own hosts were bewildered and babbled loud noises, the gods and humans being bewildered as well. When the arrow was released the firmament and the circle of the Earth with its mountains was immediately burnt by garlands of flames.

45-46. On seeing this the Lord of the demons ascended with his army to take refuge in the city, but Śiva too went swiftly and burnt the demon's triple-city. Then whilst all the enemies of the daityas, dānavas and rākṣasas were watching, the fiery energy in the demon's body was destroyed in the sun's body.[136]

---

[136] "was destroyed in the Sun's body": That is, Tripura's fiery energy became mingled with the much greater energy of the Sun, and in this way it was neutralized.

47-53ab. A voice then appeared in the sky, saying, "The demon has been liberated! He has been killed by Śiva." After that the gods and sages eulogized the three-eyed Śiva, and the multitudes of heavenly musicians sang as did the wandering singers who were engrossed in the Vedas. Groups of nymphs danced and the kiṃnaras played musical instruments. The divine sages such as Nārada and so forth, released showers of flowers and the gods, free of anxiety, went to their own homes with Śiva's permission. After making obeisance to Maheśa, killer of the demon Tripura, the calm sages again became occupied with their appropriate religious duties, and the demon being now dead, all people on the earth who were conversant with the Vedas and the auxiliaries to the Vedas, again performed fire offerings, sacrifices, gift-giving and acts of devotion with great perseverance. The multitudes of the Lords of hosts such as Śaila, and all the members of assemblies, bowed to the three-eyed Śiva.

53cd-54. After he had divided up the huge chariot to the accompaniment of cries of victory, music and the sound of celestial drums, he went joyfully to Kailāsa, the well-adorned king of mountains. Thenceforth his real name became famous as "Enemy of Tripura."

55-56. The power of the thousand names and the capability of that mantra uttered by Mahāgaṇapati has just been described. Nobody else but me knows it, nor has it been communicated to anybody else. By listening to it or reciting it a person will obtain the fruition of all his desires.

CHAPTER FORTY-EIGHT

Pārvatī's Reappearance

Vyāsa said:

1-2. I have just heard this long tale about Tripura's killing. However, I want to hear where Pārvatī, the Earth-mother, stayed. Where and how did she reappear on the day the demon-king was burnt? Brahmā, narrate all this in detail.

Brahmā said:

3-8. The great demon was burnt in the evening of the full moon in the month of Kārttika and just as described previously, the battle was very fierce on that day. Since all the gods worshipped Śiva, killer of the gods' enemy, who was flushed with victory, men on Earth offer gifts of light on that day. On that day they also bathe, give gifts, engage in recitation and sacrifices and so forth. Since it occurs often, it is traditionally called Abundance. Yet if on that day they do not perform a great festival for Śiva, Tripura's enemy, they never achieve victory and their merit is consumed. Hence they worship Śiva at dawn on full moon day, as a result of which an evil act committed during the night is destroyed. Similarly, evil performed from birth is destroyed by worshipping at midday and evil acquired over several births by worshipping in the evening, sage.

9-16. Listen, as I am now going to relate Śivā's reappearance. After she had learnt about his death[137] at Śiva's hands, Śivā's fear disappeared. Pārvatī, the Earth-mother, then reappeared from the mouth of a cave in the Himālayas and saw that the terrible mountain was infested with deer, tigers and lions. But failing to see Śiva, she became mentally agitated because of her separation from him and frightened, she lamented bitterly, "Oh, father! Oh, Śiva! You are omniscient Sadāśiva, so how can you not acknowledge me when I am utterly alone in the fierce forest weeping like an osprey? When will you appear to me? Have you forgotten me? Hara, I cannot stay alive and bear this separation! And you too, father, where are you? Don't you hear my grief? Apart from you to whom can I go for refuge? Whatever am I going to do? Know that I have reappeared from within you[138]

---

[137] "His death": That is, Tripura's death.

[138] "from within you" jaṭharāt tava: Lit. "from within your belly". I take this to denote her re-appearance from the cave in the mountain which is metaphorical of her own father Himavat, also a mountain.

because of Śiva and so you must now reunite Śiva with me. Search quickly for my excellent Śiva, because I will throw my body from this precipice if you don't."

Brahmā said:

17. Having heard her voice, superb even though she was weeping, a certain fisherman came and spoke to Himavat.

The fisherman said:

18-24. There was an especially lovely girl with full hips who was adorned with every ornament and was wearing ear-ornaments which were like the sun in splendour as well as a beautiful shining diadem glittering with many jewels. On her brow there was a four cornered jewel decorated with sixteen pearls, a string of pearls opulent with jewels, gold and flowers rested in between the parting of her hair and on her delicate nose there was a golden pearl. Two lovely bracelets were on her arms, there were bracelets on her wrists and she also wore a ring on her finger, one rich in jewels and flashing with gold. A garland of flowers and pearls was hanging on her glittering bodice and on her linen covered hips there was a beautiful girdle of gold and jewels. Two lovely anklets were jingling from a golden chain on her ankles and on each of her toe rings there was also some superb ornaments. As such her body was absolutely faultless, yet this woman was distressed and weeping bitterly. I saw and questioned her, but she didn't speak to me. Still, she mentions your name.

Brahmā said:

25. After hearing this, the wise Himavat quickly went to his daughter and whilst comforting her, he spoke to her in words filled with purpose.

Himavat said:

26-28. Beautiful-browed woman, cause of creation, preservation and destruction, endowed with every good quality, possessing all powers and faultless, why are you grieving? Great goddess, you are capable of doing something, of changing it and of undoing it, you have achieved all your desires and you exist within all beings. Śivā, you are really not separated from Śiva because you exist in everything. Accordingly, you will unite yourself with Śiva who is the cause of your happiness.

29-31. Telling her to get up and taking hold of her, he returned to his own home and Pārvatī rejoiced when she saw Menā there with her son, yet she sighed deeply, so eager was she to see Śiva. After bowing to her father she said, "Tell me the best way–a vow, gift-giving or austerity, all of which are difficult to perform–to get Śiva. Father, as before I will undertake a most severe austerity."

Brahmā said:

32. After he had reflected in his mind for a moment, her father spoke to her about a remedy which would bring about a rapid success in this affair. Hear about it sage!

Himavat said:

33-39. Listen, Pārvatī, and I will talk about adoration to Vighnarāja. It gives accomplishment in the law, profit sensuosity and liberation and is the best way of getting Śiva. The gods, Viṣṇu etc., and the sages, Nārada etc., did it and achieved their goals, such as Indra's position, for example. Brahmā too gained the capability to create through its favour and the Lord of all, Gaṇeśa, gave Viṣṇu the capacity to protect. In addition Śiva's capability of violent destruction was due to him and the Lord of all, the remover of obstacles, gave Śeṣa the capability of supporting the Earth. The gods, Brahmā, and so forth, do not know his real appearance, nor do the sages. He is inaccessible to words and inaccessible to the mind. The Lord must be seen in his real appearance as having an elephant's face. As he is worshipped in that form at the beginning of all undertakings, worship the Lord of All in the way I have described.

CHAPTER FORTY-NINE

Description of the Ritual for an Earthen Image of Gaṇeśa

Pārvatī said:

1-2. Repository of compassion, Lord of the mountains, you are my father. Tell me at once about the worship of the Lord of all, Gaṇeśa, teacher of the worlds. I will have continual happiness after finding Śiva, something which will bring benefit for people in the world.

Himavat said,

3. Because of my affection for you, goddess, and for the benefit of beings I will tell you this auspicious, superlative, secret teaching. With your mind intent, listen!

4-17. After arising at daybreak one should go in a southwestern direction, and having first covered the ground with strips of grass and wood, whilst standing, but not crawling, the wise man should remove some dirt. After he has discharged his urine and faeces, he should make himself pure as previously described.[139] Then after he has cleaned his tongue and teeth, he should go to a river, a pond, a pool, a lake or even a well in order to bathe. After he has taken an initial bath with mud on his body, he should take a bath with water, accompanied by mantras. Then he should make a mark on his forehead with clay, sandalwood or kuṅkum powder. After he has put on two washed garments, seated himself on a clean seat and carefully completed all the obligatory rites, he should grind up some soil which is fine, soft, free of small stones, very clean, moistened with water and does not come from an anthill. And when the wise man has made himself a lovely auspicious image of Gaṇeśa resplendent with four arms and complete in all its parts,

---

[139] "as previously described": Perhaps this refers to the purification rituals prescribed at 3.13-20.

holding the appropriate weapons such as the axe etc., and after he has placed that handsome, solid image on a pedestal and has washed his hands, he should diligently assemble all the materials for worship, such as water etc., eight uncrushed perfumes, red flowers and bdellium. Then after bringing one hundred and eight excellent, pure blades of green or white dūrvā grass with three, five or seven leaves, he should bring for the Lord a ghee lamp, an oil lamp and a variety of pure offerings, comprising sweet meats, cakes, spicy sweet meats and a rice pudding with ground sugar, very fine boiled rice with juice from the khādira tree which is mixed with powdered betel nut and camphor together with various seasonings, betel mixed with cloves, cardamom and vegetable fibres as well as fruits such as those from the plantain and the grape, the rose apple, mango and bread fruit etc., and coconuts as they grow in their seasons, the appropriate instruments for many kinds of ārati offerings and something made of gold as a present for the priest.

18-24. When all the requisite materials have been brought together in this way and he is stationed in a secluded spot where he has seated himself on a seat made of kuśa grass and the skin of a black antelope, he should undertake the removal of ghosts and the stilling of breaths. Before setting the directions he should bow to the gods such as Gaṇeśa, etc., and then, in accord with the method in the Āgamas, he should consign the syllables pertaining to the inside and outside of the body and he should display hand-signs such as the saṃnidhāna etc., in accord with his teacher's method. After he has performed the consigning of letters[140] on the six parts of the body and has completely purified the implements for the ritual, he should meditate on Gajānana in his form where he has one tusk, ears like winnowing fans, an elephant's face and four arms, where he is carrying an elephant's hook and a noose and sweet meats in his hands, and where he is wearing a garland of red flowers on his neck and another lovely one on his hand. And as one who gives

[140] These verses refer to the tantric ritual of finger tracing particular letters of mantras onto specific parts of the body.

boons to his devotees, is constantly accompanied by Siddhi and Buddhi, who gives good fortune and intelligence to men and accomplishment in the law, power, sensuosity and liberation, on the one whom the supreme sages led by Brahmā, Rudra, Viṣṇu and Indra eulogize. (Meditation)

25. Come, bearer of the universe who is worshipped excellently by the gods and demons, Lord of those who have no lords, who is omniscient and worshipped by the gods. (Invocation)

26. God, sit on this celestial golden lion-throne with its many jewels that I have offered. (Seat)

27. God, Lord of the gods, Lord of all, accept this foot-ablution, consisting of water taken from all the sacred fords and contains uncrushed sacred flowers. (Foot ablution)

28. O Power Unfailing, I have given you gold,
Betel with areca nut, jewels, betel nuts, fruit,
Pearls, coral, eight fragrances and uncrushed flowers.
Make profitable this offering of water for the guest. (Water for the guest)

29. Lord, sip this water with its smell of camphor, sesamum and cloves, water of the highest quality I have requested from all the sacred fords such as the Ganges. (Water for sipping)

30. And accept this sesamum, lovely because of its softness, scented with the fragrance of the Aśoka, Campaka, mimosa, jasmine and mogara trees. (Bath for auspiciousness)

31. For your bath I have offered pure milk. It is absolutely vivifying for all beings, helps accomplish the sacrifice and has been produced by the cow of plenty. (Milk for the bath)

32. Accept this choice sour milk I have offered for your bath. All people like it, it is pure and it is produced from cow's milk. (Sour milk for the bath)

33. For your bath I have also offered ghee produced from fresh butter as it is the food of the gods, part of the sacrifice and a cause of satisfaction to everyone. (Ghee for the bath)

34. God, for your bath I have offered honey produced by the red bee. It increases everyone's fiery energy and gives nourishment to everyone. (Honey for the bath)

35. In order for you to bathe, take this ground sugar I have offered to you. It was produced from the essence of sugarcane, is quite captivating and free of impurities. (Ground sugar)

36. In order for you to bathe I have brought a treacle produced from the essence of sugar-cane. It gives nourishment, is the cause of delight for everyone, is sweet and the cause of every kind of sweetness. (Treacle)

37. Accept this mixture of honey and milk, topped up with clarified butter, honey and curds, which I have brought for your worship in a brass drinking vessel covered with brass. (The offering of honey and milk)

38. Lord of the gods, accept this well-scented water for bathing correctly. It was taken at my request from every sacred ford, Lord. (Pure water)

39. Accept this pair of red garments I have offered. They defend the modesty of the gods and are exceedingly fine and priceless. (The garment)

40. Accept, Supreme Lord, this resplendent sacred thread with its jewels and gold, offered devoutly. (Sacred thread)

41. With your permission I will place on each of your limbs these many golden ornaments encrusted with many jewels. (Ornament)

42. Be compassionate, God! On your twelve limbs I am going to smear red sandalwood of the highest quality blended with eight perfumes. (Sandalwood)

43. Lord of the world, accept this rice mixed with sandalwood paste which I am going to offer for ornamentation on your tilaka. (Uncrushed rice)

44. Lord of the Earth, accept the flower of the pātala, karṇikāra, bandhūka, red lotus, mogara and mālatī. Accept this enchanting garland with its bilva leaves set with buds and a variety of lotuses. (Flower)

46. Accept this bdellium incense I have offered for your ten limbs. It causes a pleasant smell and destroys all evil. (Incense)

47. Omniscient god! Lord of all worlds! Accept this auspicious lantern of the highest quality which removes darkness. Obeisance to you, God of gods! (The lantern)

48-52. Accept this pudding of unsurpassable cooked rice pudding with ground sugar and various kinds of cooked food which is embellished with many splendid spices and curds, milk and ghee, with cloves and cardamom as well as crushed pepper and round cakes made of pulse fried in oil and decoctions made with milk. And crushed trigonella grains with butter milk mixed in water, with rājikā grains, crushed ground beans, pepper, pumpkin, cumin seed and hiṅgu seasoning, as well as round cakes which are prepared, well-cooked and then roasted, together with pulse cakes, large round cakes, sweet meats, flour cakes and small round sweet meats. And an offering consisting of the five immortal substances[141] with thin cakes made of rice, an excellent broth with salt, hiṅgu seasoning, turmeric and salt. (Food offering)

53-55. Eat this food agreeably and drink as you will this fragrant water which instills complete satisfaction. The world is satisfied when you are satisfied, notwithstanding that you are always satisfied. Now I am going to give you well-scented water to be taken before and after the meal and I am going to give you some more water for purifying your saliva.

56-57. Accept these fruits, Lord of the gods: bread fruit, mango, apple, sweet lime, pomegranate etc., grapes, cooked plantain, jujube berries and date fruits, coconuts, oranges, figs, water melon and cucumber. And I am going to give you some more water for purifying your saliva.

58. Accept this nice sandal wood powder of the highest quality which is made from many pure substances and is to be rubbed on your body and hands. (Hand powder)

59-61ab. Accept this nice sweet smelling powder named Abira for adorning the parting of your hair. It comes from bamboo essence and contains sweet śālūra. Let it be coloured with red dye and juice from the khādira tree mixed with powdered betel nut and camphor as well as betel nut containing lotus filaments mixed with cardamom and cloves. (Betel nut)

---

[141] The five immortal substances are milk, curds, butter, honey and sugar.

61cd-62ab. God, in your presence I am going to make available an honorarium of gold in order to gain perfect results in case the ritual has too much or too little. (The honorarium)

62cd-63. Supreme Lord, accept this beautiful garland bound with auspicious lotuses and red, white and yellow flowers. (The garland)

64. And I have offered twenty-one blades of dūrvā grass having three or five yellow or white leaves. (Blades of dūrvā grass)

65. God, I will perform twenty-one circumambulations and at each step you cause my evil acts to be destroyed, Lord of the gods. (Circumambulation)

66. Accept these visually pleasant lamps placed in a vessel made of gold, brass, silver or copper. (The waving of the lights)

67. Supreme Lord, accept this ārati lamp fired by five wicks. It is a lamp and, like a pleasant moon, it prevents one from going astray. And just as its ashes are purificatory, so must you remove evil.

68. Then seating oneself and making one's mind absolutely immoveable, one should eulogize him with various kinds of eulogies, wise-sayings and recitations of his one thousand names.

69. "Lord of the weak, repository of compassion
God, waited upon by the hosts,
Eulogized by the perfected ones, Girijā, Śeṣa,
Viṣṇu, Śiva, Brahmā and the brahmins,
Hindrance of all evils, utterly skilful,
Lord of the triple-world, Lord,
Make my devotion fruitful!
Forbear with all my transgressions!"

70. Goddess, after worshipping the image in this way and bowing prostrate, one should recite this mantra to the one who gives absolute perfection.

CHAPTER FIFTY

The Tale of the Vow of the Fourth during the Conversation between Pārvatī and Himavat

Pārvatī said:

1. I do not know that mantra, Lord of the mountains, so tell it to me so that I can obtain Gaṇeśa's favour and approach Śiva auspiciously.

Himavat said:

2. Goddess, there are a variety of mantras which give a great variety of perfections and those mantras of Gaṇeśa are without number, but I will tell you some of them.

3-6. One who has completed placing letters on his body and has already assumed the appropriate lotus position and completely controlled the apertures of his body,[142] should then undertake a recitation suitable to his own inclination. A hundred thousand or fifty thousand mantras of one syllable, a million or ten thousand mantras of six syllables, ten thousand mantras with five, eight or ten syllables or of twenty-eight syllables should be recited. Various types of these kinds of mantras can be recited for the accomplishment of one's wishes. Now, Pārvatī, with your mind fully concentrated, listen to my speech.

7-15ab. Strong-vowed woman, take this excellent mantra which has one syllable, and this one which has six syllables, and make your beginning on the fourth day of the bright half of the month of Śravaṇa. Perform this personal service for just one month and it will be enough. You will easily obtain Śiva and any other thing you want. When a man or a woman worships a single earthen image they are given whatever is desired such as wealth, sons, cattle, and so on. By worshipping two images a man will achieve the unachievable, and by worshipping three

---

[142] "controlled the apertures of his body" niyamya khāni: M takes this to refer to the senses, which is a valid alternative.

images he obtains a kingdom, jewels and success in everything. Whoever would attain accomplishment in the law, power, sensuosity and liberation should worship four images, and by worshipping five images one will gain the entire earth. By the worship of six images one will become the cause of creation, preservation and destruction, and by the worship of seven, eight or nine images one becomes omniscient and by god's favour knows the past, present and future. By worshipping ten images the thirty-five thousand myriads of gods including Śiva, Viṣṇu, Indra and Agni, as well as the hosts of sages such as Sanaka etc., are worshipped. By the worship of eleven images one becomes overlord of the eleven Rudras and by worshipping twelve images one will obtain the kingship over the twelve Ādityas.

15cd-19. During exceptionally difficult times one should perform worship with an increasing number of images up to the number of one hundred and eight and one will obtain as much as that.[143] By performing one hundred thousand rituals day after day one obtains a great liberation. One who wishes for release from a prison should construct five images and after twenty-one nights he will be released by Gaṇeśa's favour, daughter. That man who is devoted to Gaṇeśa and produces seven images each day for five years will be freed from great evils. From birth to death a man might worship one image made of earth, but Gaṇeśa, Vighnanāśana, can be known only when he is seen.[144]

20-33. A person should worship Gaṇādhipa in respect of all his activities because the god will certainly be pleased with his rite, even if the person himself is not. When experiencing pain from any kind of disease one should worship three images of the highest quality for nine days and all pain will be removed. If an image is made of gold, silver, copper, yellow brass, pearls or coral, it gives absolutely everything. When a vow of the

---

[143] "one will obtain as much as that": tāvat tattad avāpnuyāt: Does this mean that one will obtain as much in quantity as that with which one worships?

[144] "only when he is seen" darśanād: That is, an appearance initiated by Gaṇeśa, which is the principal way in which a bhakti deity makes himself known to his devotees.

following kind has been completed, you will obtain your wish, goddess. As soon as the fourth day in the month of Bhādrapada has arrived a great festival should be diligently performed on that day to the extent of one's resources. One must stay awake at night by listening to songs, music and stories about him. At the clear daybreak, after having bathed, one should worship the boon-giver, the Lord Gaṇeśa, as before. Then one should begin the offering in the fire. In a pit, a subsidiary pit or on plain ground one should sacrifice, the oblations offered being a tenth of the number of recitations made. One should then offer an oblation signalling the end of the ritual and then a bali offering. Afterwards one should honour one's teacher with money, a cow and a piece of land, then satisfy the brahmins and complete the rest of the fire sacrifice. With a tenth portion of that one should satiate the deceased fathers and with another portion one should feed the brahmins who know the Vedas, their wives and anyone else. One should give them clothes, ornaments and an honorarium in accord with one's capacity to do so, and one should give corselets to the women and young girls. One should not cheat in money matters when nourishing Gaṇanātha with Siddhi and Buddhi, rather one should conduct oneself to the extent of one's wealth. Then one should diligently consume a meal with one's friends and on a later day, one should joyfully place an image on a vehicle drawn by men which should be beautifully adorned with gods, flags, banners and umbrellas, and preceded by youths fighting battles with staves. Going then to a large lake, one should get into the water, throw the image in and return to one's house to the accompaniment of tunes, songs and music.

CHAPTER FIFTY-ONE

Pārvatī said:

1-4. I am pleased with your immortal words, father, but remove this doubt that I still have, Himālaya! Who previously performed this vow, Earth-holder, who described it to whom and who gained what success from it? Answer this in detail and remove my doubt. The person who asks about the auspicious tale of Gajānana, the one who speaks about it and the other who hears about it are three people who partake of merit and their birth, life, knowledge and actions are fruitful.

Brahmā said:

5. She put this particular question and Himavat told her about the many people who performed this vow for the boon-giving Gaṇeśa.

The Mountain said:

6. Pārvatī, listen and I will narrate this old discussion which contains a traditional account of that vow that causes absolute success.

7-8ab. Once when Śiva, the teacher of the world, was comfortably seated on Kailāsa, the best of mountains, amusing himself happily with the gods, heavenly musicians and supreme sages, six-faced Skanda, whose fiery energy is great, questioned him after having bowed to him and eulogized him.

Skanda said:

8cd-11ab. God of gods, Lord of the worlds, cause of security for your devotees, through your favour I have heard many celestial tales, but father, I have still not had enough, even after having drunk that ambrosia-like liquid. Now, tell me about the god's auspicious vow conferring success on every ambition, the performance of which produces successes which fall into the hands of accomplished men because of the boon-giver's favour.

Śiva said:

11cd-12. What you have asked is good, Skanda, as it promotes everyone's good. Son, I will gladly tell you about that vow pleasing to Gaṇeśa which is the best of vows and gives huge success in the world.

13-17. Skanda, son of the Kṛttikās, even without prayers, offerings, and so on, and without sacrifices and gifts, it is effective in respect of all the aims of men. Skanda, it causes absolute success, increases one's sons and grandsons and in addition, this superlative vow quickly brings a king or a prince as well as their advisers under subjection. The power of that vow instantly frees a man from great and lesser evils accrued over many lives. A man on the Earth is a vessel for all successes, but on the Earth there is nothing giving satisfaction like that vow of Gaṇeśa.

Skanda said:

18. Father, in what month should this superlative vow occur, what rules are pertinent to it and who previously performed it? If you have compassion for me, tell me all about it!

Śiva said:

19-24. On the fourth day of the bright half of the month of Nabhaḥ, after bathing one should go to one's teacher's house where, after bowing to the teacher, subsequently honouring him according to the ritual and gratifying him with the very best of ornaments, clothes and water for purifying the mouth and feet, one should duly begin the vow with his permission, saying, "Lord, you alone are the illustrious Gaṇeśa, so teach me the vow of Gaṇeśa which brings about absolute success and gives what one wants, Venerable teacher." After he has taught the vow, one should accompany him to the bank of the Ganges or to a pool excavated by the gods, and one should bathe in it according to the precept, smearing oneself with wet dough made of sesamum, mustard and Dhatrī, and after performing the obligatory rite, one should return home, six-faced Skanda. Then after sitting on a clean seat and worshipping Gaṇādhipa, one should begin the vow in the manner of the teacher's instructions.

25-30. After making an image of Gaṇeśa out of clay on the fourth day of Śravaṇa, one should worship it daily until the fourth day of Bhādra. Remaining in a vow of celibacy one should perform the vow of the highest quality by fasting, eating only one meal or by not asking for food at night. In the evening of every second day, being in a composed state the devotee should eat food appropriate for sacred occasions. and he should perform the vow whilst eating sweet honey. Daily recitation is then prescribed, six-faced Skanda, irrespective of whether one recites a mantra of Gaṇeśvara which has six syllables, eight syllables or indeed, just one syllable, ten syllables, Skanda, or even twelve syllables, a million or just ten thousand. And whilst meditating tirelessly day and night on the god Gajānana, one should perform a fire sacrifice of ten parts, half of that or half of that.

31-41. When the fourth day of the month of Bhādra has come one should construct out of gold, to the amount of a pala or half of that, an auspicious image of Gajānana having a rat or a peacock as his vehicle. After constructing a small pavilion, one should then place a quantity of grain in it, after which one should set up a gold, silver or copper plate on which a lid of gold, silver or copper should be placed. After wrapping up the lid and the water pot, containing five blossoms and five jewels, in two pieces of cloth one should, to the accompaniment of root mantras and mantras described earlier, place the Lord on a seat which has previously been set up for his worship, six-faced Skanda. After meditating on the god Gajānana and evoking him with the highest joy, one should provide the seat, the foot ablution, water for sipping from the palm and, Skanda, a bath containing water to be offered to the guest and gems, rendered auspicious by the immortal foods. A pair of red garments and a sacred thread of the highest quality should also be provided. One should then adorn the supreme Lord with ornaments of various kinds, uncrushed fragrants, incense, lights and various kinds of offerings. And one should feed the supreme Lord with a rice pudding, boiled rice, sweet meats, cakes and cakes of fried pulse etc., the five immortal foods and seasonings. Then one should place some unguent on his hand, also some fruit and betel nut and give an honorarium of gold, an umbrella, a fan and a fly-whisk. After one has offered flowers with the recitation of mantras and has waved some lights before the image, one should recite some eulogies and one should honour the brahmins after reciting the one thousand names.

42-47ab. Remaining awake during the night to the accompaniment of auspicious singing and dancing, bathing and performing the obligatory rite according to the precept when the clear dawn breaks, one should worship the god as aforesaid. One should then perform a fire sacrifice and after making an offering with various sacrificial substances, one should honour one's teacher by presenting the teacher with gold, sesamum, land and cows etc., and to the other brahmins one should give an extensive honorarium. Afterwards one should feed one hundred and eight brahmins, more if one has the capacity, otherwise just twenty-one. And to the weak, blind and miserable one should give food including rice pudding and on receipt of an excellent benediction one should once again offer an honorarium. One should then silently and diligently feed oneself, one's friends and relatives.

Śiva said:

47cd-48. Skanda, I have just narrated to you the auspicious vow of the boon-giver which gives liberation and carnal enjoyment to men as well as bringing every desire to fruition. On this very subject I am now going to tell you an old tale.

49-52ab. Once there was a king named Kardama who was greatly occupied with the Law. He protected the ocean-bounded Earth with his own power and captivated by his good qualities, the gods remained constantly in his house. Once due to the influence of fate Bhṛgu went to his house, whereupon, after standing up, the king beckoned him, whose great esteem precedes him, to a splendid seat and honoured him as if he were his teacher. Whilst that best of sages was eating the king addressed this speech to him.

The king said:

52cd-57ab. Illustrious sage who knows all truths, answer whatever I ask you! Who was I in a previous birth and what good action did I perform which has caused me to get a kingdom like this which is free of enemies, one which other kings did not get and which others will not get? Even gods, demons, snakes and heavenly musicians honour me! Sage, behold my wealth which is the equal of Kubera's fortune. Any jewel-like thing that exists in the triple-world is brought here by its own power. Any object I wish for, I see in my house. Tell me what karma has brought this about, Lord, because I want to continue acting in a way conducive to merit,[145] best of meritorious men.

Bhṛgu said:

57cd-63. Most splendid of kings, I will tell you this because of your respectful conduct. In your previous existence you were an undefiled, but weak, warrior, undertaking activities in order to support your household. Yet the work you were doing yielded no result for you. Hurt by the terribly harsh words of your wife and children, you went to the impenetrable forest without first having consulted your sons and wife. Wandering about all over the place you saw Saubhari whilst he was in the siddha posture surrounded by the bulls of sages and reciting great wisdom to his pupils that was destructive of anguish. On seeing the celestial Saubhari and the other groups of sages, King, you fell prostrate to the ground and they greeted you, and when he directed you to do so, you sat on the sage's seat. Obtaining a favourable moment, you respectfully questioned that celestial sage.

The warrior said:

64-66ab. Lord, I am tormented terribly by the anguish caused by recurring existence and I have been terribly wounded by the wordy barbs of my friends, wife and children. Even so my heart

---

[145] "acting in a way conducive to merit" puṇyam: That is, perform actions which, because they are ajudged to be meritorious, will lead to positive rebirths in the future.

feels no loathing towards my cruel friends, but I am terribly distressed by thirst, hunger, heat and cold, sage. Tell me some way of passing over this ocean of anguish.

Śiva said:

66cd-67. After he had heard his speech Saubhari became filled with pity and he thought about a way to destroy his anguish. Then he spoke to the warrior about freeing him from all his evil.

The sage said:

68-70. I will tell you about a vow which you must perform with a resolute mind. Merely by performing it there will be an end to all your anguish. Brahmins, kṣatriyas and vaiśyas as well as brahmanical sages who have performed it have become free of all anguish and have obtained the unsurpassed perfection of the boon-giver, Gaṇeśa. It gives accomplishment in the law, power, sensuosity and liberation.

CHAPTER FIFTY-TWO

The Traditional Narration in the Conversation between Himavat and Pārvatī

The warrior said:

1. Who indeed is this Gaṇeśa? What is his nature, his appearance and his innate disposition? What does he do and how did he originate? Tell me everything!

The sage said:

2-7. That one is Brahma, eternal, without impetuosity, without grief,

Whose form is knowledge, who is the highest truth.

The good call him Gaṇādhipa,

As being without beginning, middle or end and of boundless width.

The sound om originates from him, the Vedas originate from him and the world originates from him. He pervades all this. Know him to be Gaṇanāyaka. Wishing to create the world, Brahmā performed very severe austerities for one hundred full years in order to gratify him. He became pleased and Brahmā then ecstatically worshipped him with various kinds of ritual actions, celestial jewels and fruits. He also gave him two young women named Siddhi and Buddhi and the gratified god, the Lord gave him a one-syllable mantra. The boon gained, Brahmā then created the entire world.

8-9ab. Previously Viṣṇu had gratified him with the six-syllable mantra. After he had completed a vow before an image of Gaṇeśa as described previously, Viṣṇu undertook an austerity for an entire year, and once he had obtained a boon from Gaṇeṣa, he protected the worlds.

9cd-10. You must understand that Gaṇeśa is praised on Earth as the one whose form consists of everything, as being without a beginning and as being the cause of all causes. Propitiate him zealously and you will be free of all anguish.

The warrior said:

11. Tell me now, Excellent sage, in what month should this unsurpassed vow be performed and by what precept?

The sage said:

12-13ab. On the fourth day of the dark half of the month of Śravaṇa, one should begin this vow and perform it with deep devotion until the fourth day of Bhādra. Perform it and you will attain all your wishes, Protector of the Earth.

13cd-17ab. After hearing[146] about this vow from him, you performed it, Strong-vowed king. As soon as the vow was completed in Saubhari's hermitage, his house[147] became celestial due to Gaṇeśa's favour. It became filled with celestial men and women, male and female servants, the sound of the Vedas and herds of cattle. His wife found herself clothed with celestial garments and adorned with many ornaments, and amazed by this, she waited expectantly with her offspring. But wondering, "When will my husband return?" she became quite anxious.

17cd-19. In the meantime, having bid farewell to the sage, you set out for your home. After leaving his celestial refuge you were searching for your own house until men who had been sent by your wife brought you back to the house. Then you really understood the power of the boon-giver and you now possess this kingdom in this life because of the power of that vow which is his.

Śiva said:

20-22ab. After he had heard Bhṛgu's speech, King Kardama became filled with joy and did everything Bhṛgu had ordered and through the power of that vow, the king came to possess detachment and intuitive knowledge. After he had indulged his carnal pleasures according to his desire and had established his sons on his own position, he went to the abode of Gaṇeśvara, from where one does not return again.

22cd-25ab. Skanda, that vow of vows is of the highest order and it causes the accomplishment of every aim. No other vow is as munificent as this vow, Skanda, so if you want to accomplish all your aims perform this vow. Heavenly musicians, dānavas, gods, sages and humans have performed it and so too have Nala,

---

[146] "after hearing": Here Bhṛgu takes up the narrative again and speaks directly to Kardama.

[147] "his house": That is, the king"s house after it has been enriched by Gaṇeśa"s favour.

Indumatī and King Candrāṅgada. They attained all their wishes and went to Gaṇeśvara's heaven.

The mountain said:

25cd-26. Everything about this great vow, including a traditional tale, has been narrated to you. Perform this vow after you have meditated in your mind on the boon-giving Gaṇanāyaka. Then, Illustrious lady, you will get Śiva. I have narrated this to you out of affection, but do not reveal this vow.

CHAPTER FIFTY-THREE

Description of Nala's Vow in the Conversation between Himavat and Pārvatī

Pārvatī said:

1. Who is Nala and why did he perform it? Tell me, father, because my mind relaxes when I listen to a short tale.

Himavat said:

2-5. Once there was a great king of the Niṣādas named Nala who was devoted to the brahmins, versed in the Vedas, a hero, generous, highly esteemed, wealthy and sage. A mighty warrior, he possessed a chariot, a sword, a bow and armour and he was accomplished in weapons, honoured by the gods, moved amongst the three worlds and was undefiled. To describe his good qualities sends even Śeṣa to silence, and of his horses, elephants, chariots, sword-bearers and bearers of fire-weapons, there is no reckoning. The gods led by Indra and also the Lords of the directions trembled because they were afraid of him.

6-8. His wife named Damayantī was an abode of beauty and she was called Damayantī because after subduing all things and taking the best parts, Brahmā created her. Damayantī represents the loveliness and sensuosity of women in the triple-world.

Furnished with many ornaments, adorned with a variety of jewellery, her neck sparkling with a pearl necklace, she shone with beauty and she was also rich in good qualities.

9-10. His excellent minister, the courageous Padmahasta, was the equal of Bṛhaspati in intelligence, the equal of Aṅgiras in polity, like Mt. Meru in stature and the equal of the ocean in depth.

11-13. Once the very proud King Nala entered his assembly hall and sat down in the midst of a circle of kings. Nymphs of beautiful demeanour danced before him and his bards eulogized him in conjunction with his hosts of sages and brahmins. But at that very moment Gautama came to the king and after the king had stood up, he respectfully ushered him into his own seat and honoured him devoutly. After that Nala questioned him.

Nala said:

14-15. I am favoured by your appearance, Great sage, so now my birth, my kingdom, my mother, my family and my life are fruitful. Quickly now, Great sage, tell me the cause of your coming here!

Gautama said:

16-17. King, I have a great desire to see your wealth which the gods in heaven such as Brahmā, Indra, Viṣṇu and Śiva, the trident bearer, praise. You are indeed wealthy in the world of mortals and you are praised by gods and mortals. Although I am always pleased, I am truly pleased having witnessed your rite of honour and your wealth. Now give me your assent and I will return to my hermitage.

The king said:

18. Knower of the Vedas and Vedāṅgas, brahmin, originator of all the śāstras, ocean of compassion, stay a moment and remove my doubt, sage.

The sage said:

19. Well asked, Great king. I will stay because I like you, but also because nāgas, kings and gods do not transgress your commands.

The king said:

20-21ab. Brahmin, I too am amazed when observing my own wealth. By what merit or austerity did this situation come about? Tell me truly, who was I in a previous birth?

The sage said:

22cd-28. In a city called Pippala which was in a country far from Gauḍadeśa you were previously a poor warrior who was undefiled and wise. Terribly wounded by the wordy barbs of your friends, wife and children, you went in disgust to a dense forest without first consulting anyone. It was filled with trees and creepers, lions, tigers, elephants and deer, lakes of cool water, aquatic plants and so forth. Whilst you were wandering here and there in the forest you saw the hermitage of Kauśika, that receptacle of austerities, which resounded with the sounds of the Vedas being chanted. After entering there you bowed to the sage because of your devotion for him. Being compassionate towards the poor and the helpless, Kauśika made you get up and observing you to be distressed he uttered this benediction, "My Gajānana, the Lord of the gods, will bring good fortune to you." After you had heard that benediction, you became very joyful, Gentle man. Then, King, you asked the brahmin about that way which gives every desire, destroys poverty, gives liberation and carnal enjoyment, and is generally favourable.

29. Kauśika then told you about the worship of Gaṇeśa.

Kauśika said:

30-31ab. Lord of men, perform Gaṇeśa's vow for just one month. Make a beautiful looking clay image of Gaṇeśa, then perform the rite according to the precept as mentioned before and listen to a short tale everyday for just a month and you will then attain success.

The sage said:

31cd. When he had heard this the protector of the earth again questioned Kauśika.

The king said:

32. I do not know this Gajānana. Describe his real appearance to me and once I have known the Lord of the god of gods, I will perform that vow of the highest quality.

33-34ab. When he had put that very question to him in such a way, that excellent sage described to him the modifications of his real form which Gajānana has effected, his true form being indescribable since it is that of the supreme Brahma.

Kauśika said:

34cd-35ab. He is the creator of all beings, their father and mother and the teacher of the world and it is upon that very Gajānana that Brahmā, Indra, Viṣṇu and Śiva meditate.

The sage said:

35cd-40. After you had heard his speech and had bowed to the Lord of sages, he gave you leave and you went to your own home. Then on the fourth day of the bright half of Śravaṇa, having begun that vow which is of the highest order, you made an image of Gaṇeśa out of clay just as prescribed and irrespective of whether you were standing, talking, silent, moving, sleeping or eating, you were meditating on the god Gajānana and so you attained unsurpassed prosperity including many elephants, chariots and horses etc., herds of cattle and heaps of money. By the power of that vow you became prosperous, endowed with male and female servants. You then gave gifts to everyone for the gratification of the gods and you joyfully constructed a very valuable temple for Gaṇeśa. Then after you had experienced carnal delights according to your wont, in time you died.

41-42. You were born in the Niṣāda country, you became a king named Nala, and from that time permanent prosperity has befallen you and you are praised by the people of the triple-world. Allow me to go now, as what you asked has been answered.

Himavat said:

43-44. So after Gautama had gone, King Nala performed that vow. He was filled with confidence because of that speech[148] and after constructing a very beautiful image and hearing Gaṇeśa's tale every day out of devotion to that one worthy of worship, he obtained all his desires by the power of that vow..

45. Beautiful-browed Pārvatī, I have just narrated to you how Nala performed that vow, the vow which Gautama described, just as it had been performed in his previous life. Nobody now is able to describe his abundant wealth.

CHAPTER FIFTY-FOUR

The Tale of Candrāṅgada

Himavat said:

1. Now I will relate what King Candrāṅgada and his wife Indumatī did, beautiful-faced Pārvatī.

2-5. In the Mālava region there was a famous city called Karṇa. The king there was the very courageous Candrāṅgada and he possessed qualities such as the capacity to make himself small and so forth, he knew the true meaning of all the śāstras, performed sacrifices, was munificent, extremely magnanimous and thoroughly conversant with the Vedas and the Vedāṅgas.

---

[148] "that speech": That is, Gautama's speech.

His divine assembly hall, which surpassed Sudharmā, enraptures the eyes and its utterly pellucid screens suspended from jewelled columns become variegated into yellows, dark blues and reds due to motes of light beautiful as the sun's splendour.

6-7. His very virtuous wife was illustrious and delighted in being obedient to her husband, her disposition was of the law, she was completely loyal and served her in-laws. Moreover, she was steady in respect of household duties and she honoured guests and the gods. The king, whose disposition was also of the law, was often sought out by his ministers.

8-15. Under the influence of fate he once went to a forest teeming with birds, deer, wild boars and antelope in order to amuse himself by hunting. Mailed in dark armour, a covering over his blue turban, wearing a finger protector and an arm protector, carrying a knife, shield and sword, the powerful warrior was mounted on his speedy horse, his bows in his hand, surrounded by multitudes of troops, advisers and attendants. Whilst he was killing wild boar and game and despatching it to the city, some bulls of rākṣasas saw the king wandering in the forest. When he saw the rākṣasas, their mouths like caves, their eyes hollow, their mouths gaping and tall as the sky, he trembled as if he were suffering from feverish cold fits. All his warriors and attendants fled after they saw them, and some went to Yama's abode, whilst others passed out and fell to the ground. After spotting the king there, who was terribly handsome like Kāma, one fierce rākṣasa woman, infatuated with desire, embraced and kissed him, but putting his ministers in her coils, she devoured his attendants.

16-21. Desperate to leave, the king left immediately and submerged himself in a pond so that the rākṣasa woman could not find him. He was then seized by some snake women who took him to a palace in the underworld. The snake maidens adorned him with clothes, ornaments and jewels and then they asked him, "Where have you come from, who are you, to whom do you belong and what are you called? Speak truly, Best of men." On hearing their speech, the overlord of men said to them, "I am called Candrāṅgada, powerful son of Hemāṅgada, and my home is in the city of Karṇa in the Mālava region. I was frightened terribly by a rākṣasa woman, entered a large pond and you ladies brought me here. Now I have answered your question. All my people were eaten whilst they were engaged in hunting with me and I am alive now only with the help of this pond water."

22ab. After hearing his speech, they then addressed the king again.

They said:

22cd-23. Become our husband now and you will succeed in everything you like as well as sexually enjoying us snake women, something that is exceptionally rare.

24-27. After he had heard this speech the excellent king said, "Mothers, I have vowed only to have one wife! How can I give that up? I will tell you the rules pertaining to those kings who are descendants of the lunar dynasty. These virtuous and gentle kings seek neither to reproach others, nor do they seek the wives of others, nor the injury of others, nor the property of others. Study, sacrificing, generosity, protecting those who come for refuge, not doing what is forbidden and preserving the precepts which pertain to the aims of life are the rules of the three classes. In respect of the brahmin class there are three rules, sacrificing etc., but hospitality is the best and is considered by all the classes to be superior."

28-30. After they had heard the king's words the young snake women became depressed and cursed him, "Be often separated from your wife." Distressed because they were agitated with lust, they bound him with iron chains. But the rākṣasa woman too was still not entirely satiated, even though because of him she had consumed the water in the pond and eaten the fish.

31-40. Meanwhile, whilst standing in her palanquin his lotus-eyed queen heard the tale from his own messenger who had escaped from the rākṣasa woman. Distressed after hearing about the king who was sunk in misfortune, she fell onto the ground, where, falling into a deep faint, she was fanned by her friends.

Weeping women repeatedly sprinkled her with cool water when she sat up, but she continued weeping and striking her breasts, head and face. And with loud cries she grieved, crying out, "Oh dear husband! Where has my husband gone now that he has abandoned me? I am pleasant in speech, perfect in every limb, submissive, I show kindness and I am constantly devoted to the command of my husband and constantly honour guests. Where will my husband eat and where will he sleep, now that he has given up his golden bed covered with the best bedclothes? And seeing that he has left behind his scented oil, how will my lovely husband bathe? Without him, who now will undertake the protection of the people and who the conciliating of children and of all people and beings in general? Has this receptacle of good qualities, this receptacle of majesty, now gone to his death? Without that great man the regions look empty to me. Where will I find happiness and where will he find happiness? Wretched high born women only experience happiness in this or the other world because of their husband. Happiness only occurs with a husband. And who will undertake the protection of the poor and those who come for refuge?"

41-42. Crying out many things like this the miserable woman became terribly distressed and tearing off ornaments, she left them far away. She then broke all her bracelets and passed out.

CHAPTER FIFTY-FIVE

The Conversation between Indumatī and Nārada

Pārvatī said:

1. What did the people do after she had passed out? Father, tell me this at length as it gladdens my heart.

Himavat said:

2. After they had wiped away their tears all the townspeople, skilled in various kinds of discourses, pondered deeply about the king's wife.

The people said:

3-10. Mother! Get up! Do not grieve! Think of your son! A tear of grief burns the dead, so be positive about your husband. For amongst mortals never has one appeared who is long-lived, Lady of the beautiful face. In the same way as people take another garment after they have thrown away a worn out one, so it is with the body. After giving up one body, another good one is taken, Lovely lady. It is quite extraordinary! A person who stands in the face of his own death and is himself subject to the law of death, grieves about another's death, but he does not think about a future separation from his own body. Everything, beginning with Brahmā and ending with stationary objects, including the universe with the ocean and moving and unmoving things, as well as ourselves, is considered to be in the power of fate and time. Accept that he is perishable, abandon your grief and get up, Pretty mother! Your husband is righteous and of a meritorious disposition and might have attained liberation, but if he is in heaven, he will return alive at some time. Now we are going to question a certain sage who has arrived here and has knowledge of the past and future. He will tell us everything. After that we are going to determine whatever must be done.

11-13. In this way Indumatī was quickly roused up by the people and, consoled by their collective statement, she wiped away her tears with her dress and then dismissed all the people who had assembled. Having got rid of all her marks of prosperity[149] she became quite haggard and stood crying, grieving and sighing, and for a while she fainted.

14-15. After twelve years had passed Nārada, celestial of appearance, came by chance to her house whilst he was rambling about. On seeing him, she lamented, immediately began speaking about her husband's situation and told him of

---

[149] "Having got rid of...": I presume this refers back to her discarding of her ornaments narrated at 1.54.41.

the distress she had endured for twelve years. After hearing her weeping, the sage spoke in order to gladden her.

Nārada said:

16-17. Do not grieve for your husband wherever he is. After veiling your head with a blue cloth, you must deck yourself with ornaments on your ears, wear auspicious saffron on your brow, bracelets on your wrists and a lovely thread around your neck.

Himavat said:

18-22. She was encouraged by the command of that truthful, omniscient sage and straight away, having caused everything to be brought, she rejoiced and did what he said. After first honouring Nārada and then inviting and honouring all the brahmins, she gave them all many gifts. Then in her joy the beautiful Indumatī had musical instruments played, sent sugar to each house and imparted her authority to the people with gifts of clothes and betel nuts. After she had respectfully bowed again to the sage Nārada, that king's daughter then inquired about the way to regain her husband.

Indumatī said:

23. Sage, where is my husband? How is he? Knower of the Vedas, by what means will he appear to me?

Nārada said:

24-28. I am going to tell you succinctly about an excellent vow which should be begun with great joy on the fourth day of the bright half of Nabhaḥ. After first making a resolve to perform the ritual and cleaning the teeth, one should have a bath at daybreak in a river, a tank or a pond. After then returning home, clothed in white, one should make an excellent, captivating clay image of Gaṇeśa with the appropriate four arms and one should resolutely worship it with the sixteen ritual practices or one should diligently take for oneself one portion of one meal per day. But if wealthy and distinguished one should put on a large festival with songs, music and food for the brahmins.

29-30ab. Perform this vow, lovely lady, and you will be reunited with your husband who has been living in captivity with the snake-maidens in Pātāla. Lovely lady, I am telling you the truth and what I say in truth is never false.

Himavat said:

30cd-35.The sage having said this to her, she diligently began the vow after the sage had left. Some days after the month of Nabhaḥ had come, she made an image of Gaṇeśa from auspicious earth in accord with the precepts described before and performed a charming ritual employing celestial fragrances, celestial garments and celestial flowers as well as many kinds of celestial offerings of fruit and gold. And with lights, handfuls of flowers, processions, acts of obeisance, eulogies, mental recitations of his names and meditations, she gratified the Lord. And to the accompaniment of songs, music, dancing etc., and gifts to the brahmins, and after she had drunk milk to the measure of four karṣas, she performed that vow of the highest quality in order to regain her husband who had been lost for so long. In accord with the sage Nārada's command it began on the fourth day of the bright half of Nabhaḥ and continued until the fourth day of Bhādra.

CHAPTER FIFTY-SIX

The Union of Śiva and Pārvatī

Himavat said:

1-8ab. After the vow was completed the snake maidens in the underworld had a change of heart because of Gaṇeśa's favour. They released the king and honoured him according to the precept with clothes and ornaments, many jewels and great wealth. After they had given the king a horse, swift as thought, they sent him out and when he had got outside of the pond and bound the horse to a large tree, some of the townspeople saw the king whilst he was bathing. After they had bowed to him, some of them asked him, "Who are you, where do you live, where have you come from and what is your name? Tell us Lord!" On hearing their speech, the excellent king, pressed with exhaustion, asked after the good health of the youthful Indumatī. The people immediately recognized him then, embraced him and said, "King, your wife has bathed and has now gone home. She has been fasting during a vow and has become lean, a veritable mass of veins. Having adopted this kind of existence whilst still young, she is now barely alive.

8cd-13ab. But others had gone to the city and declared the news to the beautiful woman and once she heard from those very reliable people about the coming of the king, she became immersed in an ocean of bliss like a yogin who gains knowledge of Brahma. Then she sent his ministers to him preceded by a body of soldiers, whilst she had the city beautified with bright coloured banners and flags. After she had diligently prepared the assembly hall and sprinkled the roads, she adorned herself with jewels, ornaments and clothes. Then she gratified the many brahmins with cows, land, gold and gifts etc., and once she had put the ārati in the hand of a reputable woman she went from the city to a lake, accompanied by singing and music.

13cd-18, But having already left and made obeisance to the bull of kings, all the ministers in turn joyfully embraced the king and bowed down to him. And when the king sat down, they too sat down with his permission. After he had satisfied all of them in turn with inquiries about their health and so on, and had honoured the people by giving them clothes and betel nuts, the excellent king went to Indumatī's regal encampment. Then he had a ritual performed by the brahmins due to his appearance after twelve years and after first worshipping Gaṇeśa, proclaiming the day to be auspicious and appropriately honouring Śiva and the brahmins with honorariums etc., he broke a bilva fruit, and leaving there he went to her. Then he saw Indumatī and she was like the thirteenth digit of the moon.

19-28. After she had made young women and their husbands wave lights around the king, she had the maidens shower him with flowers and rice grains, at the same time wiping her eyes which were flooded with tears of joy. Full of joy and grief, these two then addressed, each other and unhindered by their grief they spoke of the anxiety caused by their mutual separation, until they were comforted by the ministers' ample words. Fetching the king they mounted him upon a huge elephant embellished with many ornaments, adorned with umbrellas and flags, resplendent with four bells and accompanied by foot soldiers. One hundred ushers were restraining it and many warriors holding fire and swords, and mounted on horses and riding in chariots went before it. On the left and right of the king a hundred thousand elephants moved easily and in front came bards, musicians and dancers who were dancing, singing and playing music, whilst rows of elephants carefully entered the city from the rear. But the sun, being covered with the dust of the troops, nothing was recognizable in that well decorated city which was without a king. Then after each had bowed to the other they went to their own homes, but the chiefs were brought to the palace and were again honoured by the king. They went home after the king had given his authorization by means of gifts of clothes and betel nut and after he had fed the priests, he ate with his kinsmen.

29-30. During the night the two slept on a beautifully made bed covered with the best quilts and furnished with coverings and cushions, yet grieving repeatedly, they both still spoke about their distress. But when soothed by the domestic chaplain they slept happily thereafter.

31-32. When the excellent king heard about the power of the vow of Vināyaka, he resolved himself to do everything done by his wife, and when the month of Śravaṇa came, King Candrāṅgada performed this vow in a great festival, beautiful faced woman.

The sage said:

33-38ab. After she had heard her father's speech, Pārvatī became extremely joyful and the month of Nabhaḥ having been reached, she diligently performed a vow. After she had diligently constructed an image and performed the rite according to the precept, and whilst she was consuming a small portion of milk and meditating on Dviradānana, Śaṅkara's heart began to waver and the trident-bearing Śiva came himself to Pārvatī's hermitage. And on Gaṇeśa's fourth when that auspicious vow had been completed the goddess saw Śiva in her own hermitage mounted on a bull. After getting up she bowed joyfully before his pair of lotus feet and honoured Śiva, who is beneficent to people, according to precept. Agitated by love, Pārvatī then spoke to Śiva.

The goddess said:

38cd-40. How could you abandon me and leave and why did you forget me? Even a moment separated from you was like an enormous period of time, Lord, so I performed this vow of Gaṇeśa which my father taught me and through the boon-giver's favour you have appeared.

Brahmā said:

41-44. At that very moment Himavat arrived and respectfully placed his hand in Pārvatī's hand, after which the gods, including the heavenly musicians, respectfully worshipped Dviradānana and, afterwards, the two Śivas, they who act benignly towards the good. Celestial drums sounded and showers of flowers fell and every one praised Gajānana with various eulogies after they had bowed to him. Śiva too gratified Dviradānana with words of triumph, then after incorporating Parvatī into half of his body and mounting a bull, he quickly went to the peak of Kailāsa and all the gods went to their own homes.

Brahmā said:

45-46. I have narrated everything, Vyāsa, which you asked about the "Glorification of the Vow" and of Gaṇanātha, Great sage. Now I am going to tell you yet another small tale, after the hearing of which a man will be freed from all his evils and will attain his desires.

CHAPTER FIFTY-SEVEN

The Conversation between Indra and Śūrasena

Bhṛgu said:

1. I have told you the Glorification in its entirety, King, and now hear once more what Vyāsa heard from Brahmā's mouth.

Somakānta said:

2. What did Vyāsa of immeasurable intellect, hear from Brahmā's mouth? Tell me, great sage, because I have still not had enough.

Bhṛgu said:

3. After he had heard this,[150] Vyāsa respectfully asked Brahmā for another tale and, faultless man, he diligently recited for that inquisitive person.

Vyāsa said:

4. Tell me more, Brahmā, about that excellent tale of Gaṇanātha as my craving to hear more of that good tale of Vighneśa is increasing.

---

[150] "After he had heard this": After Vyāsa had heard the tale recited in the previous chapter.

Brahmā said:

5. Vyāsa, listen to another of my absorbing tales about what those people, beginning with Śūrasena, experienced concerning Gajānana.

6-9. In the middle country, in a delightful city called Sahasrā, there was a very powerful king called Śūrasena who was thoroughly conversant with the Vedas and the Vedāṅgas. He was rich, handsome, generous to his people, a sacrificer and a protector of his people. He possessed the three powers, was proud, accomplished in the six virtues, intelligent in the application of the four stratagems, a killer of enemies, endowed with four kinds of strength and he was devoted to the gods and brahmins. The entire earth was always under his subjection and his city on the Earth shone more than Indra's city.

10-11. His wife was called Puṇyaśīlā as she was distinguished for her merit and in the sphere of the triple-world there was nobody like her in beauty. By her qualities of loyalty to her husband she became accomplished in modesty, a genuine Arundhatī, and by avoiding the fault of envy she was quite simply a genuine Anasūyā.

12-15. Once when he was seated in the royal assembly hall and surrounded by his ministers, who were most excellent heroes, he saw moving in the sky an excellent vehicle. It looked like a fire and stole the fiery energy from one's eye. The courtiers, fond of listening to singing, were with the king and in their agitation asked what it was and despatched messengers to investigate. The messengers then departed in order to observe the vehicle which so resembled the sun. But due to a glance from one of the king's messengers, the leprous son of a vaiśya, the vehicle fell to the ground.

16-20. After returning from there they then announced to the king, "Great king, that vehicle causes merit[151] and it is divine, but even though it shines intensely, it fell to earth because of a leprous glance." Absolutely overjoyed, the king then mounted his horse and went there with a pair of his ministers, eager to see

---

[151] "causes merit": That is, because it is associated with divinity.

the vehicle. Accompanied by his own subjects and to the strains of many musical instruments, he reached the vehicle, still thinking about his great luck. There they saw Śakra and leaving their vehicles, they bowed to him, furnished as he was with various decorations and accompanied by all the hosts of gods.

21-25. With his hands folded in supplication the king said to Indra, killer of Bali, "This ground is now auspicious, my birth is auspicious, my previous births have produced success and all our eyes are now auspicious,[152] Husband of Śaci, because, whilst in the world of mortals, I and my attendants have experienced this vision of you, to whom the worlds and the gods led by Brahmā and Śiva are subject. You do not become visible other than as the result of the performance of one hundred horse sacrifices, so I do not know by virtue of what merit all these people have now seen you, nor how your vehicle fell onto the Earth. Tell me now, Lord, and destroy the doubts I have! Where have you been and where will you go?"

Indra said:

26. Hear about this great wonder Nārada narrated to me. I will tell it to you, so listen attentively, King.

Nārada said:

27-28. Śakra, I went to the world of mortals, to the hermitage of Bhruśuṇḍin, who, having assumed Gaṇeśa's appearance, was reciting continuously. By meditating on him, I then realized the quite amazing phenomenon that his appearance represented. That sage, who had Gajānana's real appearance then honoured me, and after I had bowed to him and bid him farewell I came to visit you. Indra, performer of one hundred sacrifices, such a likeness has not been seen anywhere on Earth.

---

[152] "all our eyes are now auspicious": Referring to the eyes of the king and all the people who have accompanied him.

Indra said:

29-33. After honouring Nārada I immediately left him and have come in intense anticipation in order to see a sage of this type. After mounting my excellent vehicle, my mind agitated like the Maruts, and seeing and honouring that sage whose body had an elephant's head, I bowed to Bhruśuṇḍin and accepted his worship. Then I departed with my retinue, eager to reach Amarāvatī. But in the meantime this vehicle has come to your city. It fell onto this piece of ground because of the glance of this evil-doing leper, your messenger. King, I have now told you everything.

Śūrasena said:

34. Tell me Lord Śakra, by what austerity did Bhruśuṇḍin attain Gajānana's real appearance? Although I have been listening to this immortal tale about him, I have still not had enough.

CHAPTER FIFTY-EIGHT

The Short Tale of Bhruśuṇḍin

Indra said:

1-4. Look here! I will tell you this ancient tale about how devotion to Gaṇanātha produced a likeness to him. In a city named Nandurā in the region of the Daṇḍaka forest there was a particularly wicked man known by the name of Kaivartaka. From childhood he was a thief, in his youth he engaged in illicit sex and now he steals openly because he avoids detection, he swears openly and his false oaths cause dissension in the heart of his enemies.

5-10. Because of this and his preoccupation with dicing and drinking the people expelled him far from his village, and so with his wife he stayed in an area of mountainous caves and woods, and killed many travellers on the road. In this manner he became wealthy and adorned his wife and daughter with many ornaments and gratified them by deceit.[153] He had a sword and he was carrying a dagger, a shield, snares, an unsurpassed bow, an iron staff and two large, full quivers on either side. Stationed in a tree top or in the hollow of a tree, he kills many people and takes different kinds of things, including clothes and jewellery, which he stores in his house and sells in a distant city. As is his wont he constantly indulges his senses in his own home, and similarly, this evil-doer also kills animals in the forest.

11-17. Once he chased someone for over two yojanas, but the person left him far behind and after faltering, he fell to the ground. Then rising with difficulty the rogue quickly departed and whilst going along the road he spotted an auspicious sacred ford of Gaṇeśvara, and to drive away his fatigue he immersed himself in it. He then returned to his own district and saw Mudgala on the road reciting a mantra and the names of Gaṇanātha. Lifting up his unsheathed sword, the man named Kaivartaka then advanced on Mudgala, determined to kill him. But his sword vanished, his dagger remained stuck in his fist and by the favour of Mudgala, devotee of Dviradānana, the mind of that evil man changed in an instant. When he saw him like that the eminent sage laughed, but he pulled himself together and asked, "Tell me, why have your weapons disappeared and why have all your snares fallen off?"

Indra said:

18. Detached and wise because he had bathed in Gaṇeśa's sacred ford and had seen the sage, he said these words to Mudgala.

Kaivartaka said:

19-23. I think a really amazing thing has happened. Because I bathed in this tank, but above all because of this vision of you,

---

153 "gratified them by deceit" toṣayāmāsa māyayā: I am uncertain of the meaning of māyā here and M is no help as he simply gives a literal translation.

brahmin, my mind has altered. Since childhood my mind has been evil and has been preoccupied with evil. I have committed countless evil acts up till now, Lord, but now, by your favour, my mind has become detached and I will not again take up these weapons of mine which have fallen. Seeing that the good extend favour to the needy and to evil-doers, extend to me your total favour and raise me up from the ocean of my own existence. Just as the mixing of jewels with base metals is not without value, so association with the good is never without worth, Great sage.

Śakra said:

24. Addressed in this way Mudgala became filled with compassion and whilst thinking specifically about the offence of abandoning a person who has come for refuge, he spoke to him.

Mudgala said:

25-26. You do not have the authority to perform a rite–such as gift-giving and so on–prescribed by the precepts. However, out of kindness I am going to tell you about the recitation of Gajānana's names, the best cause of absolute perfection for men.

27-30. Kaivartaka then respectfully bowed to the sage Mudgala, who placed his hand on his head, making him feel safe. He then taught him that mantra called "Obeisance to Gaṇeśa," after which he placed his own staff in the ground in front of him and said joyfully, "Until I return and until this staff sprouts buds, sit in one position, eat air, and your mind concentrated, recite this name. And you must put water at the base of the staff every morning and evening without fail."

Indra said:

31-34. Then Mudgala instructed the man named Kaivartaka who remained there, alive but wishing for nothing, after the sage had disappeared. Sheltering in the shade of a tree in the forest and having placed himself in the front of the sage's staff, stationed in one position he recited that short mantra of the name. He was without food and without desire, a veritable gaṇa[154] who had conquered his senses and possessed self-mastery. And so at the end of a thousand years that staff sprouted buds and, his body enclosed in an anthill latticed with vines, he became expectant of the sage's return.

35-39. Due to fate the sage Mudgala then came to that spot and when he remembered the staff, he also remembered Kaivartaka. Roaming about, the sage saw the fine staff that had sprouted and also Kaivartaka whose body had been overrun by an anthill. The excellent austerity he had performed was difficult even for sages to perform, but that assiduous sage comprehended it with a mere glance. After that best of sages had entirely removed the anthill on his body, he sprinkled his entire body with charmed water and then that best of sages spoke to him who now had acquired a celestial body, which because of its trunk resembled a two handed Gaṇeśa, and was reciting an auspicious name of Vināyaka.

40-47. Roused by the sage, his eyes opened, but from his eyes there sprang up fire. It was like lightning in the heavens and it began to burn the triple world until it was restrained by the sage. After he had paid homage to the compassionate sage, his own teacher, full of joy he embraced him, as a son does with his father. Mudgala then instructed that man named Kaivartaka and honoured that son who had re-emerged from the anthill. The sage Mudgala then diligently performed his name giving, and, King, because an elephant's trunk had come out from between his eyebrows, he was called "Bhruśuṇḍin." Mudgala then told him a single-syllable mantra, after which he gave him these boons: "You will be an excellent sage, you will be honoured by the perfected ones, heavenly musicians and the gods led by Indra, and in the same way that the god Gajānana is meditated upon and is considered to be a destroyer of evil, so too will you

---

154 That is, he becomes a members of the Hosts (gaṇa in the plural) who collectively make up Gaṇeśa's semi-divine followers.

be as well, and Bhruśuṇḍin, you will be famous. The man who has a vision of you will become one who achieves his purpose and as a result of my proclamation you will enjoy good health for one hundred thousand kalpas."

48-50. Whilst Mudgala was offering him various kinds of boons, the gods led by Indra and the sages led by Nārada came to see him and after bowing to him, they said, "Bhruśuṇḍin, because of this vision of you our birth, knowledge, austerity, parents and renown now mean something. You alone are Gaṇanātha and we must worship you, sage."

51-53. After he had honoured and bowed to them all and dismissed them, he assumed the lotus position again and recited the single syllable mantra, having put a captivating image of Gaṇeśa before himself. He worshipped daily by means of the sixteen ritual practices and his hermitage shone with its creepers, trees, lakes and ponds, and animosity[155] between lions and deer and mongoose and cobras was absent from there.

54-56. Then at the end of a hundred years Gajānana became pleased and he said, "You have my appearance, so why are you undertaking austerities? You have achieved your purpose and at the end of your life you will attain union. This place will become very famous as 'Namalā' and much success will be given to men who perform personal service here. By seeing an image of me here a person will not experience rebirth again, a person who is without sons will gain sons and a person who wants knowledge will obtain knowledge.

57. Everything you had asked me has been told to you, Śūrasena, Excellent king. What else do you want to hear?

---

[155] "animosity... was absent": An indication of the combined power of the mantra and the sage's austerity is its capacity to inhibit the natural instincts of animals.

CHAPTER FIFTY-NINE

The Tale of the Vow called the Saṃkaṣṭacaturthī

Brahmā said:

1. Vyāsa, after Śūrasena had heard the excellent speech of Indra, who is attended by the Maruts, he was pleased because he had heard an immortal tale and he questioned him again.

Śūrasena said:

2. In what way does your vehicle go to heaven, Lord of the gods? Show me that way, Lord, or tell me how I can do it for you.

Brahmā said:

3. The question being put, Indra, killer of the gods' enemies, smiling, again addressed the king whilst all the people were listening.

Brahmā said:

4-5. Were a certain person–a brahmin or a kṣatriya–to perform this vow of the Saṃkaṣṭacaturthī in your city, Excellent king, and if his merit acquired over a year was correctly offered, Enjoyer of the earth, this vehicle will set out immediately, but not otherwise, even with ten thousand men.

The king said:

6-7. Tell me, sage, what is this vow of the Saṃkaṣṭacaṭurthī, what is its merit, its result, its ritual and of whom is it the worship? Who performed it in the past and will it produce success when performed now? Indra, kindly tell me all this at length.

Śakra said:

8-12. In this connection there is told this ancient legend which concerns a conversation between the great Nārada and Kṛtavīrya. On Earth there was a strong king called Kṛtavīrya who was disposed to the truth, munificent, a sacrificer, proud and a great chariot warrior. He had mastered his senses, was moderate in respect of food, honoured the gods and brahmins, and of his warriors, elephants, charioteers and all his archers, who reside in the region of the Sahya mountains, there is no reckoning. In his palace there were golden couches and vessels, but nowhere was there a cooking bowl made of udumbara wood. He had twelve thousand brahmins who ate together as a group.

13-14. His wife was called Sugandhā and she was devoted to the law, loyal to her husband, her husband was her life, indeed she was an exceptionally captivating woman in the triple-world. Very lovely in her many ornaments, she was well disposed towards guests, brahmins and gods.

15-19. Yet these two, husband and wife, were sonless, even though they had intercourse. To obtain a son they both undertook vows, gift-giving of all types, austerities, minor restraints and other sacrifices which involved many honorariums. They also visited many sacred fords and sacred places because of their wish to obtain a son, but even with that no son appeared because of evil acts they had committed in previous births. One day, after the distressed king had summoned his advisers and had given them his kingdom, seal, treasury, subjects and his sovereign lands, in fact, had given them everything, husband and wife both went to a magnificent forest where, clothed in buckskins and deer skins, they undertook austerities. They conquered their senses, conquered their desire for food and ate withered leaves and air.

20-22. Then Nārada, who with a mere glance had observed these two as just described, spoke to Kṛtavīrya's father who was in the world of the deceased ancestors, "Because he has no son your son is near to death. Kṛtavīrya will be in the world of death tomorrow and he will die the next day. But if he had a son who would show him the world of heaven, he could then live, or when dead, go to heaven."

23-25. Nārada left after he had said this, but whilst still on Earth he saw an amazing thing. Bhruśuṇḍin's parents, his two sons, wife and daughter, were upside down in the fierce Kumbhīpāka hell which was filled with blazing flames. Yama's messengers were striking them and they uttered many pitiful cries. After Nārada, a repository of compassion, had heard their weeping, he came and spoke to Bhruśuṇḍin of their distress.

Nārada said:

26-28. The hosts of gods led by Indra and the sages led by Kapila came to visit the man who had Heramba's appearance and they said, "As a result of what transgression are your parents, wife, sons, daughters and servants cooking in this cooking pot in Yama's world? And given that you have gained wisdom, why then are you not aware of this?[156] Great sage, you must act diligently to rescue your ancestors."

29-31. After he had heard this speech uttered by the sage, Bhruśuṇḍin became quite pained and blazed like a fire, being very distressed because of his father's pain. He then thought about a way to effect their rescue, and perceiving one by deep meditation, Bhruśuṇḍin, who knows what is secret, then offered the prosperity produced from the vow of the Saṃkaṣṭacaturthī. Then, placing an auspicious liquid on his hand and meditating on the god Gajānana, he spoke, entreating the god Gajānana for the sake of his deceased ancestors.

Bhruśuṇḍin said:

32. If I devoutly undertake the Gaṇanātha vow for you, quickly rescue my elders with your power.

33-35. After he had said this he poured the liquid onto Gajānana's hand and as soon as the water had been poured, all of them, their appearance that of gods, ascended vehicles and

[156] "why then are you not aware of this...": That is, of their plight.

attained Gaṇeśa's heaven by virtue of Gajānana's favour, being attended by nymphs, praised by celestial sages and chorused by celestial musicians. And there were other men, evil-doers, in the Kumbhīpāka hell and all of them, too, went in vehicles to Gaṇeśvara's heaven.

36-37. I have now told you the greatness of this vow, due to the merit of one day of which, all of these went the way of the good. Not even a residue of the merit of one who diligently undertakes this Saṃkaṣṭa vow can be calculated. Hence, through its power my vehicle should move.

CHAPTER SIXTY

The Narrative of the Vow of the Fourth

The king said:

1. When they had escaped from the Kumbhīpāka hell and had gone to
heaven, what strategy did Kṛtavīrya's father adopt then?

Indra said:

2-7. Distressed because he had heard from Nārada about the cessation of his own lineage, he went immediately to Brahmā's world and visited lotus-seated Brahmā. After he had bowed to him he asked the reason for the cessation of his lineage, saying, "My son is exceedingly righteous, he is eloquent, a performer of sacrifices, he is devoted to guests and the gods and he is very proud. Brahmā, to obtain a son he eagerly performed many rites, so why does he still not have a son, Lord of the gods? Having entrusted his kingdom to his ministers, he has located himself in the forest, eating wind. Virtually all that is left of him is bone and he will die today or tomorrow. He committed an evil deed in a former life, because of which he will die, Lord. Be compassionate, lotus-born Brahmā, and tell me a way to further his lineage and I will communicate it to him."

8-17. After hearing this Brahmā made a pleasing speech, "Listen, and I will describe your son's previous birth. Previously a low caste man in a city, he was named Sāma. His activities were evil in the extreme and a sight of him was destructive of merit. Out of greed for money, he once killed twelve peaceful brahmins on the road and left them in a cave. After he had taken everything belonging to them, he returned to his own house at the rising of the moon on the night of the fourth day of the dark fortnight of Māgha, King. Having immediately summoned his son with the words, 'Gaṇeśa, Gaṇeśa', he ate happily with him as he had not yet had water or food. In time your son died, but through the merit arising from the Saṃkaṣṭacaturthī vow which had been performed inadvertently[157] at the rising of the moon on the night of the fourth day of the dark fortnight, King, he went to Vināyaka's abode, that which gives happiness. He was mounted on an excellent vehicle and hosts of nymphs were regarding, praising and honouring him with celestial flowers. In consequence of just a remnant of your merit he became a king named Kṛtavīrya, your són who is now your son on Earth. With the destruction of his mass of evil a son will be born to him, faultless man."

18. After he had heard Brahmā's speech the excellent king became confused and he asked further about a stratagem for the destruction of the evil.

Kṛtavīrya's father said:

19. Brahmā, how can this evil caused by the killing of brahmins be destroyed? Tell me, Ocean of compassion, even if what is to be done is very difficult.

---

[157] "performed inadvertently." This refers to Sāma's act of calling his own son "Gaṇeśa, Gaṇeśa" on the appropriate night.

Brahmā said:

20. If your son correctly performs the vow called Saṃkaṣṭacaturthī, he will be freed from evil.

The king said:

21. How is this auspicious vow performed and in what month, Brahmā? Tell me everything about that which will destroy this evil, Lord.

Brahmā said:

22-29. If the fourth day falls on a Tuesday in the dark fortnight of Māgha one should begin it when the moment is an auspicious one and the moon is in an auspicious form. After cleaning one's teeth one should wash twenty-one times, then one should perform the obligatory rituals and later on recite the mantra. In a state of silence and avoiding criticism of others, one should fast and as a rule give up betel nut and avoid offensive activity. One should also avoid drinking water, injuring others and backbiting. At the end of the day one should bathe with a moist mixture of sesamum oil and myrobalan and in order to please Gaṇeśa one should recite according to the precepts a single mantra, a six-syllable mantra, a Vedic mantra or his name mantra. Then with the mind stilled, one should meditate on Gajānana, god of gods. For a muhūrta one should then worship Gaṇanāyaka by means of the sixteen ritual procedures and a variety of offerings including sweet meats, large round cakes, flour cakes, modakas, pulse cakes, fluids, various foods, condiments which can be licked and sucked, various fruits, areca nut and betel, honorariums and so forth, lamps, twenty-one pieces of dūrvā grass and flowers.

30-33. Beginning with a mantra at moon-rise and after offering worship with a valuable gift to the lunar day, then to Gajānana and afterwards to the moon, and then having bowed and repeatedly requested forbearance, one should devoutly feed twenty-one brahmins in accord with one's capacity, but if unable to do so one should fully gratify ten or twelve Brahmins with honorariums. Then after hearing a tale one should feed oneself appropriately whilst remaining silent, after which one should pass the remainder of the night in singing and music.

34-38ab. King, if this vow is performed diligently for one year a man will have an excellent son as all his evils will be destroyed or he will obtain any other wish of which he might think. All his difficulties will be removed and he will not be frightened of a hostile army. If whilst standing at the base of a śamī tree, engaged in fasting and reciting, a blind, dumb, a stupid or a lame man should perform this vow from the rising of the moon until its decline, he will obtain what he wants and there can be no doubt that he will gain a kingdom, wealth, sons and wives. One by one in each of the months beginning with Śravaṇa, one should eat sweet meats and ghee etc., until the year is completed and then one will achieve ultimate success.

Kṛtavīrya's father said:

38cd. But why is the fourth Tuesday declared to be special?

39. Kindly tell me, Brahmā. I am bent down in deference and though I have been hearing this auspicious tale about Gajānana, I have still not had enough.

CHAPTER SIXTY-ONE

The Tale of the Aṅgāracaturthī Vow

Brahmā said:

1. King, after you have become attentive, listen and I will tell you succinctly about the greatness of the fourth Tuesday.

2-7. In the city of Avantī there was a great sage called Bhāradvāja who was wise, conversant with the Vedas and the Vedāṅgas, well versed in all the śāstras, devoted to performing the fire sacrifice and ever engaged in teaching his pupils. Residing on a river bank, this sage was devoted to personal service. But when the sage unexpectedly saw a sensuous woman, he became filled with lust, and overcome by Kāma's arrows he collapsed onto the ground. His body terribly aroused, his semen spilt and the semen fell into a hole in the ground, out of which there arose a young boy who looked like a japā flower. Being affectionate towards him the Earth carefully tended him, her own offspring and she considered her parents and her family to have become auspicious because of him.

8. When he was seven years old he questioned his mother, "Why is this human body I inhabit red and who are my father and mother? Tell me exactly!"

The Earth said:

9. The semen of the sage Bhāradvāja spilt and fell onto me. Then you were born, son and I have brought you up well.

Her son said:

10. Now, mother, show me that sage, that repository of austerity.

Brahmā said:

11-13ab. Taking him the goddess Earth then went to Bhāradvāja and after she had bowed to him, she placed her son in front and said, "Sage, you must claim him now as he is your grown up son who sprang from your semen." With his assent the Earth returned to her own splendid abode and Bhāradvāja rejoiced and embraced his son whom he had just obtained. After kissing his head, he joyfully placed him on his hip.

13cd-15. When a very auspicious astrological moment came, the sage performed the Vedic initiation and after teaching him the Vedas, the śāstras and an auspicious Gaṇeśa mantra, he said, "Undertake personal service for a long time in order to gladden Gaṇeśa. When he is fully satisfied he will give you all your heart's desires."

16-19. Then the sage[158] assumed the lotus position on the bank of the Narmadā, fully restraining his senses and meditating directly on Heramba.[159] In the meantime he recited the supreme mantra, ate air and became very lean. In this way he performed a severe austerity for a thousand years and at the clear rising of the moon on the fourth day of the bright fortnight of Māgha, Gaṇanātha manifested to him his real form as the world elephant. He was wearing celestial clothes, he had the moon on his forehead, his hands were glittering with various weapons, he had a comely trunk, shining teeth and earrings on his flapping ears. Adorned with various ornaments he resembled a myriad of suns.

20-24. The boy saw that form of the god standing before him and after he had bowed and got up he eulogized the Lord of the universe, "Obeisance to you who removes obstacles! Obeisance to you who causes obstacles! To the Lord of the gods and demons! To the one who strengthens all the powers! To the one who is wholesome! To the eternal one! To the one without qualities! To the one who cuts through qualities![160] Obeisance, best of those who know Brahma! Obeisance to the one who causes the destruction and the preservation! Obeisance to you, support of the world. Obeisance, protector of the three worlds! To the one who is the origin of Brahma, to the knower of Brahma, to Brahma, to the one who takes Brahma's form! To the one whose real appearance can be characterized, yet not characterized! Obeisance to the one who discloses that which is difficult of characterization!"

---

[158] "Then the sage...": I presume this refers to the boy who as Bhāradvāja's son could be considered a sage.

[159] Heramba = Gaṇeśa.

[160] "to the one who cuts through qualities" guṇacchide: I am uncertain of the meaning of this compound and in his rendering M also gives no hint as to its meaning. If chid were to be taken in the sense of "destroy, annihilate", it might refer to a function of Gaṇeśa as the destroyer of the cosmos in the sense that the basic constituents of the cosmos are the three guṇas.

25a-d. Eulogized like this the supreme Gajānana became pleased and being exceedingly joyful, he addressed the young boy in polished words.

Gajānana said:

25ef-26. I am satisfied with your fierce austerity, that eulogy and also with your devotion. Because of your fortitude whilst still just a child, I am going to give you some cherished boons.

Addressed in this way the Earth's son made this speech to Gajānana.

Bhauma said:

27. Because of your appearance my birth and my sight
Have become auspicious, Lord of the gods.
My knowledge and family are auspicious too, Lord.
The Earth with its mountains, and so on, is also auspicious.
The eye, austerity and everything else by which
You are seen are auspicious, Lord of all.
The voice in which you are eulogized,
By one who is confused, as also the place, is auspicious.

28-30. If you are satisfied, Lord of the gods, let me remain permanently in heaven. Gaṇeśa, I want to drink ambrosia with the gods and, Cause of good fortune, my name must become famous in the triple-world. Lord, a merit-giving vision of you occurred for me on the Fourth. As a consequence, let it[161] always give merit through your favour and remove all difficulties and give their wishes to those who perform the vow.

Gaṇeśa said:

31-33. Son of the Earth, you will drink ambrosia in the appropriate way with the gods and you will become famous in the world under the name Maṅgala. In addition, since you are the son of the Earth and because of your redness you will be called Aṅgāraka. Men on Earth will perform the Aṅgāraka-

161 "it": referring to the Fourth, not to the vision.

caturthī and they will not experience problems in any of their affairs, as the merit produced from that Saṃkaṣṭi vow lasts for a year. No doubt of it.

34-35ab. Child of supreme austerity, you undertook that vow of the highest quality, the best of vows, and so you will become a king in the city of Avantī. Just by praising it a mortal will achieve all his desires.

35cd-38. After he had given these boons in this way, the god Dviradānana disappeared. Then Maṅgala diligently erected an image of the god which had an elephant's trunk on its face, ten arms and was beautiful in all its limbs. And he erected a tempe which brought joy to Gajānana and he gave the nane "Auspicious-image" to the god of gods. Thereafter that becane a sacred place giving the desires of every person and liberation to all those who perform personal service, worship or gaze at the image there.

39-45. Then the god Vināyaka sent an excellent aerial vehicle of the highest quality and his own hosts to bring Bhauma to him. On reaching there they forcibly brought Bhauma in his bodily form to Gaṇeśa and that was a virtual miracle.[162] King, after that Bhauma became famous in the triple-world, both moving and stationary, and because Bhauma had attained his goal and drank ambrosia with the gods in heaven the Saṃkaṣṭacaturthī became connected with Bhauma. In consequence of this, the Fourth associated with Tuesday became famous on Earth. The image called Maṅgala, which confers all benefits, became famous as Cintāmaṇī because it gives things as soon as they are thought of. As Cintāmaṇī it became famous west of the township of Pārinera where it removes all obstacles. At the rising of the moon it is now worshipped by the perfected men and heavenly musicians and it gives all cherished objects such as sons, grandsons, etc., and wealth.

---

[162] It is regarded as a miracle because humans rarely ever go to heaven in bodily form.

CHAPTER SIXTY-TWO

Description of the Moon's Curse and Favour

Brahmā said:

1-4. King, once I went to Kailāsa, Śiva's home, and when I entered his assembly hall I saw that Nārada had arrived. He gave Śiva one new fruit but Gaṇapa, though still a young boy, asked Śiva for it. Śiva then asked me who the fruit should be given to and I replied, "To the young boy." Śiva gave it to him, but Gaṇeśa became angry.

5. Then I, Brahmā, having returned home, endeavoured to create, however Vighnakara created an obstacle to that was utterly extraordinary.

6-11. Assuming a ferocious appearance, he terrorized me. However, whilst I was reeling about, the moon saw him, so fiercesome, and laughed at the supreme Dviradānana and his hosts. Utterly enraged he then cursed the moon, saying, "It is my injunction that you must not be seen in the triple-world. Whenever someone sees you he will become possessed of great evil."[163] After he had cursed him in this way the god left for his own home, accompanied by his followers. But wretched and tarnished, the moon dissolved into a pool of anxiety and wondered, "Did I inadvertently commit some childish mischief against the ultimate cause of the universe who possesses qualities such as smallness, etc., that I have become invisible to everyone, colourless and dirty? Praiseworthy and beautiful in shape, I pleased the gods with my digits. How could this happen?"

12. At this point the gods heard the violent curse placed on the moon and led by Agni and Indra they went to where Gajānana was and there the multitudes of gods addressed the ultimate cause of obstacles.

---

[163] That is, the act of seeing the moon now it is has been cursed will produce great evil for whoever sees it.

The gods said:

13.You, God of gods, you are praised by the worlds!
Lord, you protect, you destroy and you create at your will!
Though without qualities, you create them, Overlord of the qualities.
To you we have now come for refuge, God!
14. Protect us, Lord! Has not the entire universe fallen into distress
Through fear of your curse on the offending moon?
Therefore, Lord of the Universe, we, the universe and the moon,
Have come for refuge. Lord of the Earth, do something!

15-17. Lord, now that the moon cannot be seen, everything has fallen into danger. You must extend your favour to the moon and to the triple-world. The three Vedas did not know your majestic appearance, so who possibly could eulogize it? Even so, everyone does eulogize you. We have now achieved our task by seeing and speaking to you. We have come to you for refuge, Imperishable god who removes distress for his supplicants.

18. Dviradānana gives accomplishment in the law, sensuosity, power and liberation, and on hearing their speech he spoke to them, very pleased as he was with their eulogies.

Vikaṭa said:

19. I am pleased with your eulogy, gods. Choose something greatly cherished in the three worlds that you cannot obtain and I will give it to you.

The gods said:

20. We all want you to favour Moon, because when he is favoured all of us will be favoured as well.

Gaṇeśa said:

21. The moon must remain invisible for one year, half of that or half of that! Ask for another boon, gods.

22-26. Then they all bowed prostrate before Dviradānana, however, he, Vikaṭa, spoke emotionally to the bowing gods. "Look why were you so keen to make this trifling speech to me? I cannot abandon those who come for refuge! Mt. Meru might shake, the sun might fall, fire might go cold or the ocean might go beyond its border, but my word will never be false. So when I am talking, you must listen to my speech, excellent gods. Whoever knowingly or unknowingly is cursed as a result of looking at the moon on the fourth day of the bright fortnight will share his deep distress."[164]

27-32. After they had heard this speech all the gods rejoiced and having bowed, they said "Om" and cast down a shower of flowers. Having taken his leave the gods immediately went to the moon and said to him, "You were very stupid to ridicule Dviradānana because by offending that excellent god you have plunged the tripleworld into danger. You committed an offence against the Leader of the tripleworld, the god who regulates the threefold universe, who is eternal, who is without qualities, constant, the real appearance of whom is that of Brahma, Gajānana, who is everybody's teacher. But with great difficulty we have pleased the Lord and seeking the good of all beings, he has set down this stipulation, "You must never be seen on the fourth day of the bright fortnight of Bhādra. You too must go for refuge to Gajānana, god of gods, for by his favour your body will be purified and you will achieve high fame."

33-38. After he had heard the god's speech he went for his own benefit to take refuge in that god who is loved by all those who come for refuge. Then to Gajānana, Lord of the gods who

[164] "will share his deep distress": Gaṇeśa cannot remove the boon placed on the moon. He can only diminish its power, and so he dissipates it by extending the curse to anybody who looks at the moon in its cursed condition.

is respectfully praised by Śiva, he recited a superlative one-syllable mantra which removes evil. And as taught by Indra, Moon performed, with intense concentration, a most severe austerity for one hundred and twenty years on the southern bank of the Ganges where every success is given. After that the illustrious Gaṇeśa became pleased and came before him wearing red garlands and red clothes, smeared with red sandal wood, having four arms, huge in body, a body red with sindura. He was illuminating the worlds with his splendour, a splendour superior to that of a myriad of suns.

39-40. On seeing that mass of splendour Moon shook terribly, but having firmly gathered courage, he clasped his hands in obeisance and he pondered mentally on the subject of Dviradānana. He bowed to him, thinking, "He has come here to give me a boon," and then with great devotion he eulogized Gajānana, god of gods.

The moon said:

41. I bow to the god Dviradānana,
He who removes obstacles for all people.
He extends accomplishment in the law, power and sensuosity for all.
Obeisance to him, Vighnanāśana.
42. Obeisance to you, to the repository of compassion, Brahma,
O God, to the universal self, O God who is dextrous in the universe.
To the seed of the universe, to the one who is the universe,
To the cause of destruction of the triple-world.
43. Let there be obeisance to you who is without desire,
Who is the three Vedas, who gives illumination to all,
Who is the light of intellect, who is Overlord of the gods,
Who is constant, who is the truth, who is ever wise.
44. This transgression was committed as an error of ignorance.
Pardon it, Bringer of compassion.

Even for you there is great error in the abandonment Of one who has come for refuge, so extend your sympathy to me!

45-50. After he had heard this speech Gajānana became very pleased and in consequence of his eulogy that god, who was completely gratified, gave him some boons, saying, "You will become just as you appeared previously and any man who looks at you on the fourth day of the bright half of Bhādra will be immediately cursed as being stupid and your stupidity[165] will be gone. In conjunction with the gods I declared that you were not to be seen on that day. When men undertake the vow on the fourth day of the dark fortnight, I must be worshipped when you arise and you too must be worshipped diligently. But if you are gazed upon intently at an unfavourable time the vow will be fruitless. Moon, stand on my forehead in the form of a digit, because that will be pleasing to me and on the second part of every month you will be worshipped.

51-55. When Moon gained this boon he became just as he was previously and with the gods he erected an image of the boon-giver. The gods and sages gave it the name "Moon-on-his-forehead." He then constructed a temple of gold adorned with jewels and respectfully worshipped it[166] with the sixteen forms of ritual practices, and when he had finished worshipping, the gods and sages gave him boons, saying, "This will become famous in the world as the 'Sacred place of Perfection,' and for those who undertake religious duties there it will bring about absolute success." Then after the gods and sages had bowed to Dviradānana, they went to their own homes, filled with joy and pleased in mind.

56. After the gods and sages had gone the god Gaṇeśa concealed his own body and when he, now called "Moon-on-his-forehead," had disappeared, Moon became almost ecstatic and having been restored to his previous condition, he then returned to his own home.

---

165 "your stupidity": That is, the moon's stupidity in ridiculing Gaṇeśa.
166 "worshipped it": That is, he worshipped the image, not the temple.

CHAPTER SIXTY-THREE

The Tale of the Dūrvā Grass

Kṛtavīrya's father said:

1-2. I asked why devotion had to be manifested at moon-rise on the fourth day of the dark fortnight and you have explained it. I also wish to hear why dūrvā grass must be procured. Tell me why blades of dūrvā grass are pleasing to Gaṇanātha.

Brahmā said:

3. Well listen, Excellent king, and I will tell you the result of procuring blades of dūrvā grass for Gaṇanātha.

4-7. In the Southern region there was a city named Jāmbā where there lived a warrior named Sulabha who had good qualities, was generous, rich and strong. He was discriminating, proud, tranquil, quite self-controlled, he knew the truth of all the śāstras and was well versed in the true object of all the Vedas. Filled with devotion, he was constantly making eulogies and hymns of praise to Vikaṭa.

7. His highly renowned wife was named Samudrā and she was virtuous and extraordinarily beautiful, her beauty being such that the nymphs cursed her. Devoted to the gods, the brahmins and guests, she charmed her husband's heart with her good qualities.

8-12. Just then a brahmin named Madhusūdana arrived, seeking alms and constantly in contemplation upon the supreme Lord. But because of his poverty he was poorly clothed and though in fact he was clothed, he seemed to be naked. On seeing him, Sulabha bowed, full of joy, but overtaken by folly he unexpectedly laughed at that excellent brahmin. However, the great sage was disturbed by that, and, his angry red eyes almost burning the triple-world, he uttered a curse: "Fool! You publicly laughed at the brahmins. So become a bull that is always drawing a plough and is in constant pain."

13-15. After learning of her husband's curse, Samudrā seethed with anger and furious as a snake that has been struck, she cursed the brahmin: "Since you are discriminating, yet have placed a curse on my husband, you will be changed into a dung eating ass, Evil brahmin." But after he had heard that curse uttered, the cruel man cursed her: "Since you, a woman, cursed me, you will become a cāṇḍāla[167] woman, poverty stricken, full of defects, eating shit and piss, a cause of inauspiciousness."

16-19. After they had cursed each other in this way and lost their bodies, which were so difficult to obtain, Sulabha became a bull drawing a plough and because of the brahmin's curse never at any time did he get a moment's rest. The brahmin Madhusūdana was born in a donkey's womb and Samudrā became a malicious cāṇḍāla woman injuring living beings. Like an impoverished piśāca she became engrossed in eating piss and shit. Her body was utterly desiccated, her teeth jagged and her feet monstrous.

20-22. One day whilst wandering in the south of the city she saw an absolutely marvellous temple of Gaṇanātha in a tangle of many trees and creepers filled with many flocks of birds. There were some yogic lords in it who were constantly occupied in personal service, some of them worshippers of Gaṇeśa abiding in a state of self-restraint.

Others had their own wishes as their goals and others were seeking wealth, liberation and sons.

23-32. Some time on the fourth day of the month of Bhādra a great festival of Gaṇanātha was being held in every house of the city, but it began to rain violently, a veritable harbinger of the great destruction.[168] Frightened of the rain the caṇḍala woman went into each of the houses, but the entire populace, striking her and so forth, threw her out of each one. After taking some fire in her hand she then went to the temple, but even there some

---

[167] The name cāṇḍāla designates the lowest social class, contact with a representative of whom is held to be highly polluting. When used as a symbol the cāṇḍāla conveys the notion of evil, filth and pollution.

[168] In the Purāṇic cosmogonic scheme the period of destruction is heralded by a great rain, amongst other things.

people struck her and she was repulsed by the yogins. Then after she had started a fire with grass she warmed up her limbs. Suddenly the wind moved a blade of dūrvā grass and under the influence of fate it fell on Gaṇanātha's head. At the same time a donkey who was frightened of the cold went to the temple and also at the same time, due to fate the bull was freed from the plough and by the weight of destiny's purpose, he came to Gaṇanātha's temple. Both of them ate the cāṇḍāla woman's grass and while the people were sleeping these two fought near Gajānana with their hooves and horns. From their mouths two blades of dūrvā grass then fell onto Gaṇeśa's trunk and foot and Gajānana was satisfied. After that, taking her staff she went up to the god, struck both the donkey and the bull and performed worship herself.

33-35ab. On hearing the sound of their hooves a man awoke from sleep and hitting her with his fists and elbows he drove her out with a staff. Intent upon flight, she was also struck with stones and so forth. Fearful about the touch of the cāṇḍāla woman and the donkey, the people bathed Gajānana with consecrated water from a sacred ford and with substances of many kinds they worshipped him with the highest devotion.

35cd-36.Once more these wicked people deliberately struck the bull, the donkey and the cāṇḍāla woman with sticks, the palms of their hands and their knees. The door to the god[169] being closed, there was no refuge for them.

37-40. However whilst those three were wandering around and lamenting piteously in harsh tones, Vikaṭa voiced this thought, "Once again[170] they have performed a ritual for me by chance and so now they have worshipped me with a piece of dūrvā grass and so on. Even though they were in difficulty they undertook a great many circumambulations, and I esteem and honour anyone who should offer me a single piece of dūrvā

---

[169] "door to the god" devadvāra: I presume this means "temple" and this is how M has taken it.

[170] "Once again...by chance": The sense of this sentence is that a ritual of which Gaṇeśa is the object of worship has taken place without the three protagonists knowing it.

grass and undertake a circumambulation on the fourth day of the bright fortnight of Bhādra. In view of that I will send them to my own home in an aerial vehicle."

41-48. Accordingly, the god despatched an aerial vehicle adorned with his own hosts as well as with the hosts of nymphs and heavenly musicians, all having his real appearance. It was accompanied by music, it was filled with flowers, fragrant substances and celestial foods, and displayed banners and flags. After collecting and putting them into the aerial vehicle where they became joyous and assumed celestial bodies, the hosts, who had Gajānana's appearance, quickly took them, with Gajānana's permission, to his home.[171] Astonishment arose in the hearts of all the people who were watching and they said, "This happy result has occurred because of their previous merit." Thereafter, having left their meditation, some of the Yogic lords went to the hosts and asked, "Tell us how they acquired this result which is auspicious and permanent. They are quite depraved and amongst them, there is not even one atom of merit. Faultless hosts, tell us why they got this happy result which is so rare. We will stop our own personal service and immediately do just that. Time goes on incalculably but no god has entered our range of sight, though we are always passionless eaters of air and perform personal services. Tell us when we will reach Gaṇeśa's home."

CHAPTER SIXTY-FOUR

The Dūrvāmāhātmya

The hosts said:

1-3. Yogins, when you have stilled your wandering minds listen to this which neither Brahmā nor Śeṣa can describe. We will describe it as far as we can, insofar as anyone can really

---

[171] "to his own home": That is, to the temple from which they had previously been expelled.

describe it. Śiva and the gods are constantly performing a eulogy to him, but really, who can adequately describe Gaṇanātha's majesty or do the same concerning his divine sport? Nonetheless, listen faultless men!

4-5. The power of blades of dūrvā grass is unknown to sages and gods and cannot be gained by sacrifices, gifts, austerities, vows or fire sacrifices. But they recite this ancient tradition about it taken from a conversation between Indra, chief of the Vasus, and the great Nārada.

6-7. Once Nārada eagerly went to visit Indra and after the sage had been given a seat and honoured with deep devotion, Indra, Vala's killer, asked him respectfully about the Dūrvāmāhātmya.

Indra said:

8ab. Why is the great Gaṇeśa, god of gods, so especially fond of a large blade of dūrvā grass, brahmin sage?

The sage said:

8cd. I will relate the excellent Dūrvāmāhātmya just as it is known to me.

9-11. In a city called Sthāvara, there was once a great sage named Kauṇḍinya who possessed strength through his austerities and was a worshipper of Gaṇeśa. His delightful hermitage was located in the southern part of the village and it was large, full of trees and creepers as well as very large ponds which were frequented by bees, geese and wild duck and in which there were full blown lotuses as well as cakravāka ducks, cranes, white water lilies and water-fowl.

12-14. But there[172] he devoted himself to meditation and undertook a massive austerity. After placing himself before a large, very pleasant four-armed image of Gaṇeśa which gave excellent boons and was worshipped with dūrvā grass, he

---

[172] "But there...": That is, he devotes himself to austerities instead of enjoying the beauties of the hermitage.

recited the superlative mantra which has six syllables and satisfies the gods. But filled with doubts, his wife named Āśrayā questioned him.

Āśrayā said:

15-16ab. Lord why are you offering a load of dūrvā grass each day to the god Gajānana? No one is satisfied by grass! If there really is merit in it, then kindly tell me so.

Kauṇḍinya said:

16cd. Listen, beloved wife, and I will tell you the excellent Dūrvāmāhātmya.

17-20. Once there was an excellent festival in the city of Dharma. All the gods with the heavenly musicians and the hosts of nymphs as well as the perfected sages, wanderers, snakes, yakṣas and rākṣasas were invited. Whilst Tilottamā was dancing her upper garment fell onto the ground and Yama saw her two large and lovely breasts. Deranged and tormented with lust, he then shamelessly sought to embrace her and kissed her on the face.

21-23. His face lowered in shame, Yama departed from that place of assembly, but as he was leaving his dripping semen spilt onto the ground. It became garlanded with flames and a man with a deformed face appeared from it. Terrifying the triple-world with the pitiless howl he made through his fangs and touching the sky with his matted hair, he scorched the entire earth and his noise utterly shook the triple-world 's pride.

24-25. Then all those who were seated in the assembly hall went to see Viṣṇu and once they had performed a hymn of praise in a variety of ways with various eulogies as seemed appropriate, they calmly petitioned him for the good of all beings. He went with them to the salubrious Gajānana and after learning from him how the man would be destroyed, they all eulogized him.

The gods and sages said:

26-31. Obeisance to the one whose real appearance is the obstacle! Obeisance to you who removes obstacles! Obeisance to you, the form of everything! Let there be obeisance to you, the witness of everything! Obeisance to the god who is great! Obeisance to you, the origin of the universe! Obeisance to you, the ocean of compassion, the cause of the preservation of the universe! Obeisance to you, accomplished in austerity, the cause of the destruction of the universe! Obeisance to you, giver of boons to your devotees! Obeisance! Obeisance to him who gives to everybody. Obeisance to you, fulfiller of all wishes for those of whom you are the sole refuge! Obeisance to you, the knower of the Vedas! Obeisance to you, the cause of the Vedas! To whom else can we go for refuge? Can anyone remove our fear? How could the cosmic destruction have occurred for these people at the wrong time. Oh! Gajānana, Lord of gods! Oh! Oh! Perpetual remover of obstacles, now that death has come are you going to disregard all of us?

32-37ab. After he had heard this speech of theirs, Gajānana, the ocean of compassion, manifested himself in front of them in the form of a child, thus removing his friends' apprehension. His face had the light of one hundred moons and it had two lotus eyes. His hair-net was bright as a myriad of suns and his body surpassed that of a myriad of Kāma's. His teeth surpassed the splendour of jasmine, his lips surpassed the colour of the bimba fruit and he had a prominent nose and contracted eye brows, lovely eyes and folds in his neck. His chest was broad, his two arms were touching his knees and he was powerful, with his belly and its deep navel glistening and his lips glistening brightly too. His heavy thighs joined to his beautiful knees were vying with the splendour of plantain trunks, he had splendid ankles, very lovely shanks and his glittering feet were like lotuses. Opulent with a variety of splendid ornaments, he was clothed in garments of great value.

37cd-38. Straight after they had seen the god like this on the ground in front of the city, the gods and sages arose, making the sound of victory and bowed prostrate on the ground just like the hosts of gods to Indra.

The gods and sages said:

39-40. Who are you, where have you come from and what are you doing? Tell us everything! We believe this truly to be Brahma in the form of a boy who has manifested himself here as the cause of evil's destruction, to save us who have assembled here after giving up our activities because we are frightened of the demonic fire.

41-44. After he had heard their speech Gajānana, his form that of a child, addressed all the gods and sages with a smile on his face, "You are right.[173] What you have said is quite true. I am here to kill this evil person who is harassing you. Willingly taking the form of a boy, I have come here quickly, gods and sages. I will tell you a way to kill him and you must do it, Faultless gods. Now that you have seen him, vigorously direct me to him and then watch out for something of the greatest interest relating to him and me."

45-47. After hearing this kindly statement they were full of joy and said to each other, "We do not know his strength. He must have descended to save the triple-world which is being harassed, but can the Lord who appears to be a boy, really kill him?" Still, after speaking in this manner they all bowed respectfully to him.

48-50. At that very moment, however, the man returned to the world of men in his real appearance as the destructive fire, burning and destroying in every direction. The weeping people made a tremendous noise and the sages who were intent upon flight straight after they had seen him, went to the young boy and said to him, "Prepare to flee quickly! If he were now to swallow us and you, just as a huge fish does with a small fish

---

[173] "You are right!" bhavanto jñānasampannāḥ: This is surely satirical as it plays on the opinion of the gods and sages that they recognize Brahma, the true recognition of which is jñāna. Of course, they are wrong as Gaṇeśa points out in his mocking tone.

and as Garuḍa with snakes, this huge fire would become permanent."

51-52. After he had heard their speech, Gajānana, the highest self, assumed a mighty form and stood like Mount Himavat, but the divine sages went far away, leaving just a boy[174] there.

(Contd.)

CHAPTER SIXTY-FIVE

The Dūrvāmāhātmya (Contd.)

Āśrayā said:

1-2ab. When the gods and sages had departed and the child who was like a mountain remained, what interesting thing happened there in regard to the boy and the "fire of time"? Great sage, quickly tell me everything in detail.

Kauṇḍinya said:

2cd-8. When Gajānana, the boy who was like a mountain, stood unmoving, the demonic fire came, unshakeable like the fire of an evil spirit, and at that very moment the earth moved, even though it was immoveable. With roars like rumbling thunder he roared at the sky and swarms of birds fell off the branches of trees onto the ground. The ocean became waterless, trees were uprooted and nothing could be discerned because of the great agitation. At that very moment the god Gajānana, appearing as a boy, restrained the fire demon by the power of illusion. Then whilst everyone was watching, he consumed him like Agastya the ocean, but the god wondered, "If he has entered my stomach to see something really miraculous, he might burn the triple-world which is in my stomach."

9-18. Indra then gave him the moon to extinguish[175] his fire and the gods and sages eulogized him as Bhālacandra, but even

---

[174] "a boy": That is, Gaṇeśa has returned to his form of a small boy.

[175] The moon is considered to be cool, hence its use in attempting to extinguish the fire.

so the fire was not extinguished because it had gone into his throat. Then Brahmā gave him two young maidens called Siddhi and Buddhi who were born from his mind. Both had eyes like lotuses, smooth tapering thighs and hair which was like the śaivala plant. Their faces were moon-like, their voices like ambrosia, their navels were well-formed, the folds in their skin were like rivers, their waists were like lotus fibres, their hands like young sprouts and they were the cause of frigidity. After he had tightly embraced them both Brahmā said, "Your fire will quiten down when you have embraced them. And by embracing them his fire quietened down a little." Viṣṇu, Kamalā's husband, gave him a very pleasing lotus, such that all the gods and men called him "Padmapāṇi." But still the fire was not extinguished, so Varuṇa sprinkled it with cold water. Śiva then gave him a snake with a thousand hoods and though it was bound with that it burst out because the snake binding it had burst. Moreover, it had not become cold and his neck[176] was on fire. One thousand and eighty-eight sages then respectfully approached him and on his head they singly placed twenty-one pieces of dūrvā grass called "Ambrosia." After that the fire became cooler and honoured by the loads of dūrvā grass, the supreme Self became satisfied. Realizing this they all worshipped Gajānana and Gajānana himself rejoiced because of the many loads of dūrvā grass.

19-22. To the gods and sages he said, "Whether it be great or small, without blades of dūrvā grass, devotion and worship performed for me is useless. Nobody will obtain the results of worship without blades of dūrvā grass. Therefore, whether it be one piece or twenty-one, dūrvā grass devoutly offered at dawn by my devotees will produce a great result. But that will not be brought about by one hundred sacrifices, gifts, masses of performances of sacred vows, fierce austerities and restraints undertaken over myriads of lives. It is gained because of dūrvā grass, gods and sages."

---

[176] That is, Gaṇeśa's neck.

Kauṇḍinya said:

23-28. After they had heard this speech the gods again honoured the supreme self, Gajānana, god of gods, with blades of dūrvā grass. Full of joy, he roared, filling the sky and earth with a vast noise. And after giving many boons to all the gods, sages and men who had rejoiced, he resumed the form of a boy. Together they named him "Extinguisher of the fire of time" and after they had erected an image of Gajānana, they all constructed a temple. The happy gods gave it the title, "Here is the Remover of Obstacles." Bathing, gift-giving, austerity and service performed there beget a perpetual result due to Vighnahara's favour. The city was called "Victory" because victory is obtained from it, and, because everyone's obstacles were removed, it became "Remover of Obstacles."

Kauṇḍinya said:

29. Everything concerning this excellent Dūrvāmāhātmya has been narrated to you. The hearing and reciting of it will destroy all evil. Now, whilst I am still reciting, listen to this ancient tradition.

CHAPTER SIXTY-SIX

The Dūrvāmāhātmya (Contd.)

Kauṇḍinya said:

1-2. Once, lady, the sage Nārada came to see Gajānana who was comfortably seated. After bowing prostrate to him for many days, he said to him, "My birth has become significant, Gajānana, because I have seen you due to my accumulation of merit."

3-5. After he had said this, his hands folded in supplication, the sage stood before him and the illustrious Gajānana, taking his hand in his own hand, summoned that great and illustrious sage to a seat. Nārada, the illustrious bull of sages, was very pleased with that and he said to Gaṇādhiśa, "I have come to tell you about something extraordinary in my mind. I will bow and approach you."

Gajānana said:

6. What is this astonishing thing you have seen? What is it that is in your mind? Tell me everything in detail and then return to your own hermitage!

Nārada said:

7-14. In the region of Mithilā there is an excellent king called Janaka, God. He is proud, generous, a master of the Vedas and their auxiliaries and he is disposed to giving gifts of food. He always honours the brahmins with clothes and ornaments of various kinds and with many honorariums. In addition, he gives great wealth to the miserable, the blind and the needy, and gives beggars everything they request. Even so, the great man's wealth is not exhausted! Wondering if that wealth increases because of Gaṇeśa's satisfaction, I went to his house in order to see that astonishing thing. But arrogant because of his knowledge of Brahma, he began laughing, and I said to him, "You are wealthy, Excellent king, and because of your deep devotion Gajānana offers you whatever you think of." But arrogantly, he said this, "I am the Lord in the triple-world. I give, I consume, I protect and I cause others to give and besides my own person,[177] nothing else exists in the triple-world. I am the creator, the cause and the act of making, Excellent sage."

---

[177] "my own person" matsvarūpam: A free translation which captures the sense of the compound within its specific context. This kind of meglomania is a recurrent theme in bhakti myths and the loss of arrogance, that is, the loss of the ego is an essential step before the attainment of devotee status can be attained.

Nārada said:

15-16. After I had heard his speech, I said to him in anger, "There is absolutely no other creator of the world than the Lord![178] But, faultless king, why are you fraudulently laying down this ordinance?[179] I will shortly expose it."

17ab. After I had said this to him, I came here to you, Ibhānana.

Kauṇḍinya said:

17cd-18. After he had heard the sage's speech, the Lord honoured him with valuable things such as celestial ornaments, flowers and sandal wood perfume. And straight after receiving permission, the sage then went to Viṣṇu in Vaikuṇṭha.

19-23. Even though he was omniscient, Gajānana too, assuming an execrable appearance, went to Mithilā to investigate the king's devotion. He became filled with wounds as if he were sick, oozing blood, inauspicious, attacked by swarms of flies and toothless. When they saw him coming in this condition some men made a cloth covering for their nose, whilst others spat at him repeatedly. Faltering, fainting, falling, yet moving again, he reached the king's door accompanied by swarms of small boys and said to the door-keepers. "Messengers! Inform the king that I have arrived, a brahmin guest who is very hungry and expects whatever food he demands."

24-27. When they had gone to King Janaka, they relayed that very speech of his and in order to see this curiosity he said to his messengers, "Bring him!" But concerning this old brahmin who was oozing blood and perspiring from fatigue, the king wondered, "Could it be the Lord who has taken this appearance? If he has come to deceive me, there might be merit in it for me, so I will concentrate my mind on him and what is to be will

[178] That is, Gaṇeśa.

[179] "fraudulently proclaiming this teaching" dharmam imaṃ... dambhenaiva karoṣi kim: A difficult use of dharma and an inadequate rendering of it. Here I take it to designate a statement of a fundamental truth in the world.

come true." At the very moment the excellent King Janaka was thinking this, the brahmin was ushered in by the door-keepers and became visible.

The brahmin said:

28-29. After hearing of your fame that is as dazzling as a moonbeam, I have come to you. Give me some food, King, as I have been hungry for a very long time. Give me food for as long as I crave it and you will accrue the merit of one hundred sacrifices, Lord of men.

Kauṇḍinya said:

30-33. After he had heard this speech he brought him into his house and after he had honoured him as prescribed, he ordered some delicacies. As much as would suffice a myriad of people was placed there, but the excellent brahmin swallowed the lot in one gulp. High quality rice was put on countless plates and when prepared as a porridge, it was placed before him, yet whatever was placed in front of him he ate in an instant.

34-39. Then the people said to the king, "He eats everything! He might be a demon! If no merit at all is gained from giving gifts to a demon, why has he been given so much?" Others said, "He may not be entirely full even when the triple-world is eaten. King, give him the grain!" Then having brought all the grain stored on the ground and in houses, as well as everything that was in city and village, they sent it to that man who certainly looked like a brahmin, yet was a guest eating everything. But when this was eaten, he had still not had enough. Messengers then said to the king, "No grain can be found anywhere." Yet even as Janaka stood downcast after hearing his messenger's statement, the insatiable brahmin, having offered his greetings at each house, said, "Give me some food."

40. The people then said to him, "The king has taken all the grain in our houses and you have eaten it all, brahmin. Your appetite must be exhausted by that!"

The brahmin said:

41. In the world there is no provider of food superior to Janaka. His fame is celebrated and as I came wishing to be filled up, how can I leave without being full?

42-43. These people having become silent, he wandered away and saw the nice house of two brahmins named Virocanā and Triśiras, a house containing no useful articles nor any basic kitchen utensils. He entered there as though he in reality was the Lord of the house.

CHAPTER SIXTY-SEVEN

The Dūrvāmāhātmya (Contd.)

Kauṇḍinya said:

1-6. Their seats were simply the earth, they both had clothes which were like the sky[180] and being naked, they both avoided contact with any of the natural elements. In addition they only ate food they had not begged. Still in the form of a brahmin, he saw that both of them were performing all the rites for the purification of living beings by using water and that the house was enveloped on all sides by mosquitoes and swarms of flies. He also observed both of them engrossed in him, worshipping an image of Gaṇeśa with singular devotion utilizing fresh shoots and flowers. Then he said to both of them, "Faultless people, listen to what I am going to say. After hearing of the fame of the king of Mithilā, I turned up here, very hungry and wishing to be filled up, but he did not fill me up. Because of his fraudulent activity[181] my vitality has not been sustained, but if something were to be given in this house it would make me full."

---

[180] "clothes which were like the sky" nabha prāvārasaṃyutau: A common metaphor for nakedness.

[181] "because of his fraudulent activity" karmaṇā dāmbhikena: I take this to refer to his reputation as a magnanimous king (66,7-10), building upon Janaka's own claim (66,13-14) that he is the most powerful being in the universe. This reputation has shown to be false by his incapacity to feed Gaṇeśa adequately.

The husband and wife said:

7-8. That very king who did not fill you up is a universal monarch, but being poverty-stricken what can we give to fill you up? The ocean is never filled up by countless river waters. so tell us, how can it be filled with a mere drop of water?

The brahmin said:

9. Even a little given devoutly will give me much satisfaction, but a lot given without devotion by a deceiver will be worthless!

These two said:

10-11ab. Excellent brahmin, there is nothing in our house. This is the curse on you. At dawn we collected blades of dūrvā grass for the worship of Gaṇanātha and we have worshipped Gaṇanātha with them, but now there is only one left.

The brahmin said:

12cd. Just that one given devoutly will be sufficient. Give it to me.

Kauṇḍinya said:

12. After she had heard the statement uttered by him, Virocanā devoutly gave him one blade of dūrvā grass, with which the brahmin was contented.

13-19. Boiled rice, rice cooked in milk and many kinds of cooked food, plus all of the many spices which can be licked and sucked, all this then appeared on the blade of dūrvā grass which Virocanā had devoutly offered. Accepting it, the brahmin ate it with the greatest delight and the devoutly offered blade of dūrvā grass having been eaten, the fire in the brahmin's belly was instantly appeased and he became full at that very same moment. Then after having delightfully embraced Triśiras, the satiated brahmin abandoned his despicable appearance and manifested himself as Gajānana. He had four arms and lotus-eyes, he was resplendent with an elephant's trunk and in his hands he was holding a lotus, an axe, a garland and a tusk. He also had a very valuable diadem and he was adorned with radiant earrings and garments of celestial cloth smeared with celestial fragrances.

20. Pleased, Gajānana said to both husband and wife, "Choose a boon immediately! Ask for anything in your heart!"

These two said:

21. Whatever our lives might be, let our devotion to you be rock-solid and, God, free us from this ocean of existence which is so difficult to cross. We are both utterly destitute and expect nothing else, Ibhānana.

Kauṇḍinya said:

22. After he had given ear to this statement, had given his affirmation to it and had again happily embraced his devotee, Triśiras, Gajānana disappeared.

23-24. It is for this reason[182] that I offer him a load of dūrvā grass. That god did not become full from unlimited eating, but with just a blade of dūrvā grass he became completely full.

25-26. What I have just correctly related, Āśrayā, is powerful and auspicious. Because of the prosperity derived from offering dūrvā grass, the hearing of it gives one every wish. Whoever should devoutly hear or tell this traditional legend becomes fulfilled in his wishes, wealth and sons and will be happy here and in the next world. And whoever has no desires, yet accomplishes devotion towards Gajānana, will attain liberation.

The hosts said:

27-30. After she had heard this traditional legend, Āśrayā had a doubt in her mind, realizing which Kauṇḍinya spoke again.

---

[182] "It is for this reason...": This answers Āśrayā's questions (See 63.14-15) addressed to him as to why he offered Gaṇeśa dūrvā grass every day.

"Āśrayā, faultless woman, listen to my speech which will remove this doubt. I know what is in your mind and I am going to speak about it. After you have picked up one blade of dūrvā grass, go quickly to Indra, then utter your benediction first and afterwards, ask for an amount of gold equivalent in weight to the dūrvā grass. Once you have received it, bring it here. Neither more nor less should be taken from his cache, Lovely-faced woman."

CHAPTER SIXTY-EIGHT

The Dūrvāmāhātmya (Contd.)

The hosts said:

1-2. As commanded by the sage, she took a single blade of dūrvā grass and went to Śakra in order to accomplish her beloved husband's wish. Āśrayā said to him, "At the command of my husband I have come to ask you for some bright gold, so give me some, Lord of the gods."

Indra said:

3. Why did you come here? If a command had been made I would have sent gold to you by my own power.

Āśrayā said:

4. The gold must be the weight of a blade of dūrvā grass, god. I will take neither more nor less than that, Husband of Śaci!

Indra said:

5. Messenger, take her to Kubera's palace immediately and he will give her bright gold equivalent to a blade of dūrvā grass.

The hosts said:

6. Then with the permission of the king of the gods, the god's messenger went with her to Kubera's palace in accord with Śakra's command.

The messenger said:

7-8ab. Indra sent this good lady, who is a sage's wife, with me. Give her gold equivalent to a blade of dūrvā grass. Now that she has reached your palace, I am going. Obeisance to you, god!

Kubera said:

8cd-9. I think this is absolutely amazing. Śakra, Āśrayā and the sage are mad and don't know how much gold is the equivalent of a blade of dūrvā grass. Will there be too much or haven't they asked for enough?

The hosts said:

10-18. And so he gave enough gold to her but fearful of her husband and in doubt whether it was too little or too large, she did not take it. He placed the blade of dūrvā grass on a goldsmith's scales, but the gold did not equal it in weight. A merchant's scales was then brought, but on that also there was no equivalence, nor was equivalence with the blade of dūrvā grass reached on the scales of an oil miller. Another balance was then fixed there and on one side of it gold was put and on the other side a blade of dūrvā grass. Then the leaf went down[183] and Kubera placed another piece of gold on it, then many others. But even then there was no equivalence between it and the dūrvā grass. Then he placed the entire wealth of the treasury on it and it was high as a mountain. However, even that was not the equivalent of the blade of dūrvā grass. Filled with surprise, Kubera then summoned his wife and said, "At my command, Lovely lady, ascend that set of scales which is in front of me. If not I will equalize it in order to preserve my own wealth." Loyal to her husband, she then ascended the scales at his command, but even she was not its equivalent. Kubera then placed his entire city in the middle of the scales, but the blade of grass did not go up.

---

[183] That is, the side of the scale holding the leaf went down.

19-24. Hearing of this from his messenger's mouth, Indra came, mounted on his elephant, and with his own wealth he himself ascended the scales. However, he too went upwards and not the dūrvā grass. Face downcast, he became anxious, wondering, "What is this?" He thought of Viṣṇu and Śiva, hoping they would ascend it, and they both came with their cities and ascended the scales. Still, however, the blade of grass did not visibly go upwards. After that, just as birds go to their own nests when the end of the day has come, Viṣṇu, Śiva, Kubera, Varuṇa, Indra, Agni and the Maruts departed and went to Kauṇḍinya, as did the gods and divine sages, the serpents, vidyādharas and the perfected sages. After they had all made obeisance to the sage, they spoke, their minds agitated.

They all said this:

25-29. As a result of seeing you, sage, our misery has now gone and there will be good fortune ahead for us because of our previous merit. It is obvious to us that your wife took our vitality,[184] but we cannot understand the power that came from one blade of dūrvā grass. Even the triple-world is not the weight of a blade of dūrvā grass. Who could truly know the power of the blade of dūrvā grass you have devoutly offered and which is on Gajānana's head? Who could really know even your power, omniscient as you are, constantly engaged in austerities and recitation, singularly devoted to Gajānana?

30. After saying this to the sage and having firstly worshipped Gajānana, they all honoured the sage and his wife. Then they sang, danced and performed a eulogy.

31. Neither Brahmā, nor Hari, nor Śiva,
Indra, the Maruts, nor Agni, Vivasvat, Yama
Śeṣa, the Moon, nor Varuṇa,
Candramas, nor the Aśvins,
Nor the Overlord of speech, nor Garuḍa,

---

[184] "took our vitality" hṛtaṃ sattvam (the latter being amended from satvam): I presume this means the piece of dūrvā grass she has placed on the scales is more powerful than the totality of the gods, the measure of power being the respective weights on both sides of the scale.

Nor Kubera, nor Aṅgiras,
Fully understand the greatness of your unknown form
By means of the celestial Vedas.

32. Then after they had all satisfied Gajānana, god of gods, in this way and had taken the sage's leave, each went to his own abode.

33-37. After becoming acquainted with this excellent Dūrvāmāhātmya, Āśrayā was filled with confidence and at her husband's command, using dūrvā grass, she worshipped Vighneśvara, god of all, whom everyone worships with dūrvā grass. She also bowed to her truth-speaking husband, Kauṇḍinya, and though quite pleased yet utterly despising herself, she said, "Because I doubted your word, there can be no woman who is as depraved as me. But now, husband, being compassionate towards all beings and especially learned, you have corrected me through your special learning, Lord. I have come to you for refuge, so forgive my mistake."[185]

38-40ab. After that, they rose in the morning and quickly gathered dūrvā grass, then made an offering of dūrvā grass to the god after they had bathed and worshipped him with singular devotion. Now that they had become acquainted with the Dūrvāmāhātmya they ceaselessly worshipped the god of gods morning and evening, putting aside sacrifice, gift-giving and the vow. Understanding this, the god Gajānana, filled with huge compassion, led them to his own home.

The hosts said:

40cd-42. We have now described this excellent and profound Dūrvāmāhātmya, a perfect description of which Śeṣa, Hari and Īśvara are incapable of giving. The triple-world is not equal in weight to one blade of it. By the recollection: "This is dūrvā grass," evil of three kinds is destroyed, because in recollecting it, the god Gajānana is recollected.

---

[185] "my mistake": That is, her mistake in not realizing why he worshipped Gaṇeśa with dūrvā grass.

43-47. The greatness of the sacred place called Cintāmaṇī has now been clearly described. The act of hearing it, of reciting it and meditating on it gives results such as bodily enjoyment and liberation. For this reason[186] an auspicious aerial vehicle was sent for these three, as from the mouth of the donkey and the bull dūrvā grass fell onto the god and a piece of dūrvā grass fell onto Gajānana. It had been taken by the destructive wind from a bundle of grass which was there to alleviate the coldness of the cāṇḍāla woman. Being fond of dūrvā grass, Vināyaka was fully satisfied and because they were now without evil, he offered his presence to those three. Merely by a whiff of dūrvā grass the Lord becomes fully satisfied, how much more if it is placed on his head with assiduous devotion.

Brahmā said:

48. King,[187] none of the sages have either witnessed or heard of the power of dūrvā grass, but you have now heard about it from a messenger's mouth.

49-53. After they had bathed and had taken blades of dūrvā grass they too worshipped Vināyaka and their servants also worshipped the splendid Gajānana with dūrvā grass. All of them acquired celestial bodies, in lustre brilliant as the sun. Wearing celestial garments and smeared with oils, they ascended an excellent aerial vehicle, whilst hearing all around them the cacophanous sounds of celestial instruments. Some went to Vināyaka's residence and assumed his own real appearance, whilst other men, citizens of towns, went to watch him at a large festival and each one worshipped him singly with twenty one pieces of dūrvā grass. After enjoying bodily delights, they too

---

[186] "For this reason...": This is not entirely clear, but the next line confirms that it was their contact with dūrvā grass which motivated Gaṇeśa to appear to them. Presumably these three words refer to the general lesson - the value in touching dūrvā grass - the previous chapters have been teaching.

[187] "King": Here the king is Kṛtavīrya, to whom Brahmā has previously (62,2) agreed to speak about the powers of dūrvā grass.

went to Gaṇeśa's abode, their aerial vehicle moving upwards because of the mass of their merit.

54-57. Therefore a devotee of Gaṇeśa must worship with dūrvā grass, but the man who negligently omits to perform worship with that shall be regarded as a cāṇḍāla and will end up in many hells. A person should never look upon his face. But whoever, even if he is an evil-doer, should worship Gajānana, god of gods, with dūrvā grass, will be purified by a vision of him. When one cannot obtain much dūrvā grass, one should worship with only one piece of it, for worship undertaken with that will be multiplied by myriads. There is no doubt of it.

Brahmā said:

58-59ab. King, the power of dūrvā grass and its associated traditional legends has been narrated to you in a variety of ways. By hearing about it evil is destroyed. This should not be told to one who has a malignant mind, but it should be communicated to a beloved son.

Indra said:

59cd-60. After he had heard this most excellent tale from Brahmā's mouth, he experienced the highest pleasure and bowed to Brahmā, with whose assent he returned to his own house, quite amazed.

CHAPTER SIXTY-NINE

Description of the Vow called Saṃkaṣṭa of the Fourth

Śūrasena said:

1. What did Kṛtavīrya's son do after that? Recite yet another tale about Gaṇanātha, Indra!

Indra said:

2-3. Well, after the excellent king had heard the tale of the Saṃkaṣṭa of the Fourth (Tuesday) and of the dūrvā grass, he became filled with anxiety, thinking, "A person without a son has no happiness. How will I have a son?"

4-8. In this situation Kṛtavīrya's son visited his father in a vision, but they could not talk to each other because their voices were stammering. However, they did embrace each other, their hearts beating with affection. Taking his son by the hand, his father then placed him on a couch and he said, "Son, you have taken great pains to get a son, so I will tell you the way to do it, faultless son. Nārada came from the world of mortals and told it to me, then I went to Brahmā's residence, son, and after making obeisance to omniscient Brahmā, I asked him, "Lotus-seated Brahmā, how will my son get a lineage?" And he recited the vow of the highest quality called Saṃkaṣṭa of the Fourth.

Brahmā said:

9. Excellent king, when that vow is completed, evil is destroyed[188] and your son will have a lineage, no doubt of it.

His father said:

10-12. At the time, it was written[189] down exactly as Brahmā declared it, so take this book and perform that vow as it should be done. If it is performed for a year, Siddhivināyaka, the god who removes all difficulties, will be pleased for that length of time. And when he is pleased you will have a son, no doubt of it.

13-14. After saying this, King, the father disappeared from his son. Then Kṛtavīrya's powerful son woke up, saw the book in his hand and remembered the object of his vision. Overwhelmed by joy and grief, he shed tears from his eyes and

---

[188] "evil is destroyed": The clear implication being that the lack of a son is evil because it destroys the lineage.

[189] "it was written": That is, the details of the vrata were written down.

whilst he was stricken with grief because he was separated from his father, he bristled with joy because he had obtained the book.

15. Meanwhile his ministers came and having surrounded the king, they spoke to him.

The ministers said:

16. Don't lose control, King! Regain your composure! Put your grief aside and tell us what has caused this grief. Because of your grief excessive grief has infected us.

Indra said:

17ab. After hearing his minister's statement Kṛtavīrya's son spoke to them.

The king said:

17cd-20. My mind is agitated because I have seen my father in a dream. He put a book of instructions concerning the vow of the Saṃkaṣṭa of the Fourth into my hand and then, at that very moment, he disappeared. Like a poor man who has lost his wealth, I am grieving because of my separation from him. But he ordered me to perform this vow in order to get a son. When I awakened, ministers, I saw a book in my hand and I shed tears of joy and grief because of that miraculous experience. This is the truth.

They said:

21-23ab. It was the father of all beings, humans, snakes and rākṣasas who had your father's appearance. That is, it was Gajānana in your father's form and as he was very satisfied, he told you a way to continue your lineage, Excellent king. How could that book be accounted for otherwise? How else could the object of this dream be true? But for his favour even your dream would be declared as being mistaken.

Indra said:

23cd-30. After he had heard the ministers' speech the king, his mind attentive, having summoned the wise men and his friends, asked them, "Brahmins, tell me about that book which I obtained because of his favour." After they had examined it they proclaimed its meaning in a large colloquy. "King, there occurred an extensive discussion between Brahmā and Kṛtavīrya in which was described the 'Fourth' which removes all difficulties. The worship of Gaṇeśa at moonrise was also described in details, the greatness of the fourth Tuesday was extensively described as well as the valuable gifts with their accompanying mantras for the moon and the gods on the lunar days. The honouring of twenty-one brahmins, the food for them and the various gifts to be given to`them were also described. Faultless king, by good fortune you have acquired the specific results[190] of offering dūrvā grass, the results of white dūrvā grass and this vow, Illustrious king, something which has neither been seen nor heard of in the world. The hearing and recollecting of it will be very beneficial and will also remove difficulties for men."

31-33. After he had heard about its meaning from the mouth of the wise men, the king was filled with both astonishment and joy and he honoured the excellent brahmins. To them and all his subjects he gave much money, grains, clothes, jewels and ornaments. Then the king summoned Atri, his family teacher, and after he had worshipped the god Vināyaka at an auspicious hour and according to the ritual, he received the auspicious one syllable mantra.

34. Senses conquered he recited that mantra,
Meditating on Gaṇeśa with singular devotion.
And for Gaṇanātha's satisfaction and to gain a son,
He performed that vow which removes difficulties.

---

[190] "you have acquired the specific results...": The sense here is that all the information which produces the results of offering dūrvā grass, etc., is found in the book given by Gaṇeśa.

CHAPTER SEVENTY

Description of the Vow of the Fourth

Śūrasena said:

1. Tell me how Brahmā taught Kṛtavīrya this success-giving vow of the highest quality called the Saṃkaṣṭa of the Fourth.

Indra said:

2. In Satyaloka the very fortunate King Kṛtavīrya bowed to the omniscient Brahmā who was comfortably seated and questioned him.

Kṛtavīrya said:

3-6ab. God of gods, disposer of the universe, destroyer of pain for those who are obeisant, tell me whatever I request of you that is in my heart! How can men who live in conditions of distress, men whose minds are confused, men whose minds are tormented by anxiety and friends who are separated, be successful in attaining something rare. How can they constantly acquire money, wealth, prosperity and sons, Lord, and what can humans do to remove all their troubles?

Brahmā said:

6cd-7ab. Listen, King, I am going to describe that vow which gives every success. By its mere performance a man will obtain whatever can be imagined.

7cd-9. During the day a person whose mind is clear should smear himself with herbs and white sesamum. Then he should make a declaration to perform the ritual and after meditating on the god Gajānana, on the night of the rising of the moon and on the fourth day of the dark fortnight, he should devoutly worship Gaṇeśa with mantras from the sacred texts, King.

The king said:

10. Brahmā, how should one worship Gajānana, god of gods? As a favour to one who has made a request, tell me this in detail.

Brahmā said:

11-16. On the night of the rising of the moon, after completing the obligatory rituals, one should worship a pedestal[191] for Gaṇeśa with uncrushed flowers on a spot that is clean, smeared with cow dung and contains a small pavilion. On the pedestal one should place a pot containing the five jewels and on top of it one should place a golden lid suitable for a pot. However, if that is unavailable one should place on top of it whatever one can–silver, copper, mere bamboo or a linen cloth. On top of that one should design a yantra as prescribed in the Āgamas. And on that one should place a golden image of Gaṇeśa with these characteristics: a single tooth, a huge body resembling burnished gold, a pendulous belly, large eyes, blazing like the sun, mounted on the back of a rat, fanned by the hosts with fly whisks and with Śeṣa as his sacred thread. One should contemplate this Gajānana. (This is the meditation)

17. "Come, Indra of the kings of obstacles! Keep me away from problems! Stay in my presence for as long as I am performing this vow!" This invocation is introduced with the mantra beginning "Thousand-headed."[192]

18. "Overlord of the hosts, may there be obeisance to you, bestower of every success! God, accept this seat and keep me away from problems!" The seat is introduced with the mantra "This alone is the Puruṣa."

19. "Son of Umā, may there be obeisance to you! Obeisance to you, God who loves modakas! Accept this water for your feet, God, and keep me away from problems!" The water for the feet is introduced with the mantra "He is of such an extent."

---

[191] "worship a pedestal": That is, one should worship the pīṭha (the pedestal on which an image can be placed) in the small pavillion.

[192] The refrain of each verse from 17-33 invokes the Puruṣasūkta.

20. "Pendulous belly, may there be obeisance to you! Accept this water for the reception and fruit and jewels, Lord of gods, and keep me away from problems!" The water for the reception is introduced with the mantra "Three parts above."

21. "Accept the five immortal substances which include milk, sour milk, ghee, sugar and honey, and keep me away from problems!"

22. "I have devoutly bathed you using water taken from the confluence of the Ganges, the Narmadā and the Candrabhāgā. Keep me away from problems!" The bath is invoked with the mantra called Puruṣasūkta.

23. "Elephant-face, obeisance to you! Accept this pair of garments, Supreme Lord, and Overlord of the hosts, keep me away from problems!" The garment is invoked with the mantra "That is the sacrifice."

24. "Vināyaka, obeisance to you! Obeisance to the Axe-carrier! Accept this sacred thread and keep me away from problems!" The sacred thread is invoked with the mantra called "From that..."

25. "Īśa's son, may there be obeisance to you! Obeisance, you whose vehicle is a mouse! Take this sandal-wood, God, and keep me away from problems!" The sandal-wood is invoked with the mantra "From that sacrifice."

26. "I have given you captivating uncrushed flowers, rice, grain and ghee. Keep me away from problems!" "Uncrushed flowers."

27. "Overlord of the hosts, accept flowers of many kinds including dūrvā grass, jasmine and campaka! Free me from problems!" The flowers are invoked with the mantra "From that comes the horse."

28. "Pendulous belly, your body large, your banner grey, accept this fragrant incense and, Lord of gods, keep me away from problems!" The incense is invoked with the mantra "From that comes the Puruṣa."

29. "Cause of the destruction of darkness and obstacles, Overlord of the thirty, accept this lamp and keep me away from

problems!" The lamp is invoked with the mantra "His is the brahmin."

30. "God, accept this food offering made from clarified butter, cooked food, sugar, milk, ladūkas, flour cakes and modakas!" The food is invoked with the mantra "The moon is his mind."

31. "Lord of the gods, take this auspicious good fruit, namely, pomegranate, mango, grapes and coconut and keep me away from problems!"

32. "God, accept this betel nut which consists of the leaves of the nagavalli, cardamom, cloves and areca nuts etc., and keep me away from problems!"

33. "Accept this honorarium of gold, God, which gives every success and causes joy for everyone, and keep me away from problems!"

34. Then after picking up twenty-one blades of dūrvā grass and with concentration complete, one should worship the god to the best of one's ability with these names:

1.Obeisance to the Overlord of hosts.
2. Obeisance to Umā's son.
3. Obeisance to the remover of evil.
4. Obeisance to him who has one tusk.
5. Obeisance to Elephant-face.
6. Obeisance to him whose vehicle is the mouse.
7. Obeisance to Vināyaka.
8. Obeisance to Īśa's son.
9. Obeisance to him who gives every success.
10. Obeisance to him who has a pendulous belly.
11. Obeisance to him who has a trunk on his face.
12. Obeisance to him who loves sweetmeats.
13. Obeisance to him who causes the destruction of obstacles.
14. Obeisance to him whom everyone praises.
15. Obeisance to the Lord of the gods.
16. Obeisance to him who has elephant's ears.
17. Obeisance to him whose sacred thread is a snake.
18. Obeisance to him who has the moon on his brow.
19. Obeisance to him who holds an axe.

20. Obeisance to the Overlord of obstacles.

21. Obeisance to him who grants knowledge.

35."Lord, accept this offering of lights made from camphor wood stalks which destroys the entire flood of evil, and free me from problems."

36."You alone create the universe, Elephant-face.
You alone protect the universe, God.
You alone destroy the universe, Lord of all.
You alone are the self of the universe shining outwards.

37. I bow to God, Lord of the hosts, the Lord,
Lord of obstacles, who is proficient in removing obstacles,
Who removes his devotee's pain, who is proficient in freeing his devotees,
Who gives knowledge, who is the cause of the Vedas, primordial."

38. Such is the homage. In this way one should eulogize him as prescribed, bow repeatedly to him and perform twenty-one circumambulations insofar as one can.

39. "Without having worshipped you first, Gaṇeśa,
There are fools who strive for goals they have resolved upon.
Inevitably they are unsuccessful in the world.
I know all your powers."

40-41. Here is the petition: "Accept this sweetmeat, Teacher, Overseer of the brahmins, who gives every success, and keep me away from troubles! I have given you this special water containing uncrushed flowers and fruits, and an honorarium as well. Keep me away from troubles!"

42. Then to the accompaniment of the sixteen ritual practices one should conduct worship with this mantra: "Om! Obeisance, Heramba, who is exhilarated by spirituous liquor. Keep me away from troubles! Homage!"

43-52. The wise man should also worship the world-protectors, led by Indra, on all sides. Insofar as he can, he should then prepare sweet meats cooked in clarified butter as well as cooked beans, sesamum, other foods and betel. Then after picking up twenty-one blades of dūrvā grass and with concentration complete, one should devoutly worship the god with this list of names: Obeisance to you, Lord of hosts, Umā's son, Giver of security, One- tusk, Elephant-face, Whose vehicle is the mouse, Vināyaka, Īśa's son, Who gives every success, Obeisance to you, who has a pendulous belly, who has a trunk on his face, who removes evils, who causes the destruction of obstacles, Lord of the immortals who is praised by everyone! Obeisance to you, Elephant-face, to you whose sacred thread is a snake! Obeisance to you, on whose brow is the moon, Obeisance to him who holds an axe! Obeisance to you, Overlord of obstacles, who grants the entirety of knowledge! One should worship the god as such and with separate pieces of dūrvā grass, saying, "Having regard to this act of worship which I have correctly performed in accord with my capability, be satisfied with it and immediately fulfil the wishes in my heart! Remove all the obstacles and evils that have beset me and by your favour I will carry out all my tasks! Bring about the removal of my enemies' wisdom and elevate my friends!"

53-55. After having requested this and bowed repeatedly to the Lord of the gods, one should perform one hundred and eight offerings with sweet meats, King, in order to complete the vow, or perform a smaller number with laḍūkas, pulse cakes and twenty-one fruits. Having then clothed oneself in a red garment one should present oneself before one's teacher, saying, "Obeisance to you, Overlord of the hosts, who gives every success that can be imagined! By this gift of sweetmeats keep me away from problems!"

56-59. After hearing this meritorious tale the self-composed man should offer water seven times to the moon, King, with this mantra: "Moon, arisen from the Milk-ocean, born from Atri's eye, you and Rohiṇī accept this water offering for the reception I have offered." One should then request forbearance from the god of gods, feed the brahmins and then feed oneself with the remainder of what was offered to the brahmins. Seven mouthfuls should be taken silently according to one's capability and at one's pleasure. All this should be performed according as prescribed in the fourth month.

CHAPTER SEVENTY-ONE

The Tale of the Vow of the Fourth

The king said:

1. In the past who has performed and revealed this vow on the Earth? Kindly tell me, Lord, what merit there is in it and what result it produced?

Brahmā said:

2-12. Long ago when Skanda had gone and Pārvatī had just performed that vow at Śiva's command in the fourth month, King, she found Skanda again in the fifth month. Long ago Agastya performed it in the third month when he was trying to drink the ocean and due to Vighneśa's favour he did drink it. In the past, Overlord of kings, Damayantī performed it in the sixth month when she was searching for Nala and she found Nala. And long ago, King, Citralekhā took away Pradyumna's son, and when Pradyumna, confused, grieving and sick with grief for his son, said, "Where has he gone? Who took him?" Rukmiṇī replied, "Listen son whilst I tell you about the vow. In the past when you were a young child six days old, Śambara took you away to his own house and because I was separated from you, my heart burnt with pain as I was wondering, 'When will I see my extraordinarily handsome son?' But on seeing the sons of other women I knew in my heart that this was proof[193] that I would have a son too. Many days passed during which I was thus disturbed in thought, but by the power of fate the sage Lomaśa then came to me. He taught me the vow of the highest quality called Saṃkaṣṭa of the Fourth, which removes all

---

[193] "this was proof": Her observation of other women with sons is proof that she too will have a son.

anxiety and I performed it four times. By its favour[194] you returned, after you had killed Śambara in battle. You too should perform that vow and then you will find your son."

13-19. Long ago Pradyumna performed it, fully satisfying Gaṇanātha and in the past, whilst he was in the city of the demon Bāṇa, Aniruddha learnt about it from Nārada. At Uddhava's command Kṛṣṇa performed this vow of the highest quality a single time and according to the rules when he was afraid to do battle with Īśvara. And after he had conquered the city of blood and had conquered the demon Bāṇa in battle, Aniruddha was immediately married to Uṣas, King. I too performed it when I wished to create, Excellent king, and due to the power of that vow a creation of great variety was accomplished. Other gods, demons and men have performed it for the mitigation of obstacles, as have sages, dānavas, yakṣas, kiṃnaras, snakes and rākṣasas. One should perform that vow when in distress or to remove difficulties when one experiences them. A vow like it produces every success in the world, but austerities, generosity, recitation, pilgrimage, a mantra or a spell can never do this.

20-21. After hearing this tale, King, one should silently feed oneself and, placing one's hands in between the knees, reflect in the heart on Gaṇeśa and then, with one's kinsmen, eat what has been left over by the brahmins. It will be successful whether it is performed over a few months or many, no doubt of it. What more can be said about it! Nothing else can give instant success.

22-24. This should not be taught to a man who is not a devotee, nor to an unbeliever, nor to a deceitful person, but it should be offered to a son, a pupil, a man intent upon devotion or an accomplished man. Indra of kings, this vow has been taught to you because you are high in the law, a bull of warriors, one who acts in the interest of people. Accordingly, of all vows,

---

194 "by its favour" tatprasādāt: the vrata is performed for Gaṇeśa and so becomes the mechanism whereby Gaṇeśa extends his favour, this in turn allowing Pradyumna to return to his own mother.

perform this one first and your tasks will be accomplished. I have not spoken falsely.

25. Whenever a man or a woman considers a task worth striving for,

This good vow should be performed.

Then all esteemed tasks will be accomplished.

What can be difficult to get when Vighnahara is pleased?

The Sūta said:

26. After he had heard this the excellent king,

Duly performed that vow to remove his difficulties.

By the power of the vow he conquered his enemies,

And with his sons he enjoyed the kingdom without impediment.

CHAPTER SEVENTY-TWO

The Tale of the Vow of the Fourth

Kṛtavīrya said:

1. Wise god, how should the concluding ceremony of that vow be performed? Because of your desire for the welfare of beings, tell me that in detail.

Brahmā said:

2-8. The concluding ceremony should be performed in the first, the fifth or the seventh month in order finally to complete the vow, Indra of men. A devout man should worship with the rite as described previously.[195] After he has constructed a small flower pavilion adorned with various cloths, beautified it all over and painted it with many colours, he should worship the Lord of gods in it on a pot as before. Then when he is self-composed he should offer water for the reception, coconut fruit,

---

195 "as described previously" in Ch. 70.

fragrant sandal-wood and flowers of various kinds, with the words, "Best of lunar days, goddess who is loved by those who are loved by Gaṇeśa, take away my problems! Goddess, accept this water for the reception! May there be obeisance to you! Pendulous belly! Obeisance to you always! You who are fond of modakas, take away my problems! God, accept this water for the reception! May there be obeisance to you! Moon, arisen from the Milk ocean, born in Atri's lineage, you and Rohiṇī accept this water offering for the reception which I have offered."

9-13. He should offer soft food, hard food, liquid food, food which can be licked and food which can be sucked and satisfy Gaṇanāyaka with many other things and fruits. He should then choose a guide and twenty-one priests for it and perform ten thousand offerings with the mantra, "You are of the hosts," or else a thousand with a root mantra, or half of that, or even just one hundred and eight. Then he should perform a food offering, pour a full oblation and, afterwards, pour out a "stream of wealth."[196] After completing the rest of the offering, he should then feed the brahmins and in accord with his capacity, he should give them a pair of garments, pots and seats as honorariums. He should not engage in cheating in money matters.

14-17ab. Afterwards he should honour his teacher with clothes, ornaments and so forth and when he has eaten some food, he should give him some sweetmeats containin fruit. And as an honorarium he should give him a golden image of Gaṇādhiśa and a pot, filled with rice boiled in milk, wrapped in red cloth. After that he should offer him a plate of sesamum in order to complete the vow, and after that he should give a tawny cow is decorated and accompanied by a calf. Then he should ask for the brahmins' sufferance with the words, "May Vighneśa be pleased."

---

[196] "stream of wealth" vasor dhārāṃ: I am uncertain about the precise meaning of these words. Monier-Williams cites vasudhāra with this meaning.

17cd. When he has completed the concluding ceremony of that vow he will obtain the result of a horse sacrifice.

The father said:

18. Brahmā taught me this vow for the benefit of beings. Now that it has been told to you, perform it diligently to obtain a son.

Indra said:

19. The wise Kārtavīrya performed this great vow in just the way that his father had described it.

20-26. This vow of the highest quality was recited and after it had been correctly explained by learned men and a golden image of Gaṇeśa with Siddhi and Buddhi was set up in a large pavilion, some brahmins recited the Vedas in one place, some a Purāṇa filled with learning in another place, whilst others engaged in singing and dancing somewhere else. The sounds of many musical instruments went to the sky and some people engaged in debate, whilst others remained impartial. The very wise king recited the superlative mantra and once he had recited it, sacrificed, honoured and fed the many brahmins, he gave ornamented cows to those who were ornamented and to the wretched, the blind and the poverty stricken he gave food and various gifts. Then from all those brahmins who were performing austerities and always spoke the truth, the king received the blessing for a son in consequence of their complete satisfaction. Due to these blessings the queen soon became pregnant and at an auspicious time she gave birth to a son who possessed the right qualities.

27-29. Enraptured by the birth of his son the king gave away many gifts and at the appropriate time the king arranged the investiture of his sacred thread and his marriage. And once he had consecrated his son who possessed both knowledge and wisdom, the king who had enjoyed the Earth, went finally to the abode of the Lord, in conjunction with the sacrificial priests, learned men and spectators. All of them went to Gaṇeśa's abode because of his merit.

CHAPTER SEVENTY-THREE

The Caturthīmāhātmya

Śūrasena said:

1. Indra, performer of one hundred sacrifices, did those two have a son at the conclusion of the vow? I have asked you, so tell me everything in detail, Lord.

Indra said:

2-4. King, whatever could not happen when Gaṇeśa is fully satisfied? As a result of his favour the king's queen became pregnant. In the ninth month she gave birth and she saw that her auspicious son had two shoulders and a pleasant face, but that he was without arms and hands. He had a fine nose and lotus eyes, but neither knees, calves nor feet. When she saw him his mother really cried.

She said:

5-7. How could I be so unfortunate as to have a boy like this? He has neither hands nor feet! Gajānana, why has he been given to me? Even though barren, I was pure, so why have I got a son like this? Hasn't the evil I committed in a previous birth already been removed? Dviradānana, how could even your favour have turned out like this? How could the commands of the brahmins[197] have produced such results for me?

8-10ab. She was striking her breast and forehead repeatedly with her hands and when she wept, every other woman who stood there wept too. On hearing their uproar the king came there too and his ministers also came there after they heard him weeping. The citizens themselves cried too after they heard them crying.

[197] "commands of the brahmins": I presume the word "commands" refers to the blessings made in 1.72.25-26.

The king said:

10cd-14. In what way,[198] God Gajānana, do you sympathize with those who are miserable? In what way have you expressed sympathy for me now and in what way do you remove evils merely as a result of recollection, Faultless god? Recitation, austerity, recollection,[199] gift-giving, worship. feeding of the brahmins, personal service and sacrifice have all been useless for me. Fate is more powerful than these, continuous exertion is useless, the result of actions can never be known, nor can the future. Just as by cutting through a mountain[200] one only gets a rat, so too has this son of mine been born to me because of an effort made in a previous life.

15ab. Then the ministers spoke to that king who was full of grief.

The ministers said:

15cd-17. Stop grieving, Protector of the Earth. How can the inevitable be otherwise? Did not Rāma recognize the deer when asked for it, but he still left![201] And didn't Yudhiṣṭhira know that he would lose when he engaged in gambling. Even so, Yudhiṣṭhira, King of dharma, went to play and after he had lost everything, went to the forest.

---

[198] "In what way...": Clearly the king's statement is a rhetorical question as he cannot comprehend how Gaṇeśa could possibly give him a deformed son after all the worship he has offered him.

[199] "of recollection": That is, of Gaṇeśa.

[200] "by cutting through a mountain": where the implication is that one is looking for jewels. The meaning of the metaphor is that not even hard work guarantees a predictable result. Fate overrides human effort.

[201] "...he still left": Rāma knew the deer was the demon Mārici in disguise, yet he still went after it because he was requested to do so by Sītā (See Rām. 3.42). Yudhiṣṭhira gambled with Śakuni as recounted in Mbh. 2.53-58 even though he knew he would lose. In this matter he had no choice because he had to accede to the power of fate and the command of his maternal uncle to engage in the gambling match (Mbh. 2.52.14-15).

18-19ab. Given such bitter lamentation,[202] there may be nothing agreeable in him, yet if that which cannot be foreseen really happens, then in the future he may well be agreeable. Just as a fruit or a flower becomes a great tree over time, so too will he, over time, truly become Lord of the Earth.

Indra said:

19cd-24. After he had heard his ministers' statement the king became attentive and said to his queen, "Get up! Get up! Don't grieve!" And the king, himself now cheerful, summoning the bulls of brahmins, performed worship to Gaṇeśa and a svastivācana. After he had performed a śrāddha for prosperity, he gave away many presents, including many garlands, ornaments, clothes, cows, jewels and various clothes to his friends, kinsmen and retainers as well as to the various musicians according to their worth, and to the captives, itinerant actors, the miserable, the blind and the poverty stricken in general. And in every house he had betel and sugar nut presented.

25-32. On the eleventh day he named him Kārtavīrya and he fed the entire town which was in a state of great festiveness. And when his son was twelve years old Dattātreya came of his own volition to his home. After Kṛtavīrya had placed his head at his feet, he bowed to him and when the sage got up, he too embraced the excellent king, who, having sat him upon a charming seat, honoured him respectfully. When he was comfortably seated and pleased, with his feet being rubbed etc., he gave him a foot stool, water for the reception, a cow, clothes, a sacred thread, incense, a lamp, an offering of various kinds of fruit, an unguent, betel and an honorarium of jewels and gold. The king said to the great sage Dattātreya, "Sage, judging by your appearance in person before my naked eye, something in a previous life has now produced merit for me. Due to your favour, Strong-vowed sage, the future will be most auspicious, as evil-doers never have a sight of people like you."

---

202 "lamentation": That is, about the son.

33. After he had heard Kṛtavīrya's speech, Dattātreya said to him, "I have come now wishing to see your extraordinary son." Thereafter, filled with joy, the king spoke again to the sage.

The king said:

34-35. Personal service, austerity and gift-giving is useless. My vow has elapsed and the Lord of the worlds has now given me this son who is a veritable spear in the heart and because of his unseemliness I have become one unworthy to be looked upon.

Indra said:

36-38. After he had fetched the boy, the king presented him to the sage, but when he saw his son the good sage shaded his lotus eyes. Realizing by meditation his deed[203] the sage addressed him again, "King, by conquering everyone this very son of yours will become a killer. Your son has been born without some limbs because you yawned at the time of the vow of Saṃkaṣṭa when you should have been awake and you did not sip water. But he will gain these limbs by some means."

The king said:

39. You have expressed that well, Lord. Have pity on me and tell me the means by which, due to your favour, my son will have his limbs.

Indra said:

40-46. Filled with pity the sage then told his son a one-syllable mantra for obtaining his limbs. Then he spoke to him once more about the devout propitiation of Gaṇeśa by means of a mantra. "For twelve years undertake restraints through eating one meal a day and fasting, Strong-vowed boy, and he will

---

[203] "his deed" tatkarma: This refers to the deed which caused the young boy to be born in a deformed state.

make an appearance to you. Merely by casting a glance on him you will have a celestial body." When he had said this to the king and had bid him farewell, the bull of sages disappeared, and after he had departed, that proud son who had no feet said to Kṛtavīrya, "Take me to the dense forest. I am going to undertake this personal service for the sake of Gaṇeśa's favour." When they heard this statement he had uttered his parents wept, but his father sent him to the forest in a pleasant palanquin. And after the servants had set him up in a hut made of leaves they returned to the city. There he remained, duly resolved in himself to perform austerities.

(Contd.)

CHAPTER SEVENTY-FOUR

The Caturthīmāhātmya (Contd.)

Indra said:

1-2. Having assumed the highest condition of devotion he was meditating on the god Gajānana and in a condition of restraint–eating only air, fasting and looking like a lump of stone–he recited the mantra his teacher had taught.

3-4. Whilst that eminent young boy who had neither hands nor feet was undergoing austerities in this way twelve years passed. After observing the perfect calm he had achieved for twelve years, Gajānana emerged out of a pool, his body made of coral, and coming face to face, he spoke, highly satisfied by his firm devotion.

Gaṇeśa said:

5-6ab. Because you have stayed for twelve years in a dense thicket in this desolate forest filled with lions and tigers, I am going to give you a boon, so be attentive to what is in your mind.

6cd-7. When he had heard this statement he had made, Kṛtavīrya's son began thinking about a body, and after bowing he addressed Dviradānana whilst various gods and sages were listening in their vehicles.

The son said:

8-9. May my devotion never deviate from your lotus feet, God, and may I have the will never to ask for anything else. However, Lord of the gods, I am going to request something in order to please my parents. Give me beauty in body[204] such as will produce complete satisfaction.

Indra said:

10-20. After hearing his speech, and having made himself tiny, Gajānana, the illusionist, entered his belly. And when he had made his entry, that son assumed a divine body, King. Kṛtavīrya's son then became thousand-armed and standing with his two feet straight, he looked like a mountain. The gods and the celestial sages rained down showers of flowers and to the sounds of celestial instruments they eulogized him and the god. Adorned with one thousand arms, Kārtavīrya then roared, and on hearing his noise, which was like the rumbling of thunder, Yama, the unflappable, became exceedingly frightened. How then could the fear of others be reckoned?[205] All the kings on Earth were afraid of him and trembled, thinking, "In battle he will shoot five hundred arrows!" Then after getting out of their vehicles, Brahmā and the rest said to him, "By recollecting you the wealth of the gods that has been lost might be restored. You will drive away that sickness which exists in the hearts of all beings. And because you embody Viṣṇu in your appearance you will be celebrated in the three worlds for the length of a kalpa

---

[204] The request made in this verse for a handsome body does not contradict the final statement he has just made in vs.8. That statement implied he would not ask for something for himself and in vs.9 he asks for something which will be of benefit to others as well as to himself.

[205] "How then could the fear of others be reckoned?": This rhetorical question receives its bite from the high degree of fear accorded to Yama in his role as god of death.

under the name of Sahasrārjuna and you will devote yourself to helping the good and protecting those who come for refuge. You will be the punisher of all enemies and the Overlord of the Earth." After they had given him these many gifts the gods, beloved of Diti, disappeared. All the kings, too, brought him elephants, horses, carriages, umbrellas, fly-whisks, lamps, chariots and other presents.

21-26. Attended by brahmins, he then had a coral image of Gaṇanātha set up in a large temple and the brahmins gave it the name of "Coral Gaṇeśa." To the brahmins he gave villages which were set aside for worship[206] and this area, which gives success, became famed on Earth as Pravālakṣetra. On that spot Śeṣa became resolved upon undertaking the support of the Earth and from Gaṇeśa he obtained many boons: a capacity to support the Earth, omniscience as well, a thousand heads and preeminence amongst the nine snake families. He was completely satisfied in his heart by this and re-established the area, which became famous under its second name of "Dharaṇīdhara." It gives a result in regard to every desire to those who hear about it and recollect it.

27. After honouring all the bulls of brahmins,
After inquiring about all the kings,
The thousand-armed man returned to his own city
To visit his mother and father.

28. However, when both of them saw him in this condition and the city as well, they both rejoiced and happily gave various gifts to the principal brahmins.

Indra said:

29-32. I have explained this wonderful, marvellous dangerous Fourth, which is auspicious and has come to the world of men because of Kṛtavīrya's son. Groups of gods and

---

[206] "which were set aside for worship": This means that the revenue derived from them was not taxed and could be used to defray the expenses of pūjās.

kings such as Candrasena have experienced it,[207] it is extraordinarily meritorious and merely a recollection of it gives success. Due to its favour Rāvaṇa obtained absolute intelligence and due to its favour the Pāṇḍavas regained their kingdom. If the merit of that vow fell into my hand, this vehicle would certainly set out for Amarāvatī.

Brahmā said:

33-35ab. In this way, King Śūrasena, who was sunk in a sweet ocean of bliss, heard about the power of this vow from Śakra's mouth and roaring, he worshipped Śakra's lotus feet and then the excellent King Śūrasena spoke to him, delighted now that he had heard this tale of celestial character about the vow of the Fourth.

He said:

35cd-36ab. My previous merit has come to fruition and that is why I have heard about this vow. Absolutely nothing in the three worlds is more meritorious than it.
36cd. After he had said this he himself undertook to perform that vow for Śakra.

CHAPTER SEVENTY-FIVE

The Caturthīmāhātmya (Contd.)

Vyāsa said:

1. What did Śūrasena, enjoyer of the Earth, do after he had diligently listened to that excellent tale from Indra's mouth?

---

207 "have experienced it": that is, they have performed the vrata Indra has just narrated.

Brahmā said:

2-7ab. He then said to the messengers, "Go to the city and bring a performer of the vow of the Dangerous Fourth here." The messengers departed quickly and inquired in house after house. Whilst wandering about they saw that a beautiful, auspicious flying vehicle had arrived. It had been sent by Gaṇapa's messengers in order to take one particular woman, an evil cāṇḍāla woman, her mouth oozing leprous muck, evil smelling because of the mass of insects and flies on her, her belly shrunken, her hair long, her nose and teeth gargantuan, filthy dirty, her ear-holes long and her voice coarse. Thinking that this was extraordinary[208] the king's messengers, having bowed to her, spoke to Gaṇanātha's servants, the messengers of the god.

The messengers said:

7cd-9ab. She he is utterly contemptible and poorly bred! How can she go to heaven? Messengers, who was she previously and how did she become like this? How did you bring her to heaven? By what merit? If it can be told to us, tell us everything.

The god's messengers said:

9cd-13. In the Baṅgāla region there was a warrior named Sāraṅgadhāra whose beautiful daughter was named Sundarā. Her voice was that of a cuckoo, her face was like the moon and in loveliness she surpassed Rati. Eight cultivated noble ladies were not worthy enough to function as her servants, with a mere glance she would infatuate the heart even of yogins and just by glancing at her lovely body some young men ejaculated semen. Infatuating everyone, she became deeply involved in the ways of prostitutes and in her very costly clothes and ornaments she

---

[208] A statement referring to the heavenly vehicle, not to the juxtaposition of cāṇḍāla woman and vehicle.

offered a variety of sensual enjoyments. In the city of Baṅgāla she became famous as a quite shameless prostitute.

14-23. She constantly deceived her husband Citranāma by profligately spending incalculable wealth his father had previously accumulated. On one occasion, at midnight, after she had left him in bed, he angrily disturbed her when she was beautifully dressed and forcibly held onto her hand. Abusing her, Citranāma, her husband, then said, "Damn you, wicked woman! You always have lovers!" After hearing his statement she became angry in herself, and then, utterly furious because she could not enjoy what she should have enjoyed.[209] And in the blind darkness, seizing a dagger in her right hand she split open his belly and he fell to the ground. Then she went to make love with the man who was the paramour of her heart and whilst she was making love there, a neighbour who was awake, becoming aware of her behaviour, went and reported it to the king. The messengers, standing in the darkness until she returned to her house, the king's messengers seized and led her to the king and with the king's permission the messengers took her outside and then killed her. Yama's messengers led her into a terrible hell where, at his command, she stood face downwards, much bitten by worms. Remembering her previous behaviour she experienced extreme pain and at the end of the kalpa she became an utterly disgusting cāṇḍāla woman in the world of mortals.

24-26. On one occasion she became drunk after drinking some liquor and slept all day, but at the first watch of night she awoke, terribly hungry. Straight away she went to beg at the house of a person who was performing a vow. She ate the food he gave her and at moonrise, due to the power of fate, she spontaneously muttered, "Gaṇeśa." Straight away Gaṇanātha sent her the auspicious flying vehicle.

---

[209] "she could not enjoy what she should have enjoyed" abhakṣyabhakṣaṇena: given her obsession with sex this compound must have a sexual meaning, suggesting a connexion with the root bhaj rather than bhakṣ.

Brahmā said:

27ab. After they had heard the speech of the god's messengers and had bowed to them, they spoke again.

The king's messengers said:

27cd-31. We saw that extraordinary thing whilst we were performing our duties. The king had prescribed this command for us. Listen to it. "Śakra got on his excellent flying vehicle in order to see Gṛtsamada. He came with the gods to Bhruśuṇḍin and after he had seen him and bowed to him, he honoured him, and after receiving his worship and his farewell, he set out for his own city. But almost straight after he began moving, his vehicle fell into Śūrasena's city because of the glance of a merchant's leprous son. Śūrasena went there and after he had made obeisance and worshipped him, he asked why the flying vehicle fell and how it would move again.

Indra said:

32. This flying vehicle will start again by virtue of the merit produced by the vow of the Dangerous Fourth. So perform it diligently for this purpose.

33-36. At the king's command, we, his messengers, came to look for it. Messengers of the god, if she is to perform this vow, she must now be brought to Śūrasena, husband of the Earth. This cāṇḍāla woman will impart the prosperity that arises from the vow of the Dangerous Fourth. Possessing two lots of merit,[210] she will return to her flying vehicle and Śakra's flying vehicle too will return to his own city. If this task is done, when it is completed, it will be pleasing to you, to her, to us, to the king and to Śaci's husband.

---

[210] "two lots of merit": I take it to mean that she will have the merit gained when (vs.26), firstly, she inadvertently uttered Gaṇeśa's name, and, secondly, when she performed the vrata. In addition, this verse must refer to two flying vehicles, the one sent by Gaṇeśa and the other one belonging to Indra.

37-44. After they had heard their speech the god's servants said, "Gaṇeśa has commanded us not to give her away to anyone else." When they had said this they got up and quickly put her in the flying vehicle, and straight away she became a truly celestial maiden wearing celestial garments and ornaments on her body. To the sounds of celestial instruments the god's messengers brought her to Gaṇeśa, and as she had gone, the king's messengers went to Śūrasena and told him all the news. As soon as they had spoken the cāṇḍāla woman's vehicle suddenly came and they noticed that it was shining and illuminating the regions and directions. Her glance fell on Indra's vehicle and through contact with the rushing air of her flying vehicle, Indra's flying vehicle went aloft, whilst all the people, sages and gods were watching, amazed. Now that Śakra had gone to Amarāvatī, they all went to their own homes and she too, in possession of a celestial body, reached Gaṇeśa's home, having lost all of her evil because of the merit accruing from the vow of the Dangerous Fourth.

45. The man who should hear or relate this correctly and diligently will attain all his wishes and his troubles will be removed.

CHAPTER SEVENTY-SIX

Brahmā said:

1. Now that he had heard about and witnessed the power produced by the vow, he resolved to perform it himself and spoke to Vasiṣṭha, the bull of sages.

The king said:

2. Tell me the right moment for the vow of the Dangerous Fourth as I want to perform the vow here and now as demonstration of its proof.[211]

---

[211] "demonstration of its proof" pratyayakāraka: demonstration of proof that the ritual is effective.

Vasiṣṭha said:

3, Excellent king, in the dark half of the month of Māgha, perform that vow of the highest quality which brings every success and gives every desire.

Brahmā said:

4-8. The extremely devout king and his wife had prepared the requisite materials with the intention of beginning that vow of the Dangerous Fourth which is of the highest quality, when in just a short while the auspicious day prescribed by Vasiṣṭha came. Then after he had taken a bath at daybreak, had performed the obligatory rituals, worshipped Gaṇeśa, pronounced a benediction to the bulls of brahmins, honoured Vasiṣṭha, received his assent from him and placed his mind on Gaṇeśa, he stood on one great toe until the sun went down, conscientiously muttering his names. In the evening he once again quickly bathed and after he had performed the evening ritual, accompanied by Vasiṣṭha, he began the appropriate worship.

9-21ab. He made a large pavilion adorned with columns of plantain wood, opulent with many ornaments and cloths, resplendent with umbrellas and chowries, shining with rows of mirrors, decorated with flower garlands, containing many lustrous jewels and radiant with rows of lamps. In its midst, upon a golden pot he set a golden image of Gaṇeśa, charming in all of its beautiful limbs, shining with many ornaments and adorned with many jewels. Then whilst the leading brahmins were reciting the Vedas and the singers were singing, all the instruments were playing and the dancers dancing, he worshipped the image with mantras from the Vedas and the Purāṇas, the sixteen ritual practices and the five immortal substances. Having placed before it a food offering consisting of the five substances and milk prepared with ground sugar, laḍūkas, flour cakes, modakas, splendid with many sauces, and fragrant water, the king presented for Gajānana's complete satisfaction fruit, betel nut, an honorarium of jewels and gold, dūrvā grass, a mantra and many handfuls of flowers. Then to the

Moon, the Gaṇanātha and the day he gave water for the reception. He respectfully honoured the brahmins, fed them and then gave them honorariums of a myriad of cows, ornaments and clothes. Then the king himself ate, as did his relatives and friends, and in the night he kept a watch to the accompaniment of songs, music and story telling. After the king had bathed again in the clear light of morning and worshipped the image of Gaṇanātha as previously, he gave Vasiṣṭha implements for worship as an honorarium.

21cd-29ab. Gajānana was satisfied with that and dispatched a flying vehicle radiating absolute splendour. Then the messengers[212] placed him, his real appearance that of Gaṇeśa, on it and this brought immediate joy to all the people who were watching. The king was moved to the world of the gods due to the power of his merit and the messengers of the god, who also had Gaṇeśa's real appearance, their heads crowned with diadems and adorned with many ornaments said to him, "Vināyaka was satisfied and so he sent this flying vehicle to you. Accordingly, we have eagerly come to see you." After hearing their speech, the protector of the Earth wept and, his body stooped, his hairs bristling, he spoke in a stammering voice. Quite blushing, King Śūrasena said to them, "There is no reason why I should see him who is beyond the sphere of thought and speech, who is the ruler of the universe, permanent, incomparable and unmanifest. The Vedas and the śāstras are unable to describe him, yet the hosts of deities led by Śiva and Brahmā constantly recollect him. If he has recollected me, messengers, then I have really experienced good fortune."

29cd-30. After they had given ear to his speech the messengers spoke to the king once more, "We do not know, King, how the power of devotees can make him who has neither characteristic nor form[213] assume a form."

---

[212] "The messengers": that is, Gaṇeśa's messengers.

[213] "who has neither characteristic nor form" nirguṇaṃ yannirākāraṃ: All three words are in the neuter gender indicating that it is the aspect of Gaṇeśa as Brahma which is in question here.

The king said:

31-32. I have one great desire. Given that the god and you were satisfied, how can I go to Gajānana whilst leaving the people of the city behind? They and I ate nothing except for halāhalā poison, so how could I possibly enjoy the highest bliss without them, faultless messengers?

33. Once again the messengers addressed him, "Your wish will be fulfilled. If not, Gajānana will angrily strike all of us."

Brahmā said:

34-42. They agreed to bring every person onto the flying vehicle. All creatures came who were intelligent and born with hands were placed there, brahmin. All of them were clad in a celestial manner with celestial garments and ornaments. They all said to each other, "What is this great wonder? How could we have made such an auspicious flying vehicle?" And others said, "It is here because of the strength of the king's merit. Just as the power of wealth might make gold out of base metal, just as an excessively evil person might attain perfection through the words of the good, so have we all been uplifted by the king's merit." Then these messengers of Vināyaka constructed a heavenly pathway, but the flying vehicle had become still and did not rise up from the earth. Utter scepticism resulted from this and the people said to one another, "How will it go to heaven? From whom comes this receptacle of ill luck? Could it ascend on a huge begging-bowl cord?" Some of them looked around everywhere and when a leper came into view, one of them said to the king, "Send the leper away! When he has got off[214] this vehicle will go aloft."

43-44. To those messengers who were seeking to banish him Śūrasena then said, "I have given up evil conduct. Everyone must be brought. Because you like me and witness everything,

---

[214] "When he has got off": the meaning of this is not entirely clear although the semantic opposition between merit and demerit residing in the flying vehicle and the leper respectively is clear.

perhaps you could kindly tell me about his life, his previous evil and also the remedy for it."

The messengers said:

45. Don't worry king! We will tell you about the leper's depraved activity, his life and the remedy for his evil.

CHAPTER SEVENTY-SEVEN

The Caturthīmāhātmya

The messengers said:

1-5. Long ago in the city of Gauḍa which was in the region of Gauḍa there was a priest who had a son, the mother of whom was Śākinī and whose wife was called Sāvitrī. In her loyalty to her husband she was a veritable Sāvitrī.[215] Affectionately they adorned their only son with ornaments and, exceedingly handsome, he looked as splendid as Kāma. His mother and father never wanted to be separated from him even for an instant. But when he attained manhood and had left his own wife he was always involved with the wives of other men and he was obsessed with maliciously criticizing other men. He became very evil and hostile towards his father's commands.

6-7. At the same time in that city there was a prostitute called Naravimohinī and she came to him with her mind set on him. Listen to what she did. She had deliberately taken her own jewels out of a small basket and placed them near his mother and father, afterwards repeatedly crying out "thievery!" After he had restored them to the prostitute he had heavy sex with her.

---

[215] Here allusion is made to the tale of Sāvitrī which is recounted in Mbh. 3.277-83, amongst other places, and where Sāvitrī is shown demonstrating tremendous loyalty to her husband, Satyavat, in the face of death-defying odds.

8-9. Then giving up all sense objects including wealth and fragrant perfumes, he became a yogin of the kind that is intent upon Brahma and he established himself in that alone. But disturbed by Kāma's fire he became intoxicated just as if he were under the influence of alcohol.

10-12. However, his exhausted father, disregarding hunger and thirst, looked for his son in every house of the city, his breath labouring because he could not find him. At midnight he asked his wife, "Where has my son Budha gone? Like someone in the night who is without a lamp, my home is worthless without him. A pool is worthless without water, so too is a woman without a child. Any sight of him will be a life saver."

Śākinī said:

13-14. I stand here filled with grief and anxiety, wearied by hunger and thirst, not knowing where my beloved son has gone. I will live if I see him, but not otherwise.

15-16. Once again taking his staff in his fist, Dūrva left and looked for his son on the road and asked after him. When he was fatigued and assailed by hunger he became confused and then concerning his son he questioned a very old, fearful śūdra named Bhīma and Bhīma said what was quite evident.

Bhīma said:

17. Your son Budha is in a brothel.
Sensuous, he is happily having sex.
It does not matter who his mother, father or son is!
You have tried for nothing, brahmin.

Dūrva said:

18. How could my son Budha become attached to a prostitute?

19-20. He then went quickly to her house where he saw his crazed son, his eyes reddened by intoxication, agitated with lust, and he said, "You are like the dark stain on the moon! How could you have been born in my family? A stone or a thorn tree is considered to be better than you! Why don't you die, mischievous man? What can there be in life for you?"

Brahmā said:

21-25. Having given ear to his father's speech, the son Budha was filled with anger and he slapped his father on the snout with his palm. He said, "Your face is like that of a worm or an insect. Why have you stopped me when I am having sex, vile man? And why has crow's dung suddenly fallen on me?" With another slap of his palm he took away his breath.[216] When his father had given up the ghost, his son said, "Viṣṇu! Śiva!" and rejoiced, then after striking him on the feet, threw him far away. After he had drunk some alcohol, he again had sex with the prostitute at his pleasure.

26-30. In the morning he went to his own house and saw his mother. Happily she embraced her son, her breasts oozing with affection, and she said, "Where have you been? Where did you stay and what did you do? Tell me in detail, child. Your father has suffered exceedingly and I too am without food and water and at night I lie awake in expectancy. Son, your father has been gone for a long time looking for you." Again and again she said, "Go and find your father!" Ordered by her in this way her son angrily struck her with a dry stick and she fell on her head on the ground. Realizing that she was senseless and after striking her on the feet, he threw her outside. And after he had taken himself to the prostitute's house he had sex, utterly ecstatic.

31-32ab. The good people, each with their own sticks, burnt these two–husband and wife, but because of his brahmin status the king did not order the vile brahmin to be punished. But when he returned home his wife had a quiet word with him.

---

[216] "took away his breath": that is, he killed him.

Sāvitrī said:

32cd-35. Wise Lord of life, listen exactly to what I am going to say. The conduct of those like you who are born in that most famous and pure class[217] should be good. Evil conduct is quite another thing and should, with discrimination, be avoided. One's duty in this world is that by which one will be happy in the other world and one's duty in youth is that by which one will be happy in old age. In the eighth month one should act so that there will be happiness during the rains and one should undertake action during the day so that one will sleep easily at night.

36-42ab. The king has forgiven you because you are a brahmin and because of his affection for your father. I am perfect in every limb, a beautiful companion, your lawful wife. How could you have left me for sex with a prostitute? Everyone would revile you, but no one will speak to you because they are afraid of you. My own kinsman says to me, "Lovely lady, what's your husband worth?," and then head down in shame I long to give up the ghost here and now. But husband, if you were willingly to make love with me day and night, nobody would say anything about you, nor would there be any large transgression if at your own discretion you make good my advice by abandoning her. A wise man[218] should cease activity done by mistake or through ignorance. I do something if it is considered suitable, but I will certainly not do something if it is unsuitable. One should not act simply on the basis of a firm resolve. The man who acts wrongly gains neither this world nor the next world.

42cd-43ab. Budha was pierced to the vitals by the barbs of that woman and filled with anger, terribly cruel and almost smouldering, he spoke.

---

[217] "pure class": referring here to the brahmin class.

[218] "A wise man should cease..." tyajed budhaḥ : this is clearly intended to be a pun on the name of Budha, Sāvitrī's husband.

Budha said:

43cd-44ab. Towards me you are shameless, cruel, arrogant, wicked and angry. You will clearly attain the fate my parents have attained.

Sāvitrī said:

44cd-45. Since there is no difference between parents and teachers, how will a person who should protect their independence protect me in this adversity?[219] For a good woman, prosperity and death in this and the next world comes at the hand of her husband.

Brahmā said:

46-49. After his wife had spoken in this way, he impetuously seized her and struck her with sticks, clods of earth, his fists and stones. Then through her previous merit she recollected Rāma in the form of her husband, but suddenly, pierced in the vitals by him, she gave up the ghost and in a divine body she went to heaven where she enjoyed the highest happiness. But in the night, after dragging her body away by the feet, he threw her far away and unchecked, he rapturously made love with the prostitute and to her Budha said, "They have all been killed because of you."

50-52ab. After much time had passed, he then went to Kālabhi's house and when he had gone to bathe the depraved man seized his wife by the hair. She was extraordinarily beautiful and he embraced and kissed her, and bringing her onto the bed he fearlessly squeezed the mound of her breast and made love with her at will, whilst she cursed him constantly.

---

[219] The point being that since he has killed his parents and has paid no attention to the teachings which originate amongst the learned, how can she expect him to be protective of her.

Sulabhā said:

52cd-54. How could my parents have given me this offensive name Sulabhā?[220] I have certainly been easy for you to get, vile man, corrupt in mind! My husband Kālabhi, a bull amongst sages, having gone to bathe, you, a depraved man, used force against me. You will become leprous in a future life and nobody will even mention your name.

55. Then the frightened Budha returned to the prostitute's house where he made love with her. After he had drunk wine though, nothing worried him.

Brahmā said:

56. How can I describe such actions as this? His merit will end and he will bring this great offence to life.

57-62. Then he died and messengers took him to Yama's abode and Yama said, "Why was he brought here when he should have been taken to the hells." After they had given ear to Yama's speech, the messengers then led him away and threw him into hell,[221] which he experienced until the drowning of creatures. Having suffered this experience he then attained birth in a vaiśya's house and in consequence of the curse of the brahmin's wife he became extremely leprous. He was a patricide, a matricide, a wife killer, a drunkard and a violator of his teacher's bed! Just from touching him a person must wash his own clothes. Moreover, since he has committed a great offence one should not mention his name. But if this man who is so evil were to leave here, this flying vehicle would go aloft. There is no doubt of it.[222]

---

[220] Note the pun on the name Sulabhā, the literal meaning of which is "easy to get".

[221] "the drowning of creatures": This refers to the destruction at the end of a kalpa.

[222] All the manuscripts conclude this chapter after vs.62ab, but GN and Wai continue for another thirteen verses. I have followed the manuscripts in treating these as the first thirteen verses of Ch.78.

CHAPTER SEVENTY-EIGHT

Brahmā said:

1-3ab. After he had heard the messengers' speech Śūrasena was severely shaken and said to them, "I was not aware of this evil activity." Then getting up again the king bowed, exceedingly pained, and said to the god's messengers, "Be kind. Tell me everything, messengers, about the way to remove all the wickedness of that evil man!"

The god's messengers said:

3cd-6ab. Get up! Get up! King, we are going to tell you a way to remove his wickedness. Become attentive and listen, Tiger amongst kings. There is a famous name of Gaṇeśa consisting of four syllables. Recite it in his ear and there will be an end to all his wickedness akin to the way that darkness totally disappears at sunrise. Since he does not have a prerogative over any other way, he should recite this name!

Brahmā said:

6cd-10ab. As a result of the messengers' statement he recited the aforesaid prayer, namely, the name of Gaṇeśa in four syllables, into the vaiśya's ear. And hearing "Gajānana" he acquired a celestial body. When all his evil had gone merely by hearing that name, he ascended the flying vehicle and illuminated all the directions and regions in the same way as the sun with its fiery splendour illuminates everything. In accord with Vighnarāja's command the messengers immediately took the flying vehicle and all the people to Vināyaka's abode.

10cd-12. Now I have narrated absolutely everything that you asked to hear, faultless man, about the power of the name and the vow, the Dangerous Fourth, which is highly meritorious, of the highest quality, proper, renowned and gives long life. Every success is given due to hearing about it, all pains are appeased, all obstacles destroyed. What else do you want to hear?

Vyāsa said:

13. I am still curious, so tell me who else performed it.

Brahmā said:

14. Rāma Jāmadagni previously performed this vow and he gained long life, knowledge, victory and fame.

Vyāsa said:

15. How was Rāma born, from whom and in whom, Grandfather? I have asked you, so tell me everything in detail.

Brahmā said:

16. In the White Island there was a great sage, Jamadagni, who knows the past, present and future and with his mind produces the creation and destruction and gives favours and disfavours. He caused the gods to tremble.

17-20. The same applied to his wife whose name was Reṇukā. Kāma's wife did not even possess a particle of her beauty, hence she became famous in the worlds just like Rati[223] and since she infatuates the universe, who can describe her? To acquire the brilliance of her eyes water-dwelling cakora birds and deer, which eat pleasant grasses, performed austerities in the forest and the moon worshipped Īśvara in order to acquire the brilliance of her face. She is without beginning or end, she is fundamental matter, the goddess, the mistress.

21-25. Rāma, who was Viṣṇu, the Lord of yoga, Hari, was born in her from the very illustrious Jamadagni who was like an embodiment of Īśvara. His body was so handsome that he was like the embodiment of Kāma's destroyer, his virility and strength were celebrated and he obeyed his mother and father. He was dedicated to honouring the gods, brahmins, teachers, wise men, cows, etc., and he was a scholar of the smṛtis, the

[223] Rati is the name of one of Kāma's two wives.

śāstras, the Vedas and the Vedāṅgas. In eloquence he was Bṛhaspati's equal, in forbearance the Earth's equal, in depth the ocean's equal and he was wholly obedient to his parents' commands. On receipt of a command from his parents, he went to Naimiṣa forest, where he concentrated his thoughts entirely on the study of various branches of learning.

26-31. He was gone, but there was still the very powerful King Kārtavīrya, before whose majesty the entire Earth was always servile. Lakṣmī remained steadfastly in him, a portion of Viṣṇu who confers the objects of all desires. In battle he simultaneously releases five hundred arrows for the destruction of his enemies and, famous for his virility and strength, he was honoured by the hosts of gods led by Indra. He had countless elephants, foot soldiers, horses and chariots and when his troops move out they cover the Earth's surface just like the clouds in the rainy season covering the sky and the sun. His enemies flee in all directions when they hear the sound of his conches, just like myriads of rutting elephants when they hear the roar of lions. When the king spontaneously makes a roar equivalent to the sound of five hundred conches, the creation shakes, Excellent sage.

32-35. On a whim he marched out with his army of four corps. He wore blue garments and had a blue parasol, his soldiers likewise. He moved to and fro across inaccessible forests, rivers and mountains, spotting many groups of animals and killing anything. Then on the peak of Sahya mountain he saw an excellent hermitage resembling the home of Śiva, the mountain dweller, on Kailāsa. The king asked his attendants who owned this excellent establishment.

The attendants said:

36-37. He is the renowned Jamadagni, the personification of another Sūrya. Very fortunate man, this sage brings favour or curse and a myriad of evils is destroyed by a sight of him. Go there if you wish and you will see him and then through your favour everyone will benefit.

Brahmā said:

38-43. After hearing this speech the king became eager to go. He halted the entire army, only taking its chiefs at that particular moment and then he went to Jamadagni, the tiger of sages, a repository of austerity, and saw him seated on kuśa grass, glowing like fire. He bowed, as did his accompaniment, his body prostrate. The soldiers then sat down in many spacious halls and in bowers with rows of trees, but the king stood before the sage. Surrounded by four soldiers, the king, powerful son of Kṛtavīrya, sat on a seat prescribed by the sage, who then honoured all of them with water for the reception, grass for seats, and so on. Then he gave them cows and with his pupils he honoured them all.

44-45. Fatigued by hunting, all the hunters submerged themselves in clean, pleasantly cool water taken from various lakes, whilst at the same time listening to the sounds of Vedic recitation, the magnificent words of the śāstras, and the words and discourses which the students uttered all around them. Then the lotus-eyed king spoke to that pre-eminent sage.

Kārtavīrya said:

46-48ab. Because this sight of you has occurred my parents are now fortunate as is my birth, my knowledge and my austerity. The tree of my merit has now fruited and I now have riches, good fortune, an auspicious family and renown. It is said that you are the supreme Brahma and there can be no doubt of that. Now that I have experienced your hospitality, I am quite satisfied in my own heart.[224]

---

[224] "Now that, ... I am quite satisified...": It is not clear whether this means he is satisfied purely with his hospitality or with the truth of the knowledge that Jamadagni is Brahma.

Brahmā said:

48cd-49. After hearing this about his Brahmic nature, smiling a little, but with his mind tranquil, the sage, even though he knew, asked him, "Who are you? To whom do you belong? What is your name and what is your business?"

The king said:

50-51. My good fortune has made it obvious to me that for self-interested kings the only goal is to observe a person like you. I am Kṛtavīrya's son and I am known as Kārtavīrya. With your assent I will return to my city purified.

The sage said:

52-55. Excellent warrior, I have heard of your great fame and, in consequence of my merit, my wish to see you has borne good results. Because of your arrival, King, my body, self, austerity, knowledge, hermitage and all my wealth are truly significant. But how can you leave without having taken any food, for might you not consider my praise in the world to be unwarranted.[225] Leave after you have eaten something, Lord. For now, afford me your protection, Lord!

The king said:

56-58. Right! It is mealtime and with your assent something should be eaten. In case there is no food, we can drink water which has been requested from learned brahmins. But, how can I drink water when I have left behind an incalculable number of soldiers? How can I eat? Brahmin, I know in my heart you do not have the capacity to feed everyone. Just by seeing you I have completed my task and now I am going.

---

[225] Jamadagni has a high reputation in the world which he considers will be diminished in Kārtavīrya"s eyes if the latter does not stay for a meal.

he sage said:

59-60. Don't worry, Royal sage! I will feed you and your army with four kinds of food. What cannot be accomplished by ascetics? Let your army come here. I invite it too, but, Lord, let it rest for the moment on this very pleasant, auspicious river bank until the food is prepared. Then you will see something of real interest.

CHAPTER SEVENTY-NINE

The Tale of Kārtavīrya

Brahmā said:

1-5ab. His heart filled with wonder, Kṛtavīrya's son left the splendid river bank after he had given ear to the sage's speech. Calling his wife, the sage told her what had happened, and then, calling the wishing cow, the two honoured her for a moment. Then both of them asked her, "Preserve us from embarrassment, Wishing cow! The king and his uncountable army have been invited to eat, and so, Auspicious cow, let there be food suitable to the taste of the king and his army. Do it immediately, otherwise truth will be violated[226] and I will have no renown in the world. Do it as you see fit!

5cd-13. When these two had requested this, the wishing cow built a large city by her own power. It contained many beautiful temples splendid with many jewelled columns and assembly halls. It was adorned with lovely pleasure gardens and enclosed gardens with many creepers and flowers, it had a profusion of many banners and flags and resounded with the notes of many musical instruments. Resplendent with multitudinous rows of eight-legged flower boxes, it also contained many rows of

---

[226] "truth will be violated" satyaṃ layaṃ vrajet: lit. "truth will be destroyed". The truth here refers to his claim that he can provide them with food.

serving vessels filled with four types of food. It was also opulently splendid with huge arches, it was bound by an encircling moat and its pleasant balcony shone with its many men-servants and maid-servants. Located in various spots there were people, some moving and some still, who were stopping people, saying, "The sage Jamadagni has not given permission to advance." Uncountable dishes of food were displayed everywhere, radiant, splendid and shining, filled with many spices, containing the five immortal foods, soup, broth and cooked food, splendid rows of dishes, food to be chewed, licked and sucked, salty food, cooked lime, mango, boiled rice, fruit of the wood apple tree, etc., and plates of camphor, cardamoms, hiṅgu seasoning and a peppery decoction.

14. Once the dishes were completed the sage then
Invited his group of students,
The son of Kṛtavīrya and his army, to eat,
Because the wishing-cow was perfectly content.[227]

15. Then the sage said to his group of pupils, "Go quickly and summon the king who is staying on the river bank."

16-17. After they had reached the king and had initially received his salutations, the pupils offered him a benediction and then communicated the sage's order, "King, proceed carefully with your army for the meal. Innumerable dishes of food containing the six flavours have been served."

Brahmā said:

18-22. After getting up from there and summoning his army, King Kārtavīrya, who had duly performed his ablutions, left with his soldiers. Then he saw the sage's abode, the like of which had not been seen nor heard of in the three worlds. When he reached the arched doorway of the house he was stopped by doorkeepers, who were looking for a signal from the sage. In turn they were stopped by groups of pupils and the king then went to the eating hall, where, placing himself in its midst, he observed the sage's wealth. In his heart he conjectured, "Neither

---

[227] Content because she has created all the food.

Śiva the destroyer, nor Viṣṇu the protector have such wealth, nor does Brahmā the creator."

23-31. Placing himself in front, the sage then introduced him to every dish, and on receiving the king's assent he presented the dishes to the soldiers, row after row, as well as to those who were to eat their meal outside.[228] When everyone was seated he summoned the king to sit down and to the accompaniment of music and discourse, they then all ate foods they had not seen before, sweet fruits and roots as well. And to each other they said, "What's this? What's that?," and they all wondered how this marvel had been achieved. They ate whatever they wanted and because they had enough everyone left some food. To every plate the sage's pupils brought washing dishes, water and clean twigs. Then all the pupils offered the rest of the food to the large herds of elephants, horses and bulls located in another extensive apartment that had been turned into a stall. The people then ate sugar-cane, grapes, mangoes, bread-fruit and pomegranates, and accepted cardamom, cloves, crushed camphor, resin from the Khadira tree and small betel nuts covered with the leaves of the Piper-betel which the sage had given them. Then the sage joyfully gave all of them ornaments and garments in accord with their status, the most valuable to the king.

The sage said:

32-35. Since I just subsist on food from the forest, what can I really give a king like you who has Viṣṇu's appearance and has got everything he wants. By accepting my order that the king and his army should eat in Jamadagni's house, you have given me renown in the triple-world and because this has been so auspicious[229] the word "excellent" has been sounded in the world. If a very wicked man accedes to this order he becomes good and in all the worlds he becomes highly famed and

---

[228] Vs. 22-23 are both difficult verses and my translation is an educated guess. I can make no sense out of the pronoun ye in 23d which perhaps should be emended to yāni except this would make the śloka hypermetrical.
[229] "because this has been so auspicious": that is, eating the food.

elevated. By acceding to my order, major misfortune will not befall you, even if you are far away.

Brahmā said:

36. Having given ear to this speech uttered by Jamadagni, the king, his mind filled with amazement, questioned him about it.

The king said:

37. No one has seen this before! Was it done by illusion or was it done by the power of austerity? Tell me truly, Firm-vowed man!

The sage said:

38. King, I have never before told a lie, even in jest, so what I am telling you is the truth. The wishing-cow did everything.

Brahmā said:

39. The fate of a simpleton is to be impolitic. A great calamity caused by a bad conjunction of planets is imminent.

40. Though the king and his army, horses etc., had eaten and though he had had enough, he resolved to take the wishing-cow and he spoke accordingly.

The king said:

41-47. I see no value in this cow for sages whose anxieties are appeased, who eat bulbs, roots and fruits, who with their minds can cause the creation and destruction, who are without desire, whose senses are conquered and who are wise. What is the value of prosperity for those who eat air in the forest, who are effective in the attainment of liberation and whose disposition is towards recitation of the Vedas? There is no use in this wishing-cow for those whose disposition is towards recitation of the śāstras, who are conversant with the meaning of the Dharmaśāstras and who are occupied with yogic exercises. Vast wealth and greatness might be suitable for great works, but a large jewel is unsuitable for you, a forest dweller. Therefore, you should gladly give this cow to me, brahmin, though you should certainly think of her as remaining in your mind, even though she is with me. Brahmin, observe propriety regarding what I have just said,[230] for if not, amongst people, what can powerful kings, in conjunction with their armies consisting of four corps, not seize in their own or a different kingdom?

Brahmā said:

48-49. After hearing this speech of weak-minded Kārtavīrya, the great sage Jamadagni fairly blazed with anger like a huge snake and that brahmin was like fire. Eyes red, he spoke to the king, all but lecturing.

The sage said:

50-52. You are a good, pure and great king, whom I requested to eat, but just like the cuckoo which foolishly nourishes the young crow, I was unaware that like a heron there was dishonesty in your heart. In the end, due to his nature a crow becomes obsessed with inedible food. I have become quite confused about this friendship with a king. Nobody in the world has seen, heard of or experienced this.

CHAPTER EIGHTY

The Tale of Kārtavīrya (Contd.)

The sage said:

1-2. When you were acting helpfully you were behaving properly, but seeking the wishing-cow, you are predetermining your own destruction.[231] Truly you are confused, King, because

---

[230] "I have just said": This refers to what the king said about ascetics devaluing material possessions.

[231] "own destruction" ātmaghātam: This cannot be read as a portent for suicide because the statement is the sage's own reflection on what will

you want the unobtainable. On your head will fall the evil[232] that is produced when the triple-world is destroyed.

Brahmā said:

3-4. Pierced by those wordy darts the king came to resemble the destructive cosmic fire and from his mouth he angrily vomited fire. In extreme anger he then spoke to the sage Jamadagni.

The king said:

5. Rogue, I have never heard an evil word from anyone. What can I do? I have endured your acerbic speech only because you are a brahmin!

Brahmā said:

6-10. Getting up from there, the king quickly gave an order to his messengers, "When you have released the wishing-cow from her post, return quickly to me!" At his command the messengers then surrounded the wishing-cow, but simply by her making the sound phut they gave up the ghost and went to heaven, and with the fire of her anger she burnt the king's other messengers. Other heroes flew to heaven because of the fury of her snorting breath, concealing the sun's disc so that nothing at all was perceptible. The regions became dark, the sky was not bright, the Earth began shaking, the shaken trees fell and the frightened soldiers ran from there in every direction.

11-20. At a distance someone struck the cow with a whip and soaring up here, soaring up there, the cow chased the army as if she were a lion after a herd of elephants or Garuḍa after snakes.

---

happen to Kārtavīrya if he persists with his quest for the wishing-cow. It certainly does not reflect Kārtavīrya"s own intention.

[232] "evil that is produced when the triple-world is destroyed": This highlights the enormity of Arjuna's act. In Purāṇic cosmogony the destruction of the triple-world at the appropriate time was held to be a proper event in terms of cosmic dharma. The view being advanced here seems idiosyncratic.

A great cry of distress then came from those fleeing warriors and KārtavĪrya, the great warrior, said to them, "Don't be afraid! When I joyfully blow my conch-shell, she will go to her dwelling in fright. Who is this wishing-cow?[233] Look at my wonderful object!" He then blew the huge conch-shell, filling the triple-world with sound, but the wishing-cow was not frightened and so all the king's servants struck her vigorously with wooden rods and clods of dirt. But from wherever she was struck on her body there came forth many armoured heroes who were fully armed. Hairy barbarians came from her hair, robbers from the area of her feet. All were produced in this way: various tribes of foreigners and also many other heroes, groups of horses, elephants and very strong charioteers. They fought there with Kārtavīrya's soldiers and when they struck them, Kārtavīrya's soldiers fell down. But like moths on a tree in the night, others assembled there. Striking and killing one another, men fell in their hundreds and when their weapons were shattered against other weapons they began wrestling.

21-28. This was the situation, and when in the tumultuous battle the weapons had been lost, the sun was covered with dust, nothing belonging to oneself or another was perceptible, they still fought one another. Then amidst the sounds of neighing, the trumpeting of elephants, roaring and the sounds of battle-drums, drums, cymbals and flutes there arose a great cry of "Kill! Kill!" Such was the situation in which there occurred a huge battle between those warriors who came from the cow and Kārtavīrya's charioteers, elephants, horses and foot soldiers and it gave nourishment to ghosts and flesh-eaters, happiness to birds and jackals, but fear to the warriors' wives. Some broke their knees and some their heads, but there is certainly no reckoning of the swords, shields, spears, bows, arrows, warriors and chariots which were destroyed. Those of Kārtavīrya's warriors who remained fell then, but the warriors who came from the cow and who were pursuing them, laughed, yet did not

---

[233] "Who is this wishing-cow?": Not so much a question as a statement of reproach.

kill them. At that moment they derided them by saying, "Has the sage done this evil thing to you? Has the king become so stupid because of a previous transgression?"

29-34. His army crushed, Kṛtavīrya's son stood up and in his hands he took five hundred arrows and a bow. Placing his left knee on the ground and vigorously drawing the bow, he shot a dense mass of arrows into the army that had come from the cow. But like a fool's behaviour or sex with a barren woman, the king's dense mass of arrows achieved no result. The excellent king repeatedly released that number of arrows, yet not one struck the wishing-cow. So when his dense mass of arrows proved useless the brave king became frustrated and quite heated. He was sick with anxiety, thinking. "Where has my ability gone?" And all those who had gone to heaven thought, "One shouldn't attack when confused," and the wishing-cow gleefully thought, "How could this battle be so easy?"

35-36. After the wishing-cow had gone Kārtavīrya went to the sage and said angrily, "Brahmin, I am now aware of your deceit." And thinking that a man who has deceit in his mind deceit should not be considered a brahmin, he took one arrow and wounded the bull of brahmins, who, with the huge arrow stuck in his heart, gave up the ghost.

38-41. Reṇukā then said to the king, "This brahmin-killing is senseless." But the king, his red eyes filled with anger, said to her, "If you do not keep silent I will now kill you too, Sage's wife!" Then the evil king angrily struck her with twenty-one arrows, but at that moment she mentally recollected the sage Jamadagni, straight after which she said to the king, "Evil cāṇḍāla, why have you committed this offence. You have struck us for no reason, so your arms will be destroyed. There is no doubt of it!"

42-43. The king left there after he had heard her speech and, overwhelmed by anxiety, he departed with the remnant of his army. In his heart he blamed himself and he was grieving over his dead soldiers. Despondent and disheartened he entered his own palace.

(Contd.)

CHAPTER EIGHTY-ONE

The Tale of Rāma

Brahmā said:

1-3. Terribly distressed at his going, Reṇukā grieved, "Where were my sons when his death occurred? Now that my husband is dead, what can I do, enclosed in this dense mass of arrows? Where has my beloved son Rāma gone, filled with so much anger. When he appears I will die."

Brahmā said:

4-5. As soon as she recollected him, Rāma went to his mother, whom he saw covered in a dense mass of arrows and his father dead, killed by the evil Kārtavīrya with a massive arrow in his heart. Like a tree broken by the wind he fell swooning onto the ground, and terribly distressed, he wept for his mother and father.

Rāma said:

6-9ab. As if the Earth is without Mt. Meru, Amarāvatī without Indra, darkness is now everywhere, all directions are now empty, because without my father this hermitage looks bad to me. Like the triple-world without the Ganges is this hermitage area, because without Reṇukā this hermitage area looks bad. However, the gods' fear[234] has gone and the sages now have no Lord. Since he was like he was because of his austerities, what form will he now take?

10-15. Saying this Rāma adopted the various bodily appearances of one who is lamenting and he thrashed around as though he were a fish out of water. Weeping, he then came again to his mother and removed the arrows, and after he had placed her neck on his lap Rāma lamented once more, distressed by his mother's distress, "Here is my mother who is quite able

---

[234] "the gods' fear": their fear of the powers of an ascetic.

to turn the triple-world into ashes. How is it that, tormented by malignant arrows, she has fallen to the ground? Until the present you never forgot me for an instant when I was playing. But on leaving me now,[235] are you eager now to go somewhere else? You have given me milk, many clothes, sweet food, roots and leaves, Splendid woman! After you leave, where will you go? Damn my life and myself, now that I am without a mother and father!"

Brahmā said:

16-17. Having heard her son's speech Reṇukā became very distressed, wiped away her son's tears and spoke, terribly agitated, "Don't grieve. I will stay at your side. Listen to this account of what happened.

18-24. There is a king, the son of Kṛtavīrya, who came to this hermitage area with his army at midday. He was respectfully honoured by your father and with his army he was duly fed, but, after he had eaten by virtue of the wishing-cow's favour, he asked for the cow. After the sage had become silent, he angrily released the cow and merely by a touch the cow created a gargantuan army consisting of four corps which fought with the king's soldiers, but they all fled, wounded. Then the king began to fight and he repeatedly shot five hundred arrows. Even though he was wounded he went back to his house and the wishing-cow went to heaven. When he returned again, this evil man angrily struck your father in the chest with a single arrow and then the rogue left after having struck me, who is without fault, with twenty-one arrows. So now you must quickly decree the evil man's destruction and because he shot twenty-one arrows into my body, render the Earth without warriors twenty-one times.

25-27. Son, I am going to say one other thing you must do. Perform our death ritual where nobody has been burnt. Invite the omniscient sage Dattātreya and maintain a thirteen day

[235] "on leaving me now" tyaktvā māṃ: That is, dying.

interval between the rituals, then we will go to heaven. Nobody else is as honest as him.

28. After she had said this Reṇukā left her body and attained an abode that was difficult to reach. The very proud Rāma did everything she had prescribed.

CHAPTER EIGHTY-TWO

Relating to Bhārgava

Brahmā said:

1-4. After he had shaved and bathed correctly as prescribed, Rāma performed a "funerary rite for those departing" just as it is described by the brahmins. And after he had undertaken the "funerary rite pertaining to the repose," he placed the fire, sanctified with a mantra, on both of them. Straight away he departed for the sage Dattātreya. On finding him through meditation Rāma bowed to that bull of sages who was wearing dirty clothes, holding a dog in his hand, dirty, emaciated and accompanied by his students. With his palms clenched in homage, that brahmin stood before him for one and a half hours.

5. Although he knew his intention, the omniscient sage Dattātreya, after welcoming Rāma, said, "Notwithstanding that I know your purpose, I want to know why you have come here."

Brahmā said:

6ab. Rāma then told that tale clearly and from the beginning.

Rāma said:

6cd-14. That king who is Kṛtavīrya's son came to my father's hermitage where he was fed with the best food including many kinds of cooked food. He ate with his army and then he asked for the wishing-cow, but when she was not given he resolved to take her by force. She was struck and then she produced various kinds of soldiers. Wounded by those soldiers, the king and his army went to his home[236] and the wishing-cow went into the sky. Later, full of anger, the king vigorously shot a massive arrow into Jamadagni's heart and he angrily directed twenty-one arrows into all my mother's limbs. I was not there, brahmin, but when I came afterwards I saw her, burnt them both in a fire enchanted by a mantra and have come here, commanded thus by my mother: "Except for Dattātreya there is nobody honest enough to perform the sacrifice. At the end of the thirteenth day, after the complete ritual has been performed, then the king, Kṛtavīrya's powerful son, must be killed and the Earth must be rendered without warriors twenty-one times." This was what my mother Reṇukā commanded me, so that is why I have come here. Therefore, be kind to me.

Brahmā said:

15. Having heard Rāma's speech that sage who was Reṇukā's friend, his heart distracted by grief, made this speech to Rāma.

Dattātreya said:

16-17. It is not desirable to quarrel with someone in whose house one has eaten excessively. If an evil man does this, its fruition will soon be seen. But now, correctly perform the obsequies for these two.

Brahmā said:

18-19. On returning to the hermitage with Dattātreya, Rāma devoutly performed the funerary rituals for his parents at the end of the second day with mantras recited by Dattātreya. When the ritual was completed the sage made up his mind to go to Kolhapur and Rāma asked, "When are you coming back again?"

---

[236] "his home" nijālayam: here nija refers to Jamadagni.

The sage said,

20. Whenever you recollect me with the thought "Come, Dattātreya," you will see me, Faultless man.

21-22. Then having performed the ritual[237] he went begging each day, thinking that he must not eat the food of someone who is impure. And on the fifth day, after he had completed the ritual, that bull of sages departed, having received assent to do so.

23-25. Meanwhile a tiger came and fearful of it, Rāma shrieked, "Mother! Mother! Where will I go?" Then because of Rāma's plea Reṇukā manifested herself headless, compelled by the affection a mother bears for her son. (If Rāma had evoked her after the twelfth day, she might have appeared splendid and fully complete in all her limbs).[238]

26-28. She said to him, "Child, tell me why I have been invoked." Her breasts oozing milk, she then affectionately embraced Rāma. On the sixth day the sage Dattātreya returned and he saw someone there who was like Reṇukā. He said to Rāma, "Why has she been summoned and come into our midst deficient in body. If she has been summoned after undergoing investiture into the status of deceased ancestor, then out of affection for you, Reṇukā should have come complete, Bull of brahmins."

Rāma said:

29. Tiger of sages, because of a childish fear I spontaneously called out "Mother!" and I saw one like her.

30-33. The brahmin[239] released a bull on the eleventh day and on the twelfth day he performed the investiture into the status of deceased ancestor for those two, and on the next day the funeral

---

[237] "having performed the ritual": I am uncertain whether this refers to the funerary ritual. M takes it to refer to daily ritual (?) and takes Dattātreya as the subject of the action concerning the ritual and the begging.

[238] "If Rāma had...": a commentarial statement made by Rāma on the previous verse.

[239] "The brahmin...": Rāma Jāmadagni.

meal and the proclamation of the day as being auspicious. After that he gave many presents to the brahmins in accord with their status. Jamadagni then went to Brahmā's world in a celestial body and the woman who was like Reṇukā stayed in various places on the earth and fulfilled all the desires of those people who practised devotion.

34. It is particularly in the Skanda Purāṇa that this glorification of her[240] has been extensively narrated, but that has not been narrated here because of its excessive prolixity.

CHAPTER EIGHTY-THREE

The Gift of a Boon to Rāma

Vyāsa said:

1-2ab. How did Rāma, just a young boy and quite alone, fight with thousand-armed Kṛtavīrya's son and his army? Tell me in detail how he conquered that great hero.

Brahmā said:

2cd. One day Rāma questioned his mother.

Rāma said:

3-5. Since the gods led by Indra shake in fear because they are frightened of him and since his army of four corps is endless like an ocean, how will I conquer him, mother? Leaving nothing out, tell me the way and also how to render the earth without warriors twenty-one times. I will do everything you say, because

---

[240] "glorification of her" māhātmyaṃ ... tasyā: Is this a reference to the Reṇukāmāhātmya attributed to the Skanda Purāṇa? Cf. M. Biardeau: "La décapitation de Reṇukā dans le mythe de Paraśurāma," in J. C. Heesterman et al. ed., Pratidānam. Indian, Iranian and Indo-European Studies Presented to Franciscius Bernardus Jacobus Kuiper on his sixtieth birthday, The Hague/Paris 1968, p.564.

through your favour there will be victory, and I will enjoy unequalled fame and renown amongst all beings.

His mother said:

6. You will have victory son. Make a propitiation to Śaṅkara and when Mahādeva is satisfied, everything that is wished for will be gained.

7-8. After he had heard her speech, bowed at his mother's feet and received her blessing, Rāma came to Kailāsa. There on a jewelled throne Rāma saw Mahādeva and he eulogized him after he had bowed to him with his palms bound together in obeisance.

Rāma said:

9. Obeisance, Lord of the gods, Pārvatī's Lord, Śambhu!

Obeisance to the universe's creator! Obeisance to the universe's supporter!

Obeisance to the universe's destroyer! Obeisance to the universe's form!

Obeisance to the universe's abode! Obeisance to the abode of the moon!

10. Cause of pure knowledge, may obeisance be to the one without qualities!

To the one who possesses shape, yet is without shape!

Obeisance to the one who transcends the śāstras, the Vedas and Vedāṅgas!

Obeisancc to the manifest and unmanifest self, whose real form is truth!

11. Obeisance to you who has transcended the qualities, to the one who reveals the three qualities! Obeisance to you who comprehends expansion, but yet is devoid of expansion!

Brahmā said:

12-13. Having given ear to this eulogy, Maheśvara was quite satisfied and after welcoming Rāma he said, "I am satisfied with your immortal words, so choose a boon from me, whatever your heart desires. Brahmin, I know you are Jamadagni, Reṇukā's son."

Rāma said:

14-17ab. Though he and his army had eaten, the evil Kārtavīrya longed for the wishing-cow and he angrily killed Jamadagni who was without fault, Lord. My mother Reṇukā was struck everywhere with twenty-one arrows. Then my mother commanded me, "Kill the evil king," and so I have come to you for refuge. Tell me the way to kill him and the way in which I by myself will render the Earth without warriors twenty-one times!

Brahmā said,

17cd-18. Mahādeva, who already understood the truth of the matter, spoke to him after he had beheld in meditation the great six-syllable mantra productive of happiness, that is the means of victory and satisfies Dviradānana.

19-20. He said to Rāma, "Diligently recite one hundred thousand of these mantras and undertake a fire sacrifice using a tenth of them, a libation for the ancestors with a tenth and a meal for the brahmins with a tenth. By this great devotion the Lord Gajānana, god of gods, will be pleased and everything will be done."

22-25. Having heard this speech, respectfully bowed to Śiva and received assent, Rāma went wandering here and there over the earth. He discovered an excellent spot filled with many trees and creepers in a region north of the Kṛṣṇa river. It was quite delightful and conducive to good success. There he performed that personal service as Śiva had prescribed. Directing the activity of his mind and his senses onto Gajānana, that brahmin repeatedly recited the great mantra, standing on one toe. In turn he sacrificed with one tenth of the recitation, he performed libations to the ancestors with one tenth of that amount and fed the brahmins with one tenth of that amount.

26-29. Then the illustrious Gajānana became pleased and manifested himself in a huge body which had four arms, possessed great powers of illusion and was exceptionally handsome. His sacred thread was a snake and he was resplendent with many ornaments, wore a diadem and ear-rings, and his face was beaming, his pleasant cheeks shining. His chest was glittering with pearls, coral and garlands, his arms were huge and in his arms he was holding sweet-meats, a tusk, a lotus and an axe. Putting a lotus on his trunk, the Lord began moving it about freely, illuminating all the directions and the regions with light.

30. Suddenly Rāma saw him and closed his eyes when he was struck by that fiery splendour. Then the brahmin eulogized him.

Rāma said:

31-34ab. Obeisance to you who looks like one thousand suns, Lord of the universe! Obeisance to you, Lord of all knowledge, granter of every success! Obeisance to you, the Lord of obstacles! Obeisance, remover of obstacles! Obeisance to you, the soul of everything, who brings pleasure to all! Obeisance to the god who is pleased with his devotees, whose foot fulfils wishes! Obeisance to the creator of the universe and obeisance to its protector! Remove this huge obstacle[241] which has caused the destruction of my austerities!

Brahmā said:

34cd-35ab. Having given ear to this eulogy, Gajānana, his fiery energy quiescent, spoke to Rāma who was still confused by his intense fiery energy.

Gaṇeśa said:

35cd-38ab. He one on whom you were meditating day and night by reciting this six-syllable mantra is I. I have come now,

---

[241] "Remove this huge obstacle" mahāvighnaṃ: That is, Gaṇeśa in his highly intimidating form.

Rāma, in order to give you a boon. Choose a boon from me, anything your heart desires. I am the creator, protector and destroyer of the many creations. The sages and the gods led by Brahmā and all the royal sages certainly do not know my appearance.[242] But I have appeared to you!

Rāma said:

38cd-40. He who is immeasurable, who sustains, creates and destroys everything, but who will not enter the range of sight of people when they utilize the Vedas, austerity, sacrifices, collections of vows, gifts, nor yoga, he is certainly you whom I have now seen because of your favour, Vighnapa. Give me just constant and rock-solid devotion! What else could one wish for!

Gaṇeśa said:

41-42. Rāma, excellent brahmin, your devotion towards me will be rock-solid. In spite of being enticed with boons, your mind is not over excited. Take my axe for crushing all enemies. Your name will become famous as Paraśurāma.

Brahmā said:

43-46. After Gajānana had given him this boon and the axe, he then disappeared whilst all the people were watching. In conjunction with the brahmins who knew the Vedas, the Vedāṅgas and the śāstras, Rāma then joyfully erected a large Gaṇeśa.[243] And having given away many gifts, he fed the brahmins and erected a solid temple with jewelled columns. Then having honoured, circumambulated and prostrated himself before Gajānana, Rāma departed for his own home, tranquil in heart.

47-50. After that Rāma sacrificed intensely for the battle against Kārtavīrya, Lord of the Earth. He killed many thousands

---

[242] "certainly do not know my appearance" naiva jānanti me rūpaṃ: This means they cannot regognize his external form as he really is.

[243] The sense is that he erected a large image of Gaṇeśa.

of kings and rendered the Earth without warriors twenty-one times. After performing a sacrifice, he then gave the earth to the brahmins as an honorarium. Taking him to be the Lord Viṣṇu after they had seen his immense strength, exceeding that of all the gods, the people then worshipped him.

Brahmā said:

50-52. Son, in a variety of ways I have concisely described to you the glorification of the god Gajānana, brahmin. Even Śeṣa cannot recite it in its entirety, Lord of sages. The man on Earth who hears this Upāsanākhaṇḍa[244] obtains all his wishes and will reach Gaṇeśa's home. There he dallies as he wishes until the destruction of all creatures.

CHAPTER EIGHTY-FOUR

On the Solicitation of Kāma

The sage said:

1. In what place did Rāma perform this absolutely miraculous austerity? Tell me, Lord of the worlds, for in spite of listening, I still have not had enough.

---

[244] This is omitted in ms.B, but is found in mss. A and D (C being absent at this point), GN and Wai. It can be conjectured that this might originally have formed a conclusion to the Ukh. B may have omitted it on the possibility that it might have been regarded as a conclusion even though the Purāṇa has nine more chapters to run. However, with the exception of those which are damaged, none of the mss. recorded in manuscript catalogues have less than ninety-two or ninety-three chapters. If this really was the end of the Ukh. we would expect the interlocutory system to be rounded off and the interlocutory activity taken back to the Sūta and the sages in Naimiṣa forest, but this is not done and the current frame interlocutors continue into the next chapter.

Brahmā said:

2-5. During the four world ages there was a sacred place famous under the name of Mayūreśvara where the Lord of the gods descended, mounted on a peacock, and killed the bull of demons named Lotus-demon. Since he was mounted on a peacock it is obvious that he is the Lord of the Peacock. It became famous when praised by the gods and sages. Rāma performed personal service there as a result of which he gained the axe and so he himself became famous in the triple-world as Paraśurāma.

6-8. But listen to this legend I am now going to tell you, excellent sage. There was a demon called Tāraka who was very strong and very bold. He performed a very harsh austerity for one thousand years and pleased with that, Brahmā gave him absolute security, saying, "You will never experience death at the hands of gods, sages, heavenly musicians, snakes nor rākṣasas, nor from their multitudes of swords and daggers. Skanda will be your death when he is born!"

9-14. Having given ear to this boon, Tāraka, both arrogant and powerful, harmed the people who were dwelling in the triple-world, sage. He cast into a place of confinement brahmins who were devoted to the recitation of the Vedas, those who were performing austerities and others who were engaged in fire sacrifices. After he had brought all the kings and snakes into subjection he then went to heaven and all the gods led by Indra went to a cave in the Himālayas. Through fear of him no sacrificial or devotional activity occurred anywhere and to all beings he had a messenger proclaim: "I alone am the Lord, the god, the brahmin and the family deity and I am the only one in the universe who should be honoured and worshipped. Anybody who at any time or place worships or does obeisance to another will be struck by a staff or he will go to Yama's abode."

15-19. The entire Earth then became empty, devoid of good people, without study of the Vedas, without sacrificial exclamations, sacrifices and gift-giving. It became utterly devoid of good conduct and the rules pertaining to the family were lost. All the sages and holy men then repaired to mountain caves and of Śambhu, Lord of the universe, they asked, "How has this demon prospered? Apart from you–the creator, protector, mother and destroyer of the worlds–to whom can we go for refuge, Lord? He burns us arrogantly like a forest fire burns the forest. If you are feeling especially destructive, destroy the universe itself, but if not, destroy this demon, Tāraka, who is harming everyone.

20-24. After soliciting him in this way they performed a difficult austerity of the highest quality, taking leaves and air as food and consuming water for nourishment. When the demon-king became ignorant of these sages in this condition he struck Brahmā, having established himself in Indra's place. Then, Sage, Viṣṇu went to the Milk-ocean to sleep and leaving Kailāsa, Śaṅkara too went into a cave. The world-protectors and world-elephants repaired to various caves and in their place the demon king established other demons. Remaining immovable, he protected the Earth and the creatures, though, as was his nature he roared and then shook the triple-world.

25. In deep voices the gods led by Indra joyfully eulogized Girijā's husband, the Lord of the mountains, who was in a mountain cave.

The gods said:

26. Overlord of the gods, whose real appearance is the moon in the sky,

Whose form is air and fire, the sacrificer, your real appearance water,

You create the unmoving and moving creatures, you protect them.

By your own wish, you alone destroy everything, Lord.

27. Remover of others' suffering, since you are the highest,

It is not fitting for you now to transfer your own glory to an enemy.

Destroy him, or else all the gods and sages

Whose minds are enveloped in the worship of the two, Śiva and Pārvatī.[245]

28. Except for you, to whom else can we go for refuge, Lord of the mountains?

Except for you, to whom else should we bow, illustrious Maheśa?

To whom else should we speak, destroyer of the wicked, Lord of Pārvatī?

Except for you, what Lord is really powerful, Lord of all?

Brahmā said:

29-33. The gods eulogized him in this way for a long time until they heard a voice from the sky, "All you gods, when Śiva has a son, he will be Tāraka's destruction. Act diligently for that." On giving ear to that voice from the sky, all the gods became filled with ecstatic joy and led by Indra the gods reached the abode of that god on Kailāsa, but they did not see Śaṅkara there. In front of them they saw Umā in the form of "primary matter" and they made themselves known to her, "Saviour who gives the knowledge of saving, save us from the evil Tāraka who has oppressed the triple-world. In order that he is destroyed, you should reflect upon the gods and sages who have fallen from their places, Mother.

34. Mother, creator and destroyer of the triple-world,

Śarvaṇi, Tripurā, a portion of whom,

Which is higher than the highest, the gods led by Brahmā eulogize,

We are bowing to you who has produced the Vedas.

Make this universe right,

You whom the gods cannot describe, Śiva's wife,

Whose beautiful body was acquired at her own wish,

---

[245] The sense of 27cd is that Śiva must destroy Tāraka, because if he does not, he will be indirectly responsible for the death of the gods and sages whom Tāraka himself will kill.

Who captivates the gods,
Who was the first of all, faultless goddess.

Brahmā said:

35-36. Solicited in this way by the gods the mother of the universe said to them, "I am aware of the voice from the sky and Śiva will happily do it. All of you go to where Śaṅkara is located. Having taken up a severe restraint, he is performing a severe austerity."

Brahmā said:

37-41. Having said this to all the gods, she assumed the appearance of a Bhil woman, on seeing whom the highest yogin would have been struck by Kāma's arrows. Then the gods too became agitated with lust and Urvaśī, Menakā, Rambhā, Pūrvacitti and Rati became embarrassed after they had seen the beauty of all her limbs. Pārvatī, the mountain-born, went to Śiva, he, Sthāṇu, who had become rigid, his eyes unmoving in meditation, meditating with his mind, muttering sacred hymns, without possessions, brahmin. And so all of those gods and the Bhil woman watched the three-eyed god.

42-43. Then Umā said to all those gods, "Here is the means for bringing happiness. This is Sadāśiva who is firm in austerity and has virtually passed beyond the body. You must persuade Kāma to arouse his bodily feelings. When Sadāśiva, who is grounded in unity,[246] is pierced by an arrow his bodily feelings will be aroused, and then he will do your job."

44-47. Then all the gods called to mind the haughty Kāma and when he had come, those who were resolved upon completion of their own task spoke to him and still others solicited the mind-born Kāma concerning his own task,[247] "Amongst beings moving and unmoving you are the Lord, and

[246] "grounded in unity": that is, absorbed in Brahma.

[247] "their own task"...his own task": The first refers to the task of the gods in general, the second to Kāma's specific task within the frame of the common execution of the gods' task.

you alone produce this creation and pervade this universe. Everyone, from the weak to the strongest, becomes filled with desire just because of you. Without you this entire universe, both moving and unmoving will be worthless, so you must undertake this task which is so important for everyone."

Kāma said:

48-50. Although I do not have the means, as commanded I will perform this task until death in order to please you. With an arrow on the soft string of a wholesome bow, the glance of a young woman and the appointment of Spring as my only assistant, gods, I will conquer all the immortals including Śaṅkara.

Brahmā said:

51. After saying this Kāma went to where Sadāśiva was located in order to enchant the god Śaṅkara for the accomplishment of the gods' task.

CHAPTER EIGHTY-FIVE

The Burning of Kāma

Brahmā said:

1. Having said this Kāma left in order to effect the gods' goal.

2-7. He beheld Śiva's home, a profusion of creepers and trees, frequented by lions and tigers as well as birds and beasts of prey. In an instant, out of illusion, he himself then created a garden, many large ponds of ambrosial water, many lotuses and trees, fragrant pastures with rose-apple, mango and jujube-trees decked with ripe fruit as well as plantain, breadfruit, coconut trees and wild dates, cardamoms, cloves, pepper trees and many other trees. Imperceptibly the fragrance went straight to Hara's nostrils and at dawn Hara beheld this extraordinary grove of sensuous desire, a profusion of many flowers and fruit trees, its waters enchanting in the moonlight. Straight away it pierced the trident-bearer's heart, and in his own mind Śiva uttered an expletive, "Damn this Aśoka grove of mine!"

8-11. With his bodily feelings aroused the god speculated on the cause of this, wondering, "Who made an impediment to my austerity? Where has this beautiful forest come from? Who is the evil person, his life now finished, who has fabricated this for no apparent reason?" His eyebrows knit, Śiva's eyes became red with anger, but terrified with fear, Kāma hid and could not be found anywhere. Then he recollected Indra and the rest, and as soon as he had recollected them, the gods went there mounted on their flying vehicles, wishing for the completion of their task.

12-19. In the meantime Madana,[248] very thin and nimble, was spotted by Śiva, who opened his third eye and burned Kāma, who is mind. The entire earth then shook, as did the sky and the underworld, and for as long as the gods said, "Don't! Don't!," the fire which came from his eye continued to burn Kāma until he remained only as ash. Then after she had made obeisance and folded her hands, desirous of the good of the triple-world, the Bhil woman respectfully solicited Maheśa, "Śaṅkara, withdraw that fire which is burning the triple-world. There is a terribly powerful, huge demon, Tāraka, who has obtained a boon from Brahmā and has overrun the triple-world, such that there is now neither Vedic recitations, nor any offerings, and all the gods have fallen from their positions. On seeing you occupied with austerities and quickly summoning Kāma, Faultless god, they sent him to arouse your bodily feelings. Yet he has become ashes because of a mistake of those excellent gods. You must now protect the gods as they have come to you for refuge! You are famous in the three worlds as a protector of those who come for refuge. Forgive the mistake of those miserable gods who are seeking refuge, Śaṅkara, bringer of compassion."

---

[248] An epithet of Kāma.

Brahmā said:

20-22. Sage, after hearing the speech she made whilst her head was lying on his foot, and having drawn back the fire, Śaṅkara, a smile on his face, said, "Get up! Get up! Because of your speech and demeanour whilst you had fallen at my feet, I have now undertaken to protect the gods." Spontaneously embracing the Bhil woman, he then took his hook and after mounting his bull, he went with her to Kailāsa.

CHAPTER EIGHTY-SIX

The Tale of Viśākha

Brahmā said:

1-6. With Śiva's embrace the Bhil woman flamed with the fire of passion, but like a little fish in a desert, there was no way in which the goddess could gain relief. She fell into some water and though she became cool and smelt fragrant, she still obtained no comfort there, nor could she get any sleep on the ground. She placed camphor and sandalwood on her terrible burning, but nothing that was cold gave her any satisfaction. After quite a while only skin and bone remained. Then going to Śiva, Lord of the mountain, Girijā spoke these words, "You won't touch me god, so I am aroused. I am scorched, but passion still oppresses me terribly. I have tried various ways to quench it, but nothing has worked. There must be some way to quench it. You do it for me, Lord!"

Brahmā said:

7-9. Having given ear to his beloved wife's speech, Hara, the dispenser of kindness, took her by the hand when they were alone and placed her on the bed. He made love to her as he pleased, overpowered by Madana who, even though he was dead, completed the great task ordered by the gods. (Yet he became renowned in the world because of the belief that "Not one archer is the equal of Kāma, the bodiless.") Whilst these two were making love sixty thousand years passed.

10-12. Having provoked Madana's behaviour, the gods and sages who had fallen from their places returned once again to Kailāsa where Hara was engrossed in love play. Realizing this they stayed silent, but their hearts were filled with anxiety. These gods who were frightened of Tāraka returned again to the cave, thinking, "When will he be killed and when will we regain our positions? When will Śambhu remove our distress?"

13-14. The gods led by Brahmā remained in an ocean of anxiety until the teacher of the gods made this speech, "Listen to me, faultless gods! You must all send Fire, his true form concealed, to Hara, and once he has made himself known to Hara he will quickly perform your job.

Brahmā said:

15ab. Then, having invited Fire, they praised him with various eulogies.

The gods said:

15cd-21. Brahmin, from you alone come all the sacrificial rites and all the householder's rites. You are cause of the waters, you are the mouth of the gods and you are the leader in the fire sacrifice because you are named Gārhapatya, etc. Lord, you alone always drink the very extensive waters of the oceans and you alone cook the six flavours in men's stomachs. At every temporal juncture it is you alone who sets in motion all humans and a person whom you leave is said to be dead and is burnt in you. Lord of the gods, you are the cause of the maintenance of life in creatures, for without you and the waters food could never be cooked. You alone are Brahmā, Rudra, and Sūrya and you also assume several other forms. Lord of the universe, you alone produce the root of anger and wherever fiery energy exists, so too does your form. Accordingly, we are soliciting you now, Benefactor of the triple-world.

22-24. Lord, Tāraka has completed the subjugation of the triple-world, you know about the voice from the sky and also about Kāma's fate. Going there in another form, you must request alms in order to rouse Pārvatī and Hara who have long been immersed in love play. When this has been done,[249] that which had to be done for us and the universe will come about.

Brahmā said:

25-30. After hearing the gods' speech he became a brahmin wearing brown garments. Taking courage, he then went to where Pārvatī and Īśvara were located, still engaged in love play. Standing outside, he said "Give alms!" three times in a protracted voice and both of them heard this sound. Surprised, they said to one another, "Where does this come from? We must get ourselves dressed." And they expressed their anxiety by saying "What should we give and to whom?" He placed his semen in Umā's two hands, but unable to hold it and knowing what was inevitable, she gave that object to the beggar, who thought, "If it is left on the ground, Hara's semen might burn the triple-world, moving and unmoving." Fearful of their curse Fire drank it, but then Fire became pregnant, embarrassed and terribly pained. Fire could not get any comfort wherever he went.

31-36. Getting up at dawn to bathe in the Ganges he performed the rites of purity and so forth, whilst the sun remained on the horizon. Six women, united in their power, came there to bathe and Agni ejaculated the semen thinking, "This is the Ganges, who is loved by Hara. She will hold it if she is able. She has a watery form and is very cold." But the women ate Śiva's semen in six portions and at that very moment Agni concealed himself whilst their clothes were off. When Fire had gone to a distant spot, each one of them went home after

[249] "When this has been done...": The point being that Śiva and Pārvatī will be aroused and have intercourse, after which Skanda will be born and Tāraka destroyed.

putting on their own clothes. But their husbands saw that their mouths were glowing brightly and knowing by means of the eye of knowledge that they were pregnant, the Lords of the sages expelled them all from their houses on the grounds that their mouths were not fit to be seen.

37-40. Returning then to the bank of the Ganges which was resplendent with reeds, each of them released their own embryo and returned to their houses, bathed and clean. After the six young women had departed, each having released her own embryo, a boy was born there who had six faces and twelve arms. Merely by the sound of his "hum," stars fell out of the sky onto the earth. He shook the entire earth, Śeṣa and also the underworld, and trees were uprooted, the sun covered by mist.

41-42. At that very moment, Nārada, of the celestial appearance, was going to see the mountain dweller on Kailāsa and on the path he saw a youth who was enormously strong and shining so brilliantly as to be difficult to behold. Recognizing him by means of his deep meditation, he came silently to Kailāsa and told Śambhu and Pārvatī all the news.

43. Knowing he was Śiva's son all the earth rejoiced, divine drums thundered and the heavenly musicians sang marvelously.

Nārada said:

44-46ab. Gaurī, as I was coming I saw your son on the road. He has six faces, twelve arms and shines like a myriad of suns. Is this not the six-faced boy whom you abandoned and who fell onto the bank of the Ganges? He is endowed with the splendour of a myriad of Kāmas and everything shakes when he roars. How could one speak coarsely of this handsome boy, Gaurī?

Brahmā said:

46cd. When he had said this and disappeared, Gaurī went to the young child.

CHAPTER EIGHTY-SEVEN

The Tale of Kārttikeya

Brahmā said:

1-6. After she had seen such a special child, her breasts affectionately trickled milk and with her hand on his heart, Satī[250] embraced her son joyfully. But in a deep voice Gaṅgā said to her, "He is my boy!" Then Fire said to the daughter of the mountain, "He is mine!" And the Kṛttikās said to her, "This young boy was born from us," and hurt, they shrieked, "This boy is ours alone!" Disputing in this way they went with Fire at their head to the Lord of the mountains, on the top of whose head there is a moon-crest, who was on Kailāsa, abode of the gods. Gaurī entered first with her own small son resting on her hips and after deliberately kissing him on the head, Śiva took him onto his own lap and utterly happy, the three-eyed god amused him.

7. Gaṅgā, Fire and the six women came to his home and Brahmā and Bṛhaspati came too, having been summoned to perform his naming. Śiva said to those two, "Perform his naming."

These two said:

8-12. He was born in the month of Kārttika so it is obvious that he should be called Kārttikeya, but also, god, his primary name is Pārvatīnandana.[251] Since he also appeared in an island of reeds,[252] he is called Śarajanma[253] and because he was born from the Kṛttikās he is traditionally called Kārttikeya. And since

---

[250] Satī is an epithet of Pārvatī.

[251] Pārvatīnandana "Pārvatī's joy".

[252] "he appeared in an island of reeds": This event is only previously referred to in 86,37 where the Kṛttikās, who have been banished by the their husbands, are to said to have returned "to the bank of the Ganges which was splendid with reeds" and where they released Skanda's embryo.

[253] Śarajanma "Reed-born".

he had these six mothers, he was called Ṣaṇmātur, and because this child will conquer Tāraka, he is Tārakajit. He will be general of the divine army, hence he is named Senānī and also Mahāsena, and he is also called Ṣaḍānana because he has six faces. He is also called Skanda because the semen was ejaculated[254] three times.

13-17. Whilst these two were proclaiming this the gods led by Indra came and they rejoiced, sang and bowed to him and also eulogized and honoured him whilst the sounds of celestial instruments pervaded the heaven, earth and underworld. Then after they had bowed to the general, they requested of him. "God, kill this demon, Tāraka, who is a thorn in the triple-world!" After consecrating him into the generalship with the various implements used in the consecration and with mantras from the Vedas and Tantras uttered by the sages, and after receiving assent from him the gods returned to their own homes. The sages calmly performed austerities as before, thinking, "Now that a general has been found, we have absolutely nothing to fear."

18-20. Like the moon in the bright fortnight he grew very rapidly and, once after soaring into the air because of his childish nature, he proceeded to seize the moon, but was stopped by Brahmā who said, "Don't be so rash!" Because of his intelligence the boy was like Bṛhaspati and because of his power like Indra. Once after bowing to Śiva who was comfortably seated with Pārvatī, he inquired about the fulfilment of all desires.

Skanda said:

21-22. Father, I have heard long auspicious tales of various kinds from you, the teacher of the triple-world, yet still I have not had enough. Tell me about that auspicious vow which brings victory over all enemies, produces every success and increases wealth and sons, God, which removes every evil and gives accomplishment in liberation, sensuosity, wealth and the law.

---

[254] "ejaculated" skanna: Hence Skanda.

The Lord said:

23-27. Skanda, you asked that well, so I will tell you about this vow which brings every success for men and is beneficial to all beings, brings about the destruction of all evil, gives accomplishment in liberation, sensuosity, wealth and the law, brings about the destruction of all enemies and increases wealth and sons, removes the mass of misfortune and brings satisfaction to Gaṇanātha. Any man who devoutly performs it is honoured by the thirty gods, wanders where he pleases and becomes the cause of creation, continuity and destruction. By a sight of him the great evil of
others is destroyed, Skanda, and of the others there is none equal to the vow of the Fourth.

28. Having given ear to this speech uttered by Śiva, the general again asked his father about the greatness of the vow.

Skanda said:

29-30. Tell me in detail the māhātmya pertaining to this vow. On which day and month should it be begun, Hara, what are its rules, what are its results and what is its proof?[255] If you are satisfied, Śaṅkara, tell me everything for the sake of the full completion of that vow which is beneficial to all beings.

CHAPTER EIGHTY-EIGHT

The Killing of the Demon Tāraka

Hara said:

1-10. I will tell you the principal ritual of that vow. One should begin the vow on the fourth day of the bright fortnight of the month of Śravaṇa. After taking a bath in the morning using a

[255] "what is its proof?": That is, the proof that it is effective.

paste of spotless sesamum, and completing all the continual and occasional rituals without being too impetuous, one becomes purified. Then, having constructed a pavilion adorned with columns of plantain wood, opulent with flowers, sugar cane and fly whisks, flashing with rows of mirrors, and having placed in its midst a pot wrapped around with two pieces of cloth, one should form an eight-leafed lotus out of sandal wood on it. After receiving one's teacher's permission one should sprinkle the materials to be used for the worship and then with the sixteen forms of ritual practice one should worship a Gaṇanāyaka constructed from gold or silver in keeping with one's capacity. Then one should offer a food offering to the god Gajānana comprising twenty-one dishes each having twenty-one pieces of food. For an honorarium one should offer twenty-one coins, gold or silver without any cheating in money matters. Then to the God of gods he should offer twenty-one pieces of white or yellowish dūrvā grass and two handfuls of flowers with mantras. One should honour twenty-one brahmins who know the Vedas and one should feed them with similar quantities of food and offer them similar numbers of gifts. Then one should bow, ask for forbearance and after that, one should request that "perfect"[256] be said.

11-13. Previously the performance of the ritual to an image of Gaṇeśa made of earth was narrated and all the kinds of rites pertaining to it were described. One should listen to what was said there and afterwards one should eat and fast in silence with one's own kinsmen, whilst meditating on Gaṇeśa. In this way one should perform a vow until the fourth day of the month of Bhādra.

14-18. On that day one should diligently perform a great festival in keeping with one's resources and one should worship Gaṇanāyaka in a ritual as described before. In the night one should remain awake to the accompaniment of the sounds of music and singing, the recitation of Purāṇas and many other

[256] "request that perfect be said": He should request the god to acknowledge that the offering was perfect.

excellent tales. One should then eulogize Dviradānana with the mantra of one thousand names and when dawn breaks, having bathed, one should worship Dviradānana. Then one should devoutly feed one hundred and twenty-one brahmins and, in keeping with one's capacity, one should give money, ornaments, clothes, gold, land and cows to them as well as to the miserable, the blind and the poor. If one is unable to do this one should only feed twenty-one brahmins.

19-20. If the image is made of metal it should be given to a brahmin. If it is something different, it should be placed on a vehicle drawn by men containing umbrellas, banners and pennants and to the accompaniment of the sounds of celestial instruments, the sounds of the Vedas being sung and boys fighting with staves. Then with considerable exertion it should be cast into a pool. After casting it away one should go home.

21-28. Whoever performs this vow once, Ṣaḍānana, will attain Gaṇeśa's abode after he has obtained all his wishes. For the sake of the creation Brahmā performed it by reciting a one-syllable mantra and Vikaṭa appeared and gave him various capabilities. Viṣṇu too obtained the capacity to protect by performing this vow and reciting the great, utterly amazing, six-syllable mantra and, thereafter, he obtained the capacity of being an avatāra at his own wish. I too performed it, son, by reciting an eight-syllable mantra.[257] Indra and Madana performed the vow, wishing to kill the demons Vṛtra and Śambara, and they were able to defeat them. I too possess various capabilities and I destroy the triple-world with its yakṣas, heavenly musicians, sages, kiṃnaras, snakes and rākṣasas. Humans, perfected men and wandering singers have performed it in order to obtain the object of their own wishes. So Skanda, boon-giver, perform this vow of the Fourth and you will be victorious in battle and famous in the triple-world. I am going to give you the six-syllable mantra, boongiver.

---

[257] In my translation I have placed GN26ab after GN24cd. Through supported neither by GN or the manuscripts this is its correct logical position in the narrative.

Brahmā said:

29-36. At an auspicious hour Śiva gave him that six-syllable mantra as a consecration, after which Skanda left to perform austerities, Excellent brahmin. In a very clean spot, one filled with trees and creepers, charming with many roots and fruits and quite resplendent with ponds and lakes, Skanda performed very harsh austerities, standing on one foot, and performed that vow as prescribed in the way that Śambhu had just described. Straight away Gajānana, the supreme self, became pleased with him in consequence of his personal service, the power of the vow and the mantra. To the general he manifested his own unsurpassed form as it should be meditated upon by yogins. It possessed a vast fiery splendour, its four arms were radiant, it was splendid with a large diadem, adorned with earrings and bracelets worn on the upper arm, had a single tusk, the moon was on its forehead and its elephant's trunk was radiant. Some of its resplendent hands were holding a tusk and a garland and its other hands were holding a noose and a hook. It was furnished with multitudes of pearls and jewels, its belly was adorned with a snake-king, it was wearing celestial garments and clothes, it was smeared with celestial perfumes, shone brightly because of the flames of its fiery energy and had the appearance of many suns.

37-38. Ṣaḍānana saw it and his eyes flashed open in amazement. His mind confused, he was wondering, "What's this? I have thought about this, yet I do not know whether it is this or something else?" Thereafter he silently mused, "Who are you and what is your name?"

Gajānana said:

39-40. I am the one upon whom you have single-mindedly meditated day and night. I have come to give you a boon, so say what your heart wishes, Ṣaḍānana, and I, Gajānana, satisfied with your austerity am going to give it to you.

41. Neither the gods led by Brahmā, nor the authors of the śāstras,

Nor the snakes led by Śeṣa,
Know your true appearance, Lord of the worlds.
Yet now it has been thoroughly shown to me, Gajānana.
42. My desire has been completely satisfied by that,
Yet in keeping with your command I will make a request, God.
Let me never be defeated,
Manifest yourself when I think of you.
43. Let me never forget your lotus-feet,
Let me be the best of the gods!
44. You were invisible and have become visible, therefore you will become famous as Lakṣavināyaka,[258] the wishing tree for the wishes of devotees.

Lakṣa said:

45-46ab. Skanda, absolutely everything you have requested will come about now, you will not forget me and I will be close when you think of me. You will have victory over enemies and pre-eminence amongst the gods.

Brahmā said:

46cd-47. The god gave these very boons and quite delighted with the strength of his austerities and his conduct he gave Skanda a peacock as his own vehicle and thereafter he became famous by the name "Mayūradhvaja."

Gajānana said:

48-49. The great demons led by Tāraka will die at your hand and I, whom devotees love, will be named Lakṣavināyaka. For a long time I will appear on this sacred place at your command, Faultless god.

---

[258] Lakṣavināyaka: "Visible Vināyaka".

Brahmā said:

50-56. Having said this Vikaṭa then disappeared from there. Then after constructing a large image and having had the brahmins set it up, Skanda gave it the auspicious name of Lakṣavināyaka. He worshipped that image with sweet meats, flowers and blades of grass numbering hundreds of thousands as well as with other kinds of appropriate things. He fed as many brahmins as could be numbered, brahmin, and after eulogizing and bowing to them, Skanda went to Śaṅkara, who brings prosperity to beings. Mounted on the peacock, he related everything to Śiva and as the god had prescribed he was called Mayūradhvaja. After he had recollected the god Gajānana and had received Śiva's benediction, Skanda left with Śiva's permission in order to kill the demon Tāraka. The divine sages consecrated him into the position of Lord over the divine army and after seeing Tāraka, that very powerful general engaged in battle. In the course of one hundred thousand years he killed him with his pike. There is, however, no possibility of describing even a portion of the battle.

57-59. When the demon Tāraka was killed, all the gods rejoiced, as did the sages, world-protectors, snakes and humans. They stayed above Skanda and released showers of flowers and then all the gods and beings each returned to their own home. Just as previously, they performed the ritual exclamations of svāhā, svadhā and vaṣaṭ.

Brahmā said,

60-61. I have recited to you the power of the god Gajānana and I have described the power of that vow as it really is. The thirty-three thousand myriads of gods could not kill this great demon, but Skanda killed him in battle due to the power of that vow and he was honoured by the deities led by Indra.

Vyāsa said:

62, Tell me! In what place did Viśākha perform that personal service with the highest concentration, Prajāpati?

Druhiṇa said:

63-64. That personal service was performed where the Lord of Ghṛṣṇa[259] was located and when it was completed there he was named Lakṣavināyaka. Ela was there and afterwards he became a king who was famous in the world. Later a city was here which became famous by that name, sage.

EIGHTY-NINE

Kāma's request for a Boon

The sage said:

1-2. I have just heard this brief narrative about the vow pertaining to Gajānana, Brahmā. But if Madana was burnt by Śaṅkara's angry fire, how is it that everyone can now see Madana? Tell me this at length, Four-faced god!

Brahmā said,

3-4. When Hara angrily opened his third eye, Rati went to Hara, having realized Madana's offence and still lamenting over the dead Kāma. After bowing prostrate, she eulogized him as seemed appropriate.

Rati said:

5. I bow to the god who is Girijā's companion,
Who has a bull on his banner, an eye on his brow,
Who protects the worlds when he is filled with sattva,
Who creates the worlds due to the rajas quality.
6. The Lord of all, who at his own volition destroys the universe,
The great Lord whose body is filled with darkness,

[259] Ghṛṣṇa is an epithet of Gaṇeśa. I do not know its meaning.

Who carries a human skull and eats people's alms,
Who fulfils everyone's aims.
7. Illustrious Maheśa who is compassionate towards the miserable,
Extend refuge to me whose beloved has gone.
The noble-minded god who on Earth
Can produce something, undo it and change it.
8. For me who has come for refuge
You must vigorously foster my success by enlivening the dead.
If not, Lord, I will render my fame inauspicious
By giving up the ghost.[260]

Brahmā said:

9. In this way she eulogized Śambhu, who became pleased and spoke to her.

Śambhu said:

10. Illustrious lady, lovely wife of Kāma, choose a boon. As I am satisfied with your eulogy I am going to grant all your heart's desires.

11. After hearing Śiva's speech, Rati was delighted and bowed to him. Even though she was terribly hurt, she spoke to the god, wishing for success.

Rati said:

12-15. Lord, if you are pleased, listen to this excellent speech. There will always be hosts of sensuous women in heaven, the earth and the underworld. Never must they have a portion of my loveliness, three-eyed Śiva. Once, having seen this very woman,[261] the resplendent gods ejaculated their semen and were embarrassed. Drive away the great shame I also

---

[260] The sense of the last part of this verse is that she will lower her reputation by committing suicide.

[261] "this very woman" yāṃ: This pronoun refers to Rati.

experienced because of that! Without Kāma, my loveliness is worthless, Śaṅkara. He is disgraced and has been burnt, and of me it is said, "This Rati is a widow." Lord of the gods, enliven me by giving me a husband, Ocean of compassion!

16. And in this way she solicited Śaṅkara, who prospers beings. Rejoicing, he spoke in a gentle voice to Kāma's wife.

Śiva said:

17-19. Lovely lady, don't worry! You shouldn't be embarrassed! Young girl, simply by you recollecting him, Kāma will become visible. He is called "Mind-born" because he is thought of in the mind. He will fulfil your desires and you will become highly thought of, because when he will be reborn in Lakṣmī by Viṣṇu, your husband will become famous amongst people under the name of Pradyumna. He will live, Illustrious woman! Go now to your home!

20-22ab. At Śiva's command she went to her own very beautiful home, then she recollected her husband, but he appeared before her without a body. By the force of the Lord's[262] wish he became visible before her and Rati, marvelling, rejoiced with her husband. Then Anaṅga[263] went to Śambhu and after bowing, he made this speech.

Anaṅga said:

22cd-27. Being without offence how have I come to be without a body, Lord of the gods? The gods led by Indra, and the sages, were oppressed by the demon Tāraka and knowing that Viśākha's birth would occur because of you, they requested me to interrupt your steadfast condition.[264] I did this particular deed for the benefit of everyone. The merit equal to that beneficial act does not exist in the triple-world, yet because of my destiny, Lord of the gods, it has become unfavourable for

---

[262] The Lord here is Śiva.

[263] Anaṅga is Kāma.

[264] "steadfast condition": This relates back to 84,44-50 where Kāma is asked to do something about Śiva.

me. Previously I was the most handsome of the thirty-three myriads of gods and everyone took me as the measure of a handsome man. How then, Lord of the gods, can I exist when I am bodiless, as if dead? So, Mahādeva, kindly extend your favour to me!

Brahmā said:

28-35. Śiva gave the one-syllable mantra of Gaṇeśa to the bowing Anaṅga and instructed him in personal service. Then Anaṅga went to the delightful Janasthāna, which gives complete success, and there, at Śiva's direction, Kāma performed that personal service. Whilst engrossed in meditation on Gaṇeśa, he performed austerities for a full hundred years, reciting the one-syllable mantra and only ever eating air, all the while accompanied by Rati. Because of that the illustrious Gajānana, god of gods, became pleased and manifested himself. He had ten arms, was adorned with a large diadem, arm-bands and delicate earrings, splendid as flashing jewels. He resembled a myriad of suns, was ornamented with a pearl necklace, was wearing celestial chaplets and clothes and was smeared with celestial fragrances. His face possessed a reddish brown trunk with vermillion on it and his hands glittered with ten weapons, his navel was enclosed by Śeṣa as an ornament and he was resplendent with many ornaments. He had the shoulders of a lion, was very splendid and terrified everyone with his sounds.

36-37. When Gajānana manifested himself the sages and gods led by Indra came with nymphs, yakṣas, kiṃnaras and heavenly musicians to the accompaniment of the sounds of the gods' instruments. One by one they devoutly worshipped the god Gajānana with the sixteen forms of ritual practice.

38. Then having got up, bowed to all the gods and all the sages, Kāma first praised the god's feet, then he lauded the god Vikaṭa who practices compassion.

Kāma said:

39-43. You are the most auspicious of the gods, your real appearance is that of the Supreme Brahma, and though you are without form, you have appeared in a form. Beloved of devotees. Now my birth is auspicious and my austerity is very auspicious because I have seen your pair of feet which free one from all evils, cause every success and give accomplishment in liberation, sensuality. wealth and the law. Now both my eyes are auspicious because they have seen that supreme man. The followers of Vedānta, Sāṃkhya, Yoga and so on do not know him, thinking silently, "He is not this, he is not that."[265] Even the Vedas are stupid in respect of him. He is the Lord of all and the pores of his skin are the endless myriads of creations. He has appeared because of this mantra, hence this mantra is indeed auspicious.

Gaṇeśa said:

44-46. Well said, Husband of Rati! Brahmā and the rest do not know me. Only when I have taken a form for you do they know me. And it is only through my favour that you have seen me Kāma. Since I am completely satisfied with your austerities and your mantra, choose all your wishes from me and I will willingly give them, Kāma.

Brahmā said,

47-49ab. After hearing the god's speech, Manobhava spoke again and to him who gives wishes when pleased, Kāma narrated in due order the entire course of events brought about by Śiva: of his becoming bodiless, Rati's lamentation, the mantra, the personal service performed for a long time and the boon Śiva gave. Then he chose a boon from Gajānana who was very pleased.

---

[265] "he is not this, he is not that": A clever use of the famous passage (Bṛhadāraṇyakopaniṣad, 2. 3, 6; 3, 9, 26) from the Upaniṣads which points to the impossibility of describing the supreme Brahma. Such iconoclastic passages are literary expressions of the hierarchical superiority of bhakti over jñāna in the various modes of approach to the deity.

Kāma said:

49cd-50. If you are pleased Illustrious god, give me a lovely body that all the gods will esteem, one which is as lovely as it previously was, and rock-solid devotion on your feet and victory over the triple-world.

CHAPTER NINETY

The Tale of Śeṣa

Gaṇeśa said:

1-5. Absolutely everything you request will be yours, Kāma. After gaining birth from my charming belly, you will have a body of absolute beauty. You will be esteemed by everyone and you will be triumphant over the triple-world. A flower, a fruit, a young sprout, the limb of a sensuous young woman and a breeze will be reminders of you. And you will conquer Hara and so on with moonlight, the lotus, sandalwood, perfume and the sound of the flamingo. You will be present in the mind whenever these are seen or recollected, and because of that you will be named "Manobhū" and "Smṛtibhū."[266] Your devotion towards my feet will be rock-solid and you will never forget it. When I am recollected I will appear before you when a great task is impending.

Brahmā said:

6-9. After the illustrious Gajanana had given these boons to Kāma, he disappeared whilst the gods and sages were watching. Then after making a large image of Gaṇeśa just as prescribed, Kāma erected it and worshipped it with cooked food – modakas, laḍukas, etc., –prepared by Rati. He named it Mahotkaṭa[267] because of its fiery energy. Then he constructed a lovely temple resplendent with jewelled columns.

---

[266] manobhūḥ "mind-born" and smṛtibhūḥ "memory-born".

[267] mahoṭkataḥ "gargantuan".

10-17ab. Born from Rukmiṇī's belly, he was abandoned in the ocean by a demon. A fish swallowed him there and a fisherman gave the fish to Śambara who presented it to Māyāvatī. When she slit it open he came out of its belly, fully grown. Nārada said to her, "This is Kāma who is fully grown because of you." He was taught various kinds of deceptions, after which he killed Śambara and through Gaṇeśa's favour he who was one became many. Armed with the many deceptions Māyāvatī had taught him, he went to the town of Sarasvatī and was known as Pradyumna. He was esteemed by all the gods as the cause of victory over the triple-world and favoured by Gajānana he became blissfully tranquil. Women such as Rukmiṇī and so on, looked at him as if he were another Kṛṣṇa, and when he stood up he was surrounded by embarrassed women.[268] Realizing from Nārada's speech that he was a son they rejoiced and embraced him whilst Rati came and bowed to him. The entire city was filled with joy when he was recognized.

Brahmā said:

17cd-19. It was in this way that this image of Gaṇeśa came to be in Janasthāna, Great sage. I also told how Rāma cut Śūrpaṇakhā's nose here, due to which the image was named Nāsikā. Modakas looking like precious stones also appeared here now. Kāma propitiated Gajānana with them and both Rati and Madana rejoiced. Śeṣa also propitiated him here with a six-syllable mantra.

Vyāsa said:

20-22. Why and how did Śeṣa propitiate Gajānana, Brahmā, and what did he get when Gaṇeśa became very pleased? As merit increases through asking, hearing and speaking about what I am asking, tell me about it in detail, Four-faced god.

---

[268] I presume their embarrassment is a consequence of Kṛṣṇa's reputation as a lover exemplified, for example, in the tenth book of the BhP.

Brahmā said:

22. You asked that well, brahmin. Become attentive, listen and I will tell you the entire ambrosial tale, Vyāsa, son of Satyavatī.

23-31. Sage, on one occasion Śambhu was comfortably seated with Pārvatī on the charming summit of the best of mountains, which was strewn with many creepers and trees and resounded with the sounds of mountain torrents. Humming bees dwelt there on golden lotuses and breezes from the flowers of the Jasmine, Mimosa, Aśoka and Campaka delighted the hearts of those dwelling on the peak of that mountain. The heavenly musicians, nymphs, yakṣas and kiṃnaras, gods, sages and snakes went there to see Girijā's husband. Some addressed him whilst bowing prostrate, the heavenly musicians sang loudly, the hosts of nymphs danced. Then they worshipped the ten-armed Hara who was seated on a tiger's skin and surrounded by Nandi, Bhṛṅgin and the hosts. On Śaṅkara's forehead there was a moon, he held a trident, a bull on his banner and the residue of ashes of cremated bodies on his head. Still others worshipped the god with ritual practices conceived mentally and some, shutting their eyes, became engrossed in meditation. Vasiṣṭha, Vāmadeva, Jamadagni, Trita, Dvita, Atri, Kaṇva, Bharadvāja, Gautama and so forth, all these Lords of sages eulogized Pārvatī's husband with various eulogies.

32-34. Whilst they were uttering eulogies Śeṣa became very arrogant, thinking, "In the three worlds I alone am the most eminent, no one else. Śiva is the most eminent and I am located on his head and so the capacity to hold up the Earth exists in me, nowhere else at all. And because I was the rope for Vāsuki and because of my high birth I have, consequently, attained immortality with the gods. Therefore, nobody is superior to me."

35-43. Then Śambhu, creator of the triple-world, Śiva, who sees everything that is to be known, knowing that arrogance was in his heart, suddenly and quietly stood up. He threw Śeṣa, who had so much arrogance, onto the ground and each of his heads became tenfold and then tenfold again. He was almost death-like for one and a half hours and from that time on he became adorned with one thousand heads. Then barely alive, Śeṣa grieved, "A decoration that is an entire snake is what I have become, an ornament of Hara, Lord of the triple-world. I do not know by what deed I have reached this condition, but like a wingless bird I cannot move. What am I going to do? Where will I go? Who will now save me? Who will tell me the best way to regain my own position? Who will remove my distress?" he wondered anxiously. Then he saw the sage Nārada going on his way and like some beggar who has found gold, the chief of serpents rejoiced. Nārada saw him in front of him, his condition very distressed, immobile, scarcely breathing, like a sage sunk in meditation. Although he had complete knowledge of the situation, Nārada still questioned Śeṣa.

(Contd.)

CHAPTER NINETY-ONE

The Tale of Śeṣa (Contd.)

Nārada said:

1-3. Why have you become so distressed and why is your fiery energy absent? How were your heads smashed and towards which sage have you behaved most disagreeably? Perhaps you have disturbed Śiva or was it your exhibition of arrogance? Tell me the cause, Śeṣa, before I tell you the remedy. Except for you, who will support the Earth with its moving and unmoving things?

4. But when he did not say anything, the sage himself spoke about a way for procuring the appropriate condition of the serpent king.

Nārada said:

5. Reflect on my speech, Śeṣa, receptacle of all the fine arts. You will hold the Earth on your head like a young boy does

with a garland of flowers and the gods led by Brahmā, Viṣṇu and Śiva will become like servants to you because of that.

Śeṣa said:

6-7ab. I had some previous merit which has made you appear suddenly before me. There is no doubt that this will be good for me. Otherwise why would there be an appearance to people who have acquired merit?

7cd-8ab. I am unable to hold up the Earth because my bodily parts are terribly agitated, so tell me a plan by which I might become as before, sage!

Nārada said:

8cd-10. I will now tell you of a great mantra of the god, Protector of snakes, with the help of which Indra and so forth have attained their respective positions. Hence I am going to give you the six-syllable mantra of Gaṇeśa and then merely by applying it, Gajānana will become visible to you. Then he will bring about any wish at all that you want.

Brahmā said:

11-13. After he had given this information to Śeṣa, Nārada disappeared and then Śeṣa, having made a highly auspicious decision to perform austerities, was effecting an absolute restraint and whilst meditating upon the god Gajānana, he uttered the excellent mantra for one thousand years. At the end of this he saw the god Gajānana before him.

14. One should meditate on him as mounted on a lion,
As having three eyes, ten arms, wearing a snake,
Wearing ear-rings and arm bracelets, a pearl necklace,
A very lovely diadem, jewelled rings and a sacred thread,
As accompanied constantly by many groups of sages and gods,
As having an elephant's trunk, an elephant's face,
A body shaped according to the wishes of his devotees,
As a boon-giver to men and gods.

15-19. Gajānana, upon whose various forms the snake had meditated, then came with Siddhi and Buddhi to appear to him. He was like one thousand suns and the sky was overpowered by his brilliance. Śeṣa too was overwhelmed by his fiery energy and was almost blinded and though he was in sound health he momentarily wondered in his heart, "What is this fiery energy, resembling the fire of destruction, which has come? If that should burn all the worlds, will this one burn only me?[269] But how can one be apprehensive if an auspicious activity is being performed? Perhaps as Nārada said, I will see Gaṇeśa."

Brahmā said:

20-23. Whilst he was sick with anxiety, Gajānana said, "Fear not! I have come as the giver of boons, ones appropriate for those who are stupid and clever. I am the one on whom you meditate day and night. Choose what is in your heart! I alone am the destroyer, protector and creator of the universe, the Lord of everything and with my fiery energy the moon, fire, the sun and the planets shine forth. My real appearance is that of the Supreme Brahma, I am satisfied with your austerities and I have manifested myself for the benefit of beings and to offer you a boon. Ask me for any possible boon you want!"

Śeṣa said:

24. God, I was overwhelmed by your fiery energy and could neither see nor speak. Your favour to me is fulfilled, now become mild, Faultless god!

Brahmā said:

25-26ab. Accordingly, as he had requested, Gajānana, the ocean of compassion, Lord of the gods, became like a myriad of moons, his fiery energy cooled. Then after bowing and eulogizing the Lord of everything, Śeṣa requested some boons.

---

[269] "If that..., this one...": Here contrasting the destructive fire which occurs during the pralaya with Gaṇeśa"s fiery energy.

Śeṣa said:

26cd-30. I praise the god Gaṇanāyaka, who is without beginning or end, who pervades everything, the Lord, the cause of the cause of the universe's creation, who has the form of everything, who is the Lord of everything, who is praised by everyone. To him I bow. To Gajānana, Gaṇādhyakṣa, the Lord who was eulogized by Viṣṇu, Garuḍa's Lord, who is overlord of the qualities, who has gone beyond the qualities, to Gaṇādhīśa, I bow. To the preserver of the knowledges, the god, god of gods, who is loved by the gods, who is loved by Siddhi and Buddhi, who gives all perfections, who gives liberation and carnal enjoyment, who removes all obstacles, to the god Gaṇanāyaka, I bow.

Brahmā said:

31. Having in this way eulogized the Lord of the gods, Dviradānana, the boon-giver, he requested some wishes. Listen, great sage!

Śeṣa said:

32-33. My austerities, my knowledge, my father, my mother and my birth, as well as my body, my multitudes of eyes and my many heads are now auspicious. My tongues which wer engaged in eulogizing you are also auspicious and because I saw your pair of feet my family and my way of living have become auspicious. Give me unimpaired adoration to you, Conqueror of everything!

34-37. Vighnarāṭ, can any possible problem be ascribed to you, Omniscient god? My heads were burst apart by Maheśa who was terribly angry because of my appalling arrogance and whilst I was flopping about on the ground I saw your lotus-feet because of Nārada's favour. Now, God, give me eminence in the triple-world and dexterity in the capacity of all my heads to hold up the Earth. Give me an immoveable position, a continuous vision of yourself, eminence in family and, since I am devoted to Śiva, closeness to Śaṅkara!

Gajānana said:

38-41ab. Since your head has become tenfold, Overlord of snakes, then adorned with a thousand faces and a thousand hoods you will be famous as an attendant of Gaṇeśa for as long as the planets, the sun and the moon exist. Your capacity to hold up the Earth will be absolute and through my favour you will have a permanent place on five-faced Śiva's fifth head. You will attain eminence amongst the snakes and you will be close to me always. You will also have anything else you want, Śeṣa.

Brahmā said:

41cd-47. He gave him these very boons and fastened him onto his own belly as a result of which Gajānana gained the name "He who has a snake fastened to his belly." To reassure him the mighty god placed his hand on Śeṣa's head and he happily showed himself to Śeṣa in his real form as the sovereign.[270] He filled the Earth, the heavens, the regions and the districts with noise and the soles of his feet were the Earth, the directions were his ears and the sun was his eyes. The plants were his ears and his nails were the mountains, the clouds were his perspiration and Brahmā was his generative organ. The entire universe was in his belly and the four oceans as well. His face is endless, he is the one, his eye is endless, he is the ruler of himself, his form is endless, his power endless and he shines brilliantly. Creations by the thousand glow on the pores of his skin.

48-50. On seeing him like this Śeṣa became almost perplexed with fear and he asked Vighneśa, "Become mild again!" Thereafter he became the ten-armed god and was mounted on a lion. That boon-giving god said, "Even the gods have not seen

---

[270] "the sovereign" virāṭ: An explicit reference to Ṛg Veda.10, 90, as the subsequent verses confirm.

this kind of thing! You have seen it now Śeṣa because of my favour and your good fortune. Your place will always be on me, in the underworld and also on Śiva. I have given you this because I am pleased. Now hold up this Earth as if it were a bunch of flowers."

Śeṣa said:

51-52. When holding the Earth on one's head one is called Earth-bearer. You and I have this celebrated name and it is famous in the world. Remaining steadfast[271] in this sacred place, fulfil your devotee's wishes!

Brahmā said:

53-55. Then Vighneśa said "Om" to him and disappeared. And having made an image like him, Śeṣa respectfully erected it and constructed a beautiful temple, opulent with many jewels. For its name he nominated "Earth-bearer." Then he carried the Earth as if it were a flower and he also became Viṣṇu's couch. He remained on the lotus-navel and was an ornament of Vighnarāja.

56. So Vyāsa, I have narrated to you the marvellous majesty of Vighneśa. In the city of Pravāla Gaṇeśa is celebrated as "Earth-bearer" and it was for this that Śeṣa undertook this propitiation, Lord.

CHAPTER NINETY-TWO

Description of Various Forms of Worship

Vyāsa said:

1. God, my mind has become exceedingly restless whilst I have been listening, so tell me another tale about Gaṇeśa!

---

[271] "Remaining steadfast": That is, reside here as an image.

Ka said:

2-5. Once when the cosmic destruction had occurred, Gajānana gave me an order, "Brahmā, at my command produce a creation that has variety." With my mind I then created seven sons. I will tell you their names: Kaśyapa, Gautama, Jamadagni, Vasiṣṭha, Bhāradvāja, Atri and Viśvāmitra. The seven were all skilled in the knowledges, and they all said to me, "Brahmā, Lord of the gods, command us!"

6-11. I knew, however, that Kaśyapa was wise and the best amongst them, and when given the command, "Do my job and create a creation which has variety," after having said "Om," he went to the forest to undertake austerities. For one thousand divine years he recited the one-syllable mantra and then the illustrious Lord Dviradānana became pleased. He had four arms, lotus eyes, was adorned with a large diadem, was holding a noose, a hook, a garland and a tooth in his hand and he was wearing lovely armlets. His throat was glittering with pearl necklaces containing jewels, precious gems and gold. On his belly was a serpent, the shining circle of which was flashing like a myriad of suns, his mouth shone, his beautiful trunk was shining radiantly and his eyes were beaming. Gajānana manifested himself like this before Kaśyapa and his feet were noisy because of the sounds of small bells on his anklets.

12-18. On seeing that god Kaśyapa danced about full of delight and after bowing, he worshipped him with many auspicious things. His palms clasped together, he said this to Gajānana who was very pleased, "My father, my mother, my austerity, my knowledge, my body and my sight are now auspicious, and the Earth is auspicious as are the creeping plants, trees and flowers. This one-syllable mantra is auspicious too, since it has caused me to see the tranquil Lord of all, Gajānana, the supreme, higher than the highest. The Vedas are stupid concerning him, the Upaniṣads have been reduced to silence and he cannot be reached by reasoning. He is the very god whom I have seen. The gods led by Viṣṇu, Śiva and Brahmā manifest themselves from him and the seven hells and the fourteen worlds go to destruction in him. He is the very god I have seen. He is the source, he is the overlord of qualities, he is accessible to teachers, he is without form and some know him as Brahma. He is the very god I have seen."

Ka said:

19-20ab. Gajānana was wholly satisfied with these ambrosial words and he spoke to Kaśyapa who was bowing to him and eulogizing him with various eulogies.

Gaṇeśa said:

20cd-22ab. Sage, I have become pleased now because of your devotion, your eulogy and your personal service. Choose a boon from me and ask for whatever is in your mind!

Kaśyapa said:

20cd-22ab. Lord, give me the capability to produce a creation that has variety, devotion upon your lotus-feet and the capacity not to forget them, for you must become visible wherever I recollect you. Also give me a son such that he can be named "Joy of Kaśyapa."

Gaṇeśa said:

22cd-23. Great sage, everything you have asked me for will come about. You will not forget your devotion to me and I will be near you during difficult times. Through my favour you will produce a creation that has variety.

Ka said:

24. After he had said this to the sage, the god immediately disappeared from there and filled with joy, Kaśyapa too then returned to his own abode.

25-31. On one occasion Kaśyapa was unexpectedly afflicted by something incorporeal and he could not gain relief anywhere. He went into his house but he could remember neither how to meditate, nor the continual, occasional and optional rituals. Seeing him so distressed in this way his fourteen wives–Diti, Aditi, Danu, Kadru, Vinatā and so on–stood before him and Kaśyapa successively made love to them in their respective houses. In time, as said before, Diti gave birth to many demons. Aditi to the gods and heavenly musicians and Danu to the dānavas. Then in succession came kiṃnaras, yakṣas, perfected ones, wandering bards, gūhyakas and animals, domestic as well as wild, the Earth, mountains, trees, oceans, rivers, creepers, grains, minerals, jewels, pearls, worms, ants, snakes and hosts of birds. Everything moving and unmoving comes from them.

32-43. On seeing his lineage born with such variety as this the wise Kaśyapa rejoiced and taught many mantras. A sixteen-syllable one for someone who has paid off a monetary debt and an eighteen- syllable one for someone who has perceived the Siddhāricakra.[272] A one- syllable one to someone and one with six syllables to another, and also a five-syllable, an eight-syllable and a twelve-syllable mantra. To someone else the bull of sages gave the great mantra. He then said this, "You must undertake personal service until the god Gajānana, who is without support and who gives every perfection, becomes visible." This he communicated to them and then they all went straight away to many places to perform austerities, and each recited his own mantra to the god when sitting, eating, sleeping and awake too. With singular devotion they recollected Gajānana, Lord of the gods, and at the end of one thousand divine years Gajānana was wholly satisfied and that ocean of compassion who has many forms manifested himself before them. In the particular form of the god a person was meditating upon, so did he appear before him as that. Before one he had a moon-like colour and four arms, but in front of another Gaṇeśvara was red with six arms, and before another he had eight huge arms and looked like a cloud. Or he had ten or twelve arms, was smoke coloured, huge and powerful or he had eighteen arms and resembled a myriad of suns. To another he

[272] "who has perceived the Siddhāricakra": This translation is a guess.

had one thousand eyes and as many arms and he appeared in his real appearance as a child, but he also appeared as a youth or an old man. Or he appeared on the back of his rat in a body of splendid form, or on a lion or on a peacock and as having an elephant's face with many mouths.

44. After seeing that god in his many forms they all happily eulogized him, their hands clasped in obeisance, bowing devoutly to the god Gajānana.

They all said:

45. Because of his unlimited power we are alive and many.
From him who is immeasurable and without quality come the qualities.

From him appears all this which is split into a threefold division.
We always bow to and revere Gaṇeśa.
46. From this omniscient one all the universe is manifested.
As seated on a lotus, pervading everything, the protector of everything,
In that way do we, the gods led by Indra and humans,
Always bow to and revere Gaṇeśa.
47. From him comes the sun, fire, earth and water.
From him comes the oceans, the moons, the heavens and the atmosphere.
From him comes the moving and non-moving things and the multitude of trees.
We always bow to and revere Gaṇeśa.
48. From him come the dānavas, kiṃnaras, the multitudes of yakṣas.
From him come the wandering bards and beasts of prey.
From him come birds and worms, from him come the plants.
We always bow to and revere Gaṇeśa.
49. From him comes intellect, the removal of ignorance for the seeker of liberation.

From him comes the riches that will bring satisfaction to devotees.

From him comes the destruction of obstacles, from him the completion of tasks.

We always bow to and revere Gaṇeśa.

50. From him comes sons and riches, from him cherished goals.

From him comes the obstacles to devotees in many forms.

From him comes grief and delusion, from him desire.

We always bow to and revere Gaṇeśa.

51. From him comes unlimited power,

And Śeṣa who became capable of assuming many shapes to hold up the Earth.

From him comes the many heavens for humans.

We always bow to and revere Gaṇeśa.

52. From him comes the words of the Vedas which are blunted in the mind,

Which always proclaim, "He is not this, he is not that."

Him, the supreme Brahma his real appearance, intellect and bliss his

being,

We always bow to and revere Gaṇeśa.

CHAPTER NINETY THREE

Description of Gajānana's Names

Brahmā said:

1-2. All of these having bowed to Gajānana and eulogized him in this way, they again addressed Gaṇādhyakṣa, "Now we have become most auspicious. Our austerities are auspicious as is our generosity, our knowledge, our sacrifices and our ancestors are auspicious as well. Now our eyes have become auspicious too since we saw Gajānana."

3-5. Dviradānana was wholly satisfied with the ambrosial words of their eulogies and spoke to them in a deep voice when they were listening, "I have not shown this particular form to Brahmā, Viṣṇu and Śiva and so forth, but though my form is without qualities, everyone has now seen it with their own eyes. I have become completely satisfied because of that eulogy and so I have come here to give boons. Ask for anything you want!"

Brahmā said:

6-7. When Vikaṭa had said this, Lord of sages, they then asked Gajānana for whatever they wanted. Because of the innumerable boons, nobody, even with four faces, can describe them in every respect. Therefore I have summarized them.

8-13. Then Gaṇādhīśa continued, "The man who would recite this eulogy[273] three times daily at each of the divisions of the day will complete all his tasks. Whoever would recite this auspicious thing with its eight verses for eight days, but eight times on the last day, will obtain eight successes. He who would recite it ten times every day for a month will effect the release of a prisoner who is to be slain by a king. No doubt of it. And one who wants to gain knowledge will get knowledge and one who wants sons will get a son. That man who is preoccupied with Gajānana and recites it with the highest devotion will obtain everything he wants." After he had said this, the god Gajānana, who has the lovely face and who supports everything, disappeared instantly whilst they were all watching.

14-15. And then they made an image of Gaṇeśa with an auspicious face, and after having set it up in a massive temple constructed with jewels, they gave it the celebrated name of "Lovely-face." After making obeisance to it and worshipping it they each returned to their own home and all the sages and people again became occupied with their own specific duties.

16-29. Some gave it the distinctive name of "One-tusk" and the heavenly musicians and kiṃnaras set up another excellent image in a splendid golden temple and after worshipping it in various ways, they determined its excellent name to be "Kapila." The gūhyakas, wandering bards and perfected ones

---

[273] The eulogy alluded to here is presumably the one found at 92, 45-52.

constructed another image and after setting it up in a large temple they bowed to it and worshipped it. They gave it the name "Having Elephant's ears," the meaning of which is obvious. By means of its power they all went to heaven in their flying vehicles. All the humans set up one called "Pot belly" and all the wild animals set up another excellent image called "Huge," after the worship of which, they went to the forest. And after the mountains and trees had erected and worshipped another image and named it "Destroyer of Obstacles," both of them[274] stayed there and through its favour these mountains and trees became famous. All the groups of birds set up an image made of gold and jewels, named it "Overlord of the Hosts" and worshipped it. All the snakes set up an image of Gaṇanāyaka, made an invocation to it and it became well known as "Smoke Banner." All the lakes set up an auspicious image and they worshipped it in great festivals under the name of "Overseer of Hosts." The multitudes of worms, insects and so on, and the hosts of plants and trees set up an excellent image celebrated as "Moon on his Forehead." Other sentient beings worshipped another large image of Vināyaka in a temple of jewels. Through the power of their devotion it became known by the designation "Elephant-face" and it gives all wishes to everyone. Each of these became famous in the triple-world and each one came to be associated with a particular species, who through the god's favour, easily became experts in their own tasks.

30-34. I lack the ability to relate their names one by one, because I have only received a summary of how the thousand names were composed. Even its essential parts can only be described to you over twelve days as they are like the fourteen jewels that appeared from the churning of the ocean. As such, I have described his glory to you in a summary form. Śeṣa cannot describe it at length, nor Śiva, nor can I, nor Hari, so what of living beings from Indra to mosquitoes, and yakṣas and rākṣasas. Vyāsa, son of Satyavatī, how could I enumerate it?

[274] "Both of them": That is, the groups of trees and mountains.

Therefore,[275] Gajānana must be worshipped in respect of all activities. An evil person who does not worship Vighnavināśana, god of gods, should be kept at a distance like a cāṇḍāla.

The sage said:

35. Tell me his twelve names in order, by the hearing and reciting of which everything becomes without obstacle.

Brahmā said:

36-42. Lovely-face, One-tusk, Kapila, Having Elephant's ears, Pot belly, Huge, Destroyer of Obstacles, Overlord of the Hosts, Smoke Banner, Overseer of the Hosts, Moon on his forehead, and Elephant-face. Whoever hears or recites these twelve names at the beginning of study, at a marriage, when entering or departing, in battle or distress, will not encounter an obstacle. For the purpose of stopping all obstacles one should meditate on the god as wearing white clothes, having the complexion of the moon and four arms. The gift in marriage of myriads of young women, myriads of sacrifices and vows, all austerities, sacred fords, altars, large amounts of gold by the thousands, myriads of gifts, austerities of the kind called kṛcchra and taptakṛcchra and vows relative to the phases of the moon do not attain to a hundredth portion of the merit of these names.

43-44ab. After rising early and becoming purified a composed man should devoutly recite this as obstacles will not befall him. He completes all his tasks and at death attains liberation. People who see him are purified like gods.

44cd-47. For this reason all the worshippers of Sūrya, Śakti, Śiva and Viṣṇu perform all their tasks only after they have recited his twelve names, yet the Gaṇeśa worshippers do this regarding him with much higher zeal. Without the clear articulation of any one of the twelve the tasks will not be completed, brahmin. Therefore, one should clearly articulate

---

[275] "Therefore": Because if one cannot enumerate all the appropriate names, one must worship Gaṇeśa before every task as a kind of lesser substitute.

each one. Indeed, whatever evil-doers and non-believers have to do will be completed, even if unwittingly they merely effect the articulation of a syllable.

48-50ab. In this way I have briefly recited to you everything concerning his greatness, Sage, and I have also described the various opinions about the results of his worship. It has been narrated to you in the same length as Viṣṇu narrated it and even he did not reach the end of the worship of Gaṇeśa. Nor did he fully know the majesty of Gaṇeśa's names.

Bhṛgu said:

50cd-52ab. I have narrated this extraordinary glory to you King, and Brahmā, who was very pleased, then described it to Vyāsa. This is the Upāsanākhaṇḍa I have described, King. If you have confidence in the hearing of it, I will recite yet another tale of Gaṇeśa which will destroy the evils affecting Somakānta.

The bard said:

52cd-58. Great sages led by Śaunaka, I have narrated the worship of Gaṇeśa to you in the course of a sequence of many tales. Brahmā had recited it to the sage Vedavyāsa and Bhṛgu narrated it to Somakānta for the destruction of his evil. Whoever would listen to this excellent Purāṇa of Gaṇeśa, will, after leaving behind all his misfortunes and experiencing many bodily enjoyments, yet still in possession of sons and grandsons, intuitive and discriminating knowledge, obtain the highest liberation because of Gaṇeśa's favour. Even after hundreds of myriads of kalpas he will not be reborn. Whoever would recite this with great devotion will enjoy the results just described, just as was obtained by Somakānta who was listening to it with great diligence.

Obeisance to Śrīgaṇeśa.